W0037063

Summary of Contents

Dreamweaver MX: Advanced ASP Web Development

Edward Apostol

Omar Elbaga

Dan Short

Rob Turnbull

© 2003 Apress
Originally published by glasshaus in 2003

ISBN 978-1-59059-195-6   ISBN 978-1-4302-5498-0 (eBook)
DOI 10.1007/978-1-4302-5498-0

Dreamweaver MX: Advanced ASP Web Development

All rights reserved. No part of this book may be reproduced, stored in a retrieval system, or transmitted in any form or by any means, without the prior written permission of the publisher, except in the case of brief quotations embodied in critical articles or reviews.

The authors and publisher have made every effort in the preparation of this book to ensure the accuracy of the information. However, the information contained in this book is sold without warranty, either express or implied. Neither the authors, glasshaus nor its dealers or distributors will be held liable for any damages caused or alleged to be caused either directly or indirectly by this book.

glasshaus

labor-saving devices for web professionals

© 2003 Apress
Originally published by glasshaus in 2003

Trademark Acknowledgements

glasshaus has endeavored to provide trademark information about all the companies and products mentioned in this book by the appropriate use of capitals. However, glasshaus cannot guarantee the accuracy of this information.

Credits

Authors
Edward Apostol
Omar Elbaga
Dan Short
Rob Turnbull

Technical Reviewers
Kapil Apshankar
Bryan Ashcraft
Midhun James
Allan Kent
Drew McLellan
Murray Summers

Proof Reader
Agnes Wiggers

Indexer
Bill Johncocks

Commissioning Editor
Simon Mackie

Brand Visionary
Bruce Lawson

Lead Technical Editor
Chris Mills

Technical Editors
Alessandro Ansa
Matt Machell
Mark Waterhouse

Publisher
Viv Emery

Project Managers
Helen Cuthill
Sophie Edwards

Graphic Editors
Rachel Taylor
Pip Wonson

Production Assistants
Paul Grove
Tina Ramwell

Cover
Dawn Chellingworth

Cover Image

The cover image of this book was created by Don Synstelien of *http://www.synfonts.com*, co-author of the glasshaus book *Usability: The Site Speaks For Itself*. You can find more of Don's illustration work online at *http://www.synstelien.com*.

About the Authors

Edward Apostol

Edward Apostol is a man of many hats, playing the role of Internet Consultant, Developer, and Instructor in E-Commerce, Wireless, and New Media Studies. Edward has been a cornerstone in the Toronto web design community, being one of the first instructors to be involved with and teach Internet development in Canada since 1997.

Edward has been involved in many projects, including work for Compaq Corporation and Lotus Corporation. His work has been featured in many industry magazines such as Create Online, and web sites such as *Macromedia.com*. Edward has also spoken at numerous conferences in North America on a wide variety of web development topics. Edward's recent accomplishments include sharing a prestigious London International Advertising Award for best in New Media (self-promotional category), for the site *http://www.shawnsfolkart.com*.

His thoughts, reflections and web experiments can be found at *http://www.edapostol.com*. Edward is currently also associated with onX Enterprise Solutions (*http://www.onx.com*) as well as Centennial College (*http://www.bccc.com*) in Toronto.

I would like to acknowledge and thank first and foremost the love of my life, Marilyn, for supporting me through my crazy work lifestyle; my parents and my brother Michael, for just "being there"; Chris Mills and the folks of glasshaus Publishing, who make this effort possible; and thanks to my many current and former students, as well as my colleagues and friends, who help push me to new limits of technical innovation.

Omar Elbaga

Starting out as a fine artist, Omar Elbaga gradually moved to computer graphic arts. He was particularly amazed by the power of the World Wide Web, so he embarked upon building small-scale sites for fun utilizing HTML and his art background. Falling in love with designing web pages and its potential, he began a career in web design. Omar has since been in the web development field for several years. With his head in computer books nearly 24 hours a day, Omar moved on to enhance his skills from web design to web programming.

Most of his work involves building database-driven web sites for small companies. Omar is currently a Tutorial Manager for *udzone.com* and runs a popular Dreamweaver MX resource site named *udnewbie.com*.

Having had the opportunity to study the Arabic language abroad for several months in an intensive course at the Fajr Center in Cairo, Omar is also a translator who translates mostly 12th century scholarly Arabic manuscripts into English. Omar is currently a senior at New Jersey City University completing a double major in English Literature and Secondary Education.

Dan Short

Daniel Short never planned to be a Web designer, it just happened. He started out in the Army tearing apart computers and eventually began putting together web sites. Dan is a devoted Macromedian (and Team Macromedia Volunteer) and uses almost the entire Macromedia Web Design Suite, including Fireworks and Macromedia Flash. He's been doing the Web gig since the end of 1998, and has had great luck building his web design business through Web Shorts Site Design. Dan helps to maintain several HTML and Dreamweaver reference sites including *dwfaq.com*, for which he created the style changer and all ASP functionality, including the Snippets Exchange and the DWfaq/Store.

He's also written articles for several resource sites, including *AListApart.com* and the Macromedia Designer and Developer Center, *http://www.macromedia.com/desdev*.

He is also a contributing author to the Dreamweaver MX Bible from Hungry Minds and Dreamweaver MX Magic from New Riders.

Rob Turnbull

Rob Turnbull is the senior developer for Lighthouse; an established new media Design Company based in Shrewsbury, UK. Clients across Europe from small businesses to blue chip companies provide an increasing workload, which includes the development of databases, web sites, multimedia presentations, interactive CD-ROMs, promotional videos and 3D artwork in both animated and still form.

His personal Web site, *http://www.robgt.com*, is primarily focused on offering help and guidance to fellow Dreamweaver and UltraDev users including tutorials and links to helpful resources and some useful extensions.

My thanks go to the invisible team working just as hard behind the scenes that actually get a book like this published; you guys have been great to work with. Perhaps more importantly, my thanks, my gratitude and my respect go to Sarah. Your care and support have been fantastic and I look forward to seeing you in the daylight hours again!

Table of Contents

Introduction

Another book on creating dynamic ASP-driven web pages with Dreamweaver MX, and an advanced one at that? Why pick this one?

What's It All About?

You probably know this already, but Dreamweaver MX is the latest version of probably the most popular integrated web development environment, and is packed with functionality to take the strain out of writing code for ASP-driven web sites. ASP 3.0 is still the most widely used server-side scripting language, enabling you to add dynamic functionality to your web sites. Anyway, that's enough padding: why is this book useful to you?

Since the authors of this book use Dreamweaver MX and ASP every day in their working lives, it contains countless practical tips on how to get the most out of using Dreamweaver MX to write ASP-based web applications. This book will build on your existing knowledge of ASP and Dreamweaver MX and develop it further. Using the information and experience distilled into this book, you'll be able to take your web applications to the next level.

Who's This Book for?

We're assuming that you already know a bit about ASP, and developing with it using Dreamweaver MX. You don't have to know ASP inside out to get the most out of this book: the focus is more on advanced uses of ASP with Dreamweaver MX. Saying that, however, this isn't a book for you if you've never used ASP or Dreamweaver before.

If you are looking for a lower-level introductory book about using Dreamweaver MX (with ASP), check out *Dynamic Dreamweaver MX*, Rachel Andrew *et* al, ISBN: 1-904151-10-8.

What Do I Need to Begin?

To use this book you need a copy of Dreamweaver MX, together with a web server capable of serving ASP pages; we used IIS 5 running on Windows 2000 during our extensive code-testing process.

A couple of chapters also feature databases; *Chapters 2* and *13* make use of Microsoft Access, and *Chapters 7* and *12* use SQL Server. We also used Flash MX for *Chapter 11*.

What's Inside?

Since Dreamweaver MX will let you create ASP applications quickly and easily using Server Behaviors, you could have easily written a site or two that uses ASP without actually seeing the code. We think it is best that you understand what's going on in the code as well, to get the most out of Dreamweaver MX's ASP functionality.

Therefore, *Chapter 1* quickly introduces the key elements of ASP VBScript syntax. Dreamweaver MX will write ASP code for you in VBScript or JavaScript, but we've picked VBScript for this book, as it seems to be the most popular choice amongst ASP developers.

In *Chapter 2*, we learn about control structures, and how to make decisions within our code. This is important for being able to display material conditionally. We also cover looping: how to repeat a process several times.

Chapter 3 gives us the low-down on functions and strings. Not only can we manipulate text and numbers, but we can also manipulate dates, as well as change text into numbers and numbers into dates. Bet you never thought you'd see the word transubstantiation in a glasshaus book!

In *Chapter 4* we examine the role objects can play in our ASP web applications. We look at the key objects provided by ASP, and discover what they can do for us: their events, methods, properties, and collections.

In *Chapter 5*, we get to grips with error handling. We'll see how to provide more meaningful error messages to help aid in the debugging process and improve site security (for example, how to stop the user finding out the structure of our application by making it go wrong). This is something we'll need with all the complex applications we'll be building.

Chapter 6 takes us through the process of creating extensions for Dreamweaver MX using VBScript. Once you're up to speed with scripting extensions (incorporating the Dreamweaver MX Server Behavior Builder), you'll be knocking out useful functionality to share with the rest of us like there's no tomorrow.

Chapter 7 brings us up to speed with stored procedures and triggers, before showing us how Dreamweaver MX can help you to get the most out of your database, using the Dreamweaver MX *Command* object.

In *Chapter 8*, we look at what might be an alternative to using a database for dynamic site content. Rather than pulling information out of a database, ASP lets us read and write files on our hard drive, so if we structure our folders right we can loop through their contents and display them neatly.

In *Chapter 9*, XML comes under scrutiny, both what it is and how to work with it in our ASP applications using Dreamweaver MX. We'll be reading and writing files using XML, as well as using Extensible Stylesheet Language Transformations (XSLT) to transform one XML file into another, to suit our data needs.

In *Chapter 10*, Sessions and cookies are top of the list for consideration. We'll find out what a Session is and how it can help us keep track of a user, and we'll discuss using cookies to provide some of the same functionality.

Chapter 11 shows us how we can integrate Flash MX with Dreamweaver MX and ASP, so easily in fact that Dreamweaver MX can add Flash buttons and text to your page without your having Flash MX installed. We'll build a simple Flash MX form, and see how to use Dreamweaver MX to connect it to ASP functionality to make use of the input we get.

Chapter 12 is the first of two case studies that bring together some of the topics covered in the rest of the book by building complete working sites using Dreamweaver MX. Our first site will be a simple web log or blog, using a database to store the information, and Dreamweaver MX to build the whole ASP site to administer and display the blog data.

In *Chapter 13*, the second case study, we build a message board or forum. Again we use a database to store the posts, but this site has to keep track of more people, as well as their potentially meandering topics of conversation.

Support and Feedback

Although we aim for perfection, the sad fact of book publication is that a few errors will slip through. We would like to apologize for any that have reached this book despite our efforts. If you spot an error, please let us know about it using the e-mail address *support@glasshaus.com*. If it's something that will help other readers then we'll put it up on the errata page at *http://www.glasshaus.com*.

This e-mail address can also be used to access our support network. If you have trouble running any of the code in this book, or have a related question that you feel that the book didn't answer, please mail your problem to the above address quoting the book title (*Dreamweaver MX: Advanced ASP Web Development*), the last 4 digits of its ISBN (**1213**), and the relevant chapter and page number.

Web Support

You'll want to go and visit our web site, at *http://www.glasshaus.com*. It features a freely downloadable compressed version of the full code for this book, in both `.zip` and `.sit` formats. You can also find details of all our other published books, author interviews, and more.

1

- The Basics of ASP and VBScript

- Naming, declaring, and outputting variables

- Data types

- Comparison, logical, and arithmetic operators

Author: Omar Elbaga

Introducing ASP

Since this is the first chapter of a book using ASP and Dreamweaver MX, we'd better go through some of the basics of ASP that it has probably been hiding from us. As well as looking at how ASP is manipulated from within Dreamweaver MX, we will also be taking a look at how the language itself works. Gaining a full understanding of how the ASP code behind your pages actually functions is essential to being able to build and debug them properly.

As you probably know, ASP stands for Active Server Pages, and is Microsoft's own server-side scripting technology. In this chapter, we will explore the syntactic essentials of ASP, and the most commonly used scripting language behind it – VBScript. Specifically, we will look at:

Gaining a full understanding of how the ASP code behind your pages actually functions is essential to being able to build and debug them properly.

- Basics of ASP script including ASP delimiters, directives, and comments
- Declaring and outputting variables
- Naming your variables
- Variable data types
- VBScript operators

Don't worry: I will be trying my best not to bore you with excessive detail, but instead take what is most important to us as web developers and keep the information as comprehensive but as concise as possible.

Go Dynamic with ASP

Active Server pages are pages saved with an **.asp** extension. They consist of two parts:

- Programmatic Code
- Embedded HTML content

ASP pages are written with a scripting language and embedded HTML. It is the scripting language and the server that work with each other to make the web page dynamic. When an `.asp` page is requested by a client over the Internet, the server runs through the sourcecode; the HTML content is sent back to the client as is, whereas the programmatic code is interpreted and the additional HTML churned out as a result is sent alongside the embedded HTML.

The programmatic code is written in one of several scripting languages. Active Server Pages can be scripted in:

- VBScript
- JavaScript
- PerlScript
- Python

Although ASP developers have several scripting languages to choose from, we will be looking at VBScript in this book, as it is probably the most popular language used to script ASP pages. Dreamweaver MX only creates pages in ASP/VBScript or ASP/JavaScript anyway.

Let's demonstrate a simple example of how ASP web pages are dynamic compared to a page only coded in HTML. Create the following examples:

```
<!- 01_static_time.htm ->

<!DOCTYPE html PUBLIC "-//W3C//DTD XHTML 1.0 Transitional//EN"
"http://www.w3.org/TR/xhtml1/DTD/xhtml1-transitional.dtd">
<html>
<head>
  <title>Static Time</title>
</head>
<body>

  The time is now 8:45 PM

</body>
</html>
```

You should see the output shown here when you access the page in your web browser:

This output won't change...

Now let's modify this page with a little ASP. Create the following example and then access it through your web browser (remembering of course that you need to run it through a web server):

```
<?xml version="1.0" encoding="iso-8859-1"?>
<!DOCTYPE html PUBLIC "-//W3C//DTD XHTML 1.0 Transitional//EN"
"http://www.w3.org/TR/xhtml1/DTD/xhtml1-transitional.dtd">
<%@LANGUAGE="VBSCRIPT" CODEPAGE="CP_ACP"%>
<html xmlns="http://www.w3.org/1999/xhtml">
<head>
  <title>Untitled Document</title>
  <meta http-equiv="Content-Type" content="text/html; charset=iso-8859-1" />
</head>

<body>
  The time is now <% Response.Write Time %>
</body>
</html>
```

You should now see something similar to the following output, depending on what time it is on your web server:

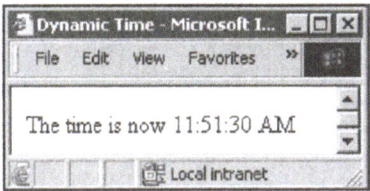

...whereas this output will be different every time it is requested

Refresh the page a few times to see how the time continues to update itself. This is what a "dynamic" page means. Also take a look at the sourcecode in your browser (for example, by selecting *View > Source* in Internet Explorer) and you will see that the ASP simply returns HTML to the client browser. The script is executed by the web server, which then sends back plain HTML.

> The script is executed by the web server, which then sends back plain HTML

Familiarize Yourself with ASP Basics

Before jumping into the details of VBScript, let us take a look at the fundamentals of constructing an ASP VBScript page. We can do so by creating a new dynamic page in Dreamweaver MX.

ASP Delimiters <% ... %>

Open Dreamweaver MX and select *File > New > Dynamic Page*. You should see the following dialog box:

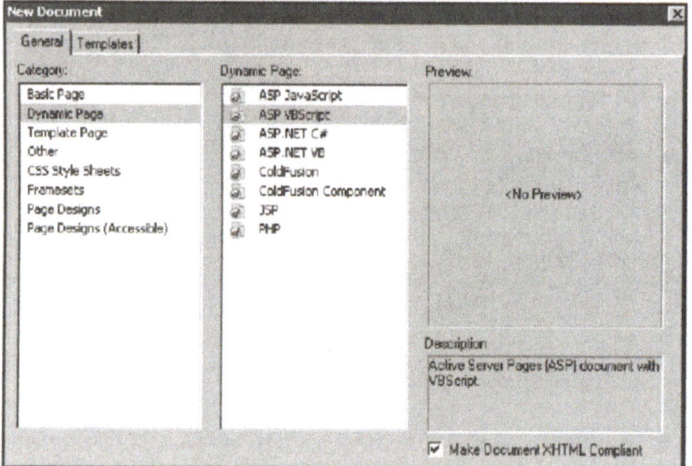

Choose your page type

Select *ASP VBScript* from the *Dynamic Page* selection. We also recommend that you check the option on the bottom right to make the page XHTML-compliant. This way Dreamweaver will generate XHTML-compliant code thereby streamlining it and making it easier and quicker to render. Hit *Create*, and when the new document is created switch the document layout to code view by selecting *View > Code*.

Note that you should keep the layout of Dreamweaver documents built in this chapter in code view since we will be looking directly into the ASP code itself.

Dreamweaver MX will create a new blank ASP page all ready to go. You should now see something similar to the following inside Dreamweaver:

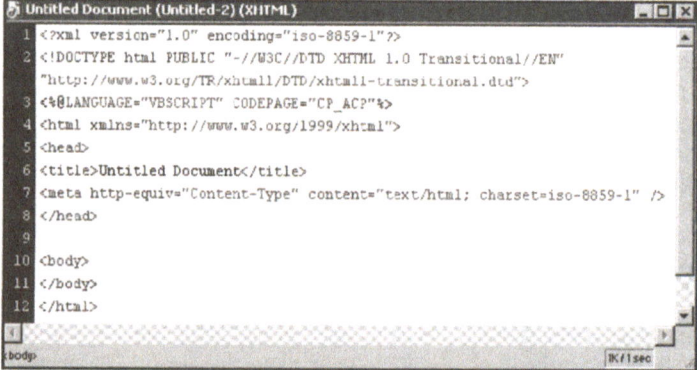

A new ASP VBScript document in Dreamweaver MX

Line three is the only ASP code on this new page:

```
<%@LANGUAGE="VBSCRIPT" CODEPAGE="CP_ACP"%>
```

This line is called an ASP **Pre-processing Directive**. **Directives** contain information that must be read by the web server before any other ASP script is processed. It tells the web server to perform certain functions before processing any ASP.

! All ASP code must go in between a ∎ set of <% ... %> delimiters. There can be more than one set on each page, but the rule remains true, and any content not inside these delimiters will be dealt with as normal HTML content.

Our new document contains two directives:

- LANGUAGE tells the server serving the ASP what scripting language is being used within our ASP sections, in our case, VBSCRIPT. If it isn't specified literally in the directive, the web server will assume VBScript as the language because it is the default language for ASP; hence, if you begin coding in JavaScript without explicitly specifying it in the directive, it will throw an error.

- CODEPAGE sets the character set the server will use to interpret the script. In our case the value is CP_ACP, which represents the default ANSI code page.

All directives must appear before any other ASP lines in an ASP page. They cannot be placed below any other ASP lines in the sourcecode. Luckily for us, Dreamweaver MX adds this line for every new dynamic page we create so we don't have to add it manually each time.

Now let's look at some of the basic ASP/VBScript constructs you really should familiarize yourself with. Here we will look at:

- Response.Write
- The <%= shortcut
- ASP/VBScript comments

Response.Write

We've already seen this in action – in our first ASP example above we used Response.Write to write the current time on the server to our web page. The main function of the Response object is to send information from the server to the client. The Write function then writes that information to the page.

Let's see how we can write a simple Response.Write statement in Dreamweaver MX – first in a new ASP page, place your cursor between the opening and closing <body</body> tags. Now go to the *Insert Panel*, select the *ASP* tab, and select the <% icon from the menu, as shown.

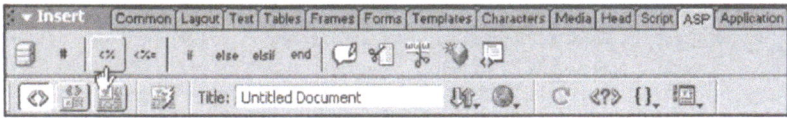

The Dreamweaver MX ASP tab.

If you don't see icons in the menu, select Edit > Preferences > General > Editing Options > Insert Panel > Icons Only.

This will insert opening and closing ASP delimiters for you in the sourcecode and also place the cursor directly between the delimiters so we can begin coding. Now we can insert a `Response.Write` statement inside the delimiters, by selecting the *Response.Write* icon, which is the icon seen above displaying the speech bubble with the pencil inside it. Do this, and our ASP code line should look like this:

```
<% Response.Write() %>
```

Now let's do something with this: update our line to the following, and save it as `response_write.asp`:

```
<% Response.Write("I'm text that came from ASP") %>
```

When we view this page, it should look like this:

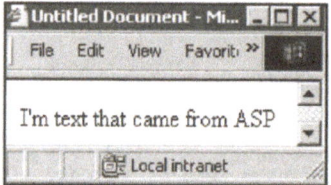

Nice and easy

Note that the text we are writing to the screen in these examples is an argument passed in the Write method of the Response Object. Unlike JavaScript, VBScript will allow you to leave out the parentheses:

```
<% Response.Write "I'm text that came from ASP" %>
```

Since we are using ASP to output mere text we can also include HTML tags inside the value – try changing our `Response.Write` line to the following (see `response_write2.asp` in the code download):

```
<% Response.Write ("I'm <em>text</em> that came from <strong>ASP</strong>") %>
```

When you view this example, it should look like this:

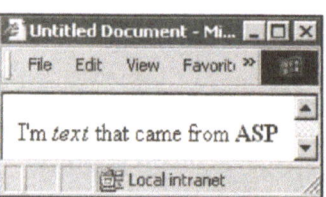

We can use Response.Write to output HTML

We have seen `Response.Write` output HTML but `Response.Write` will more often be used to output variables in typical ASP (see the *Working with Variables* section later in this chapter).

If you want to output a string of text you need to surround it with double quotes, for example `Response.Write("hello")`. Variables we want to output are not surrounded with double quotes, for example `Response.Write(Time)`, as we saw in our first example.

The <%= Shortcut

Instead of writing out `Response.Write`, we can use a shortcut instead: `<%=`.

Let's try this – take the last example we looked at, and replace `<% Response.Write` with `<%=`. Your ASP line should now look like this:

```
<%= ("I'm <em>text</em> that came from <strong>ASP</strong>") %>
```

This is equivalent to:

```
<% Response.Write("I'm <em>text</em> that came from <strong>ASP</strong>") %>
```

When you view this page in your browser, you should see the same output as before.

It is faster to use the shortcut method when you want to insert single lines of ASP code in between HTML blocks. Note that when using the shortcut method, you must close each separate write statement. For example, you could replace:

...when using the shortcut method, you must close each separate write statement

```
<%
  Response.Write("I'm <em>text</em> that came from <strong>ASP</strong>")
  Response.Write("I'm another line that came from <strong>ASP</strong>")
%>
```

with this:

```
<%=("I'm <em>text</em> that came from <strong>ASP</strong>") %>
<%=("I'm another line that came from <strong>ASP</strong>") %>
```

The following code, however, would throw an **error**:

```
<%=("I'm <em>text</em> that came from <strong>ASP</strong>")
   ("I'm a second line that came from <strong>ASP</strong>")
%>
```

Dreamweaver MX has a button that automatically writes out `<%= %>` for you: it has <%= on it, and you should have seen it in our earlier screenshot of the Dreamweaver MX ASP tab. The button can be found on the *ASP* tab on the *Insert Panel*. You can also select *Insert > ASP Objects > Output*.

Commenting Code

ASP has its own way of commenting code, as follows:

```
<%
  ' I'm a comment to help make your code clearer
%>
```

Any text appearing after a single quote character will be regarded as part of the comment until the text appears on the next line. For example:

```
<%
  ' I'm a comment to help make your code
  clearer
%>
```

In the example above, the word *clearer* will not be regarded as part of the comment, but rather as ASP code. It will skip the first line and try to read the text *clearer*. This would throw an error when the page is viewed because the text *clearer* means nothing in ASP; it is not ASP code. Hence the single quote needs to be at the beginning of each comment line, so you would need to change the comment like this:

```
<%
  ' I'm a comment to help make your code
  ' clearer
%>
```

In JavaScript you can wrap multiple lines with

```
/* <multiple lines> */
```

For example:

```
<%
  /* I'm a comment to help make your code
  clearer */
%>
```

Note that, whereas JavaScript has a method of commenting multiple lines in one shot, VBScript has no way of doing this, so you have to place the single quote character in front of each comment line.

Actual ASP code can go underneath or above these comments within the same opening and closing delimiters. For example:

```
<%
  ' output the text Hello World
  Response.Write "Hello World"
  ' done outputting, now output the text Goodbye
%>
```

Code Readability *refers to how readable your code is to yourself and others. This refers to good commenting and writing style.*

You can keep comments inside their own separate delimiters or include them inside an ASP code block. Do whatever makes the code more **readable** to you and others for that specific block.

Also bear in mind that ASP comments will **not** appear in the HTML output. They are different from HTML comments, because, like all ASP code, ASP comments are server-side not, client-side, and will have been processed out of the code by the time it appears on the client. They are only for use by those writing or updating the code.

Importance of Commenting Code

Commenting your code is extremely important. Let's say you have coded an entire discussion board application (which by the way, we will develop in this book's second case study) then you are required to open the code after a few months to update it. It's likely that the code will look so confusing to you that you may think you no longer know any ASP!

Looking at large volumes of code can be overwhelming, so comments are necessary to show you what each bit of code does, and to help you unravel and understand it. If your own code looks bad enough in these circumstances, imagine looking at someone else's code without comments!

Try to consistently comment what is going on throughout your application, so that by the end you have basically summarized what the code is doing through the collective comments. Even if the code is very simple, you should briefly mention what it is doing in the context of the rest of the application. For example:

```
' Sends Book ID to query page to be retrieved by user
```

The actual ASP code for an action like this is not very hard to recognize for any ASP coder, but let's say you are looking at the code and you just can't remember why you are sending this URL parameter anywhere. So many things are usually happening for several reasons in a web application that you need to clarify the various actions by commenting. When you comment on what the code is doing, it serves as a reference for the **logic behind the code**, which makes it easier for third parties to read through it and know what is going on.

> *When you comment the code, it makes it easier for third parties to read it*

Comments Help with Debugging

Comments also assist you in debugging your application. Let's say you have some code that is throwing an error and you're not sure what part of the code is actually causing the error. You might go back into the code, rewrite or even delete a particular section, and test the page again. What if the error still occurs? This means it couldn't have been the code you played with. So now you have to change that code back to the way it was and play around with other sections.

Using comments to comment out parts of the code allows you to force the web server to ignore ASP code without having to delete it (and then rewrite it when it turns out not to be the section that is causing the error). For example, consider the following code:

```
<%
  Dim svUserID = 12
  Dim ckbookName = "Dynamic Dreamweaver MX"

  Response.Write (svUserID)
  Response.Write ("Your book:")
  Response.Write (ckBookName)
%>
```

It might not be obvious at first glance what is causing the error, but by placing a single quote in front of the second Response.Write statement, you would remove the error from the code, and the server would no longer throw an error when trying to interpret your code – therefore, it must be this line that is at fault.

This testing method could just as easily be applied to any of the other lines in the code, without the danger of actually deleting lines that aren't at fault.

Debugging refers to editing or revising code when it does not accomplish the task(s) intended by the coder.

VBScript Basics

Now we have finished looking at a few essential basics of ASP, let's go on to look at some basic features of the VBScript language. Specifically, we will look at:

- Variables
- Data Types
- Operators

Working with Variables

What is a variable? A **variable** is like a placeholder or an allocation set in memory for a value. It can hold a value of your choice. It is considered empty until a value is placed inside it. Let's declare our first variable. Place the following code inside the HTML body of a new Dreamweaver ASP/VBScript document:

```
<%
Dim firstName
firstName = ("Omar")
%>
```

This creates a variable called `firstName` with the value `Omar`. The first line declares that the variable exists, telling the computer to put aside space for it in memory; the second line then gives a value to that variable.

The keyword `Dim` is used to declare variables. Keep in mind that it does not give them a value; it simply declares them. When the `Dim` keyword is executed, a slot is set for the variable in the web server's memory, and the computer is made aware of the variable's name. You must then give the variable a value.

Dimming variables is not essential; you could simply do the following without declaring the variable explicitly:

```
<%
firstName = ("Omar")
%>
```

The system will understand on its own that you are creating a variable named `firstName` with `Omar` as its value without the separate dimming, and Dreamweaver MX itself very often does not explicitly declare variables.

So Why Dim Variables?

Although explicitly declaring a variable in VBScript is not obligatory, it can be tremendously helpful in some circumstances. Dimming variables serves as a tracking system for all the variables on the page. If they are not explicitly dimmed, the web server cannot help you if you have misspelled a variable during printout. For example:

If they are not explicitly dimmed, the web server cannot help you if you have misspelled a variable during printout

```
<%
  myVariable = "Omar"
  Response.Write myVarible
%>
```

When you execute this page in your browser, no error will be thrown, even though we intended to print the `myVariable` variable to the screen, but ended up misspelling its name. Since we have not explicitly declared our variables, `myVarible` could simply be another variable the server does not know about. Now let's use the `Option Explicit` directive, which forces the web developer to explicitly declare every variable (we will see a lot more on using `Option Explicit` in *Chapter 5* of this book):

```
<% Option Explicit %>
<%
  Dim myVariable
  myVariable = "Omar"
  Response.Write myVarible
%>
```

When you view this page in a browser, an error will be displayed informing you that the variable `myVarible` is undefined. Dimming variables, along with `Option Explicit`, allows the web server to give you a helping hand.

One last thing to note is that unfortunately Dreamweaver MX does not always explicitly declare all variables, so using `Option Explicit` may cause an error when used in a Dreamweaver MX page. You should check your code rigorously to make sure problems don't occur if you do decide to use `Option Explicit`.

Outputting Variables

Now we get to the fun part! Let's display our variables on the page. Although the variable is set whether we display it or not, it is not much use unless we then do something with it. If you recall from the previous section, we use `Response.Write` to output to the client browser. Enter the following into a new ASP VBScript page, and save it as `output_variable.asp`:

```
<%
  firstName = "Omar"
  Response.Write(firstName)
%>
```

When you view this page in your browser you should see the name displayed on the screen:

Outputting variables is as easy as outputting text

Remember that you could also use the `<%=` shortcut to output the variable.

```
<% firstName = "Omar" %>
<%=firstName %>
```

Variable Scope?

The variables we are referring to are local variables. They persist only within the page they are declared on. They are not global, that is, available to pages throughout the entire site. What we mean by this is that if we declared a variable on a page like so:

```
<% userInitials = "OE" %>
```

This variable called `userInitials` cannot be retrieved on other pages. It can only be used on the current page.

There are ways of getting local variables to exist across pages, to make them global. There are also variables that have different scopes such as **Session**, **Cookie**, and **Application** variables, which can be used directly across pages. This is useful when we want to make information persist across different pages (sometimes referred to as maintaining state). You will learn more about global variables, maintaining state with sessions and cookies, and application variables in *Chapters 4* and *10*.

Let's look at a small example just to demonstrate how global variables span over multiple pages. Create the following page:

```
<!- local_variables1.asp ->
<% userInitials = "OE" %>
```

Now create this second page, which tries to print out the variable from the first page:

```
<!- local_variables2.asp ->
<% Response.Write(userInitials) %>
```

When you access the second page in the browser you will notice that nothing is printed out because the variable does not exist on the page. The variable is local to the first page and cannot be accessed from a second page; once the client leaves the first page it does not exist any more.

Let's see how global variables are handled by creating and using a session variable. Create the following page:

```
<!- global_variables1.asp ->
<% Session("userInitials") = "OE" %>
```

Now create this second page which tries to print out the Session variable from the first page.

```
<!- global_variables2.asp ->
<% Response.Write(Session("userInitials")) %>
```

Execute the first page global_variables1.asp and then access the second variable global_variables2.asp and you should see the initials displayed on the second page. We can display this variable on any page, from the point where the line was executed until the Session expires You will learn more about Session variables in *Chapter 10*.

If the expiry time is not specified within the ASP code, then by default sessions expire on the web server after ten minutes.

Data Types

There are different types of data that you will want to hold in variables, such as integers, text, currency, dates, etc. Here we will discuss some of the most common ones you will encounter.

Integer

An integer is any whole number. For example, 1, 240, -5000, etc. Let's see an example:

```
<%
  userAge = 23
  userID = 2120
%>
You are <%=userAge %> years old and your user ID is <%=userID %>.
```

You should see the following when you view the page in your browser (see integer.asp in the code download):

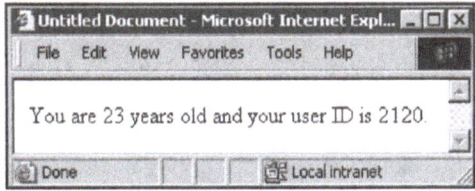

Displaying integer variables

In the example above, we create two variables, the first one named userAge with a value of 23, and the second named userID with a value of 2120. There are different data types related to the integer such as byte and long.

You won't have to worry much about these intricate details, as VBScript will discern all of this internally, without you having to know which specific data type has been selected; however it is useful to know what is going on behind the scenes.

These data types hold different ranges of numbers. For example, strictly speaking, an integer can hold a range of number values between -32,768 and 32,767 (for any numbers outside this range, we would use the long data type.), and a byte data type holds a range of number values between 0 and 255.

String

A string data type contains any sequence of numbers, letters, and/or symbols. Strings are surrounded by double quotes. Please remember this as the data type can be changed to an integer by accident if you leave off the double quotes around a number. Let's see an example:

```
<%
  userState = "New York"
  userHomeTelephone = "212-555-5555"
%>
```

```
You are from <%=userState %> and your telephone # is <%=userHomeTelephone %>.
```

You should see the following when you view the page in your browser (see `string.asp` in the code download):

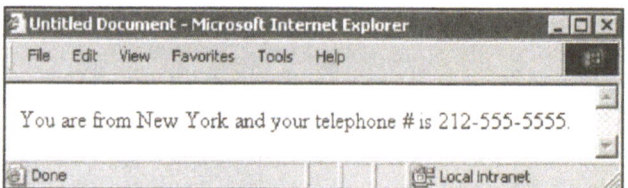

We couldn't have had this telephone number as an integer because of the dashes...

In the example above we created two variables, the first variable named `userState`, with a value of `New York`, and the second variable named `userHomeTelephone`, with a value of `212-555-5555`. We then printed the values to the screen. These characters are treated as text and not integers.

Bear in mind that the value for the `userHomeTelephone` is **not** an `Integer`, but a `String`. Remember that it is surrounded by double quotes, which make it a string. The `String` is the only data type surrounded by double quotes.

Let's see what happens if we remove the double quotes from the value of the `userHomeTelephone` variable.

```
<%
  userState = "New York"
  userHomeTelephone = 212-555-5555
%>
```

```
You are from <%=userState %> and your telephone # is <%=userHomeTelephone %>.
```

You should see the following when you view the page in your browser:

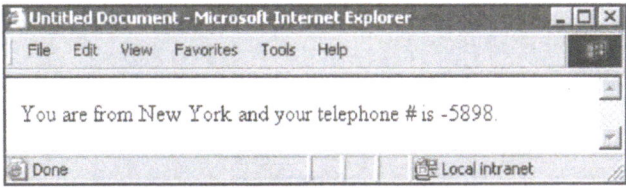

... because VBScript would get confused!

What happened? *-5898* doesn't look like a phone number, at least not in the US or the UK!

Well, since there are no double quotes around the number values, the web server treats them as `Integer`s and since the dash symbol (-) mathematically is a character that stands for subtraction, it performs a mathematical computation on the numbers: `212 - 555 - 5555 = -5898`.

The result of this computation is printed out when we output the variable. Oops! We didn't intend this, but this shows you the difference between numbers when they are `Integer`s and when they are `String`s.

When the numbers are of `String` data type you **cannot** perform any mathematical computation on them (unless you change them to `Integer` data types using the `CInt` function, discussed in *Chapter 3*). If you will be performing computations on numbers then make sure you do make them `Integer`s. For example, we cannot add the following variables:

```
<%
  userAreaCode = "212"
  userZipCode = "05646"
%>

<%= (userAreaCode + userZipCode) %>
```

If you view this page in your browser you will see the following:

Although you see a number, it did not add `212` to `05646` (the result would have been `5858`). It simply **concatenated** the two `String`s together, considering the plus symbol (+) as a concatenation character. In ASP both the symbols `+` or `&` can be used as concatenation symbols.

That's what you get when you try to add two string variables together

Concatenation simply means "bringing things together", not adding things mathematically, but rather simply putting them together, side-by-side. We will get into concatenation in more detail later in this chapter.

What happens if you leave out the double quotes around the value `New York`? In this case the page will throw an error when it is viewed – the characters `New York`, if not a `String` value, mean nothing in VBScript.

Note on Careful Coding
When you are coding, you need to be careful not to introduce bugs or errors into your code by doing things like forgetting double quotes around your strings. Bugs or errors in your code are not always obvious, nor will the page necessarily throw an error when the code is not acting how you want it to. Something totally unintended could be happening with your code without you even knowing it, so stay focused! Some advice is to always try to keep in mind the big picture of your web application even as you code the minor aspects.

Boolean

A Boolean variable holds a value of either `True` or `False`. This can come in the form of `Yes` or `No`, or `1` or `0`. `0` can represent `False` and any non-zero number can represent `True` (in VBScript, when returning these values as integer data types, `True` would return `-1` and `False` would return `0`). Let's take a look at this example:

```
<%
  mailingListOn = True
%>
```

For example, we could have collected this information from a form, telling us whether or not the user wants to be on a mailing list.

> *You will usually check a Boolean value in order to cause different things to happen in your application*

The Boolean data type is normally used within **control structures** (which you will learn more about in *Chapter 2*), when you need to know whether to perform certain actions. You will usually check whether a particular Boolean value is `True` or `False` in order to cause different things to happen in your application based on these values (such as the mailing list above – users who selected `True` will get the mailing list, users who didn't won't).

Now let's look at a more practical example for Boolean variables (`boolean.asp`):

```
<%
  userName = "omar"
  userEmail = "omar@udnewbie.com"
  showEmail = False
%>

Hi <%=userName%> <% If showEmail = True Then %><%=userEmail %><% End If %>
```

When viewed in a browser, this example looks like so:

Good thing we didn't want our e-mail displayed

In this example we create a variable for the username and for the e-mail. We then use a Boolean variable labeled `showEmail` to decide whether a user wants their e-mail appearing on the web page, and check the variable's value using an `If` control statement. In the case above the answer is `False` or No, so the control is resolved as False, and the e-mail address is not displayed. If the Boolean value is changed from `False` to `True`, the e-mail address will be displayed.

The only potentially confusing section of this code block is `<% If showEmail = True Then %><% End If %>`. Don't be thrown off by this. You haven't learned about control statements yet, but you will in *Chapter 2*.

An Aside: Finding Out a Variable's Data Type

VBScript has a built-in function that can identify the data type of any variable for you – `TypeName`. (You will learn all about built-in functions in *Chapter 3*.) The variable you want to learn the data type of should be put after `TypeName`, inside parentheses. Once you use this function you can print out the data type onto your screen. Let's see an example (`typename.asp`):

```
%
  userName = "omar"
  showEmail = False
%>

<%= TypeName(userName) %><br />
<%= TypeName(showEmail) %>
```

When you view this page in your browser you will see the following:

The `userName` variable is a `String`, while the `showEmail` variable is a `Boolean` value.

The results of our data type checking

Date

A variable with a **Date** data type simply means that the value is a date. In fact, a date variable can contain the date and/or the time. There are various VBScript functions that can also format the date in different manners.

> *There are various VBScript functions that can format the date in different manners*

To demonstrate an example of a variable with a `Date` data type, let's use VBScript's built-in `Date` function to display the current date at the web server on the screen. Enter the following example into new Dreamweaver MX page, and save it as `date.asp`:

```
<%
   webserverDate = Date()
   Response.Write (webserverDate)
%>
```

When you view this page in your browser, you should see a display similar to the following:

You'll want to check your computer settings if you get this result

Now let's see what data type the value of this variable has by using the `TypeName()` function to decipher it:

```
<%
   webserverDate = Date()
   Response.Write TypeName(webserverDate)
%>
```

The code above will return the following in your web browser:

Although it displayed like string earlier, it's actually a Date

It is still possible to use `String` or `Integer` data types to reflect the date, but using the actual date data type makes things a lot easier and also allows us to use the many built-in date formatting and manipulation functions to change the style of the date and/or time; we'll be covering the most frequently used ones in *Chapter 3*.

Empty and Null

Empty and **Null** are not data types but rather descriptions of the value of certain data. It is very important to be aware of them because web developers will too often run into these kinds of values, especially when dealing with user interaction on a web site. Users will sometimes leave data fields blank or fail to initialize data. `Empty` and `Null` deal with these kinds of values.

`Empty` refers to **uninitialized variables**. It means that no beginning value has been assigned for the variable. `Empty` variables are 0 in a numeric context, or zero-length in a string. Let's see an example (`empty.asp`):

Users will sometimes leave data fields blank or fail to initialize data

```
<%
  Dim userHomeTelephone 'declared variable with no initialized value following
  Response.Write TypeName(userHomeTelephone) 'print variable data type
%>
```

In the above example we declare a variable named `userHomeTelephone` but do not give it a value. When you view this page in your browser you should see the following:

Un-initialized variables are Empty

Bear in mind that, once any value is given to the variable, it will have a conventional data type; not an `Empty` value. Let's give our variable a value:

```
<%
  Dim userHomeTelephone 'declared variable with no initialized value following
  userHomeTelephone = "212-555-5555"
  Response.Write TypeName(userHomeTelephone) 'print variable data type
%>
```

When you view this page in your browser, you will see that the variable has a `String` data type. `Empty` values will most likely be encountered with variables that hold values directly obtained from the user, such as form fields. You will also experience `Empty` values when data in a database column has been removed.

`Null` simply refers to **no data**; it indicates the absence of any valid data. The only time a variable is `Null` is when a `Null` value has explicitly been placed in it. `Null` data is most often encountered in database tables. For example, a record column will have `Null` data when no data has been placed in it. Without accessing a database, the only way to demonstrate a `Null` value in an ASP script example is by explicitly giving a variable a `Null` value:

```
<%
  Dim userHomeTelephone
  userHomeTelephone = Null
  Response.Write TypeName(userHomeTelephone) 'print variable data type
%>
```

When you view this page in your browser, you will now see that the variable data type is `Null`.

Naming Your Variables

There are certain rules that must be followed when naming variables so that the web server can be able to recognize them. Let's make this as simple as possible. It can be summarized in two points:

- Variable names can contain numbers and letters only, with the exception of the underscore character (_). This means that periods, dashes, and spaces are not allowed.

- The first character of a variable name must be a letter. An underscore or number cannot begin a variable name.

That's it! Here are examples of legal variable names:

- userName
- user_name
- My_Number
- Str_Address
- strAddress

Here are examples of illegal variable names:

- _userName
- 2pac_shakur
- my number
- India.arie

Another point to mention (not really a rule so much as much as an inherent condition) is that VBScript reserved words cannot be used as the name of an entire variable. The keyword `Dim` cannot be used to name a variable obviously, although `Dimdim` is allowed, not that I can see why you would ever use this name!

Good Variable-Naming Conventions

When you name your variables, you should **use descriptive names**, names whose meanings can be instantly recognized at first glance. Do not try to save time by using mere initials or shortcuts for names, as anyone (including you) who has to read your code at a later date will have difficulty understanding them.

For example, don't try to use the initials `UN` to name a variable that contains a user name. What does UN stand for? United Nations? Name the variable `userName`, `user_name`, etc.

Feel free to begin your variable names with the variable type. For example, you may name a variable that will stand for an age `int_userAge`, as it is likely to be an integer. The same goes for other variable types. Here is a list of commonly used prefixes for the various data types:

- `Integer` – int
- `String` – str
- `Currency` – cur
- `Boolean` – bol
- `Date` – dt

Purists will say that you should choose a method for naming your variables and stick with it. If you do decide to use specific prefixes for your variable names then always use them. If you use a specific style such as lower camel case (for example `myFirstName`, `machineProductCode`), then do so consistently. It's really a personal decision, but try to do it one way and stick to that way whenever you code. Keep **code readability** in mind for yourself and for others.

VBScript Operators

Operators are the characters that allow you to do real work with your data; you would be unable to do anything with your data otherwise. You have already seen a few operators in this chapter such as the equals sign (=), the dash (-), and the plus sign (+). In this section we look at:

- Comparison Operators
- Logical Operators
- Arithmetic Operators

Now let's look at these three different groups in turn.

Comparison Operators

These operators compare the values of two expressions and return a Boolean value of `True` or `False` depending on the result. These operators are normally used with control statements, which we haven't covered yet (control statements will be covered in *Chapter 2*). The most important thing is to understand what each comparison operator stands for and which Boolean value two compared expressions would return.

The comparison operators are:

- =
  Expression on the left **is equal** to the expression on the right

- <>
  Expression on the left is **not equal** to the expression on the right

- <
  Expression on the left is **less than** the expression on the right

- >
  Expression on the left is **greater than** the expression on the right

- <=
  Expression on the left is **less than or equal to** the expression on the right

- >=
  Expression on the left is greater than or equal to the expression on the right

Let's look at some examples to understand these better. For example, take the following two variables:

```
<%
  mikesAge = 45
  rachelsAge = 24
%>
```

Let's have a look at what happens when we compare these variables to each other with the different operators:

- `mikesAge = rachelsAge`
  Returns `False` because 45 does not equal 24

- `mikesAge <> rachelsAge`
  Returns `True` because 45 does not equal 24. Remember that the <> symbol stands for inequality

- `mikesAge < rachelsAge`
  Returns `False` because 45 is not less than 24

- `mikesAge > rachelsAge`
  Returns `True` because 45 is greater than 24

- `mikesAge <= rachelsAge`
  Returns `False` because 45 is not less than, or equal to 24

- `mikesAge >= rachelsAge`
  Returns `True` because 45 is greater than, or equal to 24

To learn more about comparison operators see the following link:
http://msdn.microsoft.com/library/en-us/script56/html/vsgrpcomparison.asp.

Logical Operators

The Logical operators are AND, OR, and NOT. These operators are often used with comparison operators to modify one side of the comparison, and you will see more practical examples in *Chapter 2*. For now, let's try to understand how these operators work.

NOT

Not is a **negation operator**. It negates the expression to its right. Hence the result is True when the expression it negates is False. Get it? Try this:

```
<%
  bol_result = NOT 10 < 9
%>
<%=bol_result %>
```

When you view this page in your browser you should see:

The negation of False is True

You might be confused and ask "Why? 10 is not less than 9!"Right, but the NOT operator changes it around, causing the expression to say "10 is NOT less than 9"is True. Try a different example:

```
<%
  bol_result = NOT 10 < 11
%>
<%=bol_result %>
```

This expression evaluates to False, because "10 is NOT less than 11"is False.

AND

AND is a **conjunction operator** that compares two or more expressions. In order for the entire expression to be True, both statements (one to the left and one to the right) have to be True. For example, 10 < 9 AND 11 < 13 returns False, because 10 is **not** less than 9 (**both** statements have to be True for the entire expression to be True). Try it (see and.asp in the code download):

```
<%
  bol_result = 10 < 9 AND 11 < 13
%>
<%=bol_result %>
```

When you view this page in your browser you should see:

All expressions involved with the AND operator must be true to return True

Let's look at another example:

```
<%
  bol_result = 20 > 14 AND 34 < 56
%>
<%=bol_result %>
```

> *All expressions involved with the AND operator must be true to return True*

In this case, the expression will return True, because 20 is greater than 14, **and** 34 is less than 56.

OR

OR is a **disjunction operator**, meaning that only one expression has to be `True` for the entire statement to be `True`, either the left or the right one. For example (see `or.asp` in the code download):

```
<%
  bol_result = 15 < 14 OR 34 > 56
%>
<%=bol_result %>
```

When you view this page in your browser you should see *False* returned, because neither of the expressions is `True`. Let's see another example:

```
<%
  bol_result = 15 > 14 OR 34 > 56
%>
<%=bol_result %>
```

In this case, *True* is returned, because (at least) one of the two expressions is `True`.

Arithmetic Operators

The arithmetic operators are the simplest of all – they are:

- ^
  Exponentiation

- *
  Multiplication

- /
  Division

- \
  Integer division

- MOD
  Modulus arithmetic

- +
  Addition

- –
  Subtraction

- &
  String concatenation

Most of these are self-explanatory, but let's go through an example for each one anyway just in case.

Exponentiation (^)

This operator raises a number to the power of the exponent value. For example (exponentation.asp):

```
<%
  int_exponent_test = 2^3
  Response.Write int_exponent_test
%>
```

When you view this page in your browser you should see the value *8* returned; the variable int_exponent_test has a value that raises 2 to the third power (2 * 2 * 2), which equals 8.

Multiplication (*)

This operator multiplies the integer on the left and the integer on the right (multiplication.asp):

```
<%
  int_multiplication_test = 2 * 3
  Response.Write int_multiplication_test
%>
```

When you view this page in your browser you should see the value *6* returned; the variable int_multiplication_test has a value that multiples 2 by 3, which equals 6.

Division (/)

This operator divides the number on the left by the number on the right (division.asp):

```
<%
  int_division_test = 3/2
  Response.Write int_division_test
%>
```

When you view this page in your browser you should see the value *1.5* returned; the variable int_division_test has a value that divides 3 by 2, which equals 1.5.

Integer Division (\)

This operator divides the number on the left by the number on the right. The difference between this and the last operator is that in this case, only the integer portion of the number is returned. If we modify our last example like so (integer_division.asp):

Remember that an Integer is a whole number

```
<%
  int_integerdivision_test = 3\2
  Response.Write int_integerdivision_test
%>
```

The value *1* is returned; the variable `int_integerdividion_test` has a value that produces the integer division of 3 divided by 2, which equals 1.

Modulus Arithmetic (MOD)

This operator divides the number on the left by the number on the right, returning only the remainder result. Keep in mind that the remainder is rounded to the nearest whole integer. Let's modify our last example again, using MOD as the operator (`modulus.asp`):

```
<%
  int_modulus_test = 3 MOD 2
  Response.Write int_modulus_test
%>
```

When you view this page in your browser you should see the value *1*; the variable `int_modulus_test` has a value that looks to see how many times 2 goes into 3, then returns the remainder. 2 goes into 3 once, with 1 left over.

Addition (+)

This operator adds the number on the left to the number on the right (`addition.asp`):

```
<%
  int_addition_test = 13 + 7
  Response.Write int_addition_test
%>
```

When you view this page in your browser you should see the value *20*; the variable `int_addition_test` has a value that adds 13 and 7, which equals 20.

Subtraction (–)

This operator subtracts the numbers(s) on the right from the number(s) on the left (`subtraction.asp`):

```
<%
  int_subtraction_test = 13 - 7
  Response.Write int_subtraction_test
%>
```

When you view this page in your browser you should see the value *6*; the variable `int_subtraction_test` has a value that subtracts 7 from 13, which equals 6.

String Concatenation (&)

This operator is different from the operators above in that it's not really an arithmetic operator. It is usually grouped with arithmetic operators because of its math-like quality of joining: it joins two or more string expressions to each other. For example:

```
<%
  int_concatenation_test = "Omar " & "Elbaga"
  Response.Write int_concatenation_test
%>
```

When you view this page (`concatenation.asp`) in your browser you should see:

The results of concatenating two strings

The variable `int_concatenation_test` has a value that concatenates "`Omar `" with "`Elbaga`"to form "`Omar Elbaga`". You can concatenate more than two strings of course, for example:

You can concatenate more than two strings

```
<%
  int_concatenation_test = "New " & "Jersey, " & "USA"
  Response.Write int_concatenation_test
%>
```

When you view this page in your browser you should see the string *New Jersey, USA*.

Operator Precedence

One last important thing to discuss is the issue of **operator precedence**. If you do not organize multiple expressions with parentheses, the web server has no way of knowing which expression you want processed first, so it will process the operators in a set order. The order in which expressions are processed is as follows, with each list going from first to last (operators appearing on the same bullet have equal operator precedence):

Arithmetic Operators:

- Exponents (^)
- Negation (–) (indicates the negative value of a numeric expression, for example -7)
- Multiplication (*), division (/ and \)
- Modulus arithmetic (Mod)
- Addition (+), subtraction (-)

Note that in mathematics BODMAS is the acronym used in helping one remember the order of operator precedence; it stands for Brackets (parentheses), Division, Multiplication, Addition, and Subtraction.

Comparision Operators:

- Equality (=)
- Inequality (<>)
- Less than (<)
- Greater than (>)
- Less than or equal to (<=)
- Greater than or equal to (>=)

Logical Operators:

- Negation (NOT)
- Conjunction (AND)
- Disjunction (OR)

Let's look at some examples; say you had the following expression in a variable (see `precedence.asp`):

```
<%
  result = 4 + 2 * 3
  Response.Write result
%>
```

When you view this page in your browser you will see the result *10*; multiplication precedes addition so the web server does the multiplication first and then the addition. The expression is processed like so: 2 * 3 = 6, then 6 + 4 = 10.

> *You can force the web server to perform the operations in a different order*

What if you really wanted to add 4 + 2 = 6, then multiply it by 3, which would equal 18? In this case you will have to use parentheses, as the web server will execute expressions within parentheses before anything else regardless of operator precedence. You can force the web server to perform the operations in a different order if you change the code as follows (see `precedence2.asp`):

```
<%
  result = (4 + 2) * 3
  Response.Write result
%>
```

When you view this page in your browser you will see the result *18*.

Summary

This chapter contains the most important basic ASP/VBScript knowledge needed before we can continue through the more advanced concepts in the chapters to come. In this chapter you have learned about:

- The basics of ASP Script
- How to declare variables and guidelines for naming them
- The different variable data types
- The VBScript operators (logical, comparison, arithmeiic) and how they are used
- The built-in operator precedence

2

- Conditional statements

- Looping through code

- Arrays

- Converting Recordsets to Arrays

Author: Dan Short

Decision Making, Loops and Arrays

The last chapter gave you a comprehensive knowledge of ASP Syntax. This chapter will put that knowledge to use by creating functions that further empower you to perform decision-making steps throughout your code.

Part of the power of server-side markup is the ability to decide what you want sent to the viewer's browser and to affect large numbers of records or objects at one time before sending them. VBScript provides a large number of functions for performing those decision-making steps and looping through large amounts of code.

Throughout this chapter we'll be putting together a bulk e-mail application that will loop through a list of subscribed users and send an individual e-mail to each one based on their preferences. Each subscriber can choose to receive either a plain-text e-mail or an HTML-formatted one.

Decision-Making Process

The bread and butter of any rich client-experience is displaying information based on the viewer's input. Whether this input comes in the form of usernames, passwords, and stored preferences in a database, or just from submitting a feedback form, you have to decide what to do with that information. To provide for these decision-making choices, we have two different types of conditional statements:

- If ... Then ... Else
- Select Case

I think you'll probably find the `If ... Then ... Else` fairly straightforward, given its plain English syntax, but we're going to cover a few of the gotchas you'll most likely run into and a few words about nesting. For example, the more complex an `If` statement gets, the harder it is to manage. A large number of `ElseIf` statements or nested `If`s can soon become impossible to keep track of. That's when you'll need to take a look at the `Select Case` statement for trimming things down.

If ... Then ... Else, ElseIf

The basic syntax for the `If ... Then ... Else` statement is exactly that. If some condition is met then do this, or else do this. Here's a simple example from `BasicIf.asp`:

```
<%
  Dim myValue
  myValue = 0

  If myValue = 0 Then
    Response.Write("myValue is equal to 0.")
  Else
    Response.Write("myValue is not equal to 0.")
  End If
%>
```

Each statement of the `If` block is on its own line for ease of reading. We can put it on fewer lines like this:

```
<%
  Dim myValue
  myValue = 0
  If myValue = 0 Then Response.Write("myValue is equal to 0.") Else
Response.Write("myValue is not equal to 0.") End If
%>
```

I don't like this second method, for reasons of readability. The action to take if the condition evaluates to `True` follows the `Then` statement; in this case, `Response.Write("myValue is equal to 0.")`.

> *The main purpose of writing conditional statements is to show or hide a particular part of a page based on a user's information*

The main purpose of writing conditional statements is to show or hide a particular part of a page based on a user's information. For example, we could show a welcome message for users that have logged into our site and a login form for those that haven't. I think you'll see that, using the first example given, putting a login form in `Response.Write` statements can be a major pain.

To remedy this, we'll need to use context switching, or move from a VBScript block of code to an HTML block and back again. Here's a simple example showing a welcome message to logged in users. We check a Session variable (which will be discussed in *Chapter 10*) that the *Login User* Server Behavior sets when a user has logged in. Notice that I've left off the `Else` statement, so nothing happens if the user isn't logged in.

```
<% If Session("MM_Username") <> "" Then %>
<p>Welcome <%= Session("MM_Username") %></p>
<% End If %>
```

In the code block above, from `ContextSwitching.asp`, the `<p>` element content is completely editable in Dreamweaver's Design View, making it easy to apply styles, change it to a heading, or whatever else you may need to do. The `Session("MM_Username")` is a session variable that is set by Dreamweaver's *Login User* Server Behavior.

If you like clicking the buttons on the Insert Bar instead of manually typing in your `If` blocks, there is an icon for each of the `If` statements (`If`, `Else`, `ElseIf`, and `End If`) in the *ASP* tab of the Insert Bar. Just click where you want your block in Design View and press the appropriate icon. The only ones that require any additional input are the `If` and `ElseIf` objects, which require you to enter your conditions in Code View.

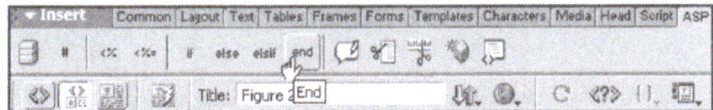

The ASP tab of the insert bar.

As you've probably experienced before, Dreamweaver also includes a few Server Behaviors used to wrap code blocks in conditional statements, depending on the results of a Recordset. In other words, you can hide or show regions of your page based on whether a Recordset returned results or not, or if you're on the first or last record of a Recordset. These are all located in the *Show Regions* menu of the *Server Behaviors* panel. Just select an area of your page to apply the behavior to, and select the appropriate *Show Region* behavior:

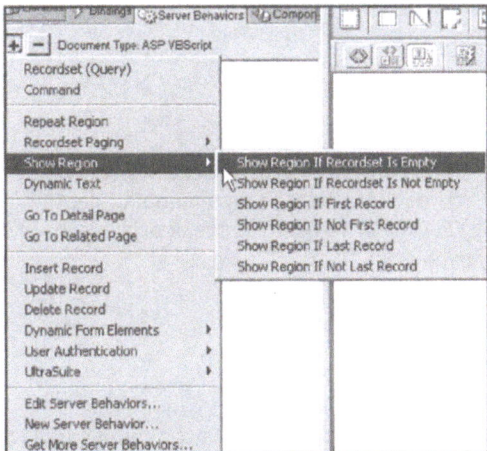

Show Region Server Behaviors.

It's also possible to string conditional statements out using AND or OR. Using these allows us control such as "If this equals True AND this equals True, then do this." This example, from `AndOr.asp`, shows both the AND and OR syntax and how the results differ:

```
<%
  Dim myValue, myName
  myValue = 0
  myName = "Dan"

  'Simple AND Condition
  If myValue = 0 AND myName = "Dan" Then
    Response.Write("All conditions met")
  Else
    Response.Write("At least one condition failed.")
  End If

  'Simple OR Condition
  If myValue = 1 OR myName = "Dan" Then
    Response.Write("At least one condition was met.")
  Else
    Response.Write("None of the conditions were met.")
  End If
%>
```

The AND and OR conditional statements can be further expanded and grouped to form extremely complex conditions. Here's another example, also found in AndOr.asp:

```
<%
  Dim myValue, myName, yourValue, yourName
  myValue = 0
  myName = "Dan"
  yourValue = 1
  yourName = "Bob"

  'Complex Condition
  If (myValue = 1 OR myName = "Dan") AND (yourValue = 1 AND yourName = "Bob") Then
    Response.Write("Both conditions tested True.")
  Else
    Response.Write("At least one of the complex conditions failed.")
  End If
%>
```

With the above example, we'd end up with "*Both conditions tested True*", since both of our conditions in parentheses tested True. You can also nest If statements to perform more complex operations. In this example, from NestedIf.asp, we're going to check and see if myValue is between 0 and 10, less than 0, equal to 0, or greater than 10.

```
<%
  Dim myValue
  myValue = 12

  If myValue > 0 AND myValue < 10 Then
    Response.Write("myValue is greater than 0 but less than 10")
  Else
    If myValue < 0 Then
      Response.Write("myValue is less than 0.")
    Else
      If myValue = 0 Then
        Response.Write("myValue equals 0.")
```

```
      Else
         Response.Write("myValue is greater than 10.")
      End If
   End If
  End If
%>
```

This complicated `If` statement certainly accomplishes what we were looking for, but the code is difficult to maintain and hard to read. Using `ElseIf` will make it much easier to see what's going on in this block of code. Here's an alternative way to write that same `If` statement, as found in `ElseIf.asp`:

```
<%
  Dim myValue
  myValue = 12

  If myValue > 0 AND myValue < 10 Then
     Response.Write("myValue is greater than 0 but less than 10")
  ElseIf myValue < 0 Then
     Response.Write("myValue is less than 0.")
  ElseIf myValue = 0 Then
     Response.Write("myValue equals 0.")
  Else
     Response.Write("myValue is greater than 10.")
  End If
%>
```

I think you'll find that code block much easier to read. The `ElseIf` statement performs the same function as the standard `If` statement. It tests to see if a condition is True and then runs a block of code if the condition is met. As soon as one condition tests True, then the appropriate action is taken and the `If` statement is exited. With the `ElseIf` statement you can also check a different condition on each line. You could potentially check the value of an infinite number of variables in one block, although that would soon get tedious since you have to reference the variable on every single line.

A bit later in this chapter, you'll be looking at an `If` statement to determine whether or not to send a particular type of e-mail to various individuals, in our e-mail application.

Select Case

If you've got a lot of options to choose between, using `If` statements can lead to your code getting messy. The `Select Case` statement allows you to use a single test expression that is evaluated once, on the `Select Case` line. This makes the code even more readable and efficient, and also helps to keep us from making any syntax mistakes along the way. It's very easy to misspell a variable name if you have to type it out 10 times in one `If` block.

> *The Select Case statement allows you to use a single test expression that is evaluated once, on the Select Case line*

Here's an example that checks a numerical entry for the appropriate month name. Notice that we also have a `Case Else` statement to output an error message if `myValue` doesn't match any of our `Case` statements. As soon as a value matches a case, the appropriate code is run, and the `Select Case` function is exited. This example is from `SelectCase.asp`:

```
<%
  Dim myValue
  myValue = 12

  Select Case myValue 'This could also be a calculation or condition
    Case 1
      Response.Write("The month is January")
    Case 2
      Response.Write("The month is February")
    Case 3
      Response.Write("The month is March")
    Case 4
      Response.Write("The month is April")
    Case 5
      Response.Write("The month is May")
    Case 6
      Response.Write("The month is June")
    Case 7
      Response.Write("The month is July")
    Case 8
      Response.Write("The month is August")
    Case 9
      Response.Write("The month is September")
    Case 10
      Response.Write("The month is October")
    Case 11
      Response.Write("The month is November")
    Case 12
      Response.Write("The month is December")
    Case Else
      Response.Write("This is an invalid value")
  End Select
%>
```

In this case, the output will be `December`, being the `Response.Write` line for `Case 12`.

You can also test for multiple values on a case line, just like you do with an `If` statement. The only difference is that you can only test against the value you use in the `Select Case` line. So something like "`Case 1 OR 2`" is also valid.

One common mistake in a `Select Case` block is to leave out the `End Select` line or the `Case Else` statement. Always make sure you're ending your blocks correctly and that you have a catch all statement for values that you didn't expect.

Looping Through Code

Looping through code, or repeating a series of steps a set number of times or until a certain condition is met, is another backbone of web applications. The ability to affect a large number of records, whether those records are being displayed or you're building a list of e-mails to send to, can make working with data much easier. If you've used Dreamweaver MX already, you'll have probably run across the *Repeat Region* Server Behavior, which is Dreamweaver's solution to displaying a list of records, using `While ... Wend`.

While ... Wend

The quickest way to loop through any data in Dreamweaver is to use the *Repeat Region* Server Behavior, which uses a `While ... Wend` loop to repeat a desired section of code until a certain condition is met. All it takes is a Recordset, a selection on your page of an action to repeat, and a few mouse clicks to iterate through a list of records using a `While ... Wend` loop. The `While ... Wend` syntax is pretty straightforward:

```
<%
  While test = true
    'Repeat this content
  Wend
%>
```

All we do is test for a specific value, and if that test is True, we repeat the contents of the `While ... Wend` statements until the test is False. To demonstrate, in `RepeatRegion.asp` I've added a connection to a database, and a Recordset (click the + icon in the *Server Behaviors* panel and choose *Recordset(Query)* – the *Simple* display is shown here) that selects data on people who have subscribed to an e-mail newsletter:

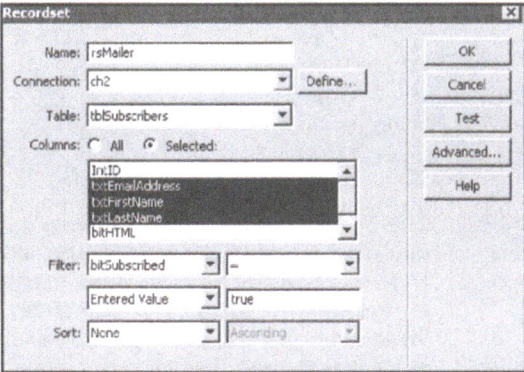

The Simple Recordset dialog.

We're just going to output the first and last name and e-mail address for each followed by a line break. Next, highlight the code you want to repeat (make sure you include the line break) and choose the *Repeat Region* Server Behavior from the *Server Behaviors* Panel – this will bring up the *Repeat Region* dialog box:

The Repeat Region dialog.

Choose how many records you want to output (in our case we've accepted the default *10*) and click *OK*. You should notice the following additions to the code:

```
<%
  Dim Repeat1__numRows
  Dim Repeat1__index

  Repeat1__numRows = 10
  Repeat1__index = 0
  rsMailer_numRows = rsMailer_numRows + Repeat1__numRows
%>
```

This code is added directly below our Recordset and determines how many rows the repeat will output. You can manually change `Repeat1__numRows` to increase or decrease the number of rows, or change it to `-1` to output all records (I'll explain how that works next).

This code is wrapped around the data we want to repeat:

```
<%
  While ((Repeat1__numRows <> 0) AND (NOT rsMailer.EOF))
%>
<%=(rsMailer.Fields.Item("txtFirstName").Value)%>
<%=(rsMailer.Fields.Item("txtLastName").Value)%>:
<%=(rsMailer.Fields.Item("txtEmailAddress").Value)%><br>
<%
  Repeat1__index=Repeat1__index+1
  Repeat1__numRows=Repeat1__numRows-1
  rsMailer.MoveNext()
Wend
%>
```

The two disadvantages to the `While ... Wend` loop are the inability to exit the loop if a condition is met inside the loop, and the inability to decide when you want to do your conditional check the `Do While ... Loop` takes care of those problems for us.

The `While` statement says "As long as the `Repeat1__numRows` variable is not equal to `0` and we're not at the end of our Recordset, keep doing everything up to the `Wend` statement". Right before the `Wend` statement, the code adjusts a few variables each time the loop is run. The `Repeat1__index` variable holds the number of records that have been shown (and is handy for displaying a running count of records), and the `Repeat1__numRows` variable holds how many more we need to show. Each time the loop is run, the `Repeat1__numRows` is decreased by one, until eventually it equals `0` or the Recordset is exhausted.

Earlier I said that you could repeat all of the rows by changing `Repeat1__numRows` to −1. The reason this works is that the `Repeat1__numRows <> 0` condition will never be met if the variable starts out below 0, since each time the loop is run, 1 is subtracted from the variable. It just keeps getting further and further away from 0.

Do While/Until … Loop

The `While ... Wend` loop is the quickest to implement in Dreamweaver, but it's not really the "correct" way to do things in ASP. `While ... Wend` has been replaced with the `Do While/Until ... Loop` statement.

Some advantages of the `Do While` loop are the ability to exit the loop if a condition is met, and the ability to perform a loop "until" a condition is met. You can also determine when the check is done, either at the beginning or the end of the loop. Here is the same repeat region we saw above, rewritten using `Do While`, with an `Exit` statement thrown in for good measure:

```
<%
  Do While ((Repeat1__numRows <> 0) AND (NOT rsMailer.EOF))
    If rsMailer.Fields.Item("txtFirstName").Value = "Daniel" Then Exit Do
%>
<%=(rsMailer.Fields.Item("txtFirstName").Value)%>
<%=(rsMailer.Fields.Item("txtLastName").Value)%>:
<%=(rsMailer.Fields.Item("txtEmailAddress").Value)%><br>
<%
  Repeat1__index=Repeat1__index+1
  Repeat1__numRows=Repeat1__numRows-1
  rsMailer.MoveNext()
Loop
%>
```

Now if the first name for a user is "Daniel", the loop will exit and the page will continue processing with the next item directly below the closing `Loop` statement.

Now, let's look at another example of how using an `Exit` statement can come in handy. The table seen here (see `ExitDo.asp` in the code download) will display all of our HTML Newsletter subscribers followed by all of our Plain Text Newsletter subscribers:

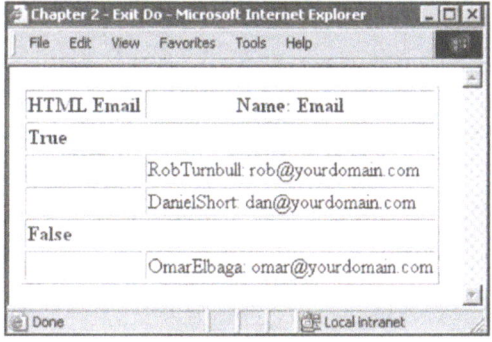

ExitDo.asp

Decision Making, Loops and Arrays

The following table, `tblSubscribers` (found in `mailer.mdb`) will store all of our data. The `bitHTML` and `bitSubscribed` fields determine whether the user wants an HTML newsletter and whether they've actually subscribed to the newsletter:

IntID	txtEmailAddress	txtFirstName	txtLastName	bitHTML	bitSubscribed
1	dan@yourdomain.com	Daniel	Short	☑	☑
3	omar@yourdomain.com	Omar	Elbaga	☐	☑
2	rob@yourdomain.com	Rob	Turnbull	☑	☑
4	simon@yourdomain.com	Simon	Mackie	☐	☐
(AutoNumber)				▣	▣

The tblSubscribers table

The only caveat for this type of nested repeat is that your Recordset needs to be sorted according to how you want to group your records first, and then sorted by whatever other means you need. In this example, we've sorted by `bitHTML`, which determines whether or not our user wants to receive HTML newsletters. Here is the code for `ExitDo.asp`:

```
<table border="1">
  <tr>
    <th>HTML Email</th>
    <th>Name: Email</th>
  </tr>
<%
  While ((Repeat1__numRows <> 0) AND (NOT rsMailer.EOF))
%>
  <tr>
    <td colspan="2">
      <strong><%=(rsMailer.Fields.Item("bitHTML").Value)%></strong></td>
  </tr>
<%
  emailType = rsMailer("bitHTML")
  Do While NOT rsMailer.EOF 'A loop while a specified condition exists.
    If emailType = rsMailer("bitHTML") Then
%>
  <tr>
    <td> </td>
    <td><%=(rsMailer.Fields.Item("txtFirstName").Value)%>
        <%=(rsMailer.Fields.Item("txtLastName").Value)%>:
        <%=(rsMailer.Fields.Item("txtEmailAddress").Value)%></td>
  </tr>
<%
    rsMailer.MoveNext()
  Else
    Exit Do
  End If
Loop

%>
<%
  Repeat1__index=Repeat1__index+1
  Repeat1__numRows=Repeat1__numRows-1
  'rsMailer.MoveNext()
Wend
%>
```

Notice that I've nested a `Do While` loop inside my regular repeat region. Right before the `Do While` statement, I set a variable to determine the e-mail type from the current record. We then enter the `Do While` statement and immediately check to see if the current record's `emailType` matches the one we set before we entered the loop. If it does, we output the record and move to the next record. If it doesn't then we exit the loop and start again.

In this way, as we move through the records, we check each one to make sure it matches the former record. If it does, we just output the record, and if it doesn't we start a new group. Also notice that I've commented out the `rsMailer.MoveNext` statement inside Dreamweaver's `Wend` block. If I remove the `rsMailer.MoveNext` statement completely, Dreamweaver will show a red exclamation mark in the *Server Behaviors* Panel, indicating that the behavior is broken. Commenting it out tricks Dreamweaver into thinking nothing's changed.

It's also possible to change when the condition of a `Do Loop` is checked, by moving the condition to the ending loop statement like this:

```
<%
  Dim intMyVar
  intMyVar = 1
  Do
    Response.Write("intMyVar")
    intMyVar = intMyVar + 1
Loop Until intMyVar = 10
%>
```

This type of `Loop` statement ensures that the loop is run at least once, since it has to go through once before it hits the `Loop` statement. You have to be especially careful with the `Loop Until` statement if you're referencing something inside the loop that doesn't exist. For example, if you do `Loop Until recordset.EOF` and you reference the Recordset inside the loop, you need to **be sure** that you actually have records in your Recordset before you enter the `Do` statement. If you don't have any records, you'll end up with an error inside your `Do` statement, because you're trying to output records that don't exist.

> ...if you do `Loop` *Until* `recordset.EOF` *and you reference the Recordset inside the loop, you need to* **be sure** *that you actually have records in your Recordset before you enter the* `Do` *statement*

For ... Next

A `For ... Next` loop allows you to cycle through a block of code a set number of times. You can loop through an array (which we'll cover soon in this chapter), or perform a calculation say ten times and then stop the loop. Using a `For` statement means that you don't have to handle the variable that does the counting – the `For` statement takes care of it for you. The default step value for the `For` statement is 1, but you can specify what the step amount is. Here's a simple `For` statement that outputs a list from 1 to 10:

> *A* `For ... Next` *loop allows you to cycle through a block of code a set number of times*

Decision Making, Loops and Arrays

2

```
<%
  Dim iCounter
  For iCounter = 1 to 10
    Response.Write(iCounter & ".<br>")
  Next
%>
```

The opening `For` statement specifies what we want our counter (the variable `iCounter`) to be and when we should stop. In this instance we want to stop when the value of `iCounter` is equal to 10. Notice that the `For` statement doesn't say "execute this code 10 times" but instead says "execute this code until the counter is equal to 10". We can also change the step value, meaning that we can say "increase `iCounter` by 2 for each iteration". Here's the syntax for the `Step` argument.

```
<%
  Dim iCounter
  For iCounter = 1 to 10 Step 2
    Response.Write(iCounter & ".<br>")
  Next
%>
```

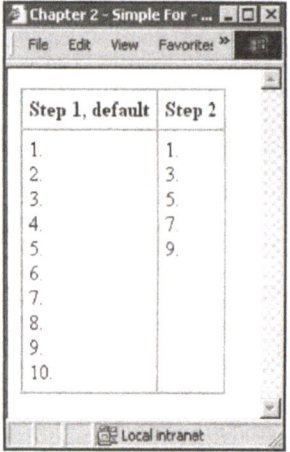

The result of this `For` loop is entirely different. The first `For` loop uses the numbers 1 through 10, whereas the second outputs all of the odd numbers between 1 to 10, because we've increased the counter by 2 each time, starting with 1. You can find this example in the code download as `SimpleFor.asp`:

Later in this chapter you'll see how to put For loops to work when working with arrays

SimpleFor.asp

> The `For Each` loop
> allows you to iterate
> through a set of
> items inside a
> collection

For Each ... Next

The `For Each` loop allows you to iterate through a set of items inside a collection (an ordered set of information) or each element inside an array. This means that you can loop through each item in a `QueryString`, form submission, or even record from a database. The concept seems a bit abstract, so it's a little easier to show an example than it is to explain. I commonly use this method for application troubleshooting. If I don't know if a `Form` or `QueryString` variable is being submitted correctly, I'll just output the entire `Request.Form` or `Request.QueryString` collection. The following code can be found as `foreach.asp` in the code download:

```
<%
  Dim Item
  For Each Item in Request.QueryString
    Response.Write(Item & ": " & Request.QueryString(Item) & "<br>")
  Next
%>
```

The result of this code when it is run with a sample querystring appended to the URL (in my case *http://localhost/chapter2/foreach.asp?var1=value1 &var2=value2&var3=value3*) would look like this:

The same can be done with the `Request.Form` collection if you need to output all of the form fields submitted to a page. A more complex example would show all of the fields in a database and each field's data type:

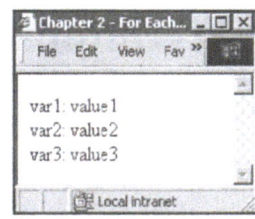

foreach.asp, displaying values from a Querystring.

```
<%
  Dim Item
  For Each Item in rsMailer.Fields
    Response.Write(Item.Name & ": " & rsMailer(Item.Name).type & "<br>")
  Next
%>
```

Take a look at `ForEachRecord.asp` to see a more advanced method that will output friendly names for the data type against the integer reference for the type. You can connect to a Recordset and output a large amount of information about each database field.

When working with `For Each`, the `Item` variable that I declared could be named whatever you want it to be. All I suggest is that it be named something meaningful. We could say "`For Each Bob in Request.Querystring`", but that doesn't really explain to someone reading our code what we're looking for. When you come back to your code six months from now, you don't want to be wondering what that `Bob` variable was for.

The Dreaded Infinite Loop

Something you're going to end up meeting, and smacking your forehead over, is infinite loops. I can't count how many times I've forgotten to add a `Recordset.MoveNext` method inside a loop and ended up sitting and waiting for the server to time out while it loops over and over. Take this code for example; the condition will never be met even if there is only one record in the Recordset:

```
<%
  Do While NOT recordset.EOF
    Response.Write(recordset("field") & <br />")
  Loop
%>
```

The reason it will never test True is because we're outputting the first record every time without ever moving to the next. If you've put an insert statement inside your Loop to add new records to your database, this is a quick way to get 10,000 new records (so I hear – I've never actually done it!). If your loop is extremely complex and you're doing a lot of database work, this could potentially bring the entire server down, so be sure that you always give yourself a way out of your loop.

Working with Arrays

> *An array is a collection of variables that comes in two different flavors: Single Dimension arrays and Multi-dimensional arrays*

An official definition of an array would be "a set of sequentially indexed elements having the same type of data". Each element of an array has a unique identifying index number. Changes made to one element of an array do not affect the other elements. In plain English an array could be considered a miniature text database, or a miniature spreadsheet that contains rows and columns of data without a physical file. You can fill arrays with whatever information you want and perform manipulations and functions on the entire array, or specific elements only.

Anatomy of an Array

An array is a collection of variables that comes in two different flavors: Single Dimension arrays and Multi-dimensional arrays. We'll cover the single dimension array first and then explain the differences in multi-dimensional arrays.

Single Dimension Arrays

The best way to explain an array is to just jump right in and create one. The simplest way to create a new array is as follows:

```
<%
  Dim myArray
  myArray = Array("item1","item2","item3","item4")
  Response.Write(IsArray(myArray)) 'Test to see if the variable is an array.
%>
```

The highlighted line in the code sample is what actually builds our array – this is a fixed-size single dimension array. The Array statement simply takes a comma-delimited list of values and builds the array, putting each value in its own indexed position. I added the IsArray function just to show that we have actually created a valid array. If the variable is an array, IsArray will return True.

Each element in the array is stored with an index starting at 0 and counting up. So, if we wanted to write each element in this array, we could do this:

```
<%
  Dim myArray
  myArray = Array("item1","item2","item3","item4")
  Response.Write(myArray(0) & "<br />")
  Response.Write(myArray(1) & "<br />")
  Response.Write(myArray(2) & "<br />")
  Response.Write(myArray(3))
%>
```

It's very important to notice that the array item numbering starts at 0, so since our array has 4 elements in it, we start at 0 and end at 3. We can also set up the same array by explicitly declaring what value goes in what array element:

```
<%
  Dim myArray(3)
  myArray(0) = "item1"
  myArray(1) = "item2"
  myArray(2) = "item3"
  myArray(3) = "item4"
%>
```

Notice that in the Dim statement we declared what size we wanted our array to be. We didn't have to do that in the previous example, because the Array statement took care of it all for us. If we're going to manually fill our array, we need to tell it how many elements we want. Again, notice the base 0 counting; we wanted 4 elements, so we declared a length of 3.

However, what if we need to add an additional item to the array later on in our code? In that case we need to use the ReDim statement, which allows us to resize our array. This code would add an additional element to myArray:

```
<%
  ReDim myArray(3)
  myArray(0) = "item1"
  myArray(1) = "item2"
  myArray(2) = "item3"
  myArray(3) = "item4"

  ReDim myArray(4)
  MyArray(4) = "item5"

%>
```

Notice that we had to declare the array with the ReDim statement at the very beginning. This sets the array as a "dynamic" array, meaning that we can add and remove elements from it using the ReDim statement. But something strange has happened now we have ReDimed our array. If we output the array contents, elements 0 – 3 are now empty!

When you resize an array, all of the old elements are removed by default. To fix that, we need to use the Preserve keyword in our ReDim statement:

```
<%
  Dim i
  ReDim myArray(3)
  myArray(0) = "item1"
  myArray(1) = "item2"
  myArray(2) = "item3"
  myArray(3) = "item4"

  Response.Write("Original array:<br />")
  For i = 0 to UBound(myArray)
    Response.Write(i & ": " & myArray(i) & "<br />")
  Next

  ReDim Preserve myArray(4)
  myArray(4) = "item5"

  Response.Write("<br />Resized (to 4) and preserved array:<br />")
  For i = 0 to UBound(myArray)
    Response.Write(i & ": " & myArray(i) & "<br />")
  Next

  ReDim myArray(5)
  myArray(5) = "item6"

  Response.Write("<br />Resized (to 5) array:<br />")
  For i = 0 to UBound(myArray)
    Response.Write(i & ": " & myArray(i) & "<br />")
  Next
%>
```

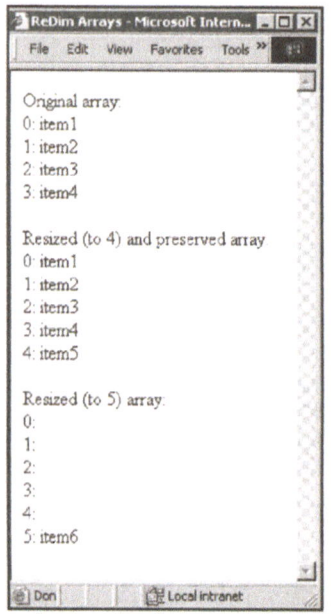

redim.asp – the effects of rediming arrays.

Here we've resized this array twice, first using the `Preserve` keyword and then without it. If you view the page in a browser (`redim.asp` in the code download) you'll end up with the following output (we'll cover those nifty `For` statements in a bit):

Notice that in the last array we don't have any of my original array elements.

Also, if you shrink an array, by `ReDiming` it to a smaller size, you'll lose any information at the end of the array, with or without the `Preserve` keyword. If we `ReDimed` `myArray` to 1 we'd lose *item3* and *item4* from the list.

Another handy way to build an array is using the `Split` function. The `Split` function has two arguments, a string to split, and a character to split the string with (that is, the string will be split where this character appears in the string). This means that we could take a sentence or a list of values in a string and split it up so that each item in the string is put into its own array element. Here's an example of splitting up a sentence:

```
<%
  Dim myArray, myString
  myString = "Don't ya just love arrays?"
  myArray = Split(myString," ")
%>
```

Now each word in myString is inside its own element in the array, since we split the string where the space character (" ") appears.

We can also Join an array, meaning we can take an array with individual elements and shove everything back into a regular string:

```
<%
  Dim myArray(4)
  myArray(0)  = "Don't"
  myArray(1)  = "ya"
  myArray(2)  = "just"
  myArray(3)  = "love"
  myArray(4)  = "arrays?"

  Dim myString
  myString = Join(myArray," ")
%>
```

The variable myString now contains "Don't ya just love arrays?" The space delimiter I added into the Join statement is optional. If you leave the delimiter off, the Join function will just squash it all together, giving us "Don'tyajustlovearrays?".

Multi-Dimensional Arrays

Now we get to the juicy part of arrays, the ability to have arrays inside arrays, termed **Multi-Dimensional Arrays**. That's right; each element of an array can have its own set of arrays. This means that we can actually store multiple bits of information (or columns) about a single array element (or row) just like we do with a standard Recordset. This also means that we can't build our array using the simple Array("value1","value2") method we used earlier. I'll walk you through setting up a multi-dimensional array for a list of country abbreviations. We're going to be using a two dimensional array for our abbreviations:

VBScript will allow for up to 60 dimensions, but I've never had to use more than two.

```
<%
  'myArray(rows,columns), numbers are zero based
  Dim myArray(2,1)
%>
```

The first difference is the Dim statement. We now have two variables, the first of which determines the number of elements (or rows, our first dimension) and the second is the number of columns for each element (our second dimension). Both of these numbers are 0-based, so our Dim statement says we want an array with 3 rows and 2 columns.

For each entry in our array, we declare it by referencing first the row and then the column we want to assign the value to. This table represents the data we are going to declare:

Row	Abbreviation (0)	Name (1)
0	UK	United Kingdom
1	US	United States
2	CA	Canada

And here are our declared variables:

```
<%
Dim myArray(2,1)
myArray(0,0) = "UK"
myArray(0,1) = "United Kingdom"
myArray(1,0) = "US"
myArray(1,1) = "United States"
myArray(2,0) = "CA"
myArray(2,1) = "Canada"
%>
```

Notice that each array is referenced by row and then column. We could continue this indefinitely, adding additional columns or rows as we see fit.

Once you get deep into a page using multi-dimensional arrays, it can get very confusing and hard to remember what number corresponds to which column. For this reason, I usually create some static variables with easy-to-remember names for referencing my columns. Here's an example of the same country array using variables to reference the column names. We first declare the variable for my column name and then set its value:

```
<%
Dim myArray(2,1)
Dim arCountryAbbr : arCountryAbbr = 0
Dim arCountryName : arCountryName = 1
myArray(0,arCountryAbbr) = "UK"
myArray(0,arCountryName) = "United Kingdom"
myArray(1,arCountryAbbr) = "US"
myArray(1,arCountryName) = "United States"
myArray(2,arCountryAbbr) = "CA"
myArray(2,arCountryName) = "Canada"
%>
```

This not only makes it easier to create our array, but also easier to reference the values later in our document. If for some reason we need to change the order of the columns in our array, it's just a matter of changing the number assigned to the friendly name.

Looping Through an Array

Now that we know how to write these wonderful arrays, what can we do with them? While it's certainly possible to reference each column of each row individually, that doesn't really make things any easier than manually putting those values on the page. That's where the wonders of the For ... Next loop come in. It's possible to loop through an array of any size from beginning to end and output all of the fields. While discussing single dimension arrays, we had the following code:

```
<%
  Dim myArray
  myArray = Array("item1","item2","item3","item4")
  Response.Write(myArray(0) & "<br />")
  Response.Write(myArray(1) & "<br />")
  Response.Write(myArray(2) & "<br />")
  Response.Write(myArray(3))
%>
```

While this works, it's obviously not very efficient – just imagine if our array contained 10,000 items! Our alternative is to use a `For ... Next` loop:

```
<%
  Dim myArray, iCounter
  myArray = Array("item1","item2","item3","item4")

  For iCounter = 0 to UBound(myArray)
    Response.Write(myArray(iCounter) & "<br />")
  Next
%>
```

The only thing we haven't covered already in this block is the `UBound` function. `UBound` stands for **Upper Bound**, and gives us the number of items in the array, starting with 0. So in this example, `UBound(myArray)` returns 3, so the `For` statement loops from 0 to 3, and outputs each array element. If we added another item to the end of our array, we wouldn't need to change our `For` loop at all.

The only problem we have now is that we will have a stray `<br />` element written after our last array element, something we didn't have when we manually output the results, and not something we really want. We just need a simple If statement to take care of that:

```
<%
  Dim myArray, iCounter
  myArray = Array("item1","item2","item3","item4")
  For iCounter = 0 to UBound(myArray)

    Response.Write(myArray(iCounter))
    If iCounter <> UBound(myArray) Then Response.Write("<br />"
  Next
%>
```

Now a `<br />` tag will be written for every array element but the last one.

While that list is handy, it's not all that impressive. Let's use our multi-dimensional array of country abbreviations to build a list menu. We're going to follow the same principles in the previous example, but we need to change our `UBound` function a bit.

```
<%
  Dim myArray(2,1)
  Dim arCountryAbbr : arCountryAbbr = 0
  Dim arCountryName : arCountryName = 1
  myArray(0,arCountryAbbr) = "UK"
  myArray(0,arCountryName) = "United Kingdom"
```

```
myArray(1,arCountryAbbr)  =  "US"
myArray(1,arCountryName)  =  "United States"
myArray(2,arCountryAbbr)  =  "CA"
myArray(2,arCountryName)  =  "Canada"

Dim iCounter
Response.Write("<select name=""countries"">")

For iCounter = 0 to UBound(myArray,1)
   Response.Write("<option value=""" & myArray(iCounter,arCountryAbbr) & """>")
   Response.Write(myArray(iCounter, arCountryName))
   Response.Write("</option>")
Next
Response.Write("</select>")
%>
```

Pull that up in our browser (countrylist.asp) and you get this:

Notice the new argument in the UBound function. For multi-dimensional arrays, you have to tell the UBound function which dimension you want the upper bound of. In our example, UBound(myArray,1) returns the number 2, since there are 3 rows. If we used UBound(myArray,2) it would return the number 1, since we have 2 columns. Remember the table we looked at earlier – the first dimension holds the rows and the second dimension holds the columns.

countrylist.asp – a dynamically populated list menu.

We now have a list of countries that we can wrap in a function and display anywhere on our site. We also don't need a database table or additional calls to the database (the less you hit a database the better). Here's an example of our list menu put into a reusable function (we'll cover functions in *Chapter 3*):

```
<%
Function CountryList(fieldName)
   Dim myArray(2,1)
   Dim arCountryAbbr : arCountryAbbr = 0
   Dim arCountryName : arCountryName = 1
   myArray(0,arCountryAbbr)  =  "UK"
   myArray(0,arCountryName)  =  "United Kingdom"
   myArray(1,arCountryAbbr)  =  "US"
   myArray(1,arCountryName)  =  "United States"
   myArray(2,arCountryAbbr)  =  "CA"
   myArray(2,arCountryName)  =  "Canada"

   Dim iCounter
   Response.Write("<select name=""" & fieldName & """>")
   For iCounter = 0 to UBound(myArray,1)
      Response.Write("<option value=""" & myArray(iCounter,arCountryAbbr) & """>")
      Response.Write(myArray(iCounter,arCountryName))
      Response.Write("</option>")
   Next
   Response.Write("</select>")
End Function
%>
```

Now any place I want to display this select menu, I can use this:

```
<%= CountryList("listmenuName") %>
```

Converting a Recordset to an Array

While working with arrays is fun and exciting, building those arrays can be a royal pain. The only way to do it in most cases is one line at a time. What if we could convert an entire Recordset into an array? This would make the load on our databases less (especially with large Recordsets) and would give us a quick and easy way to get a large two-dimensional array filled with data.

If you're dealing with extremely large arrays, stick with a Recordset: putting that much information into a variable could have adverse effects on server performance. There's no hard number you should stop at, but some simple experimentation should show you what does and doesn't work.

Let's assume that we have 500 e-mail addresses in our database, and we need to output the first name, last name, and e-mail address for each user and send them an e-mail. We're going to need to access the database quite a lot:

```
<%
  While NOT Recordset.EOF
%>
<%= Recordset("firstname") %> <%= Recordset("lastname") %>:
<%= Recordset("email") %>
<%
  Recordset.MoveNext
Wend
%>
```

If we count up all the hits to the `Recordset` object, we get a total of 2500:

- One for each field of each 500 records: 1500
- One for each MoveNext statement: 500
- One for each .EOF check: 500

To convert our Recordset to an array, we just require one hit to the object, and one line of code:

```
<% Recordset.GetRows() %>
```

The `GetRows` function takes the Recordset and converts it to a two-dimensional array with the columns arranged in the same order as the `SELECT` statement for your Recordset, or in the order they were defined in the database if you use `SELECT *`. This means that if we had:

```
"SELECT firstname, lastname, e-mail FROM tblSubscribers"
```

our array would look like this:

	firstname(0)	lastname(1)	e-mail(2)
0	Daniel	Short	dan@yourdomain.com
1	Rob	Turnbull	rob@yourdomain.com
2	Omar	Elbaga	omar@yourdomain.com
...	...	...	...
n-1*	Simon	Mackie	simon@yourdomain.com

Our array, generated from our Recordset. Here, n is the total number of records in the Recordset.

One thing you need to watch out for is that the `GetRows` method puts the rows in the second dimension and the columns in the first, opposite to what we covered earlier with standard two-dimension arrays.

Putting It All Together

All this information is great, but now let's put what we've learned to some practical use by building the e-mail application I mentioned earlier. To get started, you'll need the `mailer.mdb` file from the code download. Create a data source for the database, then go into Dreamweaver MX and create a new site and set up a connection to the database in the Databases Panel.

Getting the Records

Create a new ASP VBScript page in your site, and call it `mailer1.asp` (see the code download for the full versions of the files we will create here). We're going to add a Recordset to the page using the *Recordset* dialog, which can be found at *Server Behaviors > + > Recordset (Query)*:

- Name the Recordset `rsEmails`, and choose your connection.

- SELECT the fields in the following order: `txtFirstName`, `txtLastName`, `txtEmailAddress`, and `bitHTML`. The order is important because we're going to set up some variables for referencing each of these fields.

- You'll also need to filter the Recordset by those users who have actually subscribed, so filter for records where `bitSubscribed = True`.

- We also need to sort by the `bitHTML` field so we can group all of our HTML and non-HTML subscribers together.

The *Recordset* dialog should now look like this:

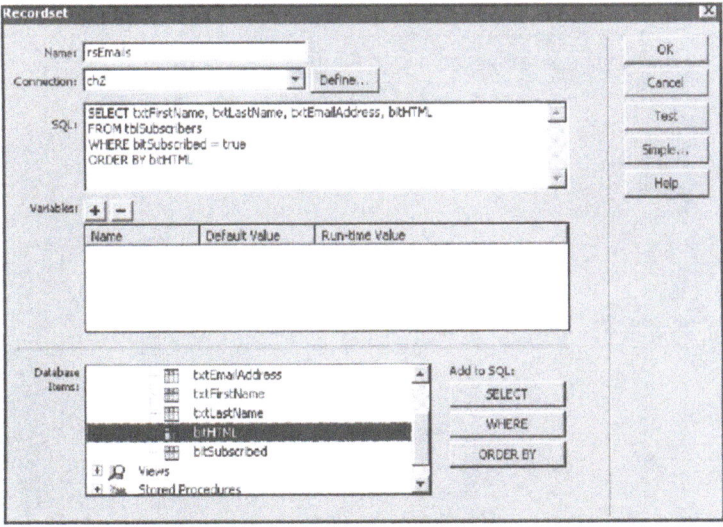

The advanced Recordset dialog.

If you test the Recordset, you should get three records returned:

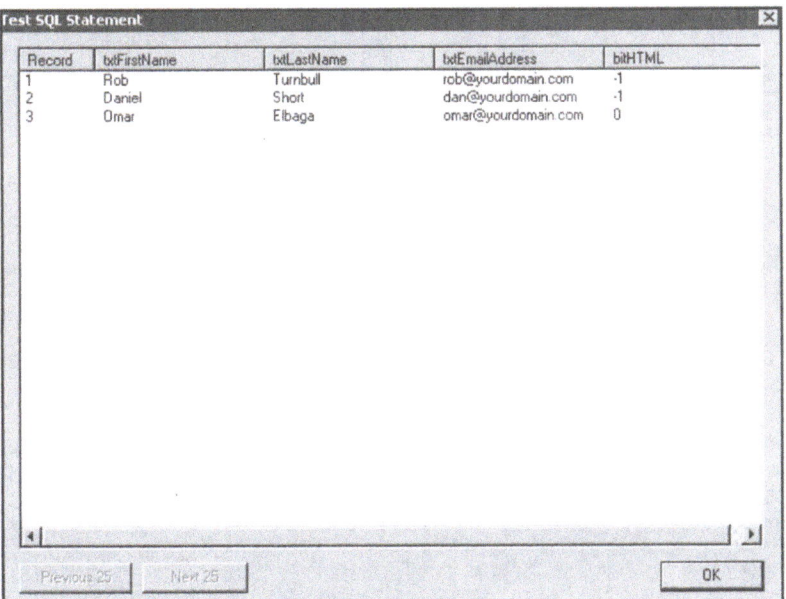

Testing our Recordset.

OK out of the Recordset dialog back to the main page, and your code should now look similar to this:

```
<%@LANGUAGE="VBSCRIPT" CODEPAGE="1252"%>
<!--#include file="Connections/ch2.asp" -->
<%
  Dim rsEmails
  Dim rsEmails_numRows

  Set rsEmails = Server.CreateObject("ADODB.Recordset")
  rsEmails.ActiveConnection = MM_ch2_STRING
  rsEmails.Source = "SELECT txtFirstName, txtLastName, txtEmailAddress, bitHTML FROM
tblSubscribers  WHERE bitSubscribed = true  ORDER BY bitHTML"
  rsEmails.CursorType = 0
  rsEmails.CursorLocation = 2
  rsEmails.LockType = 1
  rsEmails.Open()

  rsEmails_numRows = 0
%>
<html>
<head>
  <title>Untitled Document</title>
  <meta http-equiv="Content-Type" content="text/html; charset=iso-8859-1">
</head>

<body>
</body>
</html>
<%
  rsEmails.Close()
  Set rsEmails = Nothing
%>
```

Building the Array and Gathering Stats

Now we need to get our data into an array and build some variables for referencing that information. Add the highlighted code to `mailer1.asp`, before the `<html>` tag:

```
  rsEmails.Open()

  rsEmails_numRows = 0
%>
<%
  Dim myArray
  myArray = rsEmails.GetRows()
  Dim arFirstName : arFirstName = 0
  Dim arLastName : arLastName = 1
  Dim arEmailAddress : arEmailAddress = 2
  Dim arHTML : arHTML = 3
  Dim iCounter : iCounter = 0
%>
<html>
<head>
```

58

Now we've exhausted our Recordset (by putting all of the records into our array) so it's safe to go ahead and close it. Grab the Recordset destruction code from the very bottom of the page and place it directly above the `<html>` element, as seen below. Save the file again, as `mailer2.asp`:

```
  rsEmails.Open()

  rsEmails_numRows = 0
%>
<%
  Dim myArray
  myArray = rsEmails.GetRows()
  Dim arFirstName : arFirstName = 0
  Dim arLastName : arLastName = 1
  Dim arEmailAddress : arEmailAddress = 2
  Dim arHTML : arHTML = 3
%>

<%
  rsEmails.Close()
  Set rsEmails = Nothing
%>
<html>
<head>
```

Now we have all of our records and no more attachment to the database. With a large number of records, this will greatly improve database performance.

Now that we have the majority of our database pieces in place, let's build the form we're going to use to do the work. We need one textarea for our plain-text newsletter and another for our HTML. We'll also have a small table that tells us how many subscribers we have and how many are getting each type of newsletter:

- Switch to Design View, add the text *Stats* to the page, and create a 3-row, 2-column table

- Add a form below that and place the text *E-mails*, followed by a separate 5-row, 2-column table inside it

Decision Making, Loops and Arrays

Add labels to the rows as seen here, and save the page as `mailer3.asp`:

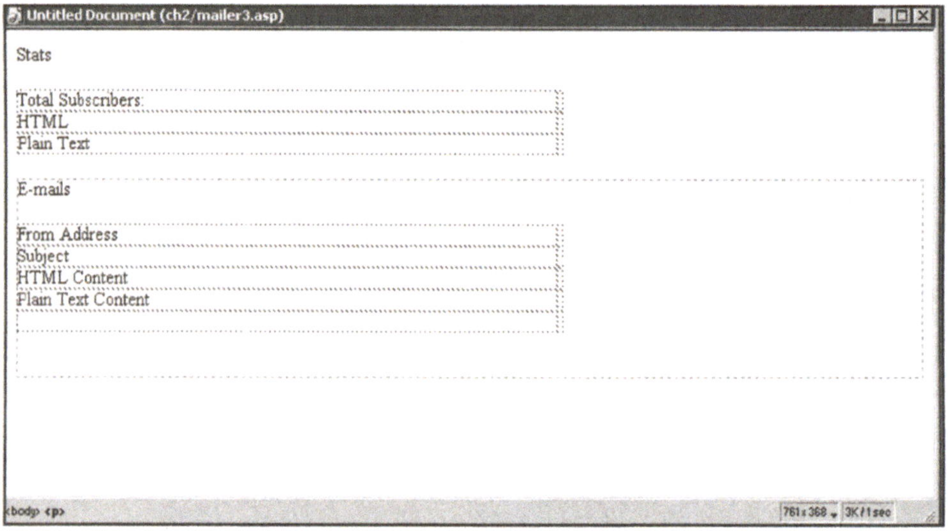

Our page layout begins to take shape.

The first table will be for our stats, and the second will be for the e-mail contents and subject.

To display the total number of subscribers, we just need to put the upper bound of the second dimension of our array (the second dimension contains the rows) plus 1 into the first row of the second column, first table cell. Remember that array counting starts at 0, so we have to add 1 to get an actual count – update that cell content as follows:

```
<tr>
  <td>Total Subscribers:</td>
<tr>
  <td>Total Subscribers:</td>
  <td><%= UBound(myArray,2) + 1 %></td>
</tr>
```

Because we've sorted our array by `bitHTML`, we can loop through the array until we hit our first plain-text subscriber (their HTML value will be False) and we have the number of HTML subscribers; update the next table cell as follows:

```
<tr>
  <td>HTML</td>
  <td><%
    For iCounter = 0 to UBound(myArray,2)
      If myArray(arHTML,iCounter) = False Then Exit For
    Next
    Response.Write(iCounter)
  %></td>
</tr>
```

Because iCounter contains the number of loops through the code, we can just output that value to see how many HTML subscribers we have.

Next, we can use that iCounter variable again to get the leftover amount, which would equal the number of plain-text subscribers; update the next table cell as follows:

```
<tr>
  <td align="right">Plain Text</td>
  <td><%= UBound(myArray,2) + 1 - iCounter %></td>
</tr>
```

Now let's test this out – save the page as mailer4.asp. If you've been following this all correctly your page should now look something like this when viewed in a web browser:

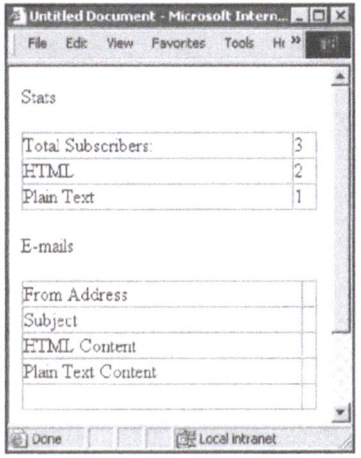

Displaying subscriber information from our database.

Send the Emails

Now we just need to add a few input fields and textareas; add the following to the second column of table 2:

- Row 1: A text field called fromAddress
- Row 2: A text field called subject
- Row 3: A textarea called htmlcontent
- Row 4: A textarea called plaintext
- Row 5: A Submit button

Save it as mailer5.asp. Now, make sure the action of the form is set to the current page, and the method is set to post. Your Dreamweaver page should now look like this:

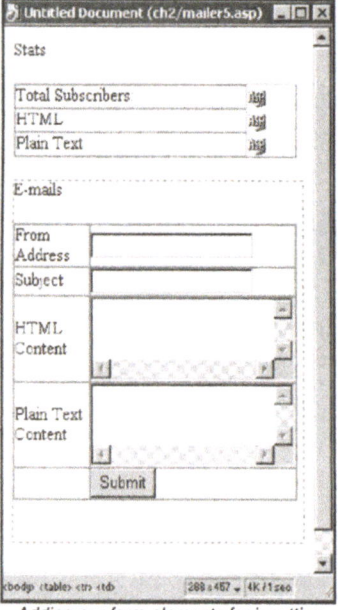

Adding our form elements for inputting the e-mail details.

Now that we have our form, all we need to do is collect the content submitted to us and send out our e-mails. The first thing we need to do is switch back to Code View and add some form checking after all of our array variables. All of our e-mail processing will be done inside the highlighted If statement below, which checks to be sure the form has been submitted:

```
<%
  rsEmails.Close()
  Set rsEmails = Nothing
%>
<%
  Dim emailsSent 'Used to store how many we send.
  If Request.Form("submit") <> "" Then

  End If

%>
<html>
<head>
```

All you need to do to use CDO mail is create an object, set the from, to, subject, and body content (as seen in the code), and send the e-mail. If you don't have CDO installed on your server check with your host to find out what type of mailer applications are available. You'll need to change the syntax of the example to fit your particular mailer application.

Next, we need to loop through our array and send an e-mail for each user. We need a For loop to get through all of the array elements and some appropriate mailer code (we're using CDO in our example, which is installed by default on all Windows 2000 servers and most Windows NT servers):

```
<%
Dim emailsSent 'Used to store how many we send.
If Request.Form("submit") <> "" Then
  For iCounter = 0 to UBound(myArray,1)
    Dim objCDO
    Set objCDO = Server.CreateObject("CDONTS.NewMail")
    objCDO.From = Request.Form("fromAddress")
    objCDO.To = myArray(arFirstName,iCounter) & " " &_
      myArray(arLastName,iCounter) &_
      "<" & myArray(arEmailAddress,iCounter) & ">"
    objCDO.Subject = Request.Form("subject")
    objCDO.Body = Request.Form("plaintext")
    objCDO.Send()
    Set objCDO = Nothing
  Next
End If
%>
```

This code works fine, but there's no test to see which type of e-mail the user elected to receive. To take care of that we're going to add a few `If` statements to test for which type of e-mail the user wants, then we'll set the appropriate MIME types and body text accordingly:

```
<%
Dim emailsSent 'Used to store how many we send.
If Request.Form("submit") <> "" Then
  Dim objCDO
  For iCounter = 0 to UBound(myArray,2)
    Set objCDO = Server.CreateObject("CDONTS.NewMail")
    objCDO.From = Request.Form("fromAddress")
    objCDO.To = myArray(arFirstName,iCounter) & " " &_
      myArray(arLastName,iCounter) &_
      "<" & myArray(arEmailAddress,iCounter) & ">"
    objCDO.Subject = Request.Form("subject")

    If myArray(arHTML,iCounter) = True Then
      objCDO.BodyFormat = cdoBodyFormatHTML 'This is where the
      objCDO.MailFormat = cdoMailFormatMIME 'HTML magic happens.
      objCDO.Body = Request.Form("HTMLContent")
    Else
      objCDO.Body = Request.Form("plaintext")
    End If
    objCDO.Send()
  Next
  Set objCDO = Nothing
End If
%>
```

Finally, after it's all done, we put a message into `emailsSent` telling the user how many e-mails were sent out, and then we output this at the top of the page, above our stats table:

```
        objCDO.Send()
    Next
    emailsSent = "<h1>" & iCounter & " e-mails were sent.</h1>"
    Set objCDO = Nothing
End If
%>
<html>
<head>
<title>emailer.asp</title>
<meta http-equiv="Content-Type" content="text/html; charset=iso-8859-1">
</head>

<body>
<%= emailsSent %>
<p>Stats</p>
<table border="1" cellspacing="0" cellpadding="5">
```

The final code for this example can be found as `emailer.asp` in the code download. When this code is run, it should produce results like those in the following screenshot (it is a good idea to enter some sample content into the form inputs too!)

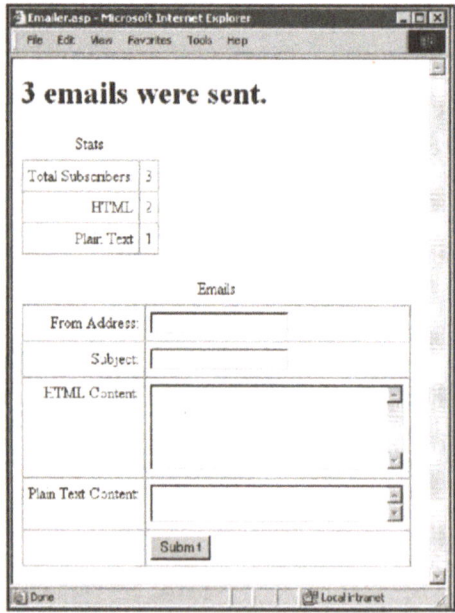

Our finished mailer application in action.

Summary

In this chapter we have looked at how to control decision-making in ASP, and how Dreamweaver can automate some of the tedious coding for us.

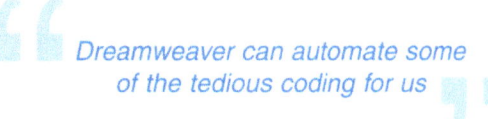

Dreamweaver can automate some of the tedious coding for us

We have seen how `If ... Then` statements can give us control over simple choices, and how using `Else` and `Elseif` can allow us to deal with more complicated options. We then saw that using `Select Case` can make things even easier if we have a long list of options to check.

We looked at how we can use a variety of loops to repeat processing, and how each one behaves slightly differently. This means that our choice of loop will depend on whether we want the processing to be carried out before or after a condition is checked, or whether it goes on while a condition is in effect. We then saw that such looping statements are a good tool for getting information out of arrays and Recordsets.

Finally, we combined what we'd seen about conditionals, loops, and arrays to build a page that will mail people with an HTML or plain-text e-mail, depending on their subscription preferences, as stored in a database.

Decision Making, Loops and Arrays

2

3

- What are they?

- Creating your own functions

- VBScript Built-in functions

Author: Omar Elbaga

Functions

Welcome to the wide world of VBScript built-in functions. In this chapter you will learn about:

- Functions and how to use them in your script
- String functions
- Typecasting functions
- Date functions

What Are They?

A function is a named piece of code that provides a particular service. You can use a function from any part of your code by making a function call, without having to rewrite the code to be executed each time. In addition to the built-in functions, you can create your own functions. Typically, a function will accept certain arguments, execute predefined code, and output a value. This helps make coding far more efficient and reusable. For example, say you had an equation that calculated shipping tax on items. Instead of having to write out the entire code for calculating the tax each time for each item, you can create one function that calculates this, accepts values as arguments, and returns the output. Then, whenever you want to execute the calculation code on an item, you would simply use the function name you created and pass the item to be calculated as an argument in the function name. The rest would be taken care of by the original function declaration that was created once at the top of your page. You would not have to re-code the calculation code each time.

Let's use some code and create a function out of it. We will try something simple at first so that the concept is clear and then move on to a more complex example. Say you just wanted to print out your name:

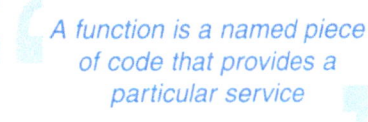
A function is a named piece of code that provides a particular service

```
Response.Write "omar"
```

Assume we had to do this over and over in our code for some reason. We can put this code into our own function and simply call on the function whenever we want to use it again. We declare a function with the following syntax:

```
Function FunctionName(parameters_if_any)

... code to be executed...

End Function
```

Say we always wanted to print out the name for display. We would create a function for it as such:

```
<%
Function printname() 'name function
Response.Write "omar" 'function process to be completed
End Function
%>
```

We can then always execute this code `Response.Write "omar"` by simply calling the function without ever writing this line out again explicitly.

```
<%
Function printname() 'name function
Response.Write "omar" 'function process to be completed
End Function
%>
```

```
<% printname() %>
```

Notice how we simply used the function we created to execute this line of code:

```
Response.Write "omar"
```

We can call the function throughout the page without having to type that line of code again. You can probably see how creating your own functions is useful for code that you may have to constantly reuse. Instead of rewriting the code over and over, you can put it into a function and simply call the function from then on.

The function needs to be declared before it can be called. You should simply put all function declarations at the top of your page, below the ASP page directive. The function name should be short but should comprehensibly describe the process it will perform.

The function we created above does not accept any parameters or arguments. But functions *can* accept arguments too. Say we wanted to print out a name frequently but not necessarily "*omar*". We can still create the function, but have it accept an argument for the name instead of being predefined. Let's readjust the function above to do this:

```
<%
Function printname(str_name)
Response.Write str_name
End Function
%>
```

Notice that we passed a variable as a parameter in the function. Then we print out that variable. Whatever goes inside the parentheses when the `printname()` function is called will take the place of the `str_name` variable in the function declaration. Let's use the function now to display various names:

```
<%
Function printname(str_name)
Response.Write str_name
End Function
%>
<% printname("tom") %><br />
<% printname("harry") %>
```

Notice how we put names to be printed as parameters inside the `printname()` function instead of as they were predefined in the original example.

What about multiple parameters? Yes, we can create a function to accept more than one parameter. To do this we simply put a comma after the first parameter and add a second parameter when declaring the function. Let's try that now. Say we wanted to create a function that multiplies two numbers together.

```
<%
Function multiplyit(int1, int2)
multiplyit = int1 * int2
End Function
%>
```

We could then pass any two numbers inside the `multiplyit()` function to be multiplied, as such:

```
<%
Function multiplyit(int1, int2)
multiplyit = int1 * int2
End Function
%>
<% multiplyit(4,5) %>
```

We can also have more complex code execute inside a function such as code that uses conditional statements. Say we wanted to check if some user input contained an offensive word for example. The code for this might look like something like this:

```
If InStr(str_usercomment, "stupid") Then
Replace(str_usercomment, "stupid", "stup**")
Else
str_usercomment
End If
```

This code checks to see if the word "stupid" appears in an imaginary variable named `str_usercomment`. If so, it changes the text "`stupid`" to "`stup**`", if not, it just returns the variable as is.

We can create a function out of this by adding the appropriate syntax:

```
<%
Function changecurse(str_usercomment)
If InStr(str_usercomment, "stupid") Then
changecurse = Replace(str_usercomment, "stupid", "stup**")
Else
changecurse = str_usercomment
End If
End Function
%>
```

In this case we declared a function called `changecurse()` that accepts the string to be checked as a parameter `changecurse(stringvariable)`. If the string contains the word "`stupid`" then we can transform it using the function:

```
<!-- changecurse_function.asp -->
<%
Function changecurse(str_usercomment)
If InStr(str_usercomment, "stupid") Then
changecurse = Replace(str_usercomment, "stupid", "stup**")
Else
changecurse = str_usercomment
End If
End Function
%>
```

```
<% mycomment = "This web site is stupid." 'any string variable %>
<%=mycomment %>
<%= changecurse(mycomment)%>
```

The following text should appear when you attempt to print out the `mycomment` variable:

This web site is stupid.

In contrast, the following text should appear when you attempt to print out the `mycomment` variable using the `changecurse()` function we created:

The `String` variable `mycomment` could be replaced with a `String` variable coming from a database or a form element.

*This web site is stup**.*

Let's try to create a simple form that submits a comment and use the `changecurse()` function to check for the word "stupid". Let's rework the page named `changecurse_function.asp` above. Leave the function declaration at the top of the page and delete the displays that utilize the `mycomment` variable. Let's add a simple comment form below the function declaration:

```
<!-- changecurse_function.asp -->
<%
Function changecurse(str_usercomment)
If InStr(str_usercomment, "stupid") Then
changecurse = Replace(str_usercomment, "stupid", "stup**")
Else
```

```
changecurse = str_usercomment
End If
End Function
%>
```

```
Comment:<br/>
<form name="frmcomment" method="post" action="changecurse_function.asp">
<textarea name="txtcomment" rows="4" cols="24"></textarea> <br/>
<input type="submit" name="submit" value="submit comment">
</form>
```

Now let's check if the form is submitted and print out the form element using the `changecurse()` function:

```
<!-- changecurse_function.asp -->
<%
Function changecurse(str_usercomment)
If InStr(str_usercomment, "stupid") Then
changecurse = Replace(str_usercomment, "stupid", "stup**")
Else
changecurse = str_usercomment
End If
End Function
%>
```

```
Comment:<br/>
<form name="frmcomment" method="post" action="changecurse_function.asp">
<textarea name="txtcomment" rows="4" cols="24"></textarea> <br/>
<input type="submit" name="submit" value="submit comment">
</form>
```

```
<%
If Request.Form("submit") <> "" Then
Response.Write changecurse(Request.form("txtcomment"))
End If
%>
```

Test the page in your browser by inputting the text "*This web site is stupid*" into the text area, and submitting the form to see what happens:

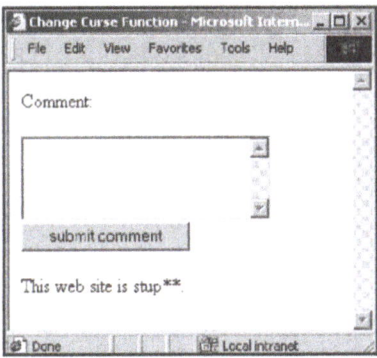

Also test the page again without using the word "stupid" to see that nothing else is changed.

In the above examples we've created three of our own custom functions: `printname()`, `multiplyit()`, and `changecurse()`. Functions perform pre-defined actions, obviating the need to recreate the code each time we want to include that functionality. Instead we create a function and simply call it by name including any arguments it requires.

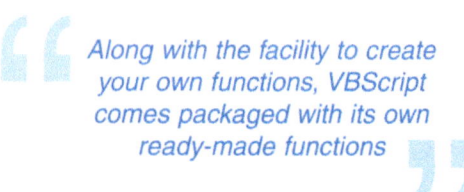

Along with the facility to create your own functions, VBScript comes packaged with its own ready-made functions

Along with the facility to create your own functions, VBScript comes packaged with its own ready-made functions, and we'll spend the rest of the chapter learning about these. These functions are built into the language originally created by the Microsoft VBScript developers; all you have to do is call the function name. There is nothing difficult about learning how to use built-in functions because they are already pre-packaged. To use them properly all you need to know is what arguments they require and what they will return. For example, there are ready-made functions to change lowercase letters to uppercase letters, convert between data types, print dates, manipulate date, time and strings and much more. We will learn about some of these functions now.

Built-In Functions

The built-in VBScript functions are intrinsic function procedures built into VBScript. Generally speaking, the functions are not divided into categories, but in order to make them easier to learn and remember I will so divide them in this chapter. VBScript has close to 100 built-in functions. Some are rarely used while others can be used on a daily basis by any ASP web developers. We will look at some of the ones that are used most.

String Functions

Function	Comments
Instr()	Returns the position of one string within another, beginning at the first character of the string.
InstrRev()	Returns the position of one string within another, beginning at the last character of the string
LCase()	Converts string to lowercase.
UCase()	Converts string to uppercase
Left()	Returns specified number of characters from the left side of a string.
Right()	Returns specified number of characters from the right side of a string.

Function	Comments
Len()	Returns the number of characters in a string.
LTrim()	Removes empty spaces on the left side of a string.
RTrim()	Removes empty spaces on the right side of a string.
Trim()	Removes empty spaces on the left and right side of a string.
Mid()	Returns specified number of characters from a string.
Replace()	Replaces part of a string with another string.

Typecasting Functions

Function	Comments
CInt()	Converts an expression to an Integer data type.
CStr()	Converts an expression to a String data type.
CBool()	Converts an expression to a Boolean data type.
CDate()	Converts an expression to a Date data type.
CCur()	Converts an expression to a Currency data type.

Math Functions

Function	Comments
Int()	Returns the whole number portion of a number.
Round()	Returns a number rounded.
Rnd()	Returns a random number less than 1 but greater or equal to 0.

Date Functions

Function	Comments
Now()	Returns the current system date and time.
Date()	Returns the current system date.
Time()	Returns the current system time.
Year()	Returns a number representing the year.
Month()	Returns a number representing the month of the year, between 1 and 12.
MonthName()	Returns the name of a specified month.
Day()	Returns a number representing the day of the month, between 1 and 31.
Weekday()	Returns a number representing the day of the week, between 1 and 7.
WeekdayName()	Returns the weekday name of a specified day of the week.
Hour()	Returns a number representing the hour of the day, between 0 and 23.
Minute()	Returns a number representing the minute of the hour, between 0 and 59.
Second()	Returns a number representing the second of the minute, between 0 and 59.
DateAdd()	Returns a date to which a specified time interval has been added.
DateDiff()	Returns the number of intervals between two dates.
DatePart()	Returns the specified part of a given date.
FormatDateTime()	Returns an expression formatted as a date or time.

Although this may look like an overwhelming list, it isn't very difficult to learn how to use them at all. You do not have to memorize all the VBScript functions. Even veteran programmers use reference books to look up functions now and then, like *ASP 3.0 Programmer's Reference*, from Wrox Press, ISBN 1-861003-23-4.

Function Power

I will divide the functions into related categories and although we will not go through every single function, we will demonstrate most of them, especially the ones that are frequently used.

String Functions

InStr

This function returns an integer indicating the position of the first occurrence of a given string found within another string. The search begins at the **beginning** of the string being searched. For example:

```
<%
Dim text, desired_location
text = "What do you want from this string?"
desired_location = inStr(text, "want") 'search for want within string

Response.Write desired_location
%>
```

The above example declares two variables: `text` and `desired_location`. The first variable is a string with the text: "`What do you want from this string?`" The second variable searches for the text `want` in the string value of the `text` variable. Lastly we print out the location.

When you view the page in your browser you should see:

13

If you count down to the letter `w` of `want` in the string "`What do you want from this string?`", it is the thirteenth character. Remember to include empty spaces when you count. The other thing to be aware of when using `inStr` is that it is case-sensitive; if we search for `Want` in our string, the function will return `0` because it isn't in the string.

Let's look at a more realistic situation in which you would use this function. Say you want to find out if some text exists in a client user's input, say in a form submission. The following code snippet displays the current browser information:

```
<%=Request.ServerVariables("HTTP_USER_AGENT")%>
```

> *You will learn more about* `ServerVariables` *in the next chapter.*

I am using Internet Explorer 5.5 so the following information is displayed on the screen:

Mozilla/4.0 (compatible; MSIE 5.5; Windows NT 5.0; T312461)

Notice that *MSIE* will appear referring to Microsoft Internet Explorer. We could use search for this occurrence in the string to find out if a client is using IE and perform a server-side browser check. Let's see an example:

```
<%
If Instr(Request.ServerVariables("HTTP_USER_AGENT"), "MSIE") Then
  Response.Redirect "ieuser.asp"
End If
%>
```

When this page is accessed, it tests to see if the user is using IE. If this is the case, it redirects to a page called `ieuser.asp`, otherwise it loads up the current page. This little script is useful when you want to redirect a specific browser.

Functions

InStrRev

This function does the same as the above function but in **reverse**. It too returns an integer indicating the position a string is found within another string, but this time the search begins at the **end** of the string being searched for. Let's try a similar example to the one we used above but change the function from `InStr` to `InStrRev`, and make the `text` variable a little longer:

```
<%
Dim text, desired_location
text = "Why do you want what you want from this string?"
desired_location = inStrRev(text, "want") 'search for want within string
Response.Write desired_location
%>
```

When you view the page in your browser you should see:

26

If you count down to the letter `w` of the first `want` from the end of the `text` variable, it is the twenty-sixth character from the beginning. The `inStrRev` function starts **searching** from the end of the `String` it is given, but still **counts** from the beginning, which can be confusing. Remember to include empty spaces when you count.

LCase

This function converts all characters of a string to lowercase. For example:

```
<%
Dim str_input, only_lowercase

str_input = "I LOVE TO WRITE IN CAPITAL LETTERS."
only_lowercase = LCase(str_input) 'convert string to all lowercase letters

Response.Write only_lowercase
%>
```

When you view the page in your browser you should see:

i love to write in capital letters.

The string with uppercase letters is set as the value of the `str_input` variable, which we transform into lowercase using the `LCase` function. The output of the `LCase` function is then assigned to the `only_lowercase` variable, which we then output to the browser. As a note, you can use the function during the `Response.Write` runtime instead of declaring a second variable. For example, this code does the same as the above:

```
<%
Dim str_input

str_input = "I LOVE TO WRITE IN CAPITAL LETTERS."

Response.Write LCase(str_input)
%>
```

This technique will work with any function, but it is better to use the first technique. Apart from allowing you to use the results of the function more than once without calling it again, if you chain a series of function calls together in this manner it becomes hard to follow what is happening. This can make it difficult to track down errors that may occur.

UCase

This function is complements the above, but instead of converting letters to lowercase, it converts letters to uppercase. For example:

```
<%
Dim str_input, only_uppercase

str_input = "something is wrong with my caps lock key today."
only_uppercase = UCase(str_input) 'convert string to all uppercase letters

Response.Write only_uppercase
%>
```

When you view the page in your browser you should see the following:

SOMETHING IS WRONG WITH MY CAPS LOCK KEY TODAY.

Left

This function returns a specified number of characters of a string starting from the left. For example:

```
<%
Dim user_comment
user_comment = "I love this site. It has so many nice resources, but it goes down
too often."
short_user_comment = Left(user_comment, 20)

Response.Write short_user_comment
%>
```

When you view this page in your browser, you should see the following:

I love this site. It

In the above example we asked for the first 20 characters of the `user_comment` variable. The `Left` function takes two parameters, the first being the `String` to cut down and the second being the desired length as an `Integer`:

```
Left(string, length)
```

We can also concatenate a symbol or desired characters to the `short_user_comment` variable. (We learned about concatenation in *Chapter 1*.) See the following example. This time let's create a simple form that collects a user comment. Assume this was entered into a database and then subsequently displayed. We might want to trim the users' comments to a certain length for formatting reasons:

```
<!--usercomments.asp-->
Comment:
<form action="usercomments.asp" method="post">
<textarea name="user_comment" cols=40 rows=6></textarea><br />
<input type="submit" name="submit" value="submit comment">
</form>

<%
If Request.Form("submit") <> "" Then
user_comment = Request.Form("user_comment")
Dim user_comment
short_user_comment = Left(user_comment, 20) & " ..."

Response.Write short_user_comment
End If
%>
```

When you view this page in your browser, enter the text "I love this site. It has so many nice resources, but it goes down too often." inside the text area and submit the form and you should see the following:

I love this site. It ...

The second block of code in the above example checks to see if the form is submitted first and then if so, it trims the value submitted in the text area form element and concatenates " ..." characters (a space and ellipsis) after the comment. This function is useful where you want to have a "preview" page containing a list of the opening few words of various messages, for example, which link to the full version.

Right

This function does the same as the Left function, but begins from the right of the string. Let's use the same example as above but replace the Left with the Right function and move the ellipsis:

```
<%
Dim user_comment
user_comment = "I love this site. It has so many nice resources, but it goes down
too often."

short_user_comment = "… " & Right(user_comment, 20)

Response.Write short_user_comment
%>
```

When you view this page in your browser, you should see the following:

... goes down too often.

Len

This function returns the number of characters in a string. For example:

```
<%
Dim user_comment
user_comment = "I love this site. It has so many nice resources, but it goes down
too often."
user_comment_length = Len(user_comment)

Response.Write user_comment_length
%>
```

When you view this page in your browser, you should see the following:

76

There are 76 characters in the string.

LTrim, RTrim, Trim

This function trims leading spaces from the **left** of a string. For example:

```
<%
Dim user_comment
user_comment = "              I love this site."

user_comment = LTrim(user_comment)

Response.Write user_comment
%>
```

When you view this page in your browser you should see the following without the leading spaces to the left of the string:

I love this site.

The RTrim function performs the same function, but trims trailing spaces to the right of the String. For example:

```
<%
Dim user_comment
user_comment = "I love this site.

user_comment = RTrim (user_comment)

Response.Write user_comment & "xxxxxxxx"
%>
```

When you view this page in your browser you should see the following without the trailing spaces to the right of the string:

I love this site.xxxxxxxx

In the above example, after trimming the right hand spaces of the user_comment variable, when I printed out the variable I concatenated a series of xs so you see that the leading spaces to the right of the user_comment have indeed been trimmed.

The `Trim` function is basically a combination of both the `LTrim` and `RTrim` functions in one. It trims leading spaces from the left and trailing spaces from the right side of a string. For example:

```
<%
Dim user_comment
user_comment = "                I love this site.              "

user_comment = Trim(user_comment)

Response.Write "xxxxxxx" & user_comment & "xxxxxxxx"
%>
```

When you view this page in your browser you should see the following without the leading spaces to the left or right of the string:

xxxxxxxI love this site.xxxxxxxx

As before, after we trimmed the spaces from `user_comment` we concatenated a series of *x*s as we print it out.

You would most likely use this function when you are collecting user information to be input into a database. You will not know how the user will input the info so to ensure that you don't have a column full of empty spaces you trim the form elements as you submit into a database.

Mid

This function is similar to those we've just seen in that it returns a specified number of characters from a `String` but it allows you to specify the starting position and length. `Mid` accepts three parameters:

- The string you want to pull characters from
- The position from which you want to begin the extraction
- How many characters you want to extract, including the character in the second parameter's position

For example:

```
<%
user_comment = "I Love You!"
desired_section = Mid(user_comment, 3, 4)

Response.Write desired_section
%>
```

We chose the third character, and we chose four characters to extract. When you view this page in your browser, you should see the following:

Love

When the specified length parameter is greater than the number of actual characters remaining in the string, the rest of the string is returned. If the length is not specified, the rest of the string starting at the specified starting position is returned.

Replace

This function replaces a specified part of a string with another string. This function requires three parameters:

- The string to be searched
- The string to be replaced
- The replacement string

For example:

```
<%
user_comment = "I Hate you."
updated_comment = Replace(user_comment, "Hate", "Love")

Response.Write updated_comment
%>
```

When you view the page in your browser you should see the following:

I Love you.

We've replaced the text *Hate* with *Love*. Note that `Replace` allows us to replace strings with others of different length.

Typecasting Functions

The term **typecasting** refers to converting between data types (we discussed data types in *Chapter 1*). It *casts* one data type to another. They are sometimes referred to as conversion functions. For example, you could use one of these functions to convert a `String` to an `Integer` or vice versa. Let's take our first example.

CInt

This function casts an expression to an integer data type. For example:

```
<%
str_result = "43" 'declare variable with string data type
Response.Write TypeName(str_result) & "<br />" 'print out current data type
int_result = CInt(str_result) 'cast str_result variable to an integer data type
Response.Write TypeName(int_result) 'print out new data type
%>
```

When you view the page in your browser you should see the following:

String
Integer

We've declared a variable with a string value and printed the data type to the screen. We then used the CInt function to convert the expression to an Integer data type and then we finally printed out the data type of the new variable.

This function comes in handy because you will often need to make sure that numerical user input is actually of Integer data type, especially if you will be performing any mathematical calculations. You can't do any mathematical calculations on numbers of a String data type. For example:

```
<%
user_age = "43" 'declare a numerical variable as a string
int_result = CInt(user_age) 'cast str_result variable to an integer data type
Response.Write TypeName(int_result) 'print out new data type
%>
```

CStr

This function is very similar to the CInt function except that it converts an integer into a String data type. Let's use an example similar to the one above but reverse the order of data types:

```
<%
int_result = 43 ' declare variable with integer data type
Response.Write TypeName(int_result) & "<br />" 'print out current data type
str_result = CStr(int_result) 'cast int_result variable to a string data type
Response.Write TypeName(str_result) 'print out new data type
%>
```

When you view the page in your browser you should now see the following:

Integer
String

Integer will appear first and *String* second because we've converted the 43 Integer to a String.

CBool

This function converts an expression to a Boolean data type. Any non-zero integer value is True while a zero integer value is False. Keep in mind that the CBool function converts only Integer data types to Boolean values. For example:

```
<%
mailing_list = 1
bool_mailing_list = CBool(mailing_list) 'convert to Boolean value
Response.Write bool_mailing_list 'print out Boolean value of mailing_list variable
%>
```

When you view the page in your browser you should see the following:

True

We declared a variable with an integer of 1, which translates to the Boolean `True`. Hence, when we convert the data type to `Boolean`, `True` prints out. Now try the same example, but using the value 0 for the variable `mailing_list`:

```
<%
mailing_list = 0
bool_mailing_list = CBool(mailing_list) 'convert to Boolean value
Response.Write bool_mailing_list 'print out Boolean value of mailing_list
variable
%>
```

When you view the page in your browser you should see the following:

False

We declared an `Integer` variable containing 0. In Boolean terms, this 0 equals `False`. Hence, when we convert the data type to `Boolean`, `False` prints out.

CDate

This function converts a valid date or time expression to a `Date` data type. For example:

```
<%
registration_date = "October 23, 2002"
Response.Write registration_date & "<br />"
Response.Write TypeName(registration_date) & "<br /><br />"

new_date = CDate(registration_date)

Response.Write new_date & "<br />"
Response.Write TypeName(new_date)
%>
```

When you view the page in your browser you should see the following:

October 23, 2002
String

10/23/2002
Date

In the code above, we declare a variable that holds a date a user may have input from our web page for example, and then we print it out to the browser along with its data type. As you see, the date is of `string` data type. We convert the variable to `date` data type using the `CDate` function, and then print out the converted date and the new data type. Lastly do not be confused by the `<br />` tags. I simply concatenated them to the end of the information to be printed out to format the output.

You can change the appearance of the dates using formatting functions, which we will get into later in the chapter. You can also use another function, `IsDate`, to check if an expression can qualify as a `date` data type. You may want to check this before attempting to convert something to a `date`. For example:

```
<%
registration_date = "October 23, 2002"
If IsDate(registration_date) Then 'check if variable qualifies as a date

new_date = CDate(registration_date) 'convert to date data type
Response.Write new_date & "<br />" 'print out new date
Response.Write TypeName(new_date) 'print out new data type

End If
%>
```

When you view the page in your browser you should see the following:

10/23/2002
Date

The code will be executed only if the date in the `registration_date` can be converted. Try the same example using a non-qualifying date and see what happens:

```
<%
registration_date = "blah blah blah"

If IsDate(registration_date) Then 'check if variable qualifies as a date

new_date = CDate(registration_date) 'convert to data data type
Response.Write new_date & "<br />" 'print out new date
Response.Write TypeName(new_date) 'print out new data type

End If
%>
```

Nothing should appear when you view this page in your browser, because "blah blah blah" cannot be converted to a date. You should use this function to validate user-input dates.

CCur

This function converts any number or numeric string into the `Currency` data type.

```
<%
str_number = "345"
Response.Write str_number + str_number & "<br />"
cur_number = CCur(str_number) 'convert numeric string to currency
Response.Write cur_number + cur_number & "<br />"
%>
```

You should see the following printout when you access the page in your browser:

345345
690

When we attempted to add the first variable (`str_number`) to itself, as you can see from the output it was actually concatenated rather than added because it was declared as a `string`. When we converted the variable to a `currency` and added the new variable to itself we received a mathematical calculation of the two numbers `345 + 345 = 690`.

Math Functions

The math functions perform particular mathematical operations on numbers such as returning the arctangent, cosine, and octal value of a specified number, although most of these will probably be rarely used in the web applications you deploy. Here are a couple of the more useful math functions:

Int

This function returns the integer part of a number:

```
<%
mynumber = 99.99

Response.Write Int(mynumber)
%>
```

When you access this page in the browser you should see:

99

From this example it should be clear that this function does not round to the nearest whole number, it simply returns the integer portion of a number.

Round

To round a number to the nearest whole number you can use the `Round` function:

```
<%
Response.Write Round(mynumber)
mynumber = 99.99
%>
```

When you access this page in the browser you should see:

100

You can also specify a number of decimal places to remain when rounding by adding the interval as a parameter. This parameter is optional:

```
Round(number, decimalplaces)
```

```
<%
mynumber = 98.768

Response.Write Round(mynumber,2)
%>
```

When you access this page in the browser you should see:

99.77

Rnd

This function generates a random number less than 1 but greater than or equal to 0.

```
<%
Response.Write Rnd()
%>
```

When you access the page in your browser you should see a random number less than 1 but greater than or equal to 0. The number that appeared in my browser was:

0.7055475

Try to refresh the page in your browser and you'll notice that a new random number is *not* generated when the browser is refreshed. To make sure a random number is generated every time the page is loaded, you must use the `Randomize` statement before you use the `Rnd` function:

```
<%
Randomize
Response.Write Rnd()
%>
```

You may wonder if it's possible to use this function to generate random numbers that are greater than one, or even below 0. In fact, it is possible, but you need a little extra code to get it to work. You can specify a range within which the function will generate random numbers; all you need to do is specify the limits of this range as follows:

```
(max - min) * Rnd + min
```

This will return a random number within the maximum and minimum numbers specified. Here is an example:

```
<%
Randomize
max = 10
min = 1

randomnumber = (max - min) * Rnd + min
Response.Write randomnumber
%>
```

This will return a random number between 1 and 10. The `Rnd` function will still return a number with trailing decimal places. You can place the variable within the `Int` function to return only the integer portion.

```
<%
Randomize
max = 10
min = 1

randomnumber = (max - min) * Rnd + min
Response.Write Int(randomnumber)
%>
```

Date Functions

The following functions all return some part of the date or time on the server. In each case, the results will be formatted according to the locale settings on the server. The examples were tested on a server with a locale setting of US.

Now

This function returns the web server's date and time. For example:

```
<% Response.Write Now() %>
```

When you view this page in your browser you should see the date and time of your web server on the screen. Here is what I got:

11/13/2002 12:01:42 PM

Date

This function is similar to Now but it only returns the **date**. For example:

```
<% Response.Write Date() %>
```

will return something similar to:

11/13/2002

Time

This function is similar to Now but it only returns the **time**. For example:

```
<% Response.Write Time() %>
```

will return something similar to:

11:33:40 PM

Year

This function returns the year. It requires a Date as a parameter. For example:

```
<% Response.Write Year(Date()) %>
```

When you view this page in your browser you should see the following:

2002

You can also use the `Now` function instead of the `Date` function as the required date parameter:

```
<% Response.Write Year(Now()) %>
```

Month

This function returns the month of a date as a number. It requires the date as a parameter:

```
<%
Response.Write Date() & "<br />"
Response.Write Month(Date())
%>
```

When you view this page in your browser you should see something similar to the following:

10/26/2002
10

MonthName

This function returns the name of the month. It requires the month as a number as a parameter. Months from January to December are represented as 1 to 12.

```
<% Response.Write MonthName(1) %>
```

When you view this page in your browser you should see the following:

January

You can include an optional parameter to have the system abbreviate the month upon display. It is `False` by default but you can force it to abbreviate by adding a parameter of `True` after the month. For example:

```
<% Response.Write MonthName(1, True) %>
```

When you view this page in your browser you should see the following:

Jan

Be aware that `MonthName(Date())` won't work, any more than `MonthName(Now())`.

Day

This function will return the day of the month as a number. It requires the date as a parameter. For example:

```
<% Response.Write Day(Date()) %>
```

When you view this page in your browser you should see something similar to the following depending on the day of the month you execute this code:

25

Weekday

This function returns the day of the week as a number. It requires one parameter, which is the date. Weekdays starting from Sunday are represented as 1 to 7. For example:

```
<% Response.Write Weekday(Date()) %>
```

When you view this page in your browser you should see something similar to the following depending on the day of the week you execute this code. I executed it on a Saturday so I got the following:

7

There is also an optional parameter allowing you to specify which day of the week should be specified as day 1. For example you might want Monday to be considered the first day. You can rearrange the above code to the following:

```
<% Response.Write Weekday(Date(), vbMonday) %>
```

I viewed this page on a Saturday so I got:

6

We specified Monday as day 1 of the week, which would make Saturday day 6. Regarding this optional parameter you can use either: `vbSunday`, `vbMonday`, `vbTuesday`, `vbWednesday`, `vbThursday`, `vbFriday`, or `vbSaturday`. It's easy to remember because you simply add `vb` to the front of the desired day of the week. Alternatively you can use the number form of the weekday (1-7), but remember that in this case Sunday is always day 1.

WeekdayName

This function returns the name of a specified weekday. The required parameter is the weekday. For example:

```
<% Response.Write WeekdayName(6) %>
```

When you view this page in the browser you should see the following:

Friday

Again remember that by default Sunday is day 1, which would make Friday day 6.

As with `MonthName`, `WeekdayName(Date())` and `WeekdayName(Now())` will not work.

Hour, Minute, Second

These three functions return exactly what they say. They all require one parameter, which is the time. Let's use all three in one example:

```
<%
Dim time_var
time_var = Time()

Response.Write time_var & "<br />"

Response.Write Hour(time_var) & "<br />"
Response.Write Minute(time_var) & "<br />"
Response.Write Second(time_var) & "<br />"
%>
```

When you view this page in your browser you should see something similar to the following depending on the time on your web server:

1:31:14 AM
1
31
14

The first printout is the entire time. The second is the hour, the third is the number of minutes, and the last is the number of seconds.

DateAdd

This function adds or subtracts a time interval (month, day, year, etc.) to a specified date, returning the new date. For example:

```
<%
Response.Write Date() & "<br />"
Response.Write DateAdd("d", 7, date())
%>
```

When you view this page in your browser you should notice that the second date displayed is 7 days in advance:

10/27/2002
11/3/2002

You can subtract a time interval from the date by using a negative number. For example:

```
<%
Response.Write Date() & "<br />"
Response.Write DateAdd("d", -7, date())
%>
```

When you view this page in your browser you should notice that the second date displayed is 7 days behind:

10/27/2002
10/20/2002

You can manipulate the following time intervals using the appropriate values:

Time Interval	Value
Day	d
Hour	h
Month	m
Minute	n
Quarter	q
Second	s
Weekday	w
Week of year	ww
Day of year	y
Year	yyyy

For example, say you wanted to add a few months to a date; you would use "m":

```
<%
Response.Write Date() & "<br />"
Response.Write DateAdd("m", 4, date())
%>
```

10/27/2002
2/26/2003

The following functions, DateDiff and DatePart, also use these values for the same purpose.

DateDiff

This function returns the time interval between two dates. The required parameters for this function are the interval you want to use to calculate, and the two dates being compared:

```
DateDiff(interval, Date1, Date2)
```

For example:

```
<%
date1 = Date() 'generate current date
date2 = DateAdd("d", 10, date1) 'add 10 days to current to create a new date

Response.Write DateDiff("d", date1, date2) 'find the difference between the 2 dates
'in terms of days
%>
```

When you view this page in your browser you should see:

10

Certainly `DateAdd` and `DateDiff` do not have to appear in the same example; we only used the `DateAdd` function to create a new date.

Refer to the interval table in the *DateAdd* section.

DatePart

This function returns a specified part of a date. For example say you wanted to return the day of the date you would do the following:

```
<% Response.Write DatePart("d", Date()) %>
```

When you view this page in your browser you should see only the day of the month:

27

Let's try to return the year:

```
<% Response.Write DatePart("yyyy", Date()) %>
```

When you view this page in your browser you should see only the year:

2002

You can return any time interval of your choice.

Refer to the interval table in the *DateAdd* section.

FormatDateTime

This function returns the date formatted in one of three fashions or the time in one of two fashions. For example to return the date in the general format, see the following example:

```
<%
Response.Write Date() & "<br />"
Response.Write FormatDateTime(Date(), vbGeneralDate)
'display date in the vbGeneralDate format
%>
```

This example should return the date in the same format.

10/27/2002
10/27/2002

The first is the default format of the date while the second date is literally specified in the default format (`vbGeneralDate`). There are two other date formats. Let's see them now:

```
<%
Response.Write FormatDateTime(Date(), vbLongDate) & "<br />"
'display date in the vbLongDate format
Response.Write FormatDateTime(Date(), vbShortDate)
'display date in the vbShortDate format
%>
```

Here is the output:

Tuesday, October 27, 2002
10/27/2002

Notice the different appearance of the two dates. Let's take a look at the two time formats:

```
<%
Response.Write Time() & "<br />"
Response.Write FormatDateTime(Time(), vbShortTime)
'display date in the vbShortTime format
%>
```

output:

1:23:00 AM
01:23

Take a look at the second time format:

```
<%
Response.Write Time() & "<br />"
Response.Write FormatDateTime(Time(), vbLongTime)
'display date in the vbLongTime format
%>
```

You will notice that the default for the `Time` function is already in the `vbLongTime` format. Here is a list of the format values you can use:

Constant	Description
vbGeneralDate	Display date in the mm/dd/yy format
vbLongDate	Display date in the long date format: weekday, month day, year
vbShortDate	Display date in the short date format, which is the default: mm/dd/yy
vbLongTime	Display time in the default time format: hh:mm:ss PM/AM
vbShortTime	Display time in the 24-hour format: hh:mm

Functions

Summary

This chapter covered the most frequently used functions. We looked at:

- How to create your own functions
- VBScript built-in Functions and how they are used in your code
- String functions
- Typecasting functions
- Date functions

Getting familiar with these functions will give you greater control of your code and user input

Getting familiar with these functions will give you greater control of your code and user input. Remember that it is not necessarily important to memorize all the built-in functions, but as you use particular functions more often in your code they will become familiar to you. You can always refer back to this chapter, looking over the functions and their use. There is nothing wrong with using a reference when you need to use functions and in some cases it can be necessary to do so.

Functions

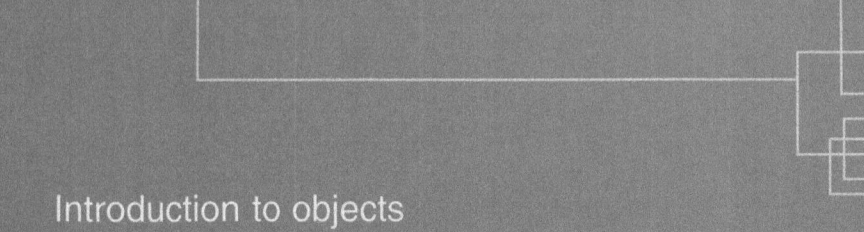

4

- Introduction to objects

- Collections

- Creating your own objects

- ASP Objects, and their properties, methods, and events

Author: Omar Elbaga

Objects, Properties, Methods, and Events

ASP provides some built-in objects (which consist of properties and methods) for you to use in your applications. Just as built-in functions can be utilized within VBScript without initializing any of the functions, these objects (considered **intrinsic**) can be used inside ASP code without first needing to be initialized. The objects are:

- Application
- Response
- Request
- Server
- Session
- ASPError
- ObjectContext

In this chapter we will discuss the Application, Response, Request, and Server objects (and their properties and methods). The ASPError and Session objects will be discussed in *Chapters 5* and *10* respectively, while the ObjectContext object is an advanced object, used to commit or abort transactions.

ObjectContext needs a lot of discussion to cover it fully, so it will not be discussed in this book. If you wish to read more about this object feel free to check out this link at Microsoft: *http://msdn.microsoft.com/library/en-us/iisref60/htm/ref_vbom_obco.asp*.

We will also be looking at collections and events, and we will have a brief look at global.asa files.

Objects

You may recall in the previous chapter that VBScript contained a wide variety of built-in functions, in addition to providing the means with which to build our own functions. In this regard, objects are similar: we can build objects to expand our web pages but we also have several built-in ASP objects that we can utilize to make our coding experience easier.

So what is an object? An object is a software representation of a real-world object, such as a tree, or a car. In theory, we could use these objects to programmatically manipulate these items. So now let's look at the built-in ASP objects, which are a similar, but rather more abstract concept.

An ASP object is a representation of an entity that you might want to manipulate using ASP, such as the server you are running your web application on, or the application itself. For example, the `Response` object is used to do things with the response that the application generates. As we have seen before, `Response.Write` allows us to write the response out on the screen.

Methods & Properties

Each object has **properties** and **methods**. Properties are the features of the object we can manipulate, and methods are the tasks an object can be used to perform.

Let's take another example of a real-world object, a computer. The properties of a computer would be modem, mouse, keyboard, hard drive, and other components that make up the computer. The methods of a computer would be typing, reading a CDROM, storing data, surfing the Web, etc.

To do useful things, object methods require information stored in the properties of their parent objects – in addition, methods may also require arguments to be passed, which can affect the values of properties.

For example, let's look at one method from our computer example: storing data. Where would you store the data, and what else do we need to know? You would store the data in one of the computer's properties, the hard drive. To do this, it is also useful to know the capacity of the hard drive, and the size of the files you want to store (a property of the data itself), so you can make sure that you have room on your hard drive to store the data. So methods can change the values of properties as well as just utilize them.

Collections

Most ASP Objects provide **collections**. With regard to ASP objects, a collection is a group of items, a data structure that stores objects. We will get into specific built-in objects below, but let's take one example to demonstrate a collection.

When we use the `QueryString` collection of the `Request` object, there may be a number of name/value pairs in the querystring, for example:

```
?userid=24&firstname=mike&lastname=odamski
```

In this case there are three items in the QueryString collection. We can then retrieve a specific querystring by identifying it using the Item property of the QueryString collection:

```
<%=Request.QueryString.Item("firstname") %>
```

We can also use the For Each loop to iterate through a particular collection and retrieve all of the items in the collection.

```
<%
  For Each Item In Request.QueryString
  Response.Write Request.QueryString(item) & "<br/>"
  Next
%>
```

Events

Another part of objects is **Events**. These are mechanisms that are generated by the objects that they belong to when something interesting occurs. For example, in our computer example, let's consider the memory size as one of its properties. The computer may need to trigger an alert to the user if he or she attempts to load a new application while the memory is full. That alert is an event of the computer object.

Events usually need **Event Handlers**, which are the special code blocks that perform an action in response to an event. For example, our full memory alert could trigger a response such as instantaneously shutting down idle applications. This response would be the event handler.

In the case of ASP-intrinsic objects, there aren't many events, although we will discuss the following two: OnStart and OnEnd. These two events can only be utilized by the Application and Session objects from within the global.asa file. We will discuss them in the *global.asa* section.

Instances

It is also important to understand what an **instance** of an object is. Plain and simple, it is a specific object, rather than just the object as a concept. Think again about the computer object. The computer design is the master object, from which instances of the computer are built. If we both bought computers, there would be two instances of the computer: my computer, and your computer.

Different instances of the computer may have differing properties: my computer might have a 17" monitor and a 5GB hard drive, while your computer might have a 15" monitor and a 10GB hard drive.

In our ASP code, we create an object, and then create instances of our object (and of the built-in objects) when we want to make use of them.

Building Objects

The two kinds of objects most ASP developers work with are ASP components and the built-in objects. Components are built by web developers; there are many books dedicated to this topic, and web sites offering ready-made components for download. It is beyond the scope of the book to discuss this in detail, but let's have a look at the basic concept behind building objects, to aid our understanding of the area.

4

Objects, Properties, Methods, and Events

When we build an object, we first need to create the original object.

```
<%
  Class Computer
    Public HardDriveGb
    Public ModemKbs
    Public NoMonitor
    Public WithMouse
  End Class
%>
```

The above example creates an object called Computer with four properties: it comes with a hard drive, modem, mouse, but it does not come with a monitor. No methods have been identified yet.

Before giving values to the properties of this Computer object we need to create an instance of this object. This requires declaring a variable for the object, and using the Set statement to make the variable an instance of the original object. It is considered good practice to begin the variable name with obj, to identify this variable as an instance of an object:

```
<%
  Class Computer
    Public HardDriveGb
    Public ModemKbs
    Public NoMonitor
    Public WithMouse
  End Class
%>
<%
  Dim obj_mycomputer
  Set obj_mycomputer = New Computer
%>
```

Note that we don't give values to the properties of the original Computer object, only the new instance, obj_mycomputer. Also bear in mind that we can create multiple instances of this object. We could now begin defining values for the properties of this object instance:

```
<%
  Class Computer
    Public HardDriveGb
    Public ModemKbs
    Public NoMonitor
    Public WithMouse
  End Class%>
<%
  Dim obj_mycomputer
  Set obj_mycomputer = New Computer

  Obj_mycomputer.HardDriveGb = "80"
  Obj_mycomputer.ModemKbs = "56"
%>
```

This computer now has an 80GB hard drive, and a 56Kbs modem. We can change the value of these properties; so let's create a method to allow us to increase the hard drive capacity. Creating a method is very similar to creating functions (refer back to *Chapter 3* if you wish). In order to increase the value of the hard drive we need to add some GB; pseudo code to do this would be as follows:

```
HardDriveGb = HardDriveGb + gigabytes
```

Let's create a method called `IncreaseHardDriveGb()` that will accept the number of GB to add as an argument to perform this action for us:

```
<%
  Class Computer
    Public HardDriveGb
    Public ModemKbs
    Public NoMonitor
    Public WithMouse
    Public Sub IncreaseHardDrive(gigabytes)
      HardDriveGb = HardDriveGb + gigabytes
    End Sub
  End Class
%>
<%
  Dim obj_mycomputer
  Set obj_mycomputer = New Computer

  obj_mycomputer.HardDriveGb = "80"
  obj_mycomputer.ModemKbs = "56"
%>
```

Now let's increase the value of the `HardDriveGb` property by 20GB, using the new method we've created:

```
<%
  Class Computer
    Public HardDriveGb
    Public ModemKbs
    Public NoMonitor
    Public WithMouse
    Public Sub IncreaseHardDriveGb(gigabytes)
      HardDriveGb = HardDriveGb + gigabytes
    End Sub
  End Class
%>
<%
  Dim obj_mycomputer
  Set obj_mycomputer = New Computer

  Obj_mycomputer.HardDriveGb = "80"
  obj_mycomputer.ModemKbs = "56"
  Obj_mycomputer.IncreaseHardDriveGb(20) 'add 20 gigabytes to hard drive property
  Response.Write Obj_mycomputer.HardDriveGb 'print out number of gigabytes
%>
```

If you viewed the output of this final code in your browser you would see:

100

If you would like to learn more about building your own custom ASP components, check out Beginning Components for ASP (Wrox Press, Alex Homer et al, ISBN 1-861002-88-2).

global.asa

`global.asa` is an optional file that you use to declare your own objects, global variables, and event handlers for the `OnStart` and `OnEnd` events, which will be accessible from any page if declared. These events are utilized by the `Application` and `Session` objects.

This page must be stored in the root of your web site directory, and needs no duplicates within sub-directories. This file should contain no displayable content, as the server will ignore it. Here is an example of a typical `global.asa` page:

```
<script language="vbscript" runat="server">

  sub Application_OnStart
  'some code
  end sub

  sub Session_OnStart
  'some code
  end sub

  sub Session_OnEnd
  'some code
  end sub

  sub Application_OnEnd
  'some code
  end sub

</script>
```

Note that all object or variable declarations need to go within the subroutines as event handlers.

Here is a brief overview of the events mentioned above:

- `Application_OnStart`: This event is triggered when the first user visiting your web site requests a page from your ASP application. The `Session_OnStart` event occurs immediately after this event

- `Session_OnStart`: This event is triggered every time a new user requests his or her first page from your application

- `Session_OnEnd`: This event is triggered every time a client's session ends, that is, whenever the session is destroyed. This can be when the client closes the browser, when the session is destroyed manually from within the code, or when the expiration time of a session set on the server passes (by default this is 20 minutes)

- `Application_OnEnd`: This event is triggered after the last user has ended the session. Since you will always have clients connecting and disconnecting, this will most likely occur when the web server has been restarted or has crashed

Let's look at an example of using these events. In the case of creating a small counter that counts how many users are connected to a web site, we could use the following code as an event handler of the `Application_OnStart` event – we would put this code inside the `global.asa` file for the site, which would make the counter accessible from any page:

```
<script language="vbscript" runat="server">

  sub Application_OnStart
  Application("numberofvisitors") = 0
  end sub

  sub Session_OnStart
  Application("numberofvisitors") = Application("numberofvisitors") + 1
  end sub

</script>
```

In the above example, once the first user accesses a page from the web site, the Application variable named `numberofvisitors` will be set to 0. Since each user gets a separate session, 1 will be added to that variable every time a visitor visits the site and starts another session. We could display the number of visitors on any page with the following code:

```
<%= Application("numberofvisitors") %> have visited our web site.
```

Some pitfalls of the `global.asa` file are that the `Session_OnStart` and `Session_OnEnd` events will only execute for users who have cookies enabled in their browser. Also, if you make any changes to the `global.asa` file you will need to stop and restart your web server and, in some cases, reboot the system.

For more information on `global.asa` files, check out the following URLs:
http://msdn.microsoft.com/library/default.asp?url=/library/en-us/iisref/html/psdk/asp/glob63vp.asp
http://msdn.microsoft.com/library/default.asp?url=/library/en-us/cdo/html/_olemsg_about_global.asa.asp

ASP Built-in Objects

Now that we have an understanding of the concepts behind ASP objects we can begin to explore the objects built into ASP.

Application Object

This object is used to share information among all users of a given application. It contains all those elements that have been declared at the application level without using the `<object>` element. An **application** refers to all the `.asp` pages in a directory and all its subdirectories. Picture a lamp in a room. The lamp illuminates all of the people in the room, so if anyone turns out the light, everyone in the room is affected by it.

Similarly, if any user at your web site edits an Application variable, everyone will see the new update. Because this object can be shared between multiple users, there are **Lock** and **Unlock** methods that are utilized to make sure users do not affect the object simultaneously. The `Application` object is shared among all users who access the application.

One `Application` object is created for your main web application, that is, your web site, but certainly you can have several Application variables within the main `Application` object.

Since only one `Application` object exists for an entire web site, it should be used to store information that is useful for the **entire** web site. You might like to follow these examples in Dreamweaver. Enter the following into a new page:

```
<!-- create_color_app_var.asp -->

<% Application("str_color") = "red" %>
<%= Application("str_color") %>
```

In the above example we've created an Application variable named `str_color` with a value of `red`, and displayed the value to the screen. When you view this page in your browser you should see:

red

Before moving on, save the page in an already defined site. For the purposes of this chapter, we'll be calling the site `Chapter04`, and for future reference we'll call this first file `create_color_app_var.asp`. Go to *Bindings > Application Variable*. A dialog box should pop up requesting the name of the Application variable: enter the name of the Application variable we created on the previous page:

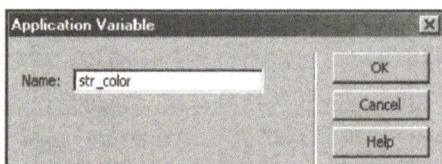

The Application variable pop-up box.

When you click *OK*, the variable should appear listed in the *Bindings* window under *Application*:

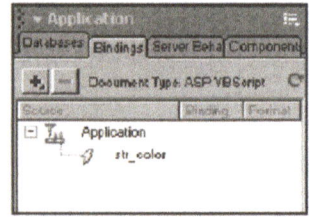

Our Application variable is now available in the Bindings window.

Our Application variable will now be ready to be used inside any web page we create within one defined site. Create another new dynamic ASP VBScript web page in Dreamweaver, and save it as `read_color_app_var.asp`. Save the page in the same defined site directory you saved the `create_color_app_var.asp` page in. You should notice that the `str_color` Application variable created on the last page appears in the *Bindings* window. Drag the variable into your document within the HTML `<body>` tags.

Once you've done this, the code to read the Application variable should be generated in your document – `<%= Application("str_color") %>`. View `read_color_app_var.asp` in your browser and the following should appear:

red

Notice that the Application variable we created in the other document can be used inside a different page. This variable can also be read from any web page created within the same root directory in which you created the initial Application variable.

Remember that all users of this site will access the same `Application` object, so the value `red` for this particular Application variable will appear for all users. The same value `red` will appear wherever this `str_color` Application variable is found. If you or any user changes the value of this Application variable, all users will see the same new value. Let's try that now. Reload the `create_color_app_var.asp` page we created earlier and change the value of the `str_color` Application variable to `blue`:

```
<!-- create_color_app_var.asp -->

<% Application("str_color") = "blue" %>
<%= Application("str_color") %>
```

Save this page, load it in your browser, and you should see the following:

blue

Now reload `read_color_app_var.asp` in your browser and you should also see the value *blue* displayed. If you still see the value `red`, you probably need to refresh your browser. Any web page within this site that reads the `str_color` variable will display the same value.

Application Methods

As mentioned before, the two methods in the `Application` object are:

- `Lock`: The `Lock` method enables you to lock the application-level variables so that only one user can modify their properties at any one time
- `Unlock`: The `Unlock` method unlocks the locked application-level variables

Why would we want to lock variables? Well, since Application variables are read by all users who access them, multiple users may try to access the same Application variable simultaneously. This may not pose a problem if the same users are simply reading the Application variable, but what happens if they are updating it? The data can become corrupted if two users attempt to update the same variable simultaneously. This is why the Application variables need to be locked if they are ever going to be updated.

Locking a variable stops it being updated by a secondary user if the primary user is still updating it. Let's try a simple counter. Add the following code to a new dynamic ASP VBScript web page called `create_site_counter.asp`:

```
<!-- create_site_counter.asp -->

<% Application("counter") = Application("counter") + 1 %>
<%= Application("counter") %>
```

Now we can lock the "`counter`" Application variable as follows:

```
<!-- create_site_counter.asp -->

<%Application.Lock %>
<% Application("counter") = Application("counter") + 1 %>
<%Application.Unlock %>

<%= Application("counter") %>
```

We've now successfully locked our Application variable, so no user can update the counter while another is still using it. View the page in your browser and refresh the page to see how the counter updates itself. Now load the page in another browser several times, and then go back to the first `create_site_counter.asp` page to see how it has updated site-wide. The first page you launched should update the variable from the position the second page left it in, meaning it will go from say, 5 to 10.

Bear in mind that you only need to lock Application variables whenever you are assigning a value to them within a code block (which is considered updating). As far as simply reading Application variables goes, there is no real need to lock them because there is no conflict.

Application variables remain in memory forever and cannot be manually expired. They only expire if the web server is restarted. So be careful not to overload your web server with superfluous Application variables.

Application Collections

The two collections in the `Application` object are:

- `Contents`
- `StaticObjects`

The `Contents` collection houses those variables that have been added to the `Application` object without using the `<object>` element (for example, through the use of an ASP script). It has three properties:

- `Item`
- `Key`
- `Count`

Using the `Item` property, you can address a specific value. For example, to set an `Item` value, you could use the following code:

```
<% Application.Contents.Item("itemname") = "myvalue" %>
```

although the following, shorthand code does the same job and looks cleaner:

```
<% Application("itemname") = "myvalue" %>
```

The `Key` property is used as a variable to specify the name of the item to retrieve when that name might not be known. Take the following example, which iterates through the `Application.Contents` collection and displays each item's variable name and value (`key.asp`):

```
<%@LANGUAGE="VBSCRIPT" CODEPAGE="1252"%>
<html>
<head>
<title>Application.Contents(key)</title>
<meta http-equiv="Content-Type" content="text/html; charset=iso-8859-1">
</head>
<body>
<%
' Create application contents
Application("a") = "This is var 1"
Application("b") = "This is var 2"
Application("c") = "This is var 3"
%>
<%
' Read them back
For Each Key in Application.Contents
  Response.Write Key & " = " & Application(Key) & "<BR>"
Next
%>
</body>
</html>
```

When you run this code in your browser, you should see the following:

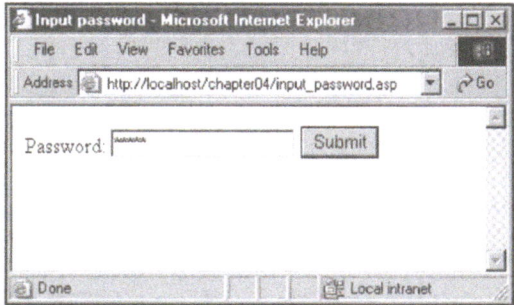

Using the Key property to retrieve the Contents collection of the Application object.

The Count property specifies the number of items in the Contents collection.

```
<%= Application.Contents.Count %>
```

There are also two methods exposed with the Contents collection, they are:

- Remove
- RemoveAll

They are fairly self explanatory. Remove enables you to remove specified Application-scoped variables while RemoveAll will remove all Application-scoped variables. The following short examples show first the removal of a specified variable, and then the removal of all variables:

```
<% Application.Contents.Remove("variablename") %>
```

```
<% Application.Contents.RemoveAll() %>
```

The StaticObjects collection contains all of the objects added to the Contents collection using the <object> element. To view a list of StaticObjects that you have created in an application, use the following example code:

```
<%
  Dim staticObject
  For Each staticObject In Application.StaticObjects
    Response.Write staticObject & " = An object<BR>"
  Next
%>
```

Response Object

The Response object gives you control over the HTTP information sent to the client. This includes setting cookies, control over existing HTTP information, and sending custom HTTP information. With this kind of control over the HTTP information, you can do many things such as checking if your client is still connected to your site, redirecting the user to various places, and stopping execution of code at your discretion.

Response Methods

You are already familiar with one of the most important methods of the Response object, the Write method (Response.Write was introduced in *Chapter 1*). Here is a list of all the methods of Response, along with a brief description of their functions:

- AddHeader: Sets the HTML header name to value
- AppendToLog: Adds a string to the end of the web server log entry for this request
- BinaryWrite: Writes the given information to the current HTTP output without any characterset conversion

- Clear: Erases any buffered HTML output – you will find some discussion of clear (in the context of the Err and ASPError objects) in *Chapter 5*

- End: Stops processing the .asp file and returns the current result

- Flush: Sends buffered output immediately

- Redirect: Sends a redirection order to the browser, causing it to connect to a different URL

It would take a fair amount of space to cover all these in detail, so in this section we will just cover the two other most important methods, End and Redirect.

Response.End

Now let's take a look at the End method. End completely terminates processing of ASP code and returns the result that was processed before termination (often called the buffer output; for more information on the buffer, see the Buffer section later on). Create the following example and save it as input_password.asp:

```
<form action="check_password.asp" method="post"
      name="frm_input_password">Password:
  <input name="txt_password" type="password">
  <input name="submit" type="submit" value="Submit">
</form>
```

The above form will simply accept a password and submit it to the next page, which we will create now – create a new page called check_password.asp, and add the following into the body of the document:

```
<%
  If Request.Form("txt_password") <> "oe123456" Then

  Response.Write "I'm terminating the rest of this page because you have entered an
  incorrect password."
  Response.End 'terminate ASP code from this point on
  End If
  Response.Write "If you see this text you have successfully gained access to the
  rest of this page."

%>
```

Refer to *Chapter 2* for more on conditional statements. Note that the embedded password is oe123456. If the user's input does not match this password, we display the message, "*I'm terminating the rest of this page because you have entered an incorrect password*", and don't process the rest of the page. If the user inputs the correct password we skip the Response.End and run the rest of the ASP code, which displays the message "*If you see this text you have successfully gained access to the rest of this page*".

Try it for yourself! Load the first page, input_password.asp, and input an incorrect password on purpose to see what happens. Next, go back and input *oe123456*.

Objects, Properties, Methods, and Events

Notice how the current result of the ASP page is returned when the page is terminated. `End` does not terminate the entire ASP script, but it does stop any more results being returned once executed. If you look at the sourcecode for this page, you'll see that no more code appears after the termination message:

The result of using Response.End to terminate a page.

Response.Redirect

The `Redirect` method allows you to redirect the client to a specified URL. This can be done for simple redirection or authentication purposes. For example, you might want to authenticate a user. If the user succeeds, you can allow them access to the rest of the page; if not, you can redirect them to another URL.

For an example, let's modify the example we saw above. Leave `input_password.asp` as is, but open the `check_password.asp` page we created above and adjust the code as follows:

```
<%
  If Request.Form("txt_password") <> "oe123456" Then

  Response.Redirect("http://www.google.com")
  Else
  Response.Write "If you see this text you have successfully gained access to the
  rest of this page. Otherwise, you would have been redirected to google.com"

  End If
%>
```

Test the example out in your browser. If you load `input_password.asp` and input an incorrect password, you will be redirected to Google. You will only gain access to the rest of the code on `check_password.asp` if you input the correct password.

You could also redirect a user to another page, such as a members-only page, if they enter a successful password. For example:

```
<%
  If Request.Form("txt_password") <> "oe123456" Then

  Response.Redirect("http://www.google.com")
  Else
  Response.Redirect("members_only.asp")

  End if
%>
```

Response Properties

Now let's have a look at the `Response` properties – here is a quick list of all of them, along with a brief description of their use:

- `Buffer`: Indicates whether page output is buffered (fully processed on the server before being sent to the browser)

- `CacheControl`: Sets a header to tell servers whether they can cache the output generated by ASP

- `Charset`: Appends the name of the characterset to the `content-type` header

- `ContentType`: Specifies the HTTP content type for the response

- `Expires`: Specifies the length of time (in minutes) before a page cached on a browser expires

- `ExpiresAbsolute`: Specifies the date and time before a page cached on a browser expires

- `IsClientConnected`: Indicates whether the client has disconnected from the server

- `PICS`: Specifies the value of a PICS rating label for a document or a site

- `Status`: The value of the status line returned by the server

For more coverage, including detailed information and examples regarding each `Response` *property, collection, and method, check out http://www.devguru.com/Technol ogies/asp/quickref/response.html.*

As with the methods, it would take a lot of space to exhaustively cover these properties, so we will just take a more detailed look at the most commonly used ones – `Buffer`, `Expires`, and `CacheControl`.

Buffer

This property records whether the server has been instructed to temporarily store ASP output until all of the ASP script in the code is processed, before sending all the output to the browser. If it is set to `True`, then it will do this; if it is set to `False`, output is sent to the browser line-by-line.

In ASP 2.0, the default value is `False`, while in ASP 3.0 the default value is `True`!

The best option for you to choose in this case really depends on the web application itself. If you have a large script that may take a long time to run, it is a good idea to set the buffer to `False` so that content is sent as soon as it is processed, otherwise the user may be kept waiting, seemingly without anything happening (and we all know user frustration is a bad thing).

Objects, Properties, Methods, and Events

In ASP 2.0, the default value is False, while in ASP 3.0 the default value is True!

If you have a small script, you could still set the property to `False`. There isn't really any advantage to setting it to `True`, except that it is a bit more elegant to have content sent in whole pages rather than in bits. It won't take too long to be processed anyhow if the script is small.

To appreciate the difference between buffering and not buffering content, let's look at a little looping example (`buffered_loop.asp`):

```
<%
  my_int =0
  Do
    my_int = my_int +1
    Response.Write my_int
  Loop Until my_int = 2000
%>
```

Since we are using ASP 3.0 (so `Buffer` is set to `True` by default), this script prints out all the numbers from 1 to 2000 in a single line of text, but it doesn't display them in the browser until it has got to the end of the loop, at which point it displays them all in one go. Now let's set the buffer to `False` so that it prints out each number as it is processed:

```
Response.Buffer = False %>
<%
my_int =0
Do
    my_int = my_int +1
    Response.Write my_int
Loop Until my_int = 2000
%>
```

Now when you view the page in your browser it will load quicker and you should notice the horizontal scroll bar getting longer until 2000 is printed, and the loop ends.

Expires

The `Expires` property specifies the length of time a page should remain cached. Let's see it in action. `Now()` gives you the current time on the server, so would need to be refreshed every second. Let's see what happens to the time when we have the page expire after five minutes. Create the following example:

```
<!-- time_cached.asp -->

<% Response.Expires = 5 %>
<%=Now() %>
```

In the above code, we use the `Response.Expires` property to make sure the page is cached for five minutes. This means that the real server time will not be displayed until the five minutes expires, or the page is manually refreshed. If you simply reload the page (say from a directory listing), you will see that the time will not be updated each time you open the page; it will do so only after five minutes.

CacheControl

On the other hand, we can use another property, `CacheControl`, to make sure that a page is never cached. This would be useful when we know a page is dynamic and we want to make sure users always see the page afresh. Let's create an example similar to the one above but make sure the page is never cached and the time appears fresh every time you reload it:

```
<!-- time_not_cached.asp -->

<%@LANGUAGE="VBSCRIPT" CODEPAGE="1252"%>
<% Response.CacheControl = No-cache %>

  <html>
  <head><title>Time Not Cached</title></head>
  <body>

  <%=Now() %>

</body>
</html>
```

The `CacheControl` should come before the `<html>` tag to make sure that it is set before any content is sent to the client.

Response and Cookies

You can also create cookies using the `Response` object, either creating new values, or overriding old values. A very practical use for a cookie is during a login. Once you authenticate a user you might set a cookie on their computer, which would then serve as proof of authentication. The syntax to create a cookie is as follows:

Cookies are pieces of information generated by the web server and stored on the user's computer as small text files. Each time the user sends a request to a site that sets a cookie, their browser will send the cookie as well.

```
Reponse.Cookies("cookie_name") = value
```

Let's try an example. Create the following example and save it as `cookie_login.asp`:

```
<form  action="cookie_login.asp"  method="post"  name="frm_input_password">password:
<input  name="txt_password"  type="password"><input  name="submit"  type="submit"
value="Submit"></form>

<%
If Request.Form("submit") <> "" Then 'check if form was submitted first

  If Request.Form("txt_password") = "oe123456" Then
  'check if correct password was entered
  Response.Cookies("ckLoggedIn") = "True" 'create cookie with value of True
  Response.Redirect("members_only.asp") 'redirect to members page
  Else
  Response.Redirect "cookie_login.asp"
  End If
```

```
  End If
%>
```

When you submit the correct password on this page (`oe123456`), you will be redirected to a `members_only.asp` page, but in addition, a cookie called `ckLoggedIn` will have been set on the user's computer, with a value of `True`. You can then easily retrieve the cookie using `Request.Cookies`, as shown, here, in the `members_only.asp` page:

```
<% If Request.Cookies("ckLoggedIn") = "True" Then %>
  The value of your ckLoggedIn cookie is: <%=Request.Cookies("ckLoggedIn") %><br/>
  Since you are logged in, you are free to view this text.
<% End If %>
```

If the correct password was entered you should see the following when you view this page in your browser:

The value of your ckLoggedIn cookie is: True
Since you are logged in, you are free to view this text.

You will learn more about the `Request` object in the next section.

Request Object

The `Request` object gives you access to the values passed in an HTTP request from a client browser to the server. The client browser will pass information directly to your script through an HTTP header, which you can retrieve using the `Request` object.

We have already seen `Request` used to retrieve a cookie value above; another example could be values passed through forms. These are passed inside an HTTP header or body, and can be retrieved using `Request.Form`.

The `Request` object collects five types of HTTP information, which it stores in the following collections:

- `QueryString`
- `Form`
- `Cookies`
- `ClientCertificate`
- `ServerVariables`

The general syntax for the `Request` object is as follows:

```
Request.[collection](variable_name)
```

It is possible to call a variable without identifying the collection type like this:

```
Request(variable_name)
```

What happens, though, if you have two variables with the same name, but in different collection types? The web server will not necessarily return the variable from the collection type you intended, instead it will return the first variable encountered (the collections are dealt with in the order listed above.) Additionally, the server will find what it's looking for quicker if it knows which collection to look in.

So, you are strongly recommended to always identify the collection type when retrieving the variable. As well as being more programmatically sound, it will also help with code maintenance when you (or someone else) comes to debug or update the code. Stating what the collection type is will make the code far easier to understand.

Let's see some real examples of retrieving these different collection types. In the interests of brevity, we won't discuss `ClientCertificate` because it is very rarely used.

QueryString Collection

The `QueryString` collection refers to the HTTP information contained in a querystring (the information appended to a URL after a question mark). For example, consider the following URL:

http://localhost/chapter04/pass_querystings.asp?username=omar&category_id=34

This URL contains two name/value pairs, *username=omar* and *category_id=34*, appended to each other with an ampersand (*&*).

Now create a new dynamic ASP VBScript web page in Dreamweaver MX and save it as `pass_querystrings.asp`. In Code View, type the text *pass QueryStrings to the next page* within the `<body>` tags. Highlight the text and click the little yellow folder to the right of the *Link* text field in the *Properties* panel:

Creating a link using the Properties panel.

When the *Select File* dialog box pops up, type `read_querystrings.asp` in the URL text field:

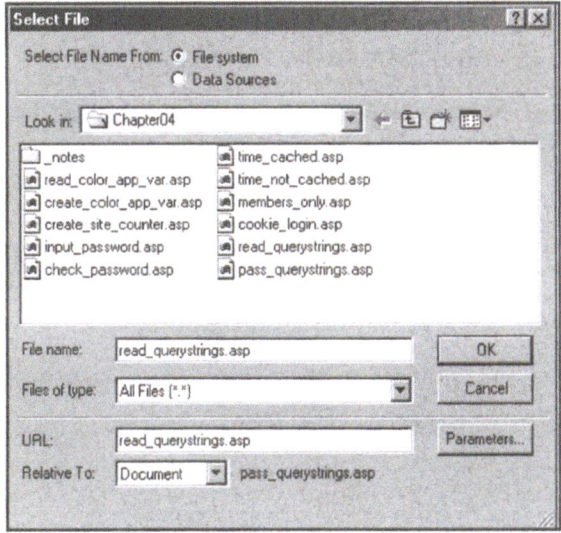

Selecting a page to link to.

Next, click the button labeled *Parameters...* and fill in the following names and values when the *Parameters* dialog box pops open:

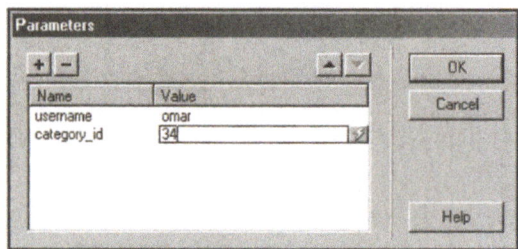

Creating some name/value pairs to pass in the querystring.

OK out of these two dialogs, and you should now see the following code in your document:

```
<a href="/read_querystrings.asp?username=omar&category_id=34">pass QueryStrings to
the next page</a>
```

We are now passing two parameters to the next page in the querystring, one named `username` with a value of `omar`, and the second named `category_id` with a value of `34`.

So let's now create the `read_querystrings.asp` page – create a new ASP VBScript document. From the *Application* panel select *Bindings > Request Variable*. When the *Request Variable* dialog box pops open, select *Request.QueryString* for the variable *Type* and type *username* for the *Name*:

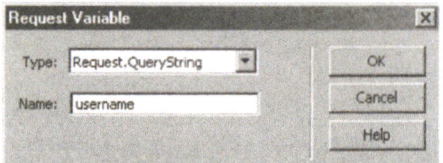

Creating Request variables – the Request Variable dialog.

Click *OK*, and then repeat this action for the `category_id` querystring. These two querystrings will now be available in the *Bindings* window:

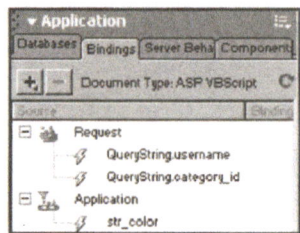

Our two Request variables are now available in the Bindings window.

You will now be able to drag these variables anywhere in your document. Drag them within the `<body>` tags to create the following code:

```
<%= Request.QueryString("username") %><br/ >
<%= Request.QueryString("category_id") %>
```

Now load the `pass_querystrings.asp` page in your browser and click the link. You should see the `read_querystrings.asp` page, with the values from the querystring on the screen. Note that the querystring values are also appended to the end of the URL in the *Address* bar:

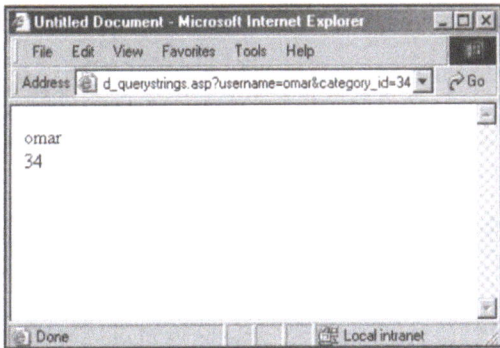

read_querystrings.asp – where our name/value pairs are passed to.

This is very useful, as values input into forms can be retrieved from the `QueryString` collection when sent using the GET method. We will look at an example of this now.

Create a new ASP VBScript document in Dreamweaver and name it `pass_form_values.asp`. Place the cursor inside the `<body>` tags and add a form. Set the `method` to `get`, the `action` to `read_form_values.asp`, and name the form `send_form_values.asp`. Now add the following into the form:

- A text field with a name of `txt_username` and a value of `John`. Select *Text* for the *Type*

- Another text field with a name of `txt_placeofbirth` and a value of `New York City`. Again, select *Text* for the *Type*.

- A button with a name of `submit` and a value of `Submit` – select *submit* for the *Type* as well

The final code in your page should look like this:

```
<form action="read_form_values.asp" method="get" name="send_form_values.asp">
  <input name="txt_username" type="text" value="John" />
  <input name="txt_placeofbirth" type="text" value="New York City" />
  <input name="submit" type="submit" value="Submit" />
</form>
```

Objects, Properties, Methods, and Events

You can easily edit your attribute values in Code or Design View by right-clicking on the element you wish to edit, and choosing the Edit Tag option from the context menu, bringing up the relevant Tag Editor dialog box.

Load this page in your browser and *Submit* the form. When you submit the form, you will get a 404 error (page cannot be found) because we haven't created the page, but take a look at the URL:

…/read_form_values.asp?txt_username=John&txt_place ofbirth=New+York+City&submit=Submit

Notice that the form values have been passed into the URL as part of the querystring. This is because we used the `get` method when submitting the form, which passes the values in the HTTP header. We can now retrieve these values like we did in the previous example:

Form Collection

The `Form` collection holds values inputted through a form submitted using the `post` method. For example, create the following form in Dreamweaver and save the document as `send_form_values.asp`:

```
<form action="receive_form_values.asp" method="post" name="frm_login">
  <label>Username</label><input name="txt_username" type="text" />
  <label>Password</label><input name="txt_password" type="password" />
  <input name="login_submit" type="submit" value="Submit" />
</form>
```

This form resembles a login form in which the username and password are sent to the server. Notice that it sends the information using the `post` method, rather than `get`, so the name/value pairs are posted to the HTTP request body, rather than being appended to the URL of the action page.

Unlike the `QueryString` collection, the `Form` collection doesn't show up in the URL window on the browser, and there is only one unique way to generate it, which is by submitting the form using the `post` method. Therefore, for reasons of security, the `post` method is the best way to submit potentially sensitive information, such as usernames and passwords.

To retrieve these values from the `Form` collection, we use `Request.Form` collection. Let's look at an example of this. Create a new document in Dreamweaver and save it as `receive_form_values.asp`. Insert the following code into the body:

```
<% If Request.Form("login_submit") <> "" Then %>

<%= Request.Form("txt_username") %> <br />
<%= Request.Form("txt_password") %>

<% End If %>
```

This code first checks to see if the form from the previous page has actually been submitted. If so, it displays the values input for both form elements: `txt_username` and `txt_password`. When the user submits the form, the form values are sent to the web server via the HTTP `post` method in the body of the HTTP request. We then use the `Request` object to retrieve those values and display them – try the example out for yourself.

Cookies Collection

The `Request` object also allows you to retrieve cookie values. While the `Response` object creates the cookies, the `Request` object retrieves them.

Retrieving cookies using the `Request` object is as simple as retrieving values from the other `Request` object collections. Let's first create a cookie and then retrieve it. Create the following example and save your page as `create_cookie.asp`:

```
<% Response.Cookies("ck_userid") = 345 'create cookie with value of 345%>
  Here is the value of the cookie named ck_userid:<br />
<%
  Response.Write(Request.Cookies("ck_userid"))
  'display value of cookie named ck_userid
%>
```

When you view this page in your browser you should see the following displayed:

345

ServerVariables Collection

The `ServerVariables` collection retrieves the values of predetermined Server variables (sometimes also known as Environment variables; information about the environment in which you are running your web applications). These variables are very often useful to web developers, as they include such data as the client's IP address, the URL of the current page and much more. When you retrieve these values you can use them within your code. For example if you have a secure login page, you might want to collect the client IP address whenever it is accessed, for security purposes.

Let's iterate through all these Server variables and display them on a page using a `For Each` loop so you can get a better idea of how many there are! We will also display the values of each Server variable (obviously, these could well differ between different servers).Add the following code to a new ASP VBScript page and save it as `get_servervariables.asp`:

```
<table border="1">
  <tr>
    <td><b>Server Variable</b></td>
    <td><b>Value</b></td>
  </tr>
  <% For Each str_key In Request.ServerVariables %>
    <tr>
      <td><%= str_key %></td>
      <td><%= Request.ServerVariables(str_key) %></td>
    </tr>
  <% Next %>
</table>
```

When you run this page, you should get something like the following in your browser:

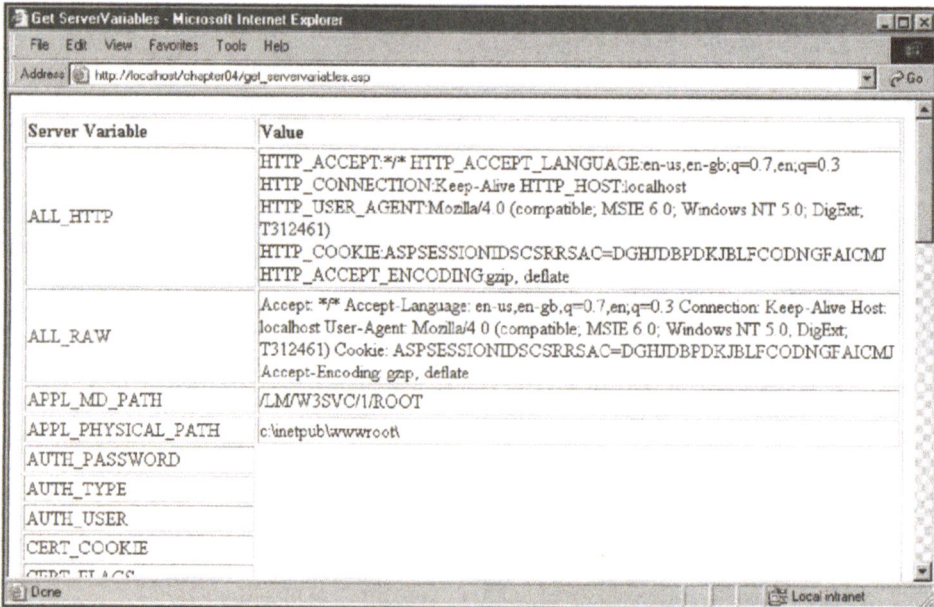

The result of requesting the serverVariables collection, and outputting it to a page.

Some Server variables don't appear, but this is because they are in fact empty.

Now let's display the client's IP address on the screen. Add the following to a new page and save it as display_ip.asp:

```
Your IP address is: <br />
<%= Request.ServerVariables("REMOTE_HOST") %>
```

If you are on a local host you will see the following displayed on the screen when the example is run:

Your IP address is:
127.0.0.1

Now let's populate a form element with a set environment. This is how Environment variables are often used. For example, say you had a registration form. While the user-entered details are being collected, you might also want to surreptitiously retrieve the user's IP address and insert it into a database for future reference. Add the following code to a new page and save it as register_form.asp:

```
<form action="register_form.asp" method="post" name="frm_register">
  Username: <input name="txt_username" type="text" /><br />
  Password: <input name="txt_password" type="password" />
<input name="hdn_ipaddress" type="hidden"
       value="<%=Request.ServerVariables("REMOTE_HOST") %>" /><br />
<input name="submit" type="submit" value="Submit" /></form>
```

When you view this page in your browser, you should see the login, but you will not see the IP address field, as it is hidden. If you view the page source, however, you should see the following:

<input name="hdn_ipaddress" type="hidden"
value="127.0.0.1">

When this form is submitted we can retrieve that hidden field just like we would the other text fields:

```
<%= Request.Form("hdn_ipaddress") %>
```

For more information, take a look at the following URL for a complete list and description of each Server variable: *http://msdn.microsoft.com/library/en-us/iisref/html/psdk/asp/vbob5vsj.asp*.

Server Object

The `Server` object provides access to methods and properties of the server.

Server Methods

The full list of `Server` object methods is as follows:

- `CreateObject`: Creates an instance of a server component
- `Execute`: Executes an .asp file
- `GetLastError`: Returns an `ASPError` object that describes the error condition
- `HTMLEncode`: Applies HTML encoding to the specified string
- `MapPath`: Maps the specified virtual path, either the absolute path on the current server or the path relative to the current page, into a physical path
- `Transfer`: Sends all of the current state information to another .asp file for processing
- `URLEncode`: Applies URL encoding rules, including escape characters, to the string

Again, it would take a lot of space to exhaustively discuss them all, so here we will just look at the most commonly used ones – `MapPath`, `HTMLEncode`, and `Transfer` methods of the `Server` object.

Server.MapPath

This method allows you to determine the physical path to a virtual directory on the server. You can do so by passing the virtual directory or filename as an argument in the `MapPath` method. For example, on my computer I have set my desktop directory as a virtual directory. I can then retrieve the physical path to the desktop folder by executing this following code in a page within the desktop virtual directory:

```
<%= Server.MapPath("/desktop") %>
```

When I view this page in my browser I get:

C:\Documents and Settings\Administrator\Desktop

Server.HTMLEncode

This method encodes HTML characters to ASCII characters and outputs the result to the browser as a `Response.Write` would. These characters are still displayed as HTML in the web browser.

This method is very useful when displaying information on your page that was submitted by a user, which you may not be entirely trusting of. For example, in guestbook or forum applications where users can freely post comments, a user could submit some malicious JavaScript that might execute and cause problems when the text is loaded. To stop this happening, you could use `HTMLEncode` to encode the HTML to ASCII, which would mean that the JavaScript would not execute.

Let's see an example. Create the following file and save it as `htmlencode.asp`:

```
Comment:<br />

<form action="htmlencode.asp" method="post">
<textarea name="str_comment" cols="35" rows="4"></textarea><br />
<input name="submit" type="submit" value="Submit" />
</form>

<% If Request.Form("submit") <> "" Then %>
<%=Request.Form("str_comment")%>
<% End If %>
```

The above code simply allows a user to submit a comment in a text area. Once the form is submitted, we display what was submitted directly underneath the form itself. Go ahead: access the page from your browser and submit some text to see how the text submitted is displayed. Now deliberately enter the following string in the form and submit it: `<b>hello</b>`.

When you submit the form you should see the following:

hello

So we can use HTML to mark up our comments. What about JavaScript? Try entering the following into the form:

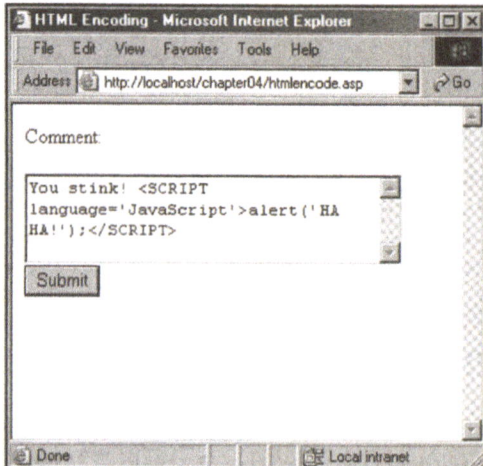

What happens if we enter a JavaScript alert into our comments box?

Submit the form and see what happens when the user's comment is displayed:

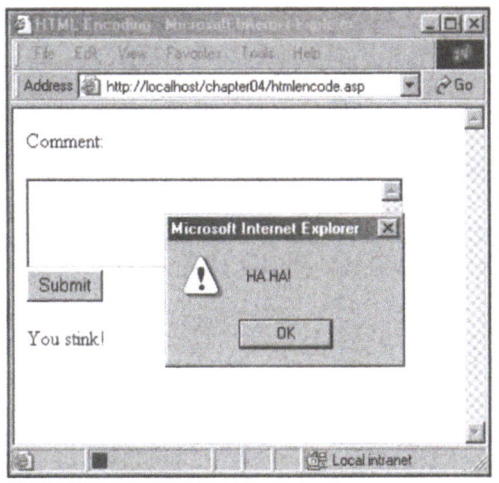

We get an annoying alert message when we submit it, that's what!

Not a pretty sight! Imagine how annoying it would be if this popped up every time you accessed the forum or guestbook? To fix this dilemma we can use `HTMLEncode` to encode the HTML characters input to ASCII characters, which would make the JavaScript useless. Make the following modification to `htmlencode.asp`:

```
Comment:<br />

<form action="htmlencode.asp" method="post">
<textarea name="str_comment" cols="35" rows="4"></textarea><br />
<input name="submit" type="submit" value="Submit" />
</form>

<% If Request.Form("submit") <> "" Then %>
<%=Server.HTMLEncode(Request.Form("str_comment"))%>
<% End If %>
```

Now access the page in your browser – now if you try submitting the same annoying JavaScript line, you should see the following:

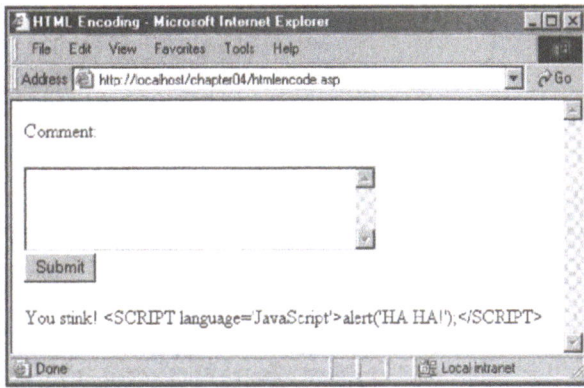

If we use Server.HTMLEncode on our submission, it isn't recognized and interpreted as JavaScript.

The comment is displayed as entered, but the JavaScript does not actually execute because the HTML characters are encoded to ASCII characters, as you will see from the sourcecode:

The source of the page, showing our ASCII-encoded HTML characters.

Server.Transfer

The `Transfer` method is similar to the `Redirect` method of the `Response` object in that it transfers the user to another URL. What `Transfer` does that `Redirect` doesn't is transfer all control of the former page to the latter page, including all objects and variables that have been given a value in an Application or Session variable, and all items in the `Request` collections such as `Form`, `QueryStrings`, etc. In essence, the Session is conserved from the first page, over to the second (see *Chapter 10* for more on sessions).

`Server.Transfer` is quicker than `Response.Redirect` because the transfer is done on the server whereas `Response.Redirect` needs to take two trips to the server to finally perform the redirection. For example, say the user requests a page with a `Response.Redirect` in it: first, a trip is made from the client to the server and back to the client to send the requested page. Then, once the `Response.Redirect` is executed, a trip is made from the client to the server and back to the client again to send the redirected page.

Summary

In this chapter we have taken a good look at some of the most important uses of the ASP-intrinsic objects. For example we saw how the `Request` object gives the web developer the ability to retrieve values from querystrings, forms, cookies, and Server variables.

We saw how we can use the `Response` object to create cookies and print values to the screen. Creating site-wide variables using the `Application` object was also discussed.

Lastly, we discussed using the `Server` object to access useful methods and properties of the server.

In this chapter we have looked at the following objects:

- Application object
- Response object
- Request object
- Server object

For more information, explore Microsoft's online documentation about ASP-intrinsic objects at: *http://msdn.microsoft.com/library/default.asp?url=/library/en-us/iisref60/htm/ref_vbom_.asp*.

4

Objects, Properties, Methods, and Events

5

- The ASP Err and ASPError objects
- Good coding practices to help avoid errors
- Creating custom error handling

Author: Dan Short

Error Handling

Any time you're dealing with dynamic data, you're most likely getting information back from the client. Unfortunately Aunt Rosemary doesn't always know what she should be sending back, the neighbor kid may actually be trying to enter malicious information into the application, and we all make spelling mistakes in our code.

To take care of some of these situations we can do some basic variable and error checking. For example, if we know that we want to insert a date into a database field, why not check to make sure the user has entered an actual valid date before committing the changes? If we have a field for age, we should usually check to make sure the user enters an integer (23) and not a string (twenty-three).

There's also a built-in function in ASP to help you find those spelling mistakes, and two error objects that will allow you to catch some of these errors. The `Err` object in ASP 2 (IIS 4 and PWS) will allow for some simple error checking, but it leaves out important trouble-shooting information like the line and column numbers where the error originated. To remedy that you need the `ASPError` object, which is available in IIS 5 and ASP 3, which is part of Windows 2000.

What do we mean by error handling though? Well, when a user inputs bad data or you have code that generates an error, you probably don't want the user to see something like this:

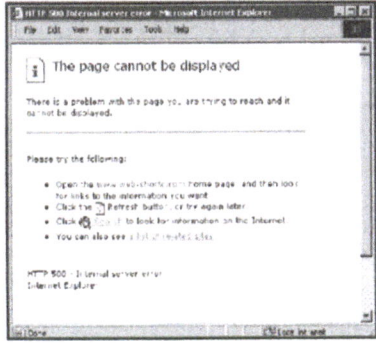

A typical default Internet Explorer error screen

> *Proper error handling will allow you to present a more user-friendly error message and can even allow you to set up a system that sends you an e-mail when a catastrophic error occurs on your site*

Not only does it not tell your user they did something wrong, but it will probably scare them away from your site. Proper error handling will allow you to present a more user-friendly error message and can even allow you to set up a system that sends you an e-mail when a catastrophic error occurs on your site.

With proper error handling included in your site, not only will your user be happy but also you'll know exactly what they did wrong so you can either add additional error checking or fix your coding blunder (but we don't make blunders, right?)

But before we get into error-handling techniques, we're going to cover some things you can do to prevent the errors in the first place.

Common Coding Practices

In order to make your code cleaner (and easier to debug) you should follow some common coding practices through your application. There are no hard and-fast-rules here, but following some simple guidelines can help make your life a bit easier in the long run.

We have already discussed the advantages of commenting code in *Chapter 1*; here we will look at checking and converting data types, and using option explicit in your code.

Check and Convert Data Types

We have already touched upon how different data types interact with each other in Chapter 1. Let's have a bit of a recap, and then look at the errors that result from data type mismatches, and how we can handle these.

The type of data you're working with is extremely important when performing certain operations. For example, you can't add strings together and can't subtract dates from an integer. When you're working with calculations and dates especially, you need to ensure that your variables have the right data type. The easiest way to explain this is with an example:

```
<%
  Dim var1 : var1 = 2
  Dim var2 : var2 = "two"
  Dim var3

  var3 = var1 + var2
%>
```

The line which adds var1 and var2 will generate the following error:

```
Type mismatch: '[string: "two"]'
```

The reason for this is that you can't add a string and an integer together. To fix this we can check to make sure that both of our variables are in fact integers before we perform our calculation. A revised code block might look like this:

```
<%
  Dim var1 : var1 = 2
  Dim var2 : var2 = "two"
  Dim var3

  If IsNumeric(var1) AND IsNumeric(var2) Then
    var3 = var1 + var2
  Else
    Response.Write("One of the vars is not numeric.")
  End If
%>
```

The `IsNumeric` function checks to see if the variable you're testing is in fact a number. If the variable is a number `IsNumeric` returns `True`, otherwise it returns `False`. In this way you can check to be sure that all of your variables are of the correct type. There are several other `Is` type functions, including `IsArray`, `IsDate`, `IsEmpty`, `IsNull`, and `IsObject`. You can also use the `VarType` function to return the type of the supplied variable. Let's go back to our previous example and output the variable type for `var1` and `var2`.

```
<%
  Dim var1 : var1 = 2
  Dim var2 : var2 = "1"
  Dim var3

  Response.Write(VarType(var1) & "<br />" & VarType(var2))
%>
```

The `Response.Write` statement returns the numbers 2 and 8. If we refer to the MSDN documentation for the `VarType` function:

http://msdn.microsoft.com/library/default.asp?url=/library/en-us/script56/html/vsfctvartype.asp

we can find out what each of the variable types are:

- 0: `vbEmpty`: Empty (uninitialized)
- 1: `vbNull`: Null (no valid data)
- 2: `vbInteger`: Integer
- 3: `vbLong`: Long integer
- 4: `vbSingle`: Single-precision floating-point number
- 5: `vbDouble`: Double-precision floating-point number
- 6: `vbCurrency`: Currency
- 7: `vbDate`: Date
- 8: `vbString`: String
- 9: `vbObject`: Automation object
- 10: `vbError`: Error

- **11**: `vbBoolean`: Boolean

- **12**: `vbVariant`: Variant (used only with arrays of Variants)

- **13**: `vbDataObject`: A data-access object

- **17**: `vbByte`: Byte

- **8192**: `vbArray`: Array

There are also a number of functions for converting variable types. Each conversion function attempts to convert the supplied variable to the new data type. For example, if we wanted to convert the string "2" to the integer 2, we would use the `CInt` function to convert it to an integer.

```
<%
  Dim myVar : myVar = "2"
  Response.Write(VarType(myVar))
  MyVar = CInt(myVar)
  Response.Write(VarType(myVar))
%>
```

That example would output the number 8 for the first `Response.Write` and the number 2 for the second. The other conversion functions include `CBool` (boolean), `CCur` (currency), `CByte` (byte number), `CDate`, `CDbl` (double), `CLng` (long), `CSng` (single), and `CStr` (string).

Option Explicit

What's the weakest part of any application during development? I bet you didn't answer yourself. If you're hand coding pages you're almost always going to misspell a variable or forget to declare something that you need. To help prevent this, you can add the `Option Explicit` declaration to your page.

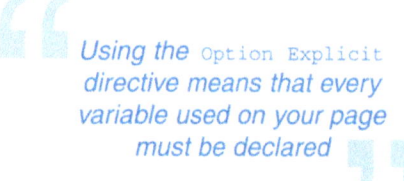

Using the `Option Explicit` *directive means that every variable used on your page must be declared*

Using the `Option Explicit` directive means that every variable used on your page must be declared. That means you can't use `myVar` unless you have `Dim myVar` sometime before the variable is accessed. How does this help you? If you misspell a variable without using `Option Explicit` then you'll just get a Null result back. If you misspell a variable when using `Option Explicit` you'll get an error saying that the variable is undefined.

Be aware that, if you're designing XHTML pages, Dreamweaver MX will add the `<?xml ... ?>` *declaration at the very top of the page, which will cause an "Expected Statement" error when you browse to the page in your browser. To fix this, just move the* `<?xml ... ?>` *tag back down to just above the* `DOCTYPE` *in your document.*

To use `Option Explicit` you need to declare it immediately after the language attribute:

```
<%@LANGUAGE="VBSCRIPT" CODEPAGE="1252"%>
<% Option Explicit %>
```

This code (`simple_error.asp`) will generate an error since `yourVar` hasn't been defined:

```
<%@LANGUAGE="VBSCRIPT" CODEPAGE="1252"%>
<% Option Explicit %>
<%
  Dim myVar : myVar = 3
  Response.Write(yourVar)
%>
```

The error you should see will be something like this:

```
Microsoft VBScript runtime error '800a01f4'
Variable is undefined: 'yourVar'
/1213/Chapter05/simple_error.asp, line 5
```

If you change the code to this, the page will work just fine:

```
<%@LANGUAGE="VBSCRIPT" CODEPAGE="1252"%>
<% Option Explicit %><%
  Dim myVar : myVar = 3
  Response.Write(myVar)
%>
```

This means that your page will throw an error any time you try to access a variable it isn't aware of. This will ensure your code is cleaner and will ensure that you don't misspell any variable names. After all, if you try to access a variable but spell it differently than when you declared it, you'll get an error.

Trapping Errors

ASP itself doesn't have any built-in error-checking mechanisms, but instead leaves it up to the scripting language to handle it – if you're using VBScript, you can use the `Err` object. The `Err` object contains all of the specific information for the last error that occurred. This means that we can trap the error and provide the user with a more useful error message than the dreaded *HTTP 500 – Internal Server Error* they would otherwise see.

If they're a bit more technically savvy they may have the *Show friendly HTTP error messages* option unchecked in their browser (you should certainly have this unchecked), and they'll see something more like this:

```
Microsoft VBScript runtime error '800a000b'
Division by zero
/chapters/04/code/error.asp, line 19
```

This is not only ugly to look at, but it gives away more information than we'd like. If our error happened on a SQL query or a connection string, then it might give information that would allow unscrupulous types to discern our database structure or worse – not a happy thought.

The `Err` and `ASPError` objects allow us to, among other things, customize our error messages so that we don't give out such information when an error is encountered. It also allows us to provide more helpful information to our users.

The Err Object

The `Err` object is a global object, meaning that it doesn't have to be instantiated. The `Err` object is therefore always available, and it will contain the last error encountered on the page. It has a number of properties, and two methods we can use to output or manipulate the error. After we take a look at those properties and methods I'll finally show you how to put `Err` to use.

Properties

You'll need to use the various properties of the `Err` object to output or catch specific errors. The following is a description of each of the properties, and an example of usage.

- `Description` – Returns a string containing a description of the error. This isn't always the most friendly error message, but will usually do the job well enough. The usage is as follows: `Err.Description()`

- `HelpFile` – The `HelpFile` property contains the actual location of a *Help* file associated with a particular error. In a VBA application this is the file that would be loaded if the user clicked the *Help* button or pressed *F1* inside an error dialog box. It isn't of much use in web applications. The usage is as follows: `Err.HelpFile()`

- `HelpContext` – If a Help file is specified in `HelpFile`, the `HelpContext` property is used to automatically display the *Help* topic identified using the context ID. Again, this property is usually used for VBA desktop type applications, and doesn't serve a real use for web applications. The usage is as follows: `Err.HelpContext()`

- `Number` – This is the actual reference number of the current error. You can reference the Microsoft documentation to find out what the error really means (see *http://msdn. microsoft.com/library/default.asp?url=/library/en-us/script56/html/vspronumber.asp*), or refernce the `Description` property. The usage is as follows: `Err.Number()`

- `Source` – This is the name of the object or application that caused the error in the first place. The usage is as follows: `Err.Source()`

Methods

You only get two methods for the `Err` object:

- `Clear` – This clears the `Err` object of the current error it's holding. This is good for getting rid of an error before continuing with additional code. The `Clear` method is automatically invoked when you execute `Exit Function`, `Exit Sub`, or `On Error Resume Next`. The usage is as follows: `Err.Clear`

- `Raise` – The `Raise` method actually generates a runtime error. This can be useful if a user meets certain criteria or tries to force some bad code into the system. You can then create your own error and do your error handling as usual. The `Raise` method just needs a number argument for you to tell it which error you want raised. Usage is as follows: You can give the method an error number, for example `Err.Raise 11` would cause a *Division by Zero* error, or you can raise a custom error of your choosing, for example: `Err.Raise vbObjectError + 12, _"mypage.asp", "My custom error"` `vbObjectError + 12` would be your custom error number (equivalent to `Err.Number`), `mypage.asp` is the page that generated the error (`Err.Source`), and `My custom error` is the description (`Err.Description`). I personally find the built-in error checking sufficient and have never had to use a custom error.

Putting it to Use

In order to enable `Err` object usage, we have to tell our page what to do when it encounters an error. The default behavior is to output the error to the page. To stop that, we use `On Error Resume Next`. That's fairly self-explanatory, but to explain further, it tells the server to just continue processing the following line after the error occurs.

Let's use the following code to do all of our testing. The following page (`error_division.asp`) will throw a `Division by 0` error every time the page is loaded, so we can see how the page reacts to our error checking.

```
<%@LANGUAGE="VBSCRIPT" CODEPAGE="1252"%>
<% Option Explicit %>
<html>
<head>
  <title>Untitled Document</title>
  <meta http-equiv="Content-Type" content="text/html; charset=iso-8859-1">
</head>
<body>
  <%
    ' Enable Error Handling
    On Error Resume Next

    ' Declare variables
    Dim intX, intY, intZ
    intX = 10
    intY = 0

    ' Divide 10 by 0
    intZ = intX / intY

    ' Check for errors
    ' If Err.Number not equal to 0 an error has occurred
    If Err.Number <> 0 Then
      Response.Write("<p><strong>The following Error has occurred:</strong></p>")
      Response.Write("Number: " & Err.Number & "<br />")
      Response.Write("Description: " & Err.Description & "<br />")
      Response.Write("Source: " & Err.Source & "<br />")
      Err.Clear
    Else
      Response.Write intX & " / " & intY & " = " & intZ
    End If
  %>
</body>
</html>
```

Notice that I've added the `On Error Resume Next` statement to the page. If you comment out that line you'll end up with the default error message we saw earlier at the beginning of this section, rather than this more friendly error.

Once an error occurs, the error information is put into the `Err` object, and we can test to see if there is an actual error. If there aren't any errors, then `Err.Number` will equal 0. If it's anything but 0, then we have an error. We can then output the details of that error (in this case, the error number and description) and what application caused the error. If we bring this page up in our browser, we end up with an easier to understand message for our user, and we can format it any way we like to make it fit the design of the rest of our site:

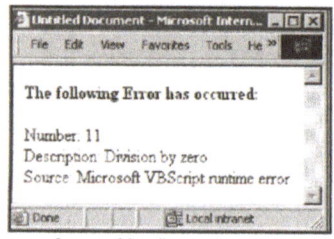

A more friendly error to output to the browser.

After we output this error message, we need to clear the error so that we can be ready for the next error that might happen. The `Err.Clear` statement takes care of that for us, setting `Err.Number` back to 0 and clearing out all of the other `Err` properties.

When your page runs into an error, it will walk up the code stack looking for any error-handling instructions. This means that if you're inside a function, it will first check for any error-handling instructions inside the function. If it doesn't find any instructions, it will go back to the calling function or page and check there. What this means is that if you put `On Error Resume Next` at the top of your page, every error on the page will be affected by this statement. If you put an `On Error Resume Next` statement inside a function, then only that function will have error checking enabled. Here's an example of error checking inside a function but not on the page.

```
<%@LANGUAGE="VBSCRIPT" CODEPAGE="1252"%>
<% Option Explicit %>
<%
  Function DivideNumbers(number1,number2)
    On Error Resume Next
    DivideNumbers = number1 / number2
    If Err.Number <> 0 Then
      Response.Write("<p><strong>The following Error has occurred:</strong></p>")
      Response.Write("Number: " & Err.Number & "<br />")
      Response.Write("Description: " & Err.Description & "<br />")
      Response.Write("Source: " & Err.Source & "<br />")
      Err.Clear
      DivideNumbers = 0
    End If
  End Function
%>
<html>
<head>
  <title>Chapter 4 Error Handling</title>
  <meta http-equiv="Content-Type" content="text/html; charset=iso-8859-1">
</head>
<body>
  <%
    Dim intX, intY, intZ
    intX = 10
    intY = 0

    'Call Function
    DivideNumbers intX, intY
```

```
    ' Divide 10 by 0
    intZ = intX / intY

    Response.Write(intZ)
  %>
</body>
</html>
```

This page (`errorFunction.asp`) will display our friendly error when we call the function, but will throw the default error when we divide the numbers outside our function.

While the number, description, and source are handy for a developer, they're not exactly user-friendly. After all, Aunt Rosemary doesn't know what a VBScript runtime error is. However, now that we know what the error number is we can write a `Select` statement to output our own custom error message. We could change the error-checking section of our code to this (see `custom_error_division.asp` for the full file):

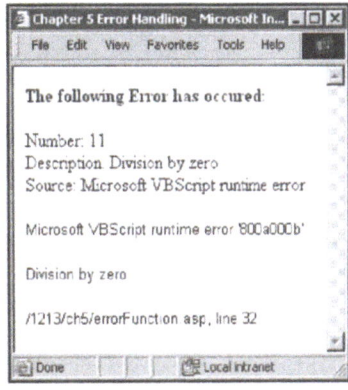

Another friendly error, but this time with more information provided.

```
If Err.Number <> 0 Then
   Response.Write("<p><strong>The following Error has occurred:</strong></p>")

   Select Case Err.Number
     Case 11
       Response.Write("You're trying to divide by 0 - you should know better.")
    'Case ... Add additional error numbers as necessary
     Case Else
       Response.Write("An error has occurred - please try again later.")
   End Select
   Err.Clear
Else
   Response.Write intX & " / " & intY & " = " & intZ
End If
```

When this page is viewed in a browser, you should see the following returned:

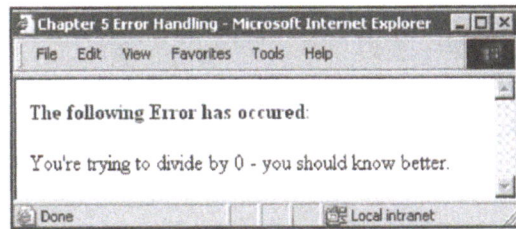

A friendly error that will prove more understandable to a user

Now that we're trapping all of the error numbers, we can output as many custom error messages as we want. We could also set up the page to e-mail us if there was a serious problem with the page (which we're going to cover in the *ASPError* section). You can find the ASP Runtime and Syntax errors through the MSDN Library:

- Runtime errors:
  http://msdn.microsoft.com/library/default.asp?url=/library/en-us/script56/html/vtoriVBScript.asp

- Syntax errors:
  http://msdn.microsoft.com/library/default.asp?url=/library/en-us/script56/html/vtoriVBScript.asp

Turning Error Handling Off Again

Now that we know how to turn error handling on, how do we turn it back off? Personally, once I have an application complete, I usually have an `On Error Resume Next` statement in a global function file (a common include used to store all of my custom functions), so every page has error checking enabled by default, since they all have that file included. But if I need to troubleshoot an individual page, I certainly don't want to disable error handling on the entire site by removing the `On Error Resume Next` statement from my global function. In order to turn error checking back on, we just use `On Error Goto 0`. This tells ASP to start using the default error-handling method again.

```
<%@LANGUAGE="VBSCRIPT" CODEPAGE="1252"%>
<%
  Option Explicit
  'Functions.asp has an on error resume next statement
%>
<!--#include file="functions.asp" -->
<%
  'Error handling is now on
  'Turn off error handling
  On Error Goto 0
  'Error handling is now off
%>
```

While using the `Err` object for error handling is better than the default (since it allows you to display an error inside your own site layout), it does have some drawbacks. The worst drawback is the fact that you can't output the line and column numbers for the error; only what the error was. This makes it much more difficult to debug a page, especially if you're depending on someone else giving you the error information. To fix that you can use the `ASPError` object, as long as you're on a Windows 2000 or XP server. You'll need IIS5 to make it work.

The ASPError Object

To cover the inadequacies of the `Err` object in IIS4, Microsoft added the `ASPError` object in IIS5. There are more properties to take note of with the `ASPError` object, and we can use these to extract quite a bit more information about the errors encountered during page processing.

The way the `ASPError` object works is fundamentally different from the `Err` object. In order to use the `ASPError` object, you'll need to set up a custom error page for your site and tell the server to use this page for all of your error processing (or have your host do it for you). You also have to fill the `ASPError` object just like you do any other object (see *Chapter 4* for more about objects.)

The `ASPError` properties are as follows (there are no `ASPError` methods):

- `ASPCode` – Returns the error code generated by IIS. You can use the MSDN Library to find out what the code refers to. The usage is as follows: `objASPError.ASPCode`

- `Number` – Returns an error code from a COM component, such as a file upload component or CDO Mail. The usage is as follows: `objASPError.Number`

- `Source` – Returns the actual sourcecode of the line that caused the error, if it's available. Usage is as follows: `objASPError.Source`

- `Category` – Returns whether the error was generated by IIS, a scripting language, or a component. The usage is as follows: `objASPError.Category`

- `File` – Returns the name of the `.asp` file that generated the error. The usage is as follows: `objASPError.File`

- `Line` – Returns the line that generated the error in an `.asp` file. The usage is as follows: `objASPError.Line`

- `Column` – Returns the column position in the `.asp` file that generated the error. The usage is as follows: `objASPError.Column`

- `Description` – Returns a short description of the error. The usage is as follows: `objASPError.Description`

- `ASPDescription` – Returns a long description of the error. The usage is as follows: `objASPError.ASPDescription`

Putting it to Use

The first thing you have to do to get `ASPError` working is to define a custom error page for your web site in

IIS – `On Error Resume Next` isn't going to work for us, as that invokes the `Err` object if there is a problem. When an error occurs in your application, IIS will `Server.Transfer` (see *Chapter 4* for more on using this) the current page to your custom error page, maintaining all of the state information (form variables and such) for the user.

To do this, go into IIS, drill down to *Default Web Site*, then right-click on it and choose *Properties*. Now click on the *Custom Errors* tab, and you should be presented with a display like this:

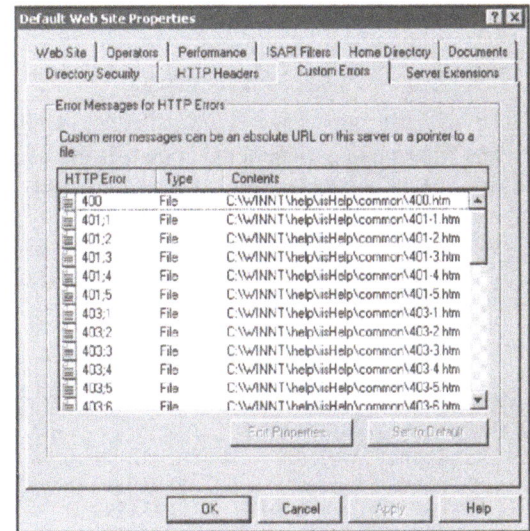

Properties for the error messages displayed within IIS.

Scroll down to the *500;100* error. The default is simply *Internal Server Error – ASP Error*. Highlight the *500;100* error and click *Edit Properties*. For the *Message Type*, click the drop-down menu and choose *URL*; next we need to enter a relative link to what you want your custom error page to be named. In our examples we're going to name it `500-100.asp`, so enter `/500-100.asp`. Your dialog box should now look like this:

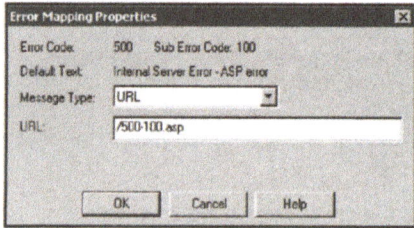

Setting our own customized server error.

Now *OK* out of these two screens.

Now that we've told the web server where to send error messages, we need to create a `500-100.asp` page. IIS has one ready for use right on your web server. By default it's located at `c:\winnt\help\iishelp\common\500-100.asp`. You can just copy this page to the root of your site and you have a custom error page that will give you a little more info than the default reporting. It's not that pretty however, so now we'll look at building one from scratch:

The first thing we need is a fresh ASP VBScript page. We then need to add our `Option Explicit` and tell the server what kind of page this is. Since it's an error page, we're going to use some properties of the `Response` object for that purpose:

```
<%@LANGUAGE="VBSCRIPT" CODEPAGE="1252"%>
<%
  Option Explicit
    If Response.Buffer Then
    Response.Clear
    Response.Status = "500 Internal Server Error"
    Response.ContentType = "text/html"
    Response.Expires = 0
  End If
%>
<html>
<head>
  <title>500-100 ASP Error</title>
```

The highlighted portion of the code tells the server the status of the page and ensures the browser won't cache the page. This prevents a previous error from being displayed by the client's browser.

Now we need to declare all of our variables and get the error passed to the page. We get the error using a method of the `Server` object, `GetLastError`. We're going to instantiate our error object and fill it with the `GetLastError` contents.

```
<%@LANGUAGE="VBSCRIPT" CODEPAGE="1252"%>
<%
  Option Explicit
  If Response.Buffer Then
    Response.Clear
    Response.Status = "500 Internal Server Error"
    Response.ContentType = "text/html"
    Response.Expires = 0
  End If
```

```
  Dim objASPError : Set objASPError = Server.GetLastError()
  Dim strServername : strServerName = Request.ServerVariables("SERVER_NAME")
  Dim strServerIP : strServerIP = Request.ServerVariables("LOCAL_ADDR")
  Dim strRemoteIP : strRemoteIP = Request.ServerVariables("REMOTE_ADDR")
  Dim strReferer : strReferer = Request.ServerVariables("HTTP_REFERER")
  Dim strEmailBody 'Used to build our email text
%>
<html>
<head>
  <title>500-100 ASP Error</title>
```

The `objASPError` object now contains all of the error information that's been passed to this page. The rest of the variables we declared will be used to e-mail us detailed error information.

Now we need to start building our e-mail. The first thing we'll do is grab all of the `ASPError` properties and list them:

```
  Dim objASPError : Set objASPError = Server.GetLastError()
  Dim strServername : strServerName = Request.ServerVariables("SERVER_NAME")
  Dim strServerIP : strServerIP = Request.ServerVariables("LOCAL_ADDR")
  Dim strRemoteIP : strRemoteIP = Request.ServerVariables("REMOTE_ADDR")
  Dim strReferer : strReferer = Request.ServerVariables("HTTP_REFERER")
  Dim strEmailBody 'Used to build our email text

  strEmailBody = "Error Details" & VbCrLf & String(20,"=") & VbCrLf
  strEmailBody = strEmailBody & "Domain Name: " & strServername & VbCrLf
  strEmailBody = strEmailBody & "Server IP: " & strServerIP & VbCrLf
  strEmailBody = strEmailBody & "Remote IP: " & strRemoteIP & VbCrLf
  strEmailBody = strEmailBody & "Referer: " & strReferer & VbCrLf & VbCrLf

  strEmailBody = strEmailBody & "ASPError" & VbCrLf & String(20,"=") & VbCrLf
  strEmailBody = strEmailBody & "ASPCode: " & objASPError.ASPCode & VbCrLf
  strEmailBody = strEmailBody & "Number: " & objASPError.Number & VbCrLf
  strEmailBody = strEmailBody & "Hex Number: 0x" & Hex(objASPError.Number) & VbCrLf
  strEmailBody = strEmailBody & "Source: " & objASPError.Source & VbCrLf
  strEmailBody = strEmailBody & "Category: " & objASPError.Category & VbCrLf
  strEmailBody = strEmailBody & "File: " & objASPError.File & VbCrLf
  strEmailBody = strEmailBody & "Line: " & objASPError.Line & VbCrLf
  strEmailBody = strEmailBody & "Column: " & objASPError.Column & VbCrLf
  strEmailBody = strEmailBody & "Description: " & objASPError.Description & VbCrLf
  strEmailBody = strEmailBody & "ASPDescription: " & objASPError.ASPDescription
%>
<html>
<head>
  <title>500-100 ASP Error</title>
```

So far our e-mail looks like this:

```
Error Details
====================
Domain Name: www.yourdomain.com
Server IP: xxx.xx.xxx.xx
Remote IP: xxx.xx.xxx.xx
Referer: http://yourdomain.com/submitpage.asp
```

```
ASPError
====================
ASPCode:
Number: -2146828277
Hex Number: 0x800A000B
Source:
Category: Microsoft VBScript runtime
File: /chapters/04/code/asperror.asp
Line: 18
Column: -1
Description: Division by zero
ASPDescription:
```

Some of the `ASPError` properties may be blank depending on the error generated. It would certainly be possible to check for empty values and then not send those variables, but it's useful to have everything, even if it's blank.

It's always nice to know what querystring and form values were sent to the page as well, so we now add two `For Each ... Next` loops (these were covered in *Chapter 2*) to send us both collections.

```
strEmailBody = strEmailBody & "Description: " & objASPError.Description & VbCrLf
strEmailBody = strEmailBody & "ASPDescription: " & objASPError.ASPDescription

Dim Item
If Request.Querystring <> "" Then
  strEmailBody = strEmailBody & VbCrLf & "Querystring Values" & VbCrLf
  strEmailBody = strEmailBody & String(20,"=") & VbCrLf
  For Each Item in Request.QueryString
    strEmailBody = strEmailBody & Item & ": " & Request.QueryString(Item) &_
    VbCrLf
  Next
End If

If Request.Form <> "" Then
  strEmailBody = strEmailBody & VbCrLf & "Form Values" & VbCrLf
  strEmailBody = strEmailBody & String(20,"=") & VbCrLf
  For Each Item in Request.Form
    strEmailBody = strEmailBody & Item & ": " & Request.Form(Item) & VbCrLf
  Next
End If
%>
<html>
<head>
  <title>500-100 ASP Error</title>
```

Now if there are querystring or form values, we'll have an e-mail similar to this:

```
Error Details
====================
Domain Name: www.yourdomain.com
Server IP: xxx.xx.xxx.xx
Remote IP: xxx.xx.xxx.xx
Referer: http://yourdomain.com/submitpage.asp
```

```
ASPError
====================
ASPCode:
Number: -2146828277
Hex Number: 0x800A000B
Source:
Category: Microsoft VBScript runtime
File: /chapters/04/code/asperror.asp
Line: 18
Column: -1
Description: Division by zero
ASPDescription:

Querystring Values
====================
var1: val1
var2: val2
```

You could continue in that vein and send additional collections, such as sending the entire `Request.ServerVariables` collection. That's left to your discretion, but anything is possible at this point, including writing errors to a database or a flat text file. The sky's the limit.

Now we just need to send our e-mail and output a simple *There was an error* message to the user of our site. Our example still won't be all that pretty to the user, but you can certainly dress this up as much as you want, and make it fit in with the rest of your site.

The final code `500-100.asp`, looks like this (also see the code download for the full version):

```
<%@LANGUAGE="VBSCRIPT" CODEPAGE="1252"%>
<%
  Option Explicit
  If Response.Buffer Then
    Response.Clear
    Response.Status = "500 Internal Server Error"
    Response.ContentType = "text/html"
    Response.Expires = 0
  End If

  Dim objASPError : Set objASPError = Server.GetLastError()
  Dim strServername : strServerName = Request.ServerVariables("SERVER_NAME")
  Dim strServerIP : strServerIP = Request.ServerVariables("LOCAL_ADDR")
  Dim strRemoteIP : strRemoteIP = Request.ServerVariables("REMOTE_ADDR")
  Dim strReferer : strReferer = Request.ServerVariables("HTTP_REFERER")
  Dim strEmailBody 'Used to build our email text

  strEmailBody = "Error Details" & VbCrLf & String(20,"=") & VbCrLf
  strEmailBody = strEmailBody & "Domain Name: " & strServername & VbCrLf
  strEmailBody = strEmailBody & "Server IP: " & strServerIP & VbCrLf
  strEmailBody = strEmailBody & "Remote IP: " & strRemoteIP & VbCrLf
  strEmailBody = strEmailBody & "Referer: " & strReferer & VbCrLf & VbCrLf

  strEmailBody = strEmailBody & "ASPError" & VbCrLf & String(20,"=") & VbCrLf
  strEmailBody = strEmailBody & "ASPCode: " & objASPError.ASPCode & VbCrLf
  strEmailBody = strEmailBody & "Number: " & objASPError.Number & VbCrLf
  strEmailBody = strEmailBody & "Hex Number: 0x" & Hex(objASPError.Number) & VbCrLf
```

```
      strEmailBody = strEmailBody & "Source: " & objASPError.Source & VbCrLf
      strEmailBody = strEmailBody & "Category: " & objASPError.Category & VbCrLf
      strEmailBody = strEmailBody & "File: " & objASPError.File & VbCrLf
      strEmailBody = strEmailBody & "Line: " & objASPError.Line & VbCrLf
      strEmailBody = strEmailBody & "Column: " & objASPError.Column & VbCrLf
      strEmailBody = strEmailBody & "Description: " & objASPError.Description & VbCrLf
      strEmailBody = strEmailBody & "ASPDescription: " & objASPError.ASPDescription

   Dim Item
   If Request.Querystring <> "" Then
      strEmailBody = strEmailBody & VbCrLf & "Querystring Values" & VbCrLf
      strEmailBody = strEmailBody & String(20,"=") & VbCrLf
      For Each Item in Request.QueryString
         strEmailBody = strEmailBody & Item & ": " & Request.QueryString(Item) &_
VbCrLf
      Next
   End If

   If Request.Form <> "" Then
      strEmailBody = strEmailBody & VbCrLf & "Form Values" & VbCrLf
      strEmailBody = strEmailBody & String(20,"=") & VbCrLf
      For Each Item in Request.Form
         strEmailBody = strEmailBody & Item & ": " & Request.Form(Item) & VbCrLf
      Next
   End If
   'Send our email
   Dim objMail
   Set objMail = Server.CreateObject("CDONTS.NewMail")

   objMail.To = "you@yourdomain.com"
   objMail.From = "me@mydomain.com"
   objMail.Subject ="Server Processing Error Details"
   objMail.Body = strEmailBody
   objMail.Send
   Set objMail = Nothing
%>
<html>
<head>
  <title>500-100 ASP Error</title>
  <meta http-equiv="Content-Type" content="text/html; charset=iso-8859-1">
</head>
<body>
  <p>An error occurred while processing this page. An e-mail has been sent to
     the site administrator. Please <a href="javascript:history.go(-1);">go back</a>
     to the previous page.</p>
</body>
</html>
```

Now if we have an error on a page of our site that doesn't contain its own `On Error Resume Next`
error checking, we should see this:

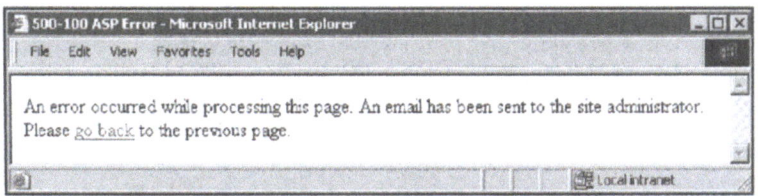

A friendly error message for the site user, plus an e-mail back to the site administrator detailing the problem – a winning error-handling combination.

You should also receive an e-mail with all of the error-checking information, provided you have changed the CDO information to send the e-mail directly to you.

Summary

In this chapter we've covered everything from checking data types to e-mailing ourselves ASP error information.

We covered how to check and see if a variable was of a specific type, how to convert the variable to the type we want, and how to output that data type. This makes it possible to ensure that we're sending good information to our database or to make sure we're adding and subtracting numbers instead of strings.

After that we covered Option Explicit and how this can point you to undeclared variables or misspelled variable references.

Finally, we covered the Err and ASPError objects, the former allowing simple error checking, while the latter allows for complex tasks such as complete error e-mails and a custom error page for your entire site.

6

- Introduction to Dreamweaver extensions

- Using the Server Behavior Builder (SBB)

- Distributing and installing your Extensions

- Extension references and recommendations

Author: Rob Turnbull

Extending Dreamweaver MX

One of the great things about Dreamweaver MX is its extensibility. The base program is an extremely powerful tool, but being able to add our own extra functionality to it by building extensions is what really gives us the ability to make the program sing as well as dance. The idea of building extensions is to speed up and simplify the process of writing code. Dreamweaver MX comes with lots of prebuilt extensions but they might not fit your particular situation, which is where extension building comes in.

There are many developers out there already producing some quite amazing extensions. There has been a growing market for commercial quality extensions for some time now and this can only be a good thing in terms of pushing back the boundaries of what is possible. Just a selection of the more common types of extensions that you can create to add functionality to Dreamweaver MX are:

- Behaviors
- Objects
- Commands
- Server Behaviors
- Panels

In this chapter we will build two simple Server Behaviors. The first will make it easy for us to maintain the paragraph formatting that our data contains when retrieved from a database. It will also include some simple validation that will prevent the code from throwing an error on the web page if there isn't any relevant data in the database. The second will conditionally show or hide an area depending upon there being database content to show in that area. If there isn't any data to show, we'll hide the area.

The order in which we go about building an extension is not set in stone, but there is an obvious progression that, if followed, will make your extension building life far easier than if you try to go about it another way. First we will write the final version of the code so we can test it to make sure it works exactly as intended. Then we will launch the **Server Behavior Builder** (SBB) and begin adding the code into there, along with the required parameters so that the SBB can build the extension interface and write the code necessary to run the Server Behavior interface and insert the correct code into our document.

It should be noted that Server Behaviors created before the release of Dreamweaver MX may or may not work due to Macromedia changing their implementation and structure. See the web page on Macromedia site for further details:

http://www.macromedia.com/software/dreamweaver/productinfo/faq/dwmx_extensions.html#1_4

Once the extensions are built, we can add some extra functionality to them, such as a *Help* button that calls an associated Help page to show users exactly how to use the extension should they get stuck. (I can't see how anyone could get stuck when using the extensions we're about to build, but we'll do it anyway so you know how it's done.)

For the purposes of this chapter, the only code we'll need to know is the code we are going to include in the Server Behavior itself; the rest of the code is written for us. If you are serious about extending Dreamweaver MX, or you simply want to create some of the other extensions (Behaviors, for instance), you should arm yourself with a thorough knowledge of JavaScript.

Anatomy of an Extension

It can take many component parts to make up an extension. The first and most obvious part is the actual piece (or pieces) of code that provides the functionality that the extension is built for. The next part is the interface that the users interact with when adding the functionality of the extension to the page. The not so obvious last part is the code that goes on behind the scenes to make all of the other parts work successfully in the Dreamweaver environment. It's not so obvious because the average user of Dreamweaver MX will very likely never directly encounter these files, yet they are very important from an extensions point of view.

The Extension Code

The first step, as we briefly touched on earlier, is to write the code out in full so that it can be tested and debugged if necessary – to make sure that the code that goes into the SBB is actually going to perform as expected.

```
1  <?xml version="1.0" encoding="iso-8859-1"?>
2  <!DOCTYPE html PUBLIC "-//W3C//DTD XHTML 1.0 Transitional//EN"
   "http://www.w3.org/TR/xhtml1/DTD/xhtml1-transitional.dtd">
3  <%@LANGUAGE="VBSCRIPT" CODEPAGE="1252"%>
4  <html xmlns="http://www.w3.org/1999/xhtml">
5  <head>
6  <title>Untitled Document</title>
7  <meta http-equiv="Content-Type" content="text/html; charset=iso-8859-1" />
8  </head>
9  <body>
10 <%
11 ' Maintain paragraphs if text exists: server behaviour
12 varMyText = (RecordsetName.Fields.Item("ColumnName").Value)
13 IF varMyText <> "" AND NOT IsNull(varMyText) THEN
14     Response.Write(Replace(varMyText,chr(13),"</p><p>"))
15 END IF
16 %>
17 </body>
18 </html>
```

The basic code we're going to turn into a Server Behavior; we're not getting lazy, we want you to see the line numbers

To do this, open up a blank ASP VBScript document and write the code between the `<body>` tags as shown on the right:

As you can see from the previous screenshot, the extension code runs from line 10 through to line 16.

Line 11 serves two purposes. The first is so we can visually identify this Server Behavior on our page and quickly know what it is going to do. The second purpose will become clear later on, but to whet your appetite now, I will just say that it will be used by Dreamweaver MX to help identify that this Server Behavior has been applied to the page so it can list it in the *Server Behaviors* panel.

Line 12 of this code is not difficult to understand, but if you ran the page you would get an error telling you that an object is expected. That's because, even though this Server Behavior will trap the error of there not being any content, currently this code is not using a proper reference to an actual Recordset or column; it is purely written for our own ease of use. When we take this code and start tweaking it in the SBB, we can quickly and easily see where we need to add parameters into the code and what we might call them: `RecordsetName` and `ColumnName`.

Line 13 takes care of the error checking for us. Line 12 assigns the value from a specified column of a Recordset to a variable. Line 13 now tests this variable for a value and, if it contains one, the code will allow the execution of line 14; if not, it will skip line 14 and nothing will be written to the screen.

Line 14 has two jobs; the first is to replace all occurrences of line breaks contained in the `varMyText` variable with closing and opening paragraph tags. The second is to write that formatted output to the screen.

The reason we replace each line break with a closing paragraph tag and then an opening one (`</p><p>`) is to take account of the fact that an initial paragraph format will have been applied to the dynamic text on the page. If you don't use paragraph formatting and would prefer to use `<br />` tags, simply change the code from:

```
(VarMyText,Chr(13),"</p><p>")
```

to:

```
(VarMyText,Chr(13),"<br />")
```

Line 15 closes the opening `IF` statement that does the error checking.

The Interface

One of the great things about building simple Server Behaviors like this one is that the SBB takes care of the code required to build the interface once we commit our Server Behavior code and the relevant parameters to it.

To do this, copy the code between lines 10 and 16 inclusive (make sure you get the opening and closing ASP tags too) and fire up the SBB by clicking *Server Behaviors > New Server Behavior...*

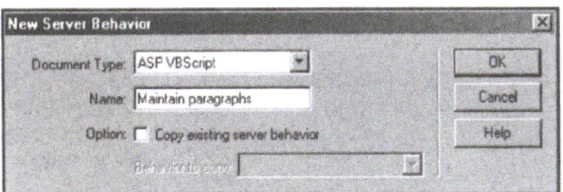

The initial New Server Behavior dialog

In the first dialog, select *ASP VBScript* as the *Document Type:* and type *Maintain paragraphs* as the *Name:* of this Server Behavior. Click *OK* to continue.

The second dialog is an empty SBB that we are quickly going to fill with our code and parameters. The empty SBB looks like this:

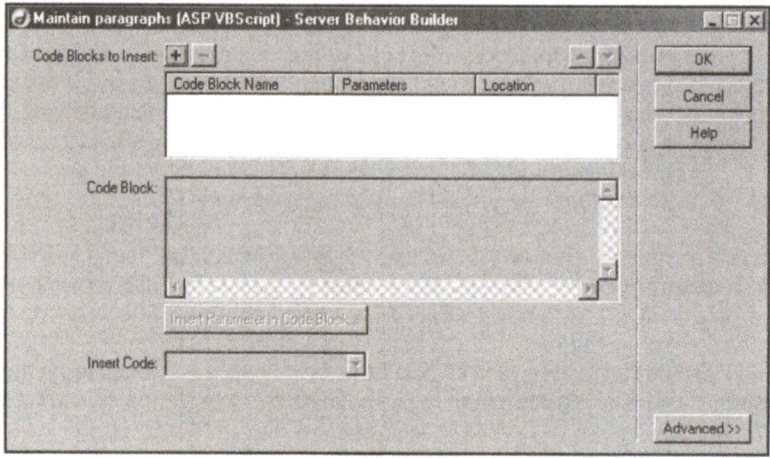

The second SBB dialog

The SBB calls each block of code that your Server Behavior needs – *Code Blocks*, logically enough!

To begin the creation process, click the ⊞ button to add a new code block. The *Create a New Code Block* dialog will pop up and ask you for a name to refer to this code block as. The default in our case will be perfect so leave *Maintain paragraphs_block1* in the dialog and click *OK* to add the new block to the SBB.

The code blocks that you add to your Server Behaviors are listed in the top window of this dialog, labeled *Code Blocks to Insert* and the corresponding code for each block is displayed in the *Code Block* window below that.

You don't have much space to work in the *Code Block* window, which is another good reason to write and test your code prior to starting the building process.

The following text is already in the *Code Block* window:

```
<% Replace this text with the code to insert
when the server behavior is applied %>
```

It is very important that the code in the Code Block pane should include the opening and closing ASP tags, whether you copied them or used the ones Dreamweaver puts in place

Highlight it all and delete it so that no code remains in the window, then paste the code that you copied from the original page into the *Code Block* window. If you didn't copy it originally, do so now and then paste it into this window.

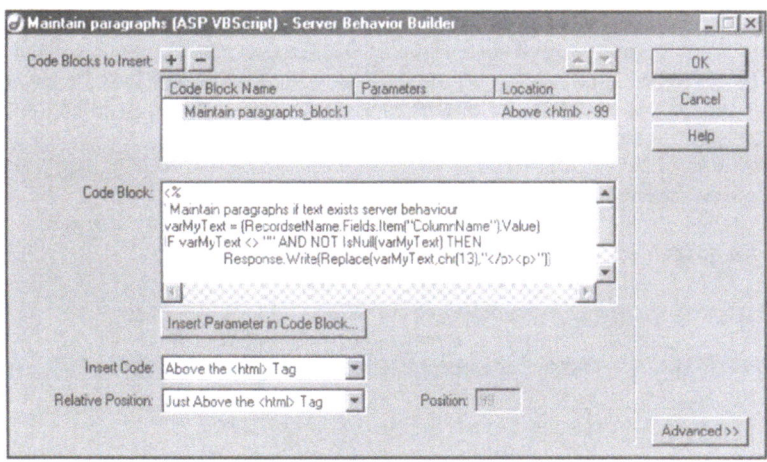
Partially completed SBB dialog

Locate the following line of code in the *Code Block* pane:

```
varMyText = (RecordsetName.Fields.Item("columnname").Value)
```

Highlight the word *RecordsetName* in the code and click the *Insert Parameter in Code Block* button.

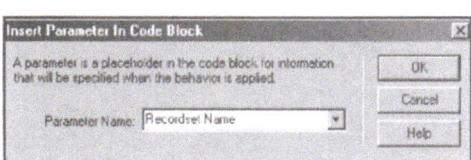
Telling Dreamweaver about our parameters

We use parameters in the SBB so it can identify which elements of our code need to be supplied by the user. It will then create form elements to cater for these parts of the code. More on that later.

The SBB uses the parameter names on the interface form it creates as labels for the form elements, so to save ourselves a little time later on we can enter a name that will be usable without our needing to edit it, such as in the previous screenshot: *Recordset Name*.

The parameter is inserted and your code is modified slightly to signify this. Where it once said *RecordsetName*, it now says *@@Recordset Name@@*. The double @ symbols wrapping our parameter name will tell the SBB that user input is required for this item and a form element will be created to cater for this. More on that when we cover the third dialog in the Server Behavior building process.

Note: If you know you won't mess it up, you can avoid highlighting and clicking the Add Parameter *button and simply type your parameters directly into your code; all you need to do is make sure that you enter the parameter correctly, surrounded by double @ symbols. One of the main advantages of using the* Add Parameter *button is that it will automatically add your parameter into your code at every location that matches the initial selection, so if you need the same piece of code to use the same parameter more than once, you should use the button method.*

Now we have added a parameter to enable the user to specify the Recordset, they will need to be able to specify which column in that Recordset should be used. To do this we need to insert our second parameter called *Column Name* in place of the word *ColumnName* in the same line of code as before. You can do this manually, by entering the parameter code required by hand, or you can click the button and add the parameter that way.

Whichever way you choose, the parameter should end up as follows:

@@Column Name@@

The completed line of code with parameters in place, should look like this:

```
varMyText = (@@Recordset Name@@.Fields.Item("@@Column Name@@").Value)
```

With the code in place, we now need to set up the rest of the dialog.

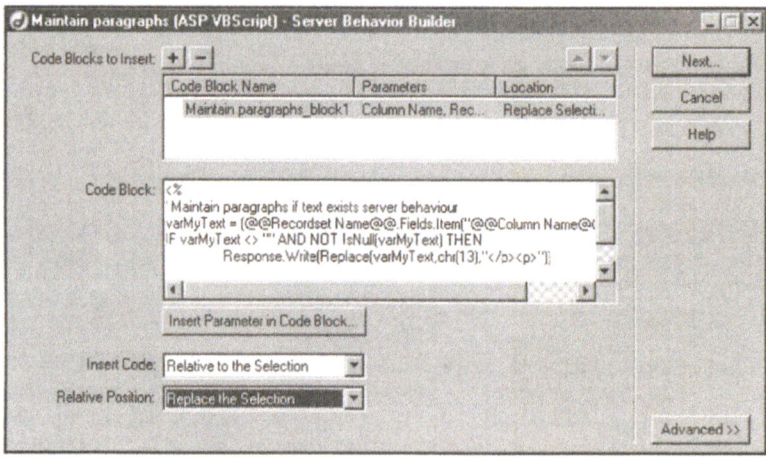

Insert Code and Relative Position drop downs and settings

At the bottom left of the dialog there are two drop-down lists that need to be set as follows:

We set these as specified because we want our code block to be inserted into the document in its entirety. If the user makes a selection prior to applying this Server Behavior, we don't want to wrap that selection with two code blocks; we want to insert a single code block in its place. If no selection is made, nothing gets replaced on the current page but the code is inserted just fine at the position of the cursor in the document.

Now click the *Advanced* button in the bottom right of the dialog to reveal a few extra items that we need to set:

The *Identifier* checkbox tells Dreamweaver MX that if this code block is found in the document it should be displayed in the list of Server Behaviors in the *Server Behavior* panel. For this single code block Server Behavior, we can leave this ticked. If you write Server Behaviors that utilize multiple code blocks, you should ensure that only one code block has this checkbox ticked.

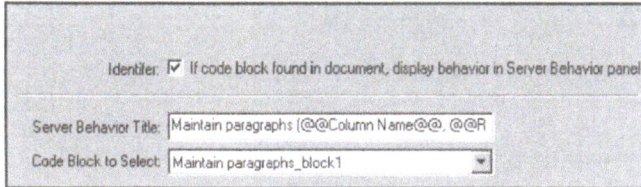

Advanced Server Behavior Builder options

" *The more complicated you make your Server Behavior, the less sense it makes to have a list of all the parameters used as the title* "

Once Dreamweaver MX has identified your code block, it needs something to display in the *Server Behavior* panel listing to reflect the fact that it knows this Server Behavior is present in the current document. The *Server Behavior Title* will be used for this purpose and the default is almost always the best option. It uses the Server Behavior name and then a list of all the parameters used in the Server Behavior. Obviously, the more complicated you make your Server Behavior, the less sense it makes to have a list of all the parameters used as it could end up being an incredibly wide title! In cases such as these, it is wise to simply use the name of the Server Behavior.

In the *Code Block to Select* list, you will only have one item available to choose, which is *Maintain paragraphs_block1*. When you create multiple code blocks in more advanced Server Behaviors than this one, the code block that is set to be the *Identifier* should also be selected as the *Code Block to Select*. We'll come back to this when we build our second Server Behavior.

Let's do one final check before continuing – your dialog should look like this:

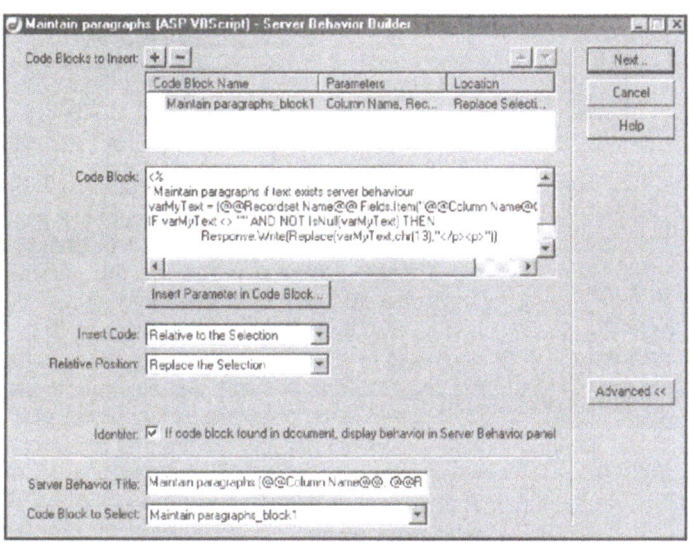

The completed Server Behavior Builder dialog

Click *Next...* to continue the SBB process in the third and final dialog called the *Generate Behavior Dialog*:

Extending Dreamweaver MX

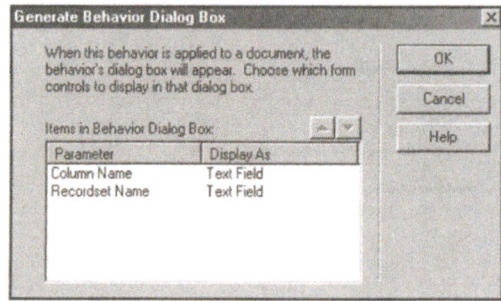

The Generate Behavior Dialog: specify what your parameters will be displayed as

Here we set up what type of form elements each of the parameters we created in the previous dialog should be represented by when presented to the user in our Server Behaviors dialog. In our case, our parameters are there to collect the name of a Recordset and the name of a column within that Recordset.

Highlight the *Recordset Name* parameter and in the *Display As* column where it currently says *Text Field*, click the gray down arrow to reveal a list of options. At the top of the list you'll see *Recordset Menu*. Select that, then click the *Column Name* parameter, click the gray arrow and select the *Recordset Fields Menu* option, which is the second one down.

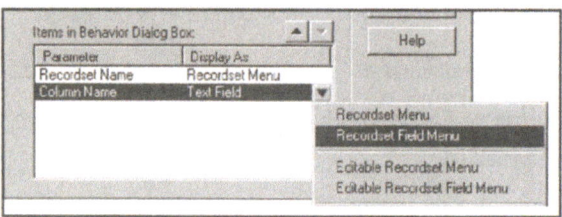

Picking the right display option for your parameter

> **You need to ensure that the Recordset and column names that you refer to actually exist**

There are several options available to us in the *Display As* list, each with its own special purpose. In this example, we use the first two options in the list, but we could just as easily have used the *Editable* versions, which are the next two options down. They give the user the opportunity of specifying a Recordset and column that don't exist on the page. This might be useful if you need to reference something that you are going to add to the page later, or perhaps something from another file that will be included in the page this Server Behavior is applied to. Either way, you would need to ensure that the Recordset and column names that you refer to actually exist or an error would occur. That is why in this case we are using the normal Recordset (and field) menus, leaving no room for user error!

The final thing you need to do here is put the parameters in the order in which you want them to appear on the Server Behavior dialog that is about to be created for you. To move one up or down, select it and click the up or down arrows to move it up or down in the list, as we've done above. The best order for these two is *Recordset Name* first, *Column Name* second.

The reason for this is the *Column Name* list will be filtered dynamically to only show the columns for the selected Recordset so it makes sense to have the user selecting the Recordset first.

Having set the order and set the types of form fields for each parameter, click *OK* and Dreamweaver MX will create the files necessary to give life to this Server Behavior.

If your code is still present on the page, after clicking *OK* you will see our new Server Behavior listed in the *Server Behavior* panel with a red exclamation mark against it. We didn't create an actual Recordset, and we used non-existent Recordset and column names in our code – luckily Dreamweaver MX recognizes that something is wrong and lets us know by displaying the red exclamation mark. If you now delete your original code and build a proper Recordset, you will be able to successfully apply your new Server Behavior to the page.

The Server Behavior is automatically added to the Server Behavior menu:

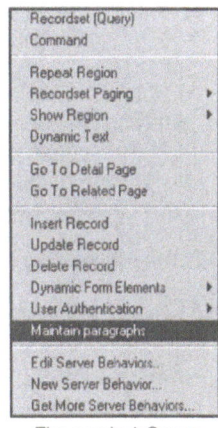

The new look Server Behavior menu

You cannot apply this Server Behavior without a Recordset being present on the page and an error message will pop up to let us know what the problem is if we try. This is all taken care of for us because of the checks that are put in place by the code that Dreamweaver MX has written for you. We'll look at these files in the next section.

To run a quick test on this Server Behavior, create a new page with a Recordset on it that will return data with multiple paragraphs of text. Click on the page to give it focus and then select the paragraph format in the *Property Inspector*. Apply this Server Behavior to the page and specify the relevant column when you do so – you should see the paragraph formatting conserved.

Behind the Scenes

The files that are created for you when using the SBB are stored in the `Configuration` folder under their specific sub folder.

Our Server Behavior was created using VBScript so the files will be located in `Configuration\ServerBehaviors\ASP_Vbs`.

If you are using one of the multi-user capable operating systems (which are Windows XP, Windows 2000, Windows NT, and Macintosh OS X) you will have your own `Configuration` folder separate from that of the program. This is to allow individual users to set up their own workspace, installed extensions and preferences in a multi-user environment, and not disturb anyone else's configurations. Assuming your drive is `C:` this folder can be found at the following location:

```
C:\Documents and Settings\<your login username here>\Application
Data\Macromedia\DreamweaverMX\Configuration\ServerBehaviors\ASP_VBS
```

Having completed our simple Server Behavior, we can see that Dreamweaver MX has created three files for us. They are:

- Maintain paragraphs.edml
- Maintain paragraphs.htm
- Maintain paragraphs_block1.edml

If you have more than one code block making up your Server Behavior, only one of them should be marked as the identifier

The first file, `Maintain paragraphs.edml`, is an XML file and is used by Dreamweaver MX to identify the files needed to run this Server Behavior. It points to the interface file and to all other participant files. The following line taken from this file illustrates the point made earlier about having a single code block ticked as the identifier. If you have more than one code block making up your Server Behavior, only one of them should be marked as the identifier.

```
<groupParticipant name="Maintain paragraphs_block1" partType="identifier" />
```

`Maintain paragraphs_block1.edml` is the file that contains our code to be inserted into the document once the parameters have been set using the Server Behavior interface. This file is also an XML file, and part of its code is used by Dreamweaver MX to identify the Server Behavior on the page. It has two methods of doing this: the complete search pattern, and the quick search pattern. If we were to change the quick search pattern from its current setting to something unique, it would save Dreamweaver MX time and speed things up for us.

The original line is as follows:

```
<quickSearch>Response.Write(Replace(varMyText,chr(13),"</quickSearch>
```

That `quickSearch` string might possibly appear in several places on your page so Dreamweaver MX is then forced to use the complete search pattern to ensure that it only flags up the actual instances of this Server Behavior on the page.

Change the original line to the following:

```
<quickSearch>' Maintain paragraphs if text exists server behavior</quickSearch>
```

This should speed up the identification process of this Server Behavior.

This new quick search is unlikely to be found liberally scattered over the code of your pages, as it is the opening comment that we used to identify what the code in our Server Behavior does.

`Maintain paragraphs.htm` is our interface file that we will use when applying this Server Behavior to our pages. If you open this page in Dreamweaver MX, you can see the complexity of code that such a simple interface requires.

By default, the SBB does not add a help button to the interface. It can't, because no Help file has been created yet and there is currently no way of adding this information into the SBB anyway: therefore, we have to do it manually. Scroll down through the code of this page to the bottom of the `scripts` section (it should be line 245) and insert the following function just before the closing `</SCRIPT>` tag.

```
function displayHelp(){
   var varConfigFolder = dw.getConfigurationPath();
   var varHelpDocument = "/ExtensionsHelp/maintainparahelp.htm";
   dreamweaver.browseDocument(varConfigFolder + varHelpDocument);
}
```

This function, called `displayHelp`, is required to add the *Help* button to the Server Behavior interface. If you just included the empty function, the button would be displayed but wouldn't do anything, which would be rather useless.

This `displayHelp` function sets up two variables, one to find the root configuration folder, and one to pinpoint the path to the actual Help file. The third line does the hard work here; it runs the Dreamweaver MX `browseDocument` command, which uses the two variables combined to locate the Help file and display it in a browser window.

Using this method means the Help document must be installed into the user's configuration folder when the extension is installed. We'll cover that in the section called *Creating the MXI file*.

If you want to host your Help files online, you would substitute the current path to the document with a fully qualified URL, such as this:

```
function displayHelp(){
    dreamweaver.browseDocument("http://www.domain.com/help/maintainparahelp.htm");

}
```

To have a Help file appear at all requires the existence of the file in the first place. We'll not go into the details of creating a simple HTML page here, as I'm sure you all know how to write a few paragraphs of text onto a page! Please bear in mind, however, that if you are going to use any images in your Help documents, you need to use document-relative paths.

Once you have created your Help file, save it as `maintainparahelp.htm` in the `ExtensionsHelp` folder in your configuration folder. Now when you click the *Help* button in your Server Behavior interface, you will be presented with a *Help* page. This isn't much use for your own extensions on your own computer but can be very useful when you come to be distributing extensions to other people who might not know how to use your Server Behavior or what it is supposed to do.

An example would be to house the extension Help file for your extension in a subfolder of the `ExtensionsHelp` folder, thus keeping the clutter to a minimum.

As for the actual extension files, if you move them into a subfolder to tidy them up, you would also be adding your own submenu to the *Server Behaviors* menu. Doing this would require you to change the relative paths that are used in the HTM file (if your Server Behavior created one, as this one did) because they are written document relative and moving them would break that document-relative path.

It is good practice to use subfolders within the default configuration structure for your own additions, such as Server Behaviors. Our example doesn't do this but you should think about keeping installations clean and tidy, and using subfolders is the way to achieve this.

For example, if you created a `glasshaus` folder under the `ASP_Vbs` folder and moved our three extension files into it, you would then need to open up the HTM file and add an extra `../` onto the seven paths of the JavaScript file references that this particular file includes (there may be more than seven in other extensions that you build). After restarting Dreamweaver MX, your subfolder (*glasshaus*) would be listed on the *Server Behavior* list and your extension would be found on its fly-out menu.

Next we'll look at exactly what you need to do with this extension of yours in order to successfully package it up ready for distribution.

Preparing for Distribution

Macromedia provide an online Exchange to which you can submit extensions for distribution. There are literally hundreds of extensions currently online and the number is constantly growing. The exchange for Dreamweaver MX can be found at
http://www.macromedia.com/exchange/dreamweaver/.

If you plan on distributing your extensions for others to use either freely or commercially, you will first need to package them in the correct format so that anyone can install them onto their computers.

Extension Manager takes care of all of the extensions for Macromedia products on your computer

The format that these files need to take is an MXP file, which stands for **M**acromedia e**X**tension **P**ackage. Fortunately, we don't need to know how to build an MXP file; the Extension Manager does that for us. This powerful little program takes care of all of the extensions that get installed into any of the Macromedia products on your computer. It also acts as a packaging tool, but to do this it needs to be fed the right ingredients. Those ingredients come in the shape of an MXI file, which is covered in the next section.

It is a good idea to set up a staging area when building extensions, so you can keep track of all the files involved very easily as they will all be in one area. Before you go any further, dig through your configuration folders and locate every part of this Server Behavior and copy them into your own staging area folder. The files will be in the `Configuration\serverbehaviors\ASP_Vbs` folder and your Help file, if you created it earlier, will be in the `Configuration\ExtensionsHelp` folder.

I have used `C:\Extensions\Maintain paragraphs` as my staging area folder name for this extension. We will create the MXI file in this staging area folder and we will store the final MXP file in this folder also. It just helps to keep things neat and tidy.

Creating the MXI file

The MXI file, **M**acromedia e**X**tension **I**nstruction file, is basically an XML file that describes all aspects of the Server Behavior. Among these properties are the name and version number of the extension, the author's name, the products to install the extension into, the description of the extension, instructions on where you'll find it in the program after installation, a list of the files that are used in the Server Behavior and where those files should be stored on the user's computer when it is installed, and any configuration changes that need to be made to the user's installation of Dreamweaver MX.

You can get an extension called **MXI Doc Type**, which will add a blank MXI document type to the *New File* dialog in Dreamweaver MX, from the following location:
http://www.dwteam.com/Extensions/.

Once you have the extension installed, you will find the new MXI file type in the *Other* section when you create a new file using the *New File* dialog

A basic, empty MXI file ready for version 1 of a Server Behavior for Dreamweaver MX looks like this:

```
<macromedia-extension
  name=""
  version="1.0.0"
  type="Server Behavior"
  requires-restart="true">

  <author name="" />

  <products>
    <product name="Dreamweaver" version="6" primary="true" required="true" />
  </products>

  <description>
  <![CDATA[
  This description will appear in the Extension Manager description window
  ]]>
  </description>

  <ui-access>
  <![CDATA[
  This ui access data will also appear in the Extension Manager description
window
  ]]>
  </ui-access>

  <files>
    <file source="" destination="" />
  </files>

  <configuration-changes>
  </configuration-changes>
</macromedia-extension>
```

To build this into a working MXI file that we can use with our extension, we need to make the following additions and alterations to this basic file:

- Change `name=""` to `name="Maintain paragraphs"`
- Change author `name=""` to `author name="Rob Turnbull"` (you can use your own name here!)

The changes to the description need to be made only to the text contained inside the square brackets of CDATA []. The reason it is spaced onto separate lines in the code is to make it easier to edit and read. It makes no difference to the computer. The description element is where you describe in a straightforward way what your extension is going to do.

6

Extending Dreamweaver MX

The changes to `<ui-access>` should follow the same principle as the description – only the text within the square brackets of `CDATA[]`. This is where you list how the user should access your Server Behavior. In our case you could write something like:

```
Access this Server Behavior by clicking Server Behaviors  > Maintain paragraphs
```

Now comes the heavy part – the files!

What we have to do here is specify the files to include in the package and their destination when they are installed onto the user's computer. This is what our `<files>` section should look like, including the Help file:

```
<files>
    <file source="Maintain paragraphs_block1.edml"
          destination="$dreamweaver/Configuration/serverbehaviors/ASP_Vbs/" />
    <file source="Maintain paragraphs.htm"
          destination="$dreamweaver/Configuration/serverbehaviors/ASP_Vbs/" />
    <file source="Maintain paragraphs.edml "
          destination="$dreamweaver/Configuration/serverbehaviors/ASP_Vbs/" />
    <file source="Maintainparagraphshelp.htm "
          destination="$dreamweaver/Configuration/ExtensionsHelp/" />
</files>
```

Each `<file>` line should be one continuous line of code.

If you were using subfolders as suggested earlier, to keep installations clean and tidy, you would simply add your subfolder name onto the end of the current destination path. For example:

```
<file source="Maintain paragraphs_block1.edml"
```

```
destination="$dreamweaver/Configuration/serverbehaviors/ASP_Vbs/glasshaus/" />
```

There are restrictions on the length of the names you can use in Server Behaviors and slightly different name lengths in the MXI file (for some strange reason!). In the SBB, the limit is 27 characters and in the name of the MXI file, the limit is 23 characters.

This code tells Dreamweaver MX to take each named file and install it into the user's configuration folders at the specified point. Taking the first file source line as an example, `Maintain paragraphs_block1.edml` will be installed into the `ASP_Vbs` folder under the `serverbehaviors` folder within the `Dreamweaver MX configuration` folder.

If you include images in your Server Behavior interface or in any documentation that you wish to install on the user's system, you need to create a separate file source line for each image and ensure that it gets installed to the relevant directory in the configuration structure.

The completed MXI file for the *Maintain paragraphs* Server Behavior should look like this:

```
<macromedia-extension
    name="Maintain paragraphs"
    version="1.0.0"
    type="Server Behavior"
    requires-restart="true">
```

```
<author name="Rob Turnbull" />

<products>
  <product name="Dreamweaver" version="6" primary="true" required="true" />
</products>

<description>
<![CDATA[
  This server behavior will maintain the paragraphs
  in database-driven text when displayed on the web page.
]]>
</description>

<ui-access>
<![CDATA[
  Access this Server Behavior by clicking
  Server Behaviors > Maintain paragraphs
]]>
</ui-access>

<files>
  <file source="Maintain paragraphs_block1.edml"
        destination="$dreamweaver/Configuration/serverbehaviors/ASP_Vbs/" />
  <file source="Maintain paragraphs.htm"
        destination="$dreamweaver/Configuration/serverbehaviors/ASP_Vbs/" />
  <file source="Maintain paragraphs.edml "
        destination="$dreamweaver/Configuration/serverbehaviors/ASP_Vbs/" />
  <file source="Maintainparagraphshelp.htm "
        destination="$dreamweaver/Configuration/ExtensionsHelp/" />
</files>

<configuration-changes>
</configuration-changes>
</macromedia-extension>
```

The empty section at the bottom of the MXI file, `<configuration-changes>`, can be used to specify changes to menus, shortcuts, server behaviors, server formats, and data sources. For example, if you create a command called `mycommand` you might want it to appear under the *Commands* menu and in your own submenu. You would use the following code:

```
<configuration-changes>
  <menu-insert appendTo="DWMenu_Commands">
    <menu name="Menu Name" id="DWMenu_Commands_Menu_Name">
    </menu>
  </menu-insert>
  <menu-insert appendTo="DWMenu_Commands_Menu_Name">
    <menuitem name="My menu item here" file="myhtmlcommandfile.htm"
              id="My_Unique_Identification_String_Here" />
  </menu-insert>
</configuration-changes>
```

The first of this pair of `<menu-insert>` tags adds a folder to the *Commands* menu called *Menu Name*. The second `<menu-insert>` adds a menu item into that folder and references the `command.htm` file that this particular command uses.

All the items you add into this part of the MXI file will update the user's `Menus.xml` file. There have been many reported problems with updating this file, some so severe that a complete re-installation of the software was needed. Many developers steer clear of modifying the `Menus.xml` file at this time because of the reported problems.

With the MXI file created and saved as `maintainparagraphs.mxi`, and all the files stored in our staging area, we can now begin the relatively simple packaging process, which will create the MXP file.

Creating the MXP File

The MXP file is the file that you can distribute to other Dreamweaver MX users, safe in the knowledge that they will be able to install it into their system.

The creation of the MXP file is done for us through the use of the Extension Manager. There are two ways of instigating the packaging process, the first is to double-click the MXI file, which, if your file associations are set up correctly, will launch the Extension Manager and automatically start the packaging process. The second method is fail-safe for everyone to use and is detailed here.

Open the Extension Manager application, make sure you've got Dreamweaver MX selected in the drop-down box near the top, and then go to *File > Package Extension*.

You now need to locate the MXI file that the packager will use to create the MXP package. Ours is stored in the staging area folder: `C:\Extensions\Maintain paragraphs`. Locate that folder in the file browser window that has popped up and select `maintainparagraphs.mxi`.

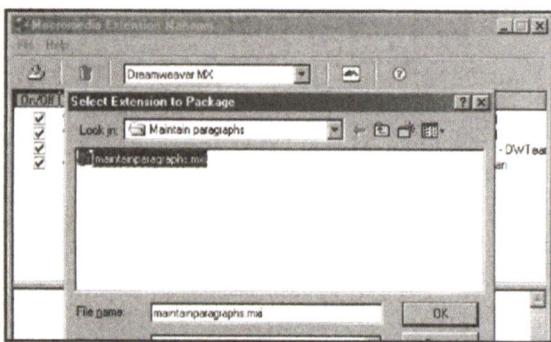

Next select the location to save the packaged extension – the same folder will be perfect so simply click *Save* to save the MXP file. The Extension Manager will default to giving the MXP file the same name as the MXI file we feed it, which again is fine.

Click *OK* in the dialog that tells us the extension has been packaged and created successfully, and that's it.

Packaging the right extension for the right product

It should be noted here that your extension has not been installed using this procedure; it has simply been packaged. You currently have the original build of this extension in your Dreamweaver MX configuration, which is why you can see and use it in the *Server Behaviors* panel, but it does not appear in the Extension Manager's list of currently installed extensions.

To test the new MXP file, to make sure that it installs everything correctly, simply remove all the original files from the configuration folders – not forgetting the Help file – and then install the extension from the new MXP you just created. You don't have to remove the original files from your configuration, but if you don't you'll be prompted to overwrite each file when you do install from the MXP.

The Second Server Behavior

At the start of this chapter we mentioned that we would be creating two Server Behaviors. The second one that we are now going to create is intended to be applied to an area of the web page that displays dynamic data that may or may not exist in the database for a particular record. If data exists, we want to display the area to the user; if data does not exist we want to hide the area from the user. The idea here is that blank space will be removed from the data display on the screen.

The code that we will need to create this Server Behavior comes in two simple parts. Part one assigns the data to a variable and then checks the content of the variable for a value. The code for that is as follows:

```
<%
' *** Hide Area If Database ColumnName Is Empty ***
varMyValue = (RecordsetName.Fields.Item("ColumnName").Value)
IF varMyValue <> "" AND NOT IsNULL(varMyValue) Then
%>
```

Part two of the code simply ends the IF statement started in part one. The code for that is as follows:

```
<%
' *** End Of Hide Area If Database Column Is Empty ***
END IF
%>
```

With the code already prepared to go into the SBB, let's get started building the Server Behavior. Click *Server Behaviors > + > New Server Behavior...* to open up the *New Server Behavior* dialog box. Select *ASP/VBScript* as the *Document Type* and enter *Hide Empty Area* as the *Name* then click *OK*.

Add an empty code block to the dialog by clicking the *Code Blocks To Insert* plus (+) button and then clicking OK to the suggested code block name – the default name of *Hide Empty Area_block1* is fine. Replace the code for block one with the first part of our Server Behavior code.

Set the *Insert Code* drop-down list to *Relative to the Selection* and set the *Relative Position* to *Before the Selection*. We do this because our finished code will be inserted before and after the user's selection on the page inserting the first part of our code (code block 1) before their selection and the second part of our code (code block 2) after their selection.

In the code, highlight the word RecordsetName and create a parameter in its place called *Recordset Name*, then replace the word ColumnName in the code with a parameter called *Column Name*. The SBB will offer to replace all instances of ColumnName when you create the *Column Name* parameter, which we don't want to do in this case. The other instance in the code is in the commented description line of the code which we can leave as it stands.

Expand the *Advanced* area of the dialog and make sure the *Identifier* checkbox is checked. In the *Code Block to Select* list, select *Hide Empty Area_block1*:

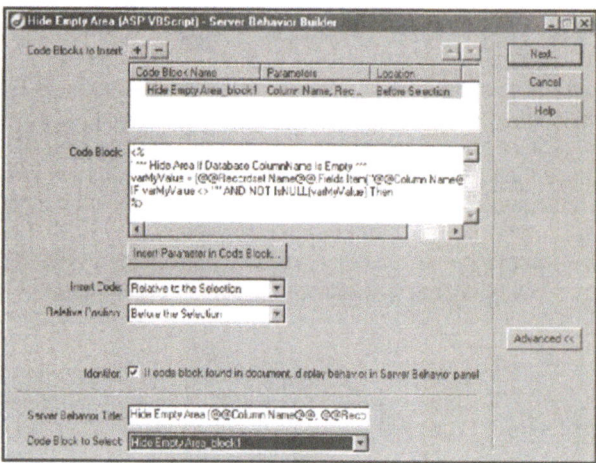

The first code block added

> We only want one identifying code block in our code

Add a second empty code block by clicking the *Code Blocks To Insert* Plus (+) button again and accepting its offer of a suitable code block name – `Hide Empty Area_block2`. Replace the code for block two with the second part of our Server Behavior code.

There are no parameters to insert into this code block so move straight to the *Insert Code* drop-down list. Set it to *Relative to the Selection* and set the *Relative Position* to *After the Selection*.

Uncheck the *Identifier* checkbox for this code block. We only want one identifying code block in our code and that will be the first code block in this case.

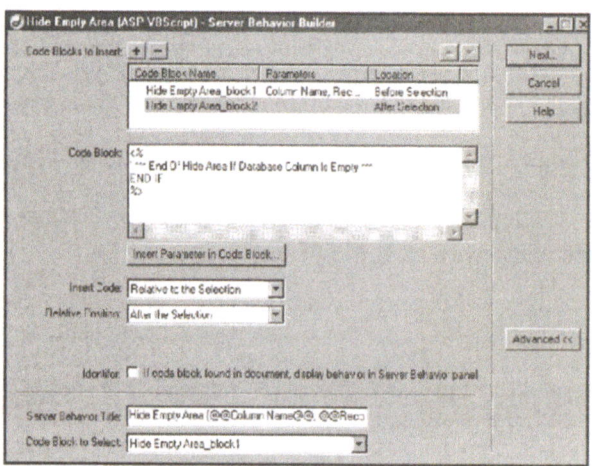

The second code block added

Click *Next* to continue to the form element selection dialog.

Set the *Column Name* parameter to *Display As Recordset Field Menu* and set the *Recordset Name* parameter to *Display As Recordset Menu.* Change the order of these two parameters so the *Recordset Name* parameter is on top of the *Column Name* parameter in the list – this will be the order in which they are presented on the form the SBB will generate. Click OK to finish the Building process.

The property inspector only displays the properties of a Recordset if it is selected in the Server Behaviors *panel, rather than the* Bindings *panel.*

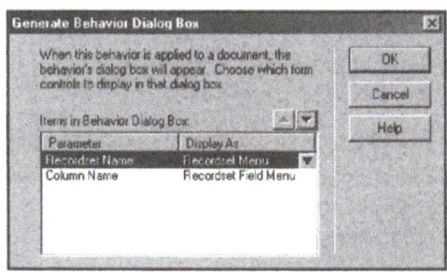

Picking the display as and order of our parameters

To test this Server Behavior, open up a page that displays dynamic content. Make a selection on the page of an area that displays dynamic data and then apply this Server Behavior by clicking *Server Behaviors > + > Hide Empty Area*. Select the same Recordset Name and Column Name of the dynamic data that is already bound to the page and click *OK* to apply it.

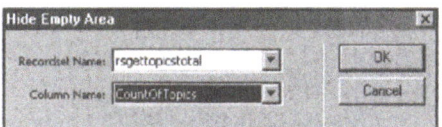

Selecting a Recordset and column

We select the same data to test that content exists. One proviso of using this Server Behavior is that your Recordset cursor needs to be set to *Static* rather than *Forward Only* (Forward-Only is the default cursor type in Dreamweaver MX). This is so your page can access the same piece of data more than once (which is not the case for Forward Only cursor types).

To change your cursor type, click the Recordset name in the *Server Behaviors* panel and change it in the property inspector.

Installing Extensions

Installing extensions is a very straightforward practice mainly because of the structure of the MXI file. You'll notice that near the start of the MXI file you have a declaration called *Products.* This tells the Extension Manager which product this extension should be installed into. In our case, we built a Dreamweaver MX extension, which is denoted by the declaration *version="6"*.

The Extension Manager

The Extension Manager is the tool used to install, uninstall, switch on or off, and package all extensions for all of your installed Macromedia products. It is an extremely useful one-stop-shop.

Extensions that you build (such as Server Behaviors) will not automatically be listed in the Extension Manager – it only lists extensions that you have actually installed using it.

Make sure you are using the very latest version of the Extension Manager application by checking your version number (*Help > About Macromedia Extension Manager*) against that found on the download page for the latest version, which can be found here: *http://www.macromedia.com/exchange/em_download/*.

You can install Server Behaviors in one of two ways. If you have the file associations correctly configured on your computer you can simply double-click an MXP file and the Extension Manager will launch and begin the installation process immediately for you – in much the same way that you can start the process of packaging extensions as discussed earlier. The other method is to open the Extension Manager and click the

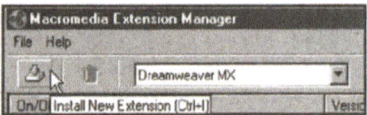

The Install New Extension icon

Install New Extension icon on the toolbar.

This pops up the *Select Extension to Install* dialog in which you need to locate the MXP file to install.

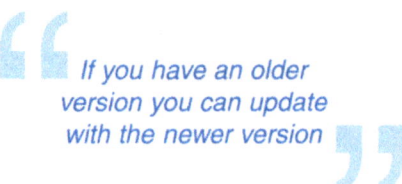

If you have an older version you can update with the newer version

Having selected the MXP file, click *Install* to start the process. You will then be asked to accept the disclaimer of liability from Macromedia. Click *Accept* (if you accept it) and installation will continue. If you already have the same extension installed, there are several possible warning dialogs that you might be presented with. If you have an older version you can update that version with the newer version. If you have a newer version already installed, you will be warned that this is the case.

The installation will always prompt you to overwrite any existing files that might already exist in your configuration. If you install several extensions from the same author, for example, that author might use the same graphic in their user interface, but every extension they produce would still need to include it in the package in case it isn't already installed. When the installation is complete, the Extension Manager will tell you. If you had Dreamweaver open while you were installing the extension, you'd be told you needed to close and restart Dreamweaver.

The Extension Manager also allows you to quickly "turn off" extensions without having to uninstall them first. You do this by un-checking the tickbox next to the extension in the *On/Off* column.

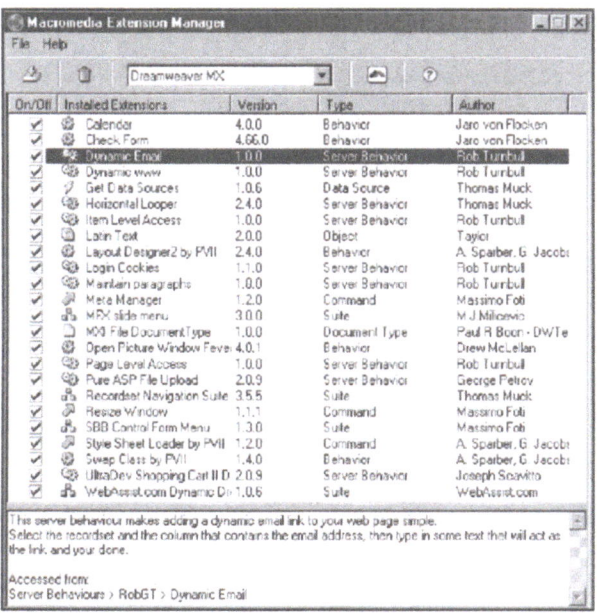

Extension Resources

Along with the Macromedia Exchange that was mentioned earlier in the chapter, there are literally hundreds of extensions to be found at various sites on the Internet. The following list of URLs will provide links to just some of the many Dreamweaver MX extensions that are not available on the Exchange. Some of the following sites were published when UltraDev was alive and well but have extensions that have been updated for Dreamweaver MX.

This list is in alphabetical order and is definitely not exhaustive!

http://charon.co.uk/
http://dreamweaverfever.com/
http://dwmxextensions.com/
http://dwteam.com/
http://robgt.com/
http://www.basic-ultradev.com/
http://www.fourlevel.com/
http://www.interakt.ro/
http://www.kaosweaver.com/
http://www.massimocorner.com/
http://www.projectseven.com/
http://www.thechocolatestore.com/ultradev/
http://www.dmxzone.com/
http://www.ultrasuite.com/
http://www.webassist.com/home.asp
http://www.yaromat.com/dw/

Personal Favorites

There are so many great extensions available, that choosing just a few personal favorites is very hard indeed. However, the following would be my choices:

- Recordset Navigation Suite
- UltraCart II
- Pure ASP Upload 2

> *I have used this extension (and its predecessors) on every site that needed Recordset paging on it.*

Recordset Navigation Suite

This extension wins my accolade of Best Extension. Its creator Tom Muck has been quite prolific in the extension scene and this was a deserving winner. I have used this extension (and its predecessors) on every site that needed Recordset paging on it. The point-and-click simplicity of the suite makes this a truly remarkable set of extensions.

This extension is available from *http://www.basic-ultradev.com/exthelp/DataNavigation/index.asp*.

UltraCart II

When it comes to creating an e-commerce site, I don't even think twice about which cart solution I'm going to use. UltraCart II is an amazing collection of extensions that make building an online store extremely easy. There are free cart extensions available for Dreamweaver MX, which are very good, but this cart is my personal favorite. If you're on a tight budget, perhaps you should take a look at the CharonCart extension, which is free.

This extension is available from http://www.thechocolatestore.com/ultradev/order/order.asp.

Pure ASP Upload 2

This extension caters for the need to upload files to the web server. In the development of an administration system, there will be times when you need to give the users of the system the opportunity of uploading files to the server, such as images of products. That's where this extension comes into its own. Ordinarily, to offer upload capabilities, you would need to register a component on the server. Pure ASP Upload is exactly that, it is purely code; a component-free solution that is very easy to use.

This extension is available from
http://www.dmxzone.com/showDetail.asp?TypeId=3&NewsId=1622.

Summary

This chapter has focused on extending the server-side capabilities of Dreamweaver MX by building two simple Server Behaviors that will help us to easily maintain the paragraph formatting of text coming from a database and to hide an area if no data exists.

Server Behaviors are only one aspect of the extensibility of Dreamweaver MX. There is plenty of room to add Behaviors, Commands, and Objects too.

Unfortunately, there isn't a builder mechanism like the SBB to help us to build these other types of extensions – instead you need to brush up on your JavaScript skills and get to work writing them by hand.

For a great learning resource, especially for building Behaviors, Commands, and Objects, dive into the configuration folder of Dreamweaver MX and open up some of the Behaviors, Commands, and Objects that are already there to see how they work.

6

Extending Dreamweaver MX

7

- Stored Procedures and Triggers

- Tables, relationships, and views in MS SQL Server

- The Dreamweaver MX Command object

- Backing up your databases

Author: Rob Turnbull

Advanced ASP Databases

It is now time to look at how we can use Dreamweaver MX to aid us in utilizing databases on our web sites.

There are many different choices of database that we can utilize on dynamic web sites, depending on what server-side language we've chosen – however, since this is a book about ASP, there are two main choices of database to go with:

- **Microsoft Access**
  Access is useful for small-scale web sites that won't be stressed with heavy usage, such as personal websites. Access can be a great learning tool if you are just starting out with databases, but it doesn't have the power and flexibility of SQL Server, so you are limited in terms of the level of database automation available to you. For example, you cannot utilize Stored Procedures or Triggers in Access.

- **Microsoft SQL Server**
  Using SQL Server will enable your web site to handle far higher traffic without the problems that can be associated with Access, such as the database crashing under stress. You also have automation features available that Access doesn't. The overall management of your database is made easier by the multitude of tools supplied, such as scheduling jobs to take care of backups etc.

This chapter will be focused solely on **SQL Server 2000**, the database of choice for ASP web sites for many reasons. It is enterprise ready, scalable, robust, and provides all the features necessary for us to get the job done, and several more that we won't need.

First we will look at **Stored Procedures**, which are precompiled collections of SQL statements stored in the database as a single unit. They speed up database interactions from your web pages by enabling you to execute a series of SQL statements with a single call and, because they are compiled on the server when you create them, they execute faster than individual statements.

Following on from stored procedures, we will look at **Triggers**. A trigger is a special kind of stored procedure that is called into play when an INSERT, UPDATE, or DELETE operation is performed on your database tables. They are primarily used for enforcing business rules but can also be used for maintaining referential integrity.

Referential integrity deals with ensuring that child records in a database are not orphaned when their parent records are deleted or updated.

Once we have covered stored procedures and triggers, we will go into Dreamweaver MX and start to make use of them through the **Command** object. We will run through a few commonly encountered sample scenarios, and come up with some simple solutions for them.

One of the more overlooked elements of data storage is backing up and restoring data. SQL Server makes this job extremely painless and very easy for us to take care of. We will end the chapter by creating a backup schedule to export our entire database to a file.

Stored Procedures

As previously mentioned, stored procedures can help to speed up the performance of your web application.

They can also cut down on the amount of network traffic required to run your application, because we don't need to pass the entire SQL query through the network to the database. The stored procedure houses the entire SQL statement, therefore, we can simply call the stored procedure, which then executes the required SQL code. We won't see much of a performance benefit when the SQL code to be executed is simple and therefore negligible in size, like a couple of straightforward SELECT statements. However, you really begin to see the benefits when you are dealing with lots of SQL.

The increased speed of using stored procedures over querying your database through other means really comes into play when they are used to enforce the business rules that your database relies upon. For example, you might need to check a user's status before they are allowed to place an order. If they are marked down as a bad creditor from past experiences, you might not want to extend their credit and so would need to catch that before adding records into your database.

You could perform all these operations on your web page, but that would require extra network traffic in gathering the initial data to check credit-worthiness before continuing. Making a single call to a stored procedure and passing a few parameters makes far more sense in this scenario.

A stored procedure is written as a block of SQL code wrapped in more defining code. The defining code gives the stored procedure its name and tells SQL Server how the procedure should be defined. The basic structure is as follows:

```
CREATE PROCEDURE procedure_name
AS
sql statements
```

You can use the keyword PROCEDURE or the shortened version of PROC if you want. They are both functionally equivalent.

In the code above, `procedure_name` should be replaced with the name of your stored procedure, and `sql statements` is where the SQL code goes.

A few stored procedure rules to bear in mind are as follows:

- Your stored procedure name may not contain any spaces, and it should not be longer than 128 characters in length.

- You do not have to specify the owner of the stored procedure in the name.

- The name of your stored procedure must follow the naming rules of all database elements in that it must be unique in the database. The only way you could have more than one stored procedure with the same name is if you are using number grouping, which looks like this:

```
CREATE PROCEDURE procedure_name ; 1
...
CREATE PROCEDURE procedure_name ; 2
...
```

The reason you might do this is for simplicity in removing these stored procedures at a later date if you need to – in this case, you would only need to use and a single DROP statement, citing the stored procedure name. Because they are numbered, they become grouped, and as such would all be dropped at the same time.

All objects in a SQL Server database are created by an owner and are identified as such in the naming conventions. For example, if `dbo.tablename` is a table in your database, `dbo` is the owner of this object.

Using Parameters

There are several extra items that can be included between the naming of the stored procedure and the AS keyword. These include parameters, which give stored procedures more flexibility.

If we pass parameters into a stored procedure, we need to declare them in the code. This is illustrated in the following example, where the stored procedure will select the order history of a user. The UserID is dynamically passed into the procedure:

```
CREATE PROCEDURE spSelectUserOrderHistory(@UserID int)
AS
SELECT * FROM tblOrders WHERE UserID = @UserID
ORDER BY OrderDate DESC
GO
```

The first line of the code assigns the name `spSelectUserOrderHistory` to the stored procedure. We then declare our variable which is preceded by an @ symbol. The UserID in the database is an integer, and when declaring variables, their correct data type must be declared with them – if the incorrect data type is declared, your stored procedure will throw an error.

Next we have a simple SELECT statement to gather all the matching orders for this UserID and return them in reverse date order, which would put the latest orders first. Lastly, we use the GO statement, which instructs SQL Server to perform the preceding section of SQL code.

You can use up to 2100 parameters in a stored procedure, which should be more than enough to cover any requirements you might have.

7

Advanced ASP Databases

71

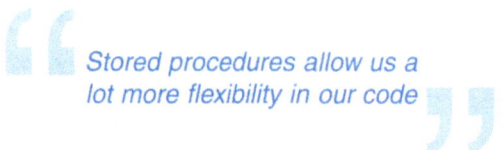
Stored procedures allow us a lot more flexibility in our code

Stored procedures allow us a lot more flexibility in our code in addition to what we have already seen. One such technique, which we'll look at now, involves using the IF statement within stored procedures.

The IF Statement

The IF statement gives us the capabilities of branching and error checking in our SQL code. We could use this type of statement for many purposes. In the following example, it tests to make sure that the parameter passed into the stored procedure is not Null before going on to SELECT the user's order history:

```
CREATE PROCEDURE spSelectUserOrderHistory(
@UserID int)
AS
IF @UserID IS NOT NULL
BEGIN
  SELECT * FROM tblOrders WHERE UserID = @UserID
  ORDER BY OrderDate DESC
END
GO
```

If you have just a single line of SQL code to execute inside the IF statement, you can omit the BEGIN and END statements, but it is good practice to use them regardless. However, you must use them if you have two or more lines of SQL code to execute.

You can also use the ELSE clause to specify more than one option in an IF statement, as you can in any other programming language. The following example expands on the previous one to give multiple choices – it can have two parameters passed into it, UserID and StartDate. Tests are performed to make sure the UserID is supplied, and that a date is supplied. If it is not, the ELSE statement will come into play.

```
CREATE PROCEDURE spSelectUserOrderHistory(
@UserID int,
@StartDate smalldatetime)
AS
IF @UserID IS NOT NULL
  IF @StartDate IS NOT NULL
    BEGIN
      SELECT * FROM tblOrders WHERE UserID = @UserID AND OrderDate >= '@StartDate'
      ORDER BY OrderDate DESC
    END
  ELSE
    BEGIN
      SELECT * FROM tblOrders WHERE UserID = @UserID
      ORDER BY OrderDate DESC
    END
GO
```

The objective of the above stored procedure is to select a user's order history from a defined point in time. If the point in time is not supplied to the stored procedure, it will simply return all past orders for the user.

Triggers

Triggers are an extra mechanism that SQL Server provides us with for maintaining business rules and data integrity. The main role of triggers is the business rules aspect, so we will concentrate on that more in this section.

> *Triggers are an extra mechanism that SQL Server provides us with for maintaining business rules and data integrity*

The primary, preferred method for maintaining data integrity is to use **Constraints**, which can be applied to individual columns or multiple columns to ensure that the data being entered into them obeys predefined rules. That doesn't mean you can't use triggers for this purpose, it's just better to use constraints, as this is exactly what they are designed for.

Triggers are basically stored procedures that only run when a specific action is performed on the table on which they are set. For example, if you insert a new record into a table and you also need to insert an empty record into several other tables at the same time for the purposes of creating related records, a trigger would be ideal to do this.

The syntax for a trigger that fires when an INSERT action is performed on the table or view specified is as follows:

```
CREATE TRIGGER trigger_name
ON table or view
FOR INSERT
AS
sql statement(s)
```

The normal naming conventions apply to triggers as with everything else in the database. When you create a trigger, it is created ON a table FOR a particular event, and will execute the defined SQL statements every time that event occurs. Once you get your head round this, the syntax of the skeleton trigger above starts to make more sense.

The SQL statements can be made up of any valid SQL.

Triggers can be useful time savers in situations where you might need data to be inserted into more than one table when an INSERT takes place. Or perhaps you might need to UPDATE or DELETE rows from other tables when an UPDATE takes place on the table on which your trigger is set.

We will look at the use of the UPDATE trigger in the following section.

The UPDATE Trigger

There are not very many occasions when you will need to update a customer ID number in your database, but should you stumble into such a situation, you'll suddenly realize that it's not only the ID number in the main customers table that needs updating, but also that in every related record this customer has in the customer orders table.

Advanced ASP Databases

Cascade Update will update all related child records in a one-to-many relationship when an update takes place on the parent record

When you create a relationship in your database between two database objects, you can set a **Cascade Update** option. Cascade Update will update all related child records in a one-to-many relationship when an update takes place on the parent record.

If you are not creating the database from scratch, or perhaps if you have to cope with a legacy system that didn't have this feature set up for you, you could bring an UPDATE trigger into play.

The following example of a trigger is based on the situation where you need to update a particular customers' ID number in the customer orders table of your database:

```
CREATE TRIGGER UpdateCustomerID
ON tblCustomers
FOR UPDATE
AS
IF UPDATE(CustomerID)
BEGIN
  DECLARE @NewCustomerID int
  DECLARE @OldCustomerID int
  SELECT @NewCustomerID = CustomerID FROM inserted
  SELECT @OldCustomerID = CustomerID FROM deleted
  UPDATE tblCustomerOrders
    SET tblCustomerOrders.CustomerID = @NewCustomerID
    WHERE tblCustomerOrders.CustomerID = @OldCustomerID
END
```

The trigger is created on the tblCustomers table and is set to watch for an UPDATE action on the table. If the UPDATE action updates the CustomerID column, the trigger kicks in and updates the CustomerID of all the related records in the tblCustomerOrders table.

When an update takes place, the old data is placed into a SQL Server table called deleted and the new data is placed into a table called inserted. In the above example, we use these tables to gather the relevant values, assign them to variables that have been declared locally to this trigger, and then we perform our update.

Now we've seen a few isolated examples to give us an idea of how these database functions work, let's go on to look at a few integrated examples, which we'll run on a sample database.

Sample Database

In order for us to experiment with examples in this chapter, we're going to need a SQL Server database, so let's create a simple database, containing:

- Some related tables
- A view
- Some Stored Procedures

In doing this, we will create some examples that are actually useful to us in real-world situations.

We accept that SQL Server is not the cheapest database to get hold of. If you do not have a copy of it available, and are reluctant to buy it, you could easily construct an equivalent database in Access, or you could get hold of an evaluation copy of SQL Server from Microsoft – see http://www.microsoft.com/sql/evaluation/trial/default.asp for more details.

In *Enterprise Manager*, expand the *SQL Server* node in the left-hand panel until you can see the *Databases* folder, as seen in the following screenshot:

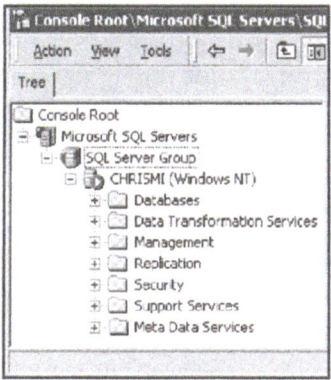

Right-click on the *Databases* folder and select *New Database...* from the context menu.

In the *Database Properties* dialog, enter the name of the database (we called it **Chapter7**):

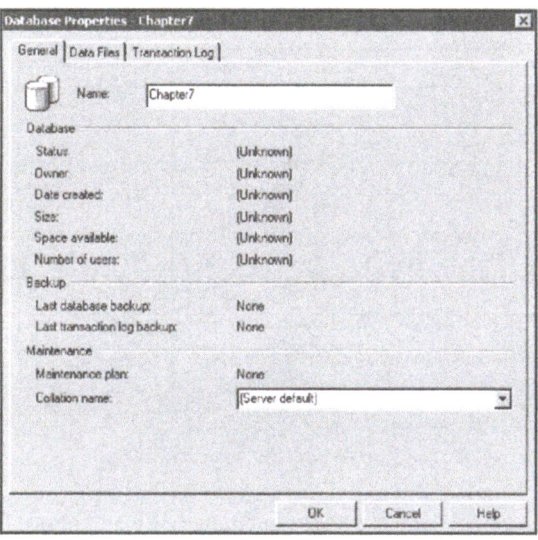

The database name is the only thing we need to enter to create an empty database so click *OK* to close the dialog and your new database object will be listed in the *Databases* folder.

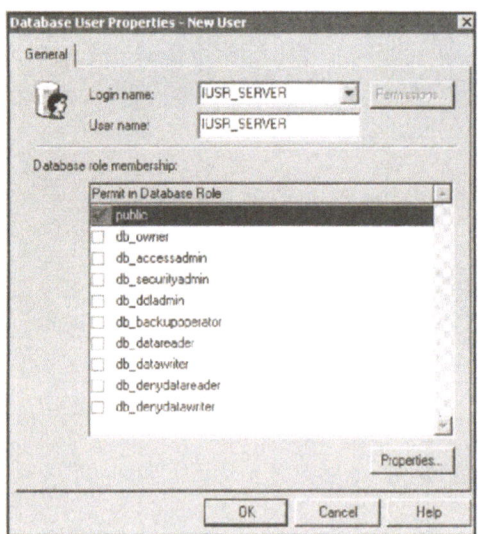

Once the database object has been created, we need to add the **IUSR** user to it so that our web application can access the data objects that it needs:

- Expand the Databases folder and select our new database

- Right-click on the Users object in the right-hand panel

- Select New Database User…

- Select the IUSR_SERVER (or your equivalent) account from the Login name drop-down list. Your dialog box should look like the following:

Click *OK*.

The Tables

Now create the following four tables in the database (we have provided a SQL script in the code download for this chapter, to do this quickly).

Column Name	Data type	Length	Allow Nulls
CustomerID	int	4	No
CustomerName	varchar	200	No
Address1	varchar	100	Yes
Address2	varchar	100	Yes
Address3	varchar	100	Yes
Town	varchar	100	Yes
County_State	varchar	100	Yes
Postcode_Zip	varchar	20	Yes
Country	varchar	50	Yes
EmailAddress	varchar	250	No
Username	varchar	30	No
Password	varchar	30	No

tblCustomers

CustomerID should be set as the primary key column, and as an identity (auto number) column with a seed and increment of 1.

tblCustomerOrders

Column Name	Data type	Length	Allow Nulls
OrderID	int	4	No
CustomerID	int	4	No
OrderDate	datetime	8	No
OrderFulfilled	bit	1	No

OrderID should be set as the primary key column, and as an identity column with a seed and increment of 1. OrderDate should have a default value of getdate(), and OrderFulfilled should have a default value of 0.

tblCustomerOrderDetails

Column Name	Data type	Length	Allow Nulls
OrderDetailID	int	4	No
OrderID	int	4	No
ProductID	int	4	No
QuantityOrdered	int	4	No
TotalPrice	real	4	No

OrderDetailID should be set as the primary key column, and as an identity column with a seed and increment of 1.

Column Name	Data type	Length	Allow Nulls
ProductID	int	4	No
ProductName	varchar	250	No
Category	varchar	50	No
Description	text	16	No
Price	real	4	No
ImageName	varchar	200	Yes

tblProducts

Assign the IUSR user SELECT, INSERT, UPDATE, and DELETE permissions on these four tables.

The Relationships

Now we can add the relationships between these tables to ensure referential integrity and to cascade updates and deletes between the tables. Doing this removes the need for us to write triggers to do the updating and deleting of child records.

Advanced ASP Databases

Right-click the *Diagrams* object and select *New Database Diagram…* from the context menu. Click *Next* on the wizard welcome screen. On the *Select Tables to be Added* screen, *Add* all of our tables except tblProducts to the diagram. Click *Next* to continue, then click *Finish* to close the wizard.

The three tables should have been added to the diagram. To make the creation of relationships easier, arrange the tables as shown here:

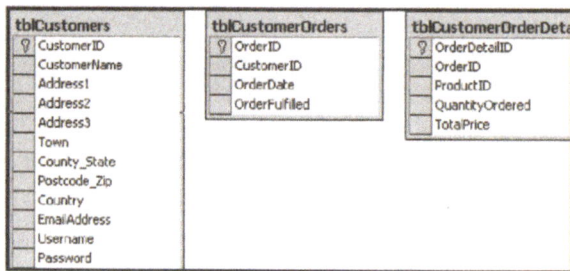

Now we can create relationships between the tables by clicking and dragging column names between them – follow the steps below to create a relationship between tblCustomers and tblCustomerOrders via the CustomerID column:

- Click the CustomerID column in tblCustomers and drag it onto the CustomerID column in tblCustomerOrders

- In the resulting *Create Relationship* dialog, ensure the correct column names are selected under the primary key table and foreign key table lists – CustomerID for both columns

- Deselect *Check existing data on creation* and *Enforce relationship for replication*

- Select *Cascade Update Related Fields* and *Cascade Delete Related Records*. Your dialog box should now look like this:

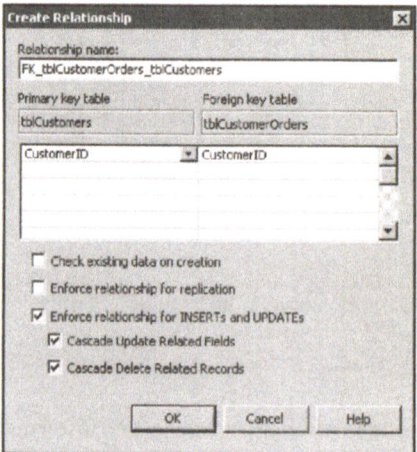

Click OK to create the relationship – this creates a one-to-many relationship between tblCustomers and tblCustomerOrders, which will allow our customers to make multiple orders.

Now create a similar relationship between `tblCustomerOrders` and `tblCustomerOrderDetails`, via the `OrderID` column. Use the exact same settings as the previous relationship.

Save the diagram and accept the dialog warning of changes to be made to the affected tables. The default name of `Diagram1` is acceptable, unless you want to specify your own for easy identification purposes.

With these relationships in place, if a customer order is deleted from the database, the order details will be deleted along with it. If a customer is deleted from the database, everything associated with them is deleted – all their orders and all their order details. This is very simple and ensures that integrity is preserved within your database!

The View

Now we can build a simple view to bring together customers and their order history. One of our stored procedures will use this view to return data to our web application.

In Enterprise Manager, expand the *Databases* Folder and the *Chapter7* database icon, then right-click on the *Views* object and select *New view...* On the menu bar, click the *Add Table* icon:

From the *Add Table* dialog, double-click `tblCustomers` and `tblCustomerOrders` to add them to the view, and then click *Close*.

The tables are added to the View Designer. Place a tick in the checkbox next to each column that you want to appear in the final view. From `tblCustomers`, we want every column except the `Username` and `Password`. From `tblCustomerOrders`, we need all columns except the `CustomerID` column.

Once all the columns are added to the view, save your view as *viewCustomerOrders*; now assign the `IUSR` user account `SELECT` permissions on this view. The reason we do this is to ensure that the stored procedure can access this query when it is called by the IUSR account. Another option would be to add DRI permissions to the view instead, which would allow the IUSR to use this query because it already has sufficient permissions to use the stored procedure that calls it.

The Stored Procedures

Now let's build some stored procedures that will help us to improve the performance of our web applications. You will find the code for the stored procedures in the code download for this chapter.

Right-click on the *Stored Procedures* object and select *New Stored Procedure...* In the *Stored Procedure Properties* dialog, enter the following code:

```
CREATE PROCEDURE spCustomerOrderHistory(
@CustomerID int,
@StartDate smalldatetime)
AS
IF @CustomerID IS NOT NULL
```

Advanced ASP Databases

```
    IF @StartDate IS NOT NULL
      BEGIN
        SELECT * FROM viewCustomerOrders WHERE CustomerID = @CustomerID AND OrderDate
>= @StartDate
        ORDER BY OrderDate DESC
      END
   ELSE
      BEGIN
        SELECT * FROM viewCustomerOrders WHERE CustomerID = @CustomerID
        ORDER BY OrderDate DESC
      END
GO
```

Your dialog box should now look like this:

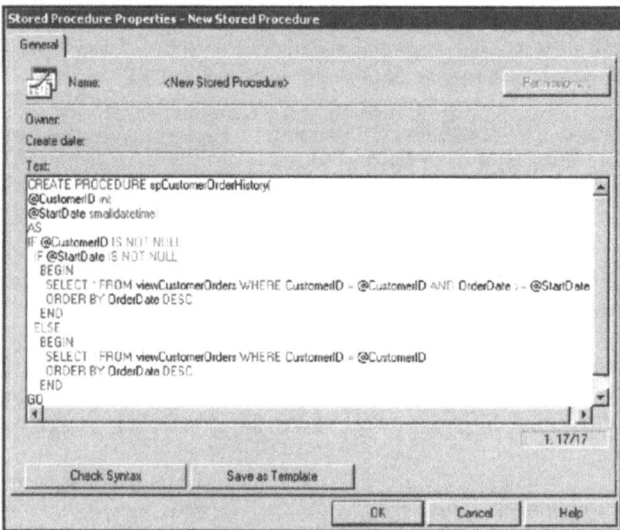

This stored procedure code checks the `CustomerID` parameter first. If it exists, we then check the `StartDate` parameter. If that exists, we perform a select on the data using both parameters. If the start date does not exist, we perform a select using only the `CustomerID`.

Click *Check Syntax* to make sure there are no obvious errors in the code (like column names that are misspelled), *OK* the successful syntax check dialog, and click *OK* on the main dialog.

There is a slight point of confusion here (a bug), as the stored procedure is now saved but the dialog box doesn't go away. To get rid of the dialog, click *Cancel* then click *No* to discard changes (we haven't made any since creating the stored procedure and saving it). Now, click the *Refresh* button on the main menu bar and your stored procedure will appear in the stored procedures list.

Now follow the above steps twice more to create another two new stored procedures that we will be using later in the chapter. Add the following code in turn to the two *Stored Procedure Properties* dialog boxes:

spUnfulfilledOrders

```
CREATE PROCEDURE spUnfulfilledOrders(
@CustomerID int)
AS
IF @CustomerID IS NOT NULL
  BEGIN
    SELECT * FROM viewCustomerOrders WHERE CustomerID = @CustomerID AND
OrderFulfilled = 0
    ORDER BY OrderDate DESC
  END
GO
```

spDeleteOrder

```
CREATE PROCEDURE spDeleteOrder(
@OrderID int)
AS
IF @OrderID IS NOT NULL
BEGIN
  DELETE FROM tblCustomerOrders WHERE OrderID = @OrderID
END
GO
```

The last thing to do is ensure that the IUSR account has EXEC permissions on all three stored procedures otherwise none of it will work:

- Right-click on a stored procedure that we just created
- Click on *Properties* from the context menu
- Click on *Permissions*
- Check the *Exec* checkbox for the IUSR Account
- Click *OK*

It's only a very simple database but it will be enough to illustrate what we are going to cover next. We'll start by looking at the *Command* object in Dreamweaver MX, and then we'll show how we can use it to speed up our database interactions when we utilize the stored procedures in our web application.

Dreamweaver MX Command Object

Having all these wonderful automation and scripting features in our database is all well and good, but if we don't make good use of them from our web applications, what's the point?

Dreamweaver MX gives us access to our stored procedures via the *Command* object, which you can access by clicking *Server Behaviors > + > Command*.

> *Dreamweaver MX gives us access to our stored procedures via the* Command *object*

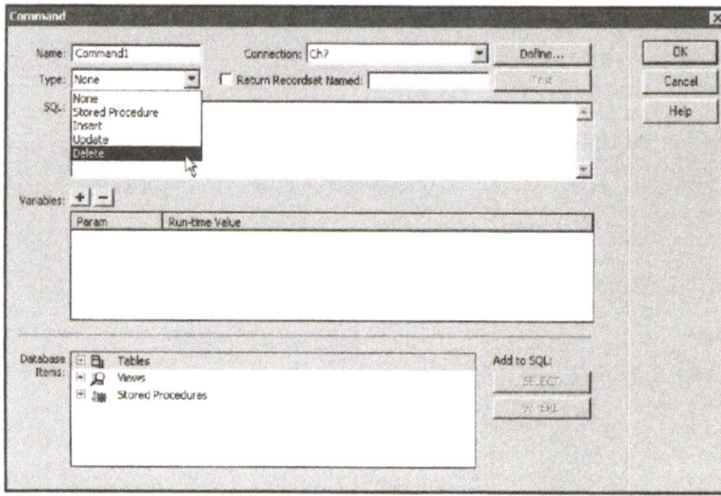

There are four types of command available to us from this dialog, which are *Insert*, *Update*, *Delete*, and *Stored Procedure*. You can see these in the above screenshot in the *Type* list.

A new command will always use a default name unless you specify one. It is good practice to name your objects in a manner that makes sense in the context of the task at hand; for example, a command to update a product might be called cmdProductUpdate.

In the following three examples, we will use the *Command* object to bring data from the database to our web pages utilizing the stored procedures we created earlier. It is assumed that you already have a site set up and your connection to the database for the site has been created. Some data in the database might help too!

> *If you need help creating a DSN to your database, check out this simple*
> *tutorial on my web site, located here:*
> http://robgt.com/tutorials/sqlserver/sqldsn.asp.
> *For help with creating DSN-less connections to your database, check out the*
> *following great resource:* http://dwteam.com/articles/ado/index.asp.

Order History

This is going to be a simple page layout created using two tables. The first will house some form elements and the second will house the returned data.

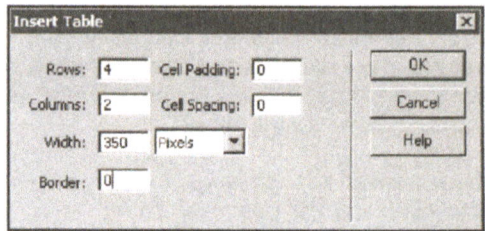

Create a new ASP VBScript page and save it as orderhistory.asp. Add a form to the page, and then insert a table with the following properties:

Now do the following to our table:

- Merge the top row and enter into it the following text: "Select a user to view their order history and optionally provide a start date"

- In row 2, type "Customer" into column 1, and add a *List/Menu* object into column 2. Call the *List/Menu* object `CustomerID`

- In row 3, type "Start Date" into column 1, and add a Text Field object into column 2. Call the *Text Field* object `StartDate`

- In row 4 column 2, add a *Submit* button

We will dynamically populate the list box from a Recordset that gathers all the users from the database. The labels will use the users names, and the values will use their ID numbers.

Now create a Recordset with the following SQL statement, calling it `rsCustomers`:

```
SELECT CustomerID, CustomerName
FROM dbo.tblCustomers
ORDER BY CustomerName
```

Click on the list box to select it, and click the *Dynamic* button [🖉 Dynamic...] in the *Property Inspector*.

In the following dialog box, add a static option to the top of the list – click the + button and type "Please select" in the *Label* column. Type "0" (zero) in the value column – we add a zero into the value column so that no results will be returned if it is selected.

Select `rsCustomers` from the *Options From Recordset* drop-down list, and `CustomerID` from the values list. The *Labels* list should already have `CustomerName` selected. If it doesn't, select it. Your dialog box should look like this:

Click *OK* to apply the code to the page.

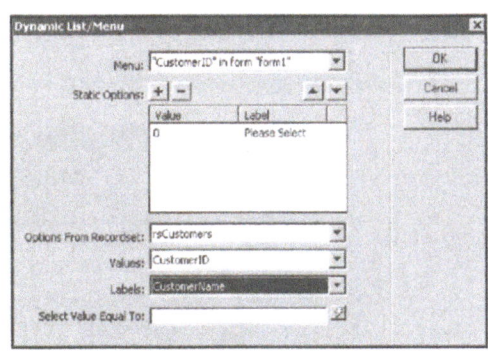

Add some space between this table and the one we're about to add (use *Shift + Enter* to add `<br />` tags to your page). Next, add another table with the following properties:

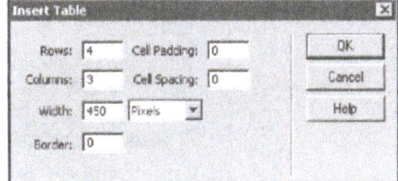

Do the following to this table:

- In row 1, type "Customer Name" into column 1, then merge the second and third columns
- In row 2 column 1, type "Order History"
- In row 3 column 1, type "Order ID"
- In row 3 column 2, type "Order Date"
- In row 3 column 3, type "Fulfilled"

Now we need to create the command to get our data from the database onto the page. Click *Server Behaviors > + > Command* and the *Command* dialog will open up.

In the *Name* field type `cmdOrderHistory`, and select your connection from the connections drop-down list. Select *Stored Procedure* from the *Type* drop-down list, tick the checkbox next to *Return Recordset Named*, and enter `rsOrderHistory` as the name of the Recordset to return.

In the *Database Items* window at the bottom of the dialog, expand the *Stored Procedures* node, highlight `dbo.spCustomerOrderHistory`, and click the *Procedure* button.

Three variables are now added to the *Variables* window:

- The first one, `@RETURN_VALUE` can be deleted because we don't need it
- `@CustomerID` should be given a Size of 4 and Default Value of 0, and make sure the *Run-time Value* entry says `Request.Form("CustomerID")`
- `@StartDate` should be given a Size of 8 and Default Value of 01/01/2001, and make sure the *Run-time Value* entry says `Request.Form("StartDate")`

Your *Command* dialog should now look like this:

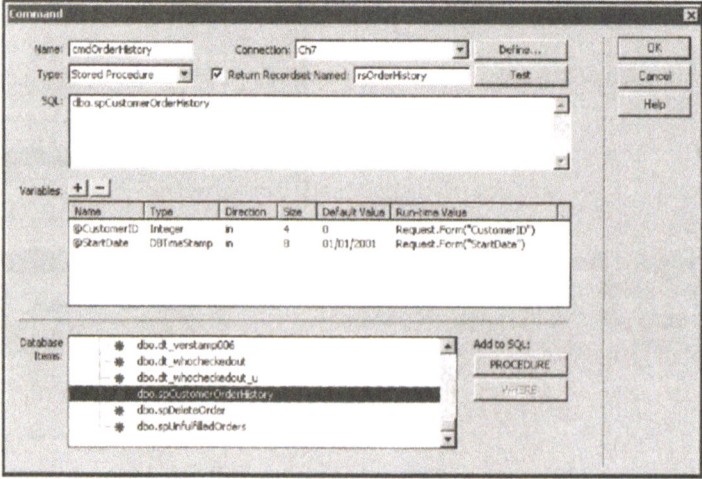

Click *OK* to create the *Command* object.

Now click the *Bindings* tab, and you will see that your `Command(cmdOrderHistory)` Recordset has been returned from the *Command* object you just created. If you expand this Recordset, all the columns that are returned from the stored procedure are visible and you can bind them to the page. That's the next step, which we'll do now.

First, drag `rsOrderHistory.OrderID` from the *Bindings* panel into the first column of the fourth row of the second table, under *Order ID*.

Perform similar operations to bind `rsOrderHistory.OrderDate` to the cell underneath *Order Date*, and `rsOrderHistory.OrderFulfilled` to the cell underneath *Fulfilled*.

> If you want to display the words *Yes* and *No* in the *Fulfilled* column instead of the *-1* and *0* that the database will give us, go into Code View and change this code:
>
> ```
> <%= rsOrderHistory.Fields.Item("OrderFulfilled").Value %>
> ```
>
> to this:
>
> ```
> <%
>   varFulfilled = rsOrderHistory.Fields.Item("OrderFulfilled").Value
>   IF varFulfilled = -1 THEN
>     Response.Write("Yes")
>   ELSE
>     Response.Write("No")
>   END IF
> %>
> ```

Now, in Design View, drag the cursor across the bottom three columns with the data bindings in them to select the entire row, and apply a repeat region to it.

To do this, click *Server Behaviors > + > Repeat Region*. Make sure you select `rsOrderHistory`, and then select *Show All Records*. This will display all the selected customers' previous orders. Now click *OK* to apply the Server Behavior.

Finally, select the entire bottom table and apply a *Show Region* Server Behavior to it. We only want this table to be displayed if there is data to show. This will also prevent any errors that might occur if the Recordset is empty.

Click *Server Behaviors > + > Show Region > Show Region If Recordset Is Not Empty*. In the resulting dialog box, select `rsOrderHistory` as the *Recordset* and click *OK* to apply this Server Behavior to the page.

If you want to add Recordset paging to these results you can choose to show a specific number of records in this dialog and then add Recordset navigation links to the page. For simplicity, we are simply showing all records.

The page is now complete – now save it and test it out. The finished page should look something like this:

7

Advanced ASP Databases

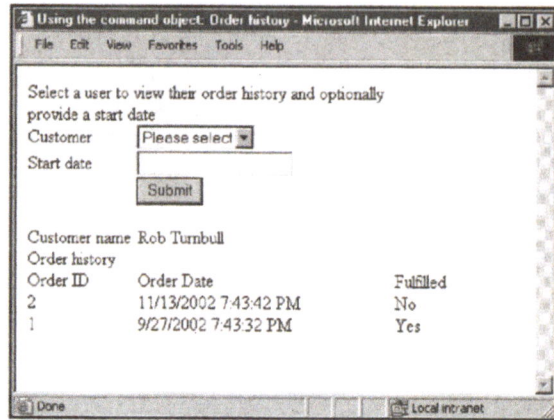

When you run the page and select a customer from the list, clicking the *Submit* button will bring back all that customers orders. If you also specify a date, the returned Recordset will be further filtered to only show the customer orders occurring on or after that date.

Unfulfilled Orders

This page will be very similar in nature to the *Order History* page, except it will only show unfulfilled orders for the selected customer. Follow the following steps:

- Make a copy of the `orderhistory.asp` page and save it, calling it `unfulfilledorders.asp`

- Delete the row containing the *Start Date* form element in the top table – we don't need it in this example page

- Replace the *Order History* heading with *Unfulfilled Orders*

- Remove the *Fulfilled* heading and the ASP code in the row below it, replacing the ASP code with the word *Cancel*. This will become a link to the `cancelorder.asp` page that we will build after completing this page

Your display should now look like this:

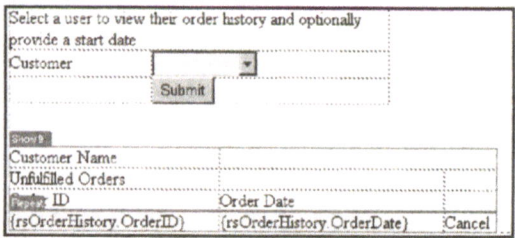

Now we need to change the `Command` object that is currently applied to this page. Click the *Server Behaviors* panel, and then double-click `Command(cmdOrderHistory)` in the list. This will open the *Command* dialog with the current settings in place.

Change the name of the command from `cmdOrderHistory` to `cmdUnfulfilledOrders`, and then change the name of the Recordset to be returned from `rsOrderHistory` to `rsUnfulfilledOrders`.

In the *Database Items* window at the bottom of the *Command* dialog, expand the *Stored Procedures* node, highlight dbo.spUnfilledOrders, and click the *Procedure* button. Two variables are added to the *Variables* window:

- @RETURN_VALUE can be deleted because we don't need it
- @CustomerID should be given a size of 4, and a default value of 0. Make sure the *Run-time Value* entry says Request.Form("CustomerID")

Your dialog should now look like this:

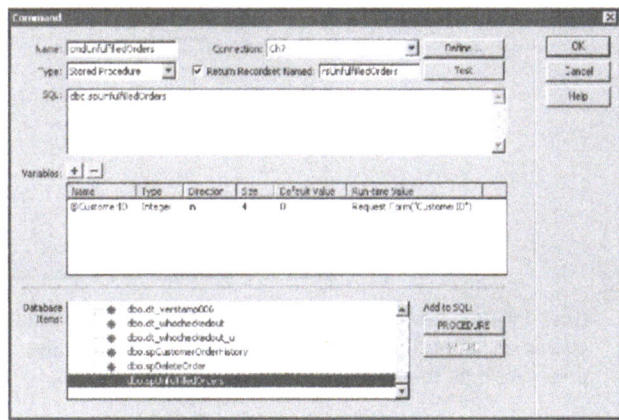

Click *OK* to update the *Command* object on this page.

Once you do that, a red exclamation mark will appear against the remainder of the Server Behaviors applied to this page, listed in the *Server Behaviors* panel will have them. This is because the Recordset that they reference is no longer part of this page. To quickly rectify this, we need to go into Code View and perform a search and replace.

Click the *Code View* icon to switch from Design View to Code View, then right-click anywhere in the code view and select *Find and Replace...* from the context menu.

We need to find rsOrderHistory and replace all instances of it on this page with rsUnfulfilledOrders. Set your find and replace dialog to do this and click the *Replace All* button to perform the action.

Now let's make our *Cancel* link:

- Select the word *Cancel* and click the folder icon next to the *Link text* field in the *Property Inspector*
- Type cancelorder.asp as the page to link to, then click the *Parameters...* button
- In the *Name* column, type OrderID and in the *Value* column click the lightning bolt icon and select rsUnfulfilledOrders.OrderID from the *Command Recordset*
- Click *OK*, *OK* again, and *OK* a third time to close the link dialog.

7

Advanced ASP Databases

Your final *Link* should look like this:

```
cancelorder.asp?OrderID=<%= rsUnfulfilledOrders.Fields.Item("OrderID").Value %>
```

The page is now complete, so save it and test it out – it should look something like this:

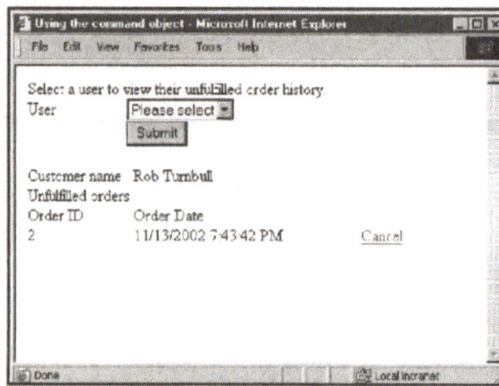

Now only unfulfilled orders will be returned from the database when a customer is selected from the customer list and the form is submitted. Don't click the *Cancel* link yet; we still need to create that page. We'll do that next.

Cancel an Order

This page will be linked to from the unfulfilled orders page and will simply run the stored procedure to delete the selected order from the database. It won't be a visual page: it will simply call the stored procedure, and then return to the unfulfilled orders page:

- Create a new *ASP VBScript* page and save it, calling it `cancelorder.asp`
- Go into Code View and delete everything except the first line which should be the page language declaration – we don't need any client-side code on this page, so we can remove the basic HTML that a new page supplies us with.

Now to add the command – click *Server Behaviors > + > Command*.

Type `cmdCancelOrder` in the *Name* field, select your connection and select *Stored Procedure* from the *Type* list. We will not be returning a Recordset so make sure this checkbox is left unchecked. The text field should also be empty.

In the *Database Items* window, expand the *Stored Procedures* node; select `spDeleteOrder` and then click the *Procedure* button. We will again see two variables added to the *Variables* window:

- Delete the `@Return_Value` variable, as we will not need it
- `@OrderID` should be given a size of 4, and a default value of 0. Make sure the *Run-time Value* entry says `Request.Form("OrderID")`

Your dialog should now look like this:

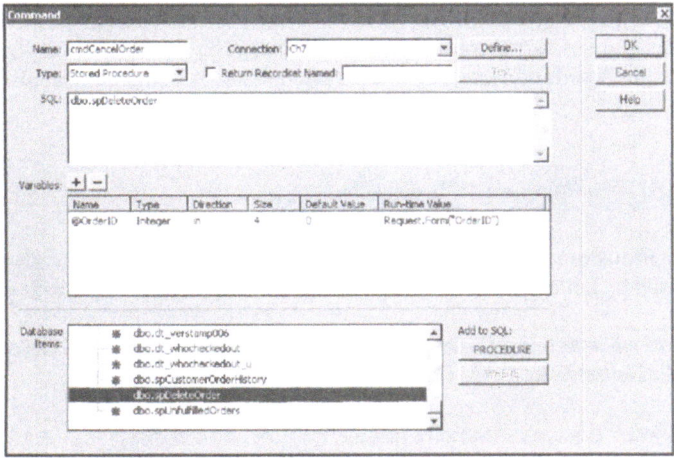

Click *OK* to add this command to your page.

Now go into Code View and add the following line of code after the command code.

```
<% Response.Redirect("unfulfilledorders.asp") %>
```

Your complete code for this page should look something like this:

```
<%@LANGUAGE="VBSCRIPT" CODEPAGE="1252"%>
<!--#include file="Connections/Ch7.asp" -->
<%

  Dim cmdCancelOrder__OrderID
  cmdCancelOrder__OrderID = "0"
  if(Request("OrderID") <> "") then cmdCancelOrder__OrderID = Request("OrderID")

%>
<%

  set cmdCancelOrder = Server.CreateObject("ADODB.Command")
  cmdCancelOrder.ActiveConnection = MM_Ch7_STRING
  cmdCancelOrder.CommandText = "dbo.spDeleteOrder"
  cmdCancelOrder.CommandType = 4
  cmdCancelOrder.CommandTimeout = 0
  cmdCancelOrder.Prepared = true
  cmdCancelOrder.Parameters.Append cmdCancelOrder.CreateParameter("@OrderID", 3,
1,4,cmdCancelOrder__OrderID)
  cmdCancelOrder.Execute()

%>
<% Response.Redirect("unfulfilledorders.asp") %>
```

That's this page completed – save it and test it out.

To test this page, you will first need to run the `unfulfilledorders.asp` page – get an unfulfilled order up, and click the *Cancel* link. Once you have selected a customer on the `unfulfilledorders.asp` page, click *Submit* to bring back their unfulfilled orders and then click the **Cancel** link to cancel the selected order. Selecting their name from the list again and resubmitting the form will show the record has been deleted. It happens so quickly that you just might not believe it did anything!

Backing Up Your Database

You can use Data Transformation Services (DTS) to do this but I prefer to create a Job and let the database get on with it. Jobs are not difficult to write if you are comfortable with your SQL skills.

In this example, we will create a Job that will back up the entire database to a file at midnight every night. Go into SQL Server Enterprise Manager, and follow the following steps:

- Right-click your database name (*Chapter7*), in the *Databases* folder and select *All Tasks > Backup Database...*

- On the *General* tab give a name to this backup job. The default should be fine

- Leave *Database – complete* selected in the *Backup* radio button group

- In the Destination area, click *Add...* and select the destination to output the backup file to. You will need to enter a filename at this point. We'll save ours as `C:\BACKUP\Chapter7backup.bak`. *OK* out of this subdialog

- In the *Overwrite* area, select *Overwrite existing media*. In this example, we are merely illustrating a complete database backup so overwriting the old database backup with the new one makes sense – in a corporate environment, you would be more likely not to overwrite the last backup, instead keeping multiple backups from different times, say, in the last week. Multiple backups can be very useful if a phantom data disappearance has occurred, and you are not sure when you last had the data

- Tick the *Schedule* check box and then click the ellipsis button ▣ to the right of the schedule text box

- In the *Schedule* dialog, click the *Change...* button and select the *Daily* radio button. The remainder of the dialog should be fine set at the defaults. It should be set to occur every day, occurring once at midnight starting on today's date with no end date specified

- Click *OK*, then *OK* again to get back to the main dialog

Your finished dialog should look like this:

Click *OK* to save the backup job. It really is as simple as that!

If you ever need to edit the schedule, or any of the other details of the backup job, you can now access it under the **Jobs** object, which is located under the *Management* folder > *SQL Server Agent* > *Jobs*.

Double-clicking the Job in the list will open up a properties sheet detailing your backup schedule on which you can change any part of it.

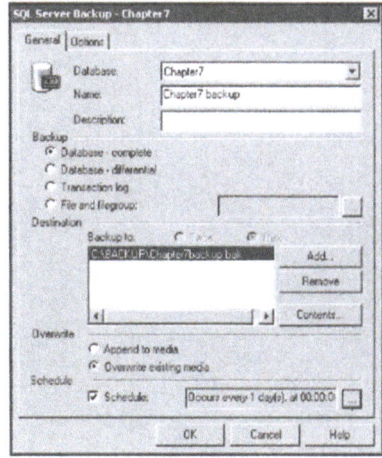

Summary

In this chapter we first covered the creation of stored procedures and triggers and showed examples of using conditional code to execute the relevant part of a stored procedure. We went on to build a basic database containing tables, views, stored procedures, and triggers and made use of those elements from within Dreamweaver MX with the aid of the *Command* object, in three simple ASP files.

Finally, we covered the creation of a backup schedule to back up your database. This is a critical step – ignoring it can have serious consequences if something terrible happens to your web server, or to the database itself.

Building a solid, well-structured database is only the starting point when it comes to building fast web pages that interact with a database. Utilizing stored procedures and triggers to take care of the business logic can offer some serious speed advantages over traditional methods, especially when performing complex operations.

I hope this chapter has offered some food for thought in terms of what might be possible in your particular situation. Explore and experiment!

Advanced ASP Databases

8

- `FileSystem` Objects collection (FSO)
- The `Server.MapPath` method
- Reading and writing text files
- Uploading files

Author: Dan Short

File Handling

Not only can we work with databases on the server, but we can also manipulate text files, folders, and other file types. There is an entire collection of **FileSystem Objects** (or **FSO**), which allow you to read, write, modify, and delete files and folders on the server. With a few handy components you can even create ZIP archives of groups of files from your ASP page.

The `FileSystem` object is in itself a collection of other objects, which include the `Drive`, `File`, `FileSystemObject`, `Folder`, and `TextStream` objects. Each of these objects also has its own sets of properties and methods (many are duplicated but each also has unique properties and methods). Twenty-odd pages isn't quite enough to cover everything you can do with FSO, so we're going to cover just some of the properties and methods of the FSO objects and collections. After that we're going to build a single page that will display image galleries based on a collection of folders.

FSO consists of a large number of child objects and collections, which give us functionality including access to drives, folders, files, and text streams. For this chapter we're going to cover a tiny bit of syntax and then we're going to jump right into an example, showing you how to use some of the more common objects, properties, and methods as we go along.

Objects and Collections

As stated in the introduction, the FSO system in ASP is itself a collection of objects and other collections. Each object can contain information about a particular folder, file, or drive and can contain additional objects (we'll iron all this out, I promise). Here's a list of the bits that make up FSO:

- `FileSystemObject` – This is the main FSO object. This is the first FSO object you'll invoke when you need to create/delete/gain information about/manipulate drives, folders, and files.

- `File`: This object is used to create, delete, or move files. You can also get specific information about a file such as filename, path, and various other properties.

- `Files`: This collection contains a list of all the files inside a folder.

- Drive: This object allows you to gather information about a drive attached to the system, such as its share name and how much room is available. Note that a "drive" isn't necessarily a hard disk, but can be a CD-ROM drive, a RAM disk, and so forth. A drive doesn't need to be physically attached to the system; it can be logically connected through a network.

- Drives: This collection (not object) provides a list of the drives on the web server, either physically or logically. The Drives collection includes all drives, regardless of type, including removable-media drives (which don't need to have media inserted for them to appear). This means that you could potentially pull files off a CD on your web server.

- Folder: This object allows you to create, delete, or move folders. You can also get specific information about a folder, such as folder names, paths, and various other properties.

- Folders: This collection contains a list of all the folders inside another folder (subfolders in common terms).

- TextStream: This object allows you to read and write text files.

Now each of the objects above contains numerous methods and properties that can be accessed. These include such gems as DateLastCreated, Name, Path, ParentFolder, Size, ShareName, and FreeSpace. The list of available properties and methods is in fact huge. You can find all of the properties, methods, objects, and collections here:

http://msdn.microsoft.com/library/en-us/script56/html/fsooriScriptingRun-TimeReference.asp

> *The FileSystemObject object (I know, confusing, isn't it?) is the daddy of all FileSystem objects*

The FileSystemObject object (I know, confusing, isn't it?) is the daddy of all FileSystem objects. You need a FileSystemObject declared before you can get access to any of the other objects and collections. This means that in order to get a list of folders, you first need a FileSystemObject object declared, and then you can get the list of folders from that object using the GetFolders method. Here's an example to try and clear this up:

```
<%
  'Create our FSO object, we'll be referring back to this object constantly
  Dim objFSO
  Set objFSO = CreateObject("Scripting.FileSystemObject")

'Stuff our folder into an object we can manipulate
  Dim objFolder
  Set objFolder = objFSO.GetFolder("c:\myfolder")
%>
```

Notice that we've first instantiated a FileSystemObject. We can now use methods against this object to create more objects. In the second highlighted line, we've added the folder c:\myfolder to the objFolder object using the GetFolder method of objFSO. The GetFolder method returns a folder object, which contains collections of files and subfolders. So if I wanted to list every subfolder under myfolder, I could do this:

```
<%
  'Create our FSO object, we'll be refering back to this object constantly
  Dim objFSO
  Set objFSO = CreateObject("Scripting.FileSystemObject")

  'Stuff our folder into an object we can manipulate
  Dim objFolder
  Set objFolder = objFSO.GetFolder("c:\myfolder")

  Dim SubFolder
  For Each SubFolder in objFolder.SubFolders
    Response.Write(SubFolder.Name & "<br />")
  Next
%>
```

The `objFolder.SubFolders` statement accesses the `SubFolders` property of `c:\myfolder`. If `c:\myfolder` had two subfolders called `subfolder1` and `subfolder2`, then this script would cause the following to be written to the browser:

There are also file collections and methods for gathering path information and file types. We're going to cover all of that as we walk through an example of building an online image gallery, using just one page that will display multiple galleries based on the folder structure.

The results of this simple ASP code

Server.MapPath

Another method we're going to use extensively is the `MapPath` method of the `Server` object. We use this method when we need to translate a value to the physical path. The `Server.MapPath` object will take a virtual path, and convert it to a physical path. This not only makes it easier for us to write lean code but it also makes our application far more portable. What if our host moves our site to a new drive, or changes the name of a parent folder we don't have control over? If we've referenced everything by an absolute path, our application will be unable to find the original directory. We'll need this to tell the FSO object which folders and files to display. The `MapPath` method takes a page-relative (meaning a relative path from the page calling the script) or root-relative path and converts it to the full directory path:

```
<body>
  <p>
  </p>
    Current Directory: <%= Server.MapPath(".") %><br />
    One directory up:<%= Server.MapPath("../") %><br />
    Two directories up:<%= Server.MapPath("../../") %>
</body>
```

If the above code was in `c:\website\mysite\www\` then the first line, `Current Directory`, would return `c:\website\mysite\www`. The `One directory up` line would return `c:\website\mysite`, and the `Two directories up` line would return `c:\website`.

> *The `MapPath` method makes it easier to move your application around without worrying about changing path information. This also makes sure that things will continue to work correctly even if your host moves your site from one drive to another.*

We're going to be using a lot of file paths with the FSO objects. If you already know the full path to the directory you can enter it manually, but the `MapPath` method makes it easier to move your application around without worrying about changing path information. This also makes sure that things will continue to work correctly even if your host moves your site from one drive to another.

Dynamic Image Gallery

The easiest way to demonstrate all of the `File` and `Folder` objects and collections is to build something using those items. We're going to be putting together a dynamic image gallery that doesn't use a database at all. We're going to use the folder structure of our gallery and the files inside those folders to build the gallery each time the page is loaded. That means that you'll be able to simply upload another file to the directory and it will instantly show up in the gallery.

> *Like any structure that you want to reuse, things have to be consistent and reliable*

Our Dynamic Image Gallery example relies on folder structure. Therefore, before we get started, we need to figure out how we're going to lay out our folders for consistency. Like any code/file structure that you want to reuse over and over, things have to be consistent and reliable, otherwise you end up writing a ton of conditional statements to account for every possibility.

Our gallery is going to consist of several different categories of shoes. We're going to be showing clogs, dress shoes, sandals, and a few others, with the possibility that we may one day add additional categories. Each gallery will have a list of thumbnails that link to a larger image.

We also want some left-hand navigation to move from gallery to gallery. This means that we need a folder for each gallery in order to be able to list all of the individual galleries. This means that we're going to create a link for the `Clogs` folder, a link for the `Sandals` folder, etc. We also need a way to determine which images are thumbnails and which are full sized. The easiest way is to use separate folders again, one for thumbnails and one for full size images. We could distinguish them by filename, but again, we'd end up writing additional code in order to check for different filenames. You'll see how this falls into place later.

After all that, this is what our folder structure will look like (you can find all the images in the code download for this chapter).

Each gallery/category has a folder with a `FullSize` folder and `Thumbs` folder. Each of these folders has identically named images that are different sizes. So `Shoes/Clogs/Thumbs/clog4.jpg` is the thumbnail counterpart of `Shoes/Clogs/FullSize/clog4.jpg`. This is going to make it really easy for us to get through all of our files and folders quickly.

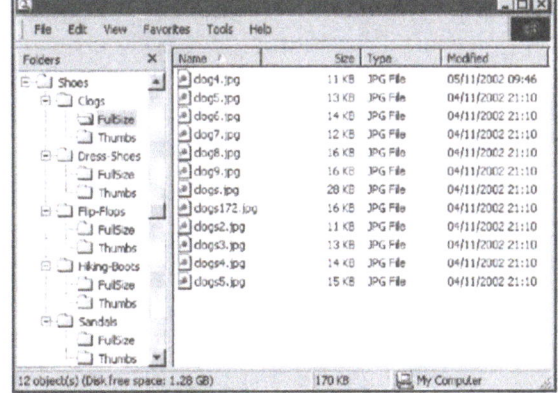

Our sample application folder structure

After we have put together all our ASP code, the end result of our labors will look something like this:

Now let's dig in, and see how we put our application together.

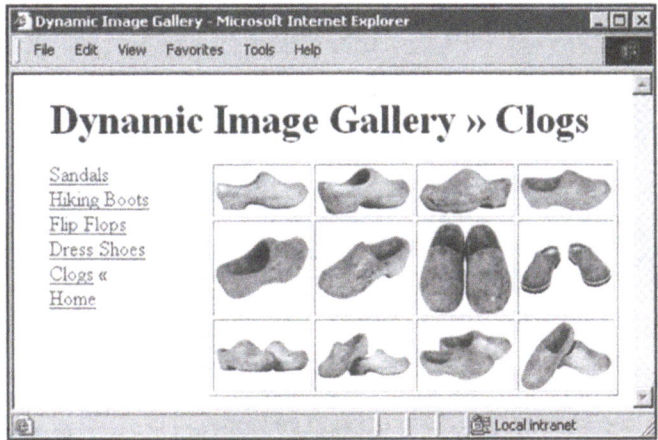

This is how the Dynamic Image Gallery application will look when finished

Playing with Folders and Files

We're going to start with a simple ASP file (`default.asp`) with a few `<div>` elements that we'll use for our layout. This is what we need to start with:

```
<?xml version="1.0" encoding="iso-8859-1"?>
<!DOCTYPE html PUBLIC "-//W3C//DTD XHTML 1.0 Transitional//EN"
         "http://www.w3.org/TR/xhtml1/DTD/xhtml1-transitional.dtd">
<%@LANGUAGE="VBSCRIPT" CODEPAGE="1252"%>
<% Option Explicit %>
<html xmlns="http://www.w3.org/1999/xhtml">
<head>
  <title>Dynamic Image Gallery</title>
  <meta http-equiv="Content-Type" content="text/html; charset=iso-8859-1">
  <style type="text/css">
  <!--
```

```
   a img {
      border: 0px;
   }
   #GalleryNav {
      position:absolute;
      left:28px;
      top:67px;
      width:125px;
      z-index:1;
   }
   #GalleryPhotos {
      position:absolute;
      left:154px;
      top:66px;
      z-index:2;
   }
   #GalleryHeader {
      position:absolute;
      left:28px;
      top:16px;
      z-index:3;
   }
   -->
   </style>
</head>
<body>
   <div id="GalleryNav"></div>
   <div id="GalleryPhotos"></div>
   <div id="GalleryHeader"></div>
</body>
</html>
```

Declaring Variables

The first thing we need to pay attention to is declaring all of the variables we're going to use on our page. We're going to be looping through files and folders, and will need to get paths for full-size images and thumbnails. We're going to divide our script into two parts: one for the navigation and

> We're going to divide our script into two parts, one for the navigation and one for the actual gallery

one for the actual gallery. Here are the variables we're going to use to build our gallery navigation, added to the GalleryNav <div> seen above. Some of these will be reused for the gallery images:

```
<div id="GalleryNav">
<%
   '=======
   'Variable Declaration
   '=======
   Dim objFSO, objFolder, SubFolder

   'Determine the folder that holds our galleries.
   'Setting this to a variable makes this page much more portable.
   Dim parentPath : parentPath = "Shoes/"
```

```
'This stores the path for the gallery we want to show.
Dim galPath : galPath = Request.QueryString("gal")

'Used to store the full path to our gallery for use with the FSO objects
Dim galPathFull : galPathFull = parentPath & galPath

'We're going to store the "name" of objects in theName to prevent hitting our
'objects too many times.
Dim theName

%>
```
`</div>`

You can see that, in the first `Dim` statement, we've created three variables for working with our folders and subfolders. `objFSO` will be our main FSO object, which we'll use to get all of the other folder and file information. `objFolder` and `SubFolder` will be used for listing our gallery folders, as I demonstrated earlier in this chapter.

The `parentPath` variable will be used to determine which folder contains all of our galleries. Setting this as a variable makes it possible to take this page and use it to display a *shirts* directory or a *socks* directory by just changing the value of this variable. We've set the variable to `Shoes/` since that's the parent folder of our galleries. You'll see how this is put to use in a bit.

In order to determine which gallery the user wants to view, we have to pass a variable somehow. We're going to pass the folder name via the `gal` Querystring, which we'll store in `galPath` so it's easy to reuse throughout the page. To complement that, we also have `galPathFull`, which puts the `parentPath` and `galPath` together to create the full path to our gallery. If we want to view the `Clogs` folder contents, `galPathFull` would contain `Store/Clogs`. We're using a Querystring so people will be able to link directly to a gallery, rather than using a form where they'd be required to submit a form in order to get to the gallery.

The last variable is the easiest. We're going to use `theName` to store (you guessed it) the name of a file or folder as we work with it. Assigning the object's name to a variable means we only have to reference that object once. Again, this will all fall into place as we go.

If we need to display the filename four or five times, we hit the object once to get the name and stuff it in our variable, and then we just reuse the variable throughout the remainder of the script. This creates less server load and can dramatically increase the speed of things if you've got a really large number of images to display

Now that we have our variables defined, we need to do a little cleanup of our Querystring variable to prevent hacking. In our `Server.MapPath` examples in the previous section, you can see that it's possible to walk up the directory structure by using relative paths (such as `../../`). This could potentially allow someone to view folders we don't want them to. To prevent that, we need to make sure that a user can't enter relative paths into the Querystring. We need to change our `galPath` variable like this:

```
'This stores the path for the gallery we want to show.
Dim galPath : galPath = Request.QueryString("gal")
```

```
'We need to clean up the gallery path, to be sure that someone doesn't try
'to walk up our directory path.
galPath = Replace(galPath,"../","")
```

```
    galPath = Replace(galPath,"/","")
    galPath = Replace(galPath,"\","")
```

Replacing "../", "/" and "\" ensures that the user can only enter simple folder names without going up or down in our directory structure.

Building Navigation and Looping Through Folders

Now that the boring part is done we can start playing with folders. First, we have to create our objects:

```
'We're going to store the "names" of objects in theName to prevent hitting our
'objects too many times.
Dim theName
```

```
'Create our FSO object, we'll be refering back to this object constantly
Set objFSO = CreateObject("Scripting.FileSystemObject")

'Stuff our folder (shoes) into an object we can manipulate
Set objFolder = objFSO.GetFolder(Server.MapPath(parentPath))
    %>
</div>
```

First, we create our FSO object, objFSO, which is a Scripting.FileSystemObject. Next, we need to build our folder object. We just use the GetFolder method of objFSO and give it the path of the folder we want to use. In this case, we're going to give it the path to our Shoes directory, which is stored in parentPath. Server.MapPath(parentPath) gives us the full folder name on the drive.

Our objFolder variable now contains a collection of subfolders and files. Since it's a collection we can loop through it just like we would an array or a Request collection, using a For Each ... Next loop (see *Chapter 2* for more on looping).

```
'Stuff our folder (shoes) into an object we can manipulate
Set objFolder = objFSO.GetFolder(Server.MapPath(parentPath))
```

```
'=======
'Loop through subfolders
'=======
'Loop through all of the subfolders in our parent folder and
'output their names with a link to display the particular gallery.
For Each SubFolder In objFolder.SubFolders
  theName = SubFolder.Name 'Get the folder's name
  Response.Write("<a href=""default.asp?gal=" & theName & """>" &_
    Replace(theName,"-"," ") & "</a>")
  'Is this the folder we're currently looking at, if so, add an indicator
  If galPath = theName Then Response.Write(" &laquo;")
  Response.Write("<br />")
Next
Set objFolder = Nothing
    %>
<a href="default.asp">Home</a></div>
```

Remember that we declared a `SubFolder` variable earlier in the page. That variable is used to store the current folder in the `SubFolders` collection of our `Folder` object (`objFolder.SubFolders`). So the `For ... Each` loop will run once for each subfolder under the `Shoes` directory, storing the current subfolder's information in the `SubFolder` variable.

On the second line in the `For ... Each` loop we've assigned the subfolder's name to the `theName` variable using the `.Name` property of the subfolder. This allows us to use the name of the subfolder multiple times without having to go back to the `objFolder` object.

We're going to replace any hyphens for the link text so we have a nice pretty name for the link

Next we need to write out a link for the user to click. Our link needs to include the `gal` Querystring so we know what gallery to show, so our link will be "`default.asp?gal=theName`". We've just reused `theName` to add it to the Querystring. After that we write out the text for our link, which will also be `theName`, the only difference being we're going to replace any hyphens for the link text so we have a nice pretty name for the link (see the *Our sample application folder structure* screenshot earlier in this section).

The final bit for each gallery link is to determine if it's the current gallery selected. We can compare `galPath` and `theName` and, if they're equal, we know that the user is viewing that particular gallery. We could change the color of the link, remove the hypertext, or (as in our example) just add a << after the gallery. After that we just add a line break and we're done. All that's left is to destroy the `objFolder` object (since we're done with it) and manually create a link to get back to the page without any gallery selected.

Displaying the Images

Now that we have all of our navigation pieces in place, we need to build the actual image gallery section. We're going to start with a simple `If ... Then` statement to see if the user has actually selected a gallery to view.

```
<div id="GalleryPhotos">
  <%
    '=======
    'Output gallery
    '=======
    If galPath <> "" AND _
        objFSO.FolderExists(Server.MapPath(parentPath & galPath)) Then
      'Do gallery stuff
    Else
      Response.Write("<p>Choose a gallery to view.</p>")
    End If
  %>
</div>
```

The `If` statement makes sure that the user has indeed chosen a gallery to view by checking `galPath` isn't empty, also checking to make sure that the gallery folder actually exists. If they entered "`../myfolder`" into the Querystring and `myfolder` doesn't exist, we don't want to throw an error. The `FolderExists` method of the FSO object will return `True` or `False` based on whether the folder path supplied actually exists.

We're also going to need some variables for building our thumbnail image gallery:

```
<%
    '=======
    'Output gallery
    '=======
    If galPath <> "" AND objFSO.FolderExists(Server.MapPath(parentPath & galPath))
Then
        Dim strFullSizeFolder, objThumbFolder, File

        'Used to track how many cells in a row.
        Dim cellCounter : cellCounter = 1

        'Used to determine how many columns we want in our display table.
        Dim numCols : numCols = 4

        'Stores cell contents and defines a generic counter
        Dim cellContents, i

        'Folder path for full size images.
        strFullSizeFolder = Server.MapPath(galPathFull & "/FullSize/")
        'Object containing all the files in the thumbs folder.
        Set objThumbFolder = objFSO.GetFolder(Server.MapPath(galPathFull & _
            "/Thumbs/"))
    Else
```

Our variables include a container for our files (`File`), a generic counter we're going to use to make sure we get the right number of cells in each row (`cellCounter`), the number of columns we want for our thumbnail table (`numCols`), a container for our table cell contents (`cellContents`), and another generic counter for use in our loops (`i`).

We've also created a variable for the full folder path to our full size images (`strFullSizeFolder`), and we've created a new object, `objThumbFolder`, which contains all of the folder contents for our thumbnail images. We've used the `GetFolder` method again to get the contents of the `Thumbs` folder.

Now we need to start outputting our images. We'll start by opening the table and looping through the images, and then we'll close the table when we're done.

```
        'Folder path for full size images.
        strFullSizeFolder= Server.MapPath(galPathFull & "/FullSize/")

        'Object containing all the files in the thumbs folder.
        Set objThumbFolder = objFSO.GetFolder(Server.MapPath(galPathFull & _
            "/Thumbs/"))
        Response.Write("<table border=""1"">")

        'Loop through all of the files in the thumbnail folder
        For Each File In objThumbFolder.Files
            theName = File.Name 'Get the filename to use throughout the loop
            cellContents = "<img src=""" & galPathFull &_
                            "/Thumbs/" & theName & """ />"

        Next
        Response.Write("</table>")
    Else
```

You should note that we're doing the same thing with the files that we did with the subfolders earlier. We're just looping through the `File` collection of the `objThumbFolder` object. As we enter the loop, we're going to clear out the `cellContents` variable, since it will still have content left over from the previous file. We then set `theName` to the file's name by using the `Name` property of the `File` we're currently using. Next we simply have to build the path to our thumbnail image, so we stuff the `<img>` tag into `cellContents`, with the `src` attribute built from our path pieces. Don't worry about the table cell information yet; we'll cover that in a bit.

There's one problem with this approach. We don't have a height and width for our images because we don't have that information stored anywhere. Without a height and width we could run into some rendering anomalies (such as tables jumping around as the browser determines the image sizes) and could actually slow page loading.

If we had the images listed in a database, we could store the height and width inside the database.

To fix this we're going to use a script from *http://www.learnasp.com/learn/graphicdetect.asp* by Daniel Gorroño Santurtzi, which reads an image file and returns the height and width of the image – you'll find the `imgsize.asp` file in the code download for this chapter. We just need to add an `#include` line to the top of our gallery page (`default.asp`) to pull in the image size functions:

```
<%@LANGUAGE="VBSCRIPT" CODEPAGE="1252"%>
<% Option Explicit %>
<!--#include file="imgsize.asp" -->
<html xmlns="http://www.w3.org/1999/xhtml">
```

With these functions now available to us, we'll grab the image size like so:

```
        theName = File.Name 'Get the filename to use throughout the loop

        'Get height and width of thumbnail using imgsize functions
        HW = ReadImg(galPathFull & "/Thumbs/" & theName)
        cellContents = "<img src=""" & galPathFull &_
            "/Thumbs/" & theName & """ height=""" & HW(0) &_
            """ width=""" & HW(1) & """ alt=""View larger image of " &_
            objFso.GetBaseName(File.Path) & """ />"
    Next
```

The `HW` variable is actually an array, which stores our image's height and width. We can then use the values in that array to write out the image height and width in our `<img>` tag. Also notice that we've added an `alt` attribute to the image. The `GetBaseName` method of the FSO object returns the filename minus any path information or the file extension. So if our image is named `myshoe.jpg` then `GetBaseName` will return `myshoe`.

Now that we have our thumbnails being written out to the page we need to write a link to our full-size image, but we also need to make sure that there is a full-size image to display in the first place. If you're turning this application over to a client, they could very well upload a thumbnail without uploading the corresponding full-size image.

...you'd probably rather have an image without a link than a link to a broken pop-up window, right?

In this situation, I think you'd probably rather have an image without a link than a link to a broken pop-up window, right?

```
cellContents = cellContents & "<img src="""" & galPathFull &_
        "/Thumbs/" & theName & """ height="""" & HW(0) &_
        """ width="""" & HW(1) & """ alt=""""View larger image of " &_
        objFso.GetBaseName(File.Path) & """ />"
```

```
    'Does a full size image exist?
    If objFSO.FileExists(strFullSizeFolder & "\" & theName) Then
        'Get height and weight of full size image from imgsize functions
        HW = ReadImg(galPathFull & "/FullSize/" & theName)
        cellContents = "<a href=""""javascript:void(0);"" _
                onclick=""""openPictureWindow_Fever('" &_
                objFSO.GetExtensionName(theName) & "','" &_
                galPathFull & "/FullSize/" & theName & "','" & HW(1) &_
                "','" & HW(0) & "','Large Image','100','100');"""">" &_
                cellContents & "</a>"
    End If
Next
```

In this new block of code we're using the `FileExists` method of the FSO object to determine if our full-size image actually does exist. The `FileExists` method returns `True` or `False`, based on whether the file path supplied to the method actually exists. Using this method we can safely build a link if the full-size image is actually there. If we wanted to, we could write an `Else` statement to clear out the `cellContents` variable if there wasn't a full-size image, and prevent any orphaned thumbnails from displaying.

You should also note that I've used a Behavior (**Open Picture Window Fever!** from *DreamweaverFever.com*, see *http://dreamweaverfever.com/grow/* and download your copy) to display my pop-ups. We first put the JavaScript into the head of the document by placing an image on the page in Design View and applying the Behavior from *Design Behaviors > + Fever > Open Picture Window Fever!* panel. Here is the interface the Behavior uses:

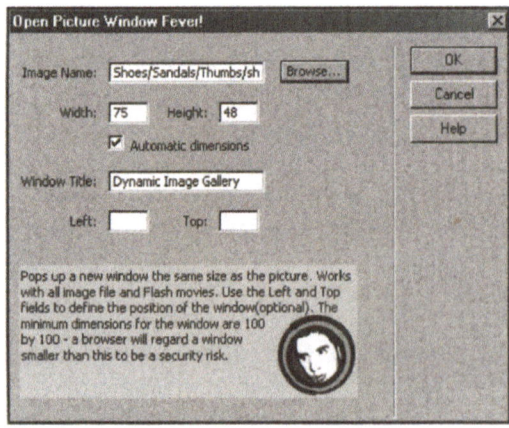

The Open Picture Window Fever! dialog

We then copied the generated JavaScript code from the new link, converted it to a VBScript string, and added it to my code block. Lastly, we simply delete the image we added to the page, leaving our Behavior's JavaScript intact.

Part of the `OpenPictureWindow_Fever` syntax is the file image type (`jpg`, `gif`, `png`, etc.) We can use the `GetExtensionName` method (I love these method names!) to grab the file extension for our full-size image.

Note again that we keep going back to that root FSO object to grab filenames, extensions, and paths from multiple files – you should reuse objects as much as possible, rather than creating additional objects. We've also reused the HW variable to store the full-size image's height and width. This makes it possible for every pop-up window to be customized to fit each full-size image. Lastly, we just wrapped the link around our cellContents variable, which already contained the path to our thumbnail image.

We now have our thumbnail and full-size image worked out, so next we need to figure out how to build our table cells. This doesn't involve the FSO object at all, instead going back to our conditional statements from *Chapter 2*.

```
          cellContents = "<a href=""javascript:void(0);""" &_
              "onclick=""openPictureWindow_Fever('" &_
              objFSO.GetExtensionName(theName) & "','" &_
              galPathFull & "/FullSize/" & theName & "','" & HW(1) &_
              "','" & HW(0) & "','Large Image','100','100');"">" &_
              cellContents & "</a>"
      End If

      Select Case cellCounter
        'If this is the first item in a row, open the row
        Case 1
          Response.Write("<tr><td>" & cellContents & "</td>")
          cellCounter = cellCounter + 1

        'If this is the last item in a row, close the row, and reset the
counter.
        Case numCols
          Response.Write("<td>" & cellContents & "</td></tr>")
          cellCounter = 1

        'Otherwise, add a cell and increment the counter.
        Case Else
          Response.Write("<td>" & cellContents & "</td>")
          cellCounter = cellCounter + 1
      End Select

    Next
```

Remember way back at the beginning we declared a cellCounter variable to determine which cell we were writing to the page? Well, the above Select Case statement compares the current cellCounter variable against the numCols variable, which determines how many cells to have in each row. If cellCounter is equal to 1, we open our row and increment our counter, since it's cell 1. If it's equal to the number of columns we want, then it's the last cell and we should end our row and reset the counter. If it meets neither of those criteria, it's a center cell, and we should just write our <td> tags and increment the counter.

At this point we're done with all of our FSO work, so we can destroy our FSO objects and do some table cleanup. We need to clean up the table to make sure that we actually write all of the necessary table cells into the table. Otherwise we'd end up with empty table cells on the final row of our thumbnail images.

8

File Handling

205

```
        Next
        'Destroy our objects
        Set objFSO = Nothing
        Set objThumbFolder = Nothing

        'If we've completed a row, or are at the beginning of a row, don't do
anything,
        'otherwise, finish the row with empty table cells.
        If cellCounter <= numCols AND cellCounter <> 1 Then
          For i = cellCounter to numCols
            Response.Write("<td> </td>")
          Next
            Response.Write("</tr>")
        End If
        Response.Write("</table>")
      Else
        Response.Write("<p>Choose a gallery to view.</p>")
      End If
    %>
</div>
```

We need to set both `objFSO` and `objThumbFolder` to `Nothing` in order to clear up those resources on the server. We also need compare our `cellCounter` against the `numCols` again to make sure we put enough empty table cells to finish up the last row in our table.

```
<div id="GalleryHeader">
    <h1>Dynamic Image Gallery<% If galPath <> "" Then _
                            Response.Write(" &raquo; " & galPath)%></h1>
</div>
```

The last thing we need to do is build the header for our gallery, so that the user has some other indication of the gallery they're viewing.

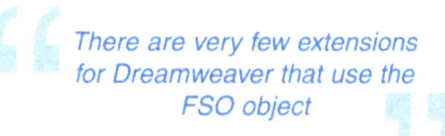

There are very few extensions for Dreamweaver that use the FSO object

And that's it. You now have a full online gallery using just one single ASP page. You'll find the entire page, `default.asp`, in the code download. Unfortunately, there are very few extensions for Dreamweaver that use the FSO object. The only one currently out there is **MFXListFolder** from *http://jjooee.media3.net/udtmp/index2.htm*, which allows you to display a list of all of the files and subfolders of a specified folder. The extension has nice code for looping through an infinite number of subfolders, allowing you to generate a page with the entire directory structure of your site.

Reading Text Files

The above example is all well and good, but what if we wanted to give each gallery its own unique description at the top of the page? With our current code base, that's simply not possible. There's no identifying information to pull a description from, so we'd need to supply this information in some way. We could build a database to store the information in, but that means dealing with relational information and just adds complexity to a very simple application.

What if it were possible to pull in text from a separate file? This would make it possible for the client to just upload a regular text file composed in Notepad containing the description they want displayed for each gallery. Or you could build an online form for them to change the content of the text file (more on this in a bit).

You could build an online form to change the content of the text file

To make this happen we need to set another standard for our application, a naming standard for our text files. We're going to have a `description.txt` file in each of our image gallery folders that will store the description for that set of images. It will contain any HTML code and text we want to be able to display; it just has to be properly formed code or it will be displayed incorrectly on the page. The result is going to be the same as if we'd copied the code out of the text file and pasted it into our document. This could potentially be handled as an include, but we'll see how this could be expanded on after we finish this simple example.

If we go back to our gallery (`default.asp`), we can just add the following code (see `default2.asp` for the full updated code):

```
<%
   '=======
   'Output gallery
   '=======
   If galPath <> "" AND _
        objFSO.FolderExists(Server.MapPath(parentPath & galPath)) Then
     If objFSO.FileExists(Server.MapPath(galPathFull & _
                                  "/description.txt")) Then
       'Display our gallery description.
       Dim objFile, objTextStream, txtFile
       Set objFile = objFSO.GetFile(Server.MapPath(galPathFull & _
           "/description.txt"))
       Set objTextStream = objFile.OpenAsTextStream(1)
       Response.Write("<p>" & objTextStream.ReadAll & "</p>")
       Set objFile = Nothing
     Set objTExtStream = Nothing
   End If

     Dim strFullSizeFolder, objThumbFolder, File
```

We've added a check to see if there is a `description.txt` file: if so, the content of that file is to be displayed. In order to display the text we need to create two more objects. The first, `objFile`, will contain the reference for `description.txt` file. The second, `objTextStream`, will act as the conduit for the text content of the file. The `OpenAsTextStream` method actually opens the text file and returns an object that can be used to read or write to the file.

These are just the numbers that ASP specifies to represent these things.

You'll notice that we pass argument `1` with this method. This means that we're opening the file to read. If we needed to write to the file (overwriting everything else in it) we'd use the number `2`, or if we wanted to append additional text to the bottom of the file we'd use `8`.

Now all that's left to do is output the content. The `ReadAll` method of the `TextStream` object reads the entire file and returns a string with the content. That's great, but what good does that really do you? You could just as easily use an include file in this instance.

But what if you wanted to use an HTML file, and just return a specific portion of it? Let's assume that we have a directory of static HTML files, and we want to be able to output a date that's in a comment on each of those pages. Let's set up each of our HTML files like this (see the HTML content of the `FileList` folder in the code download):

```
<html>
<head>
  <title>Page 1</title>
</head>
<body>
  <p>This is 1.html </p>
  <p>Date: <!--StartDate-->Feb 2, 2002<!--EndDate--></p>
</body>
</html>
```

Notice that the second paragraph element has two comments wrapped around the date. We have an entire folder filled with files that each have this same setup, and we want to be able to have an index page that displays each of these dates with a link to the particular file associated with it. With the `TextStream` objects we can read information out of any text-based file. We'll use this to get the date out of each of our files with a bit of simple string manipulation. We're going to use this function to find specified start and end tags, and return the content in between those two tags. The following is found at the end of the `default.asp` for this example, in the `FileList` folder:

```
<%
  Private Function GetString(strStartTag, strEndTag, strHTML)
    'Declare variables
    Dim intStart   'Holds the start position in the file
    Dim intEnd     'Holds the end position in the file
    'Get the start position in the file of the tag
    intStart = InStr(1, LCase(strHTML), strStartTag, 1)

    'If the start tag exists
    If NOT intStart = 0 Then
      'Get the end position of the HTML tag
      intStart = intStart + Len(strStartTag)

      'Get the position in the file of the closing tag for the element
      intEnd = InStr(intStart, LCase(strHTML), strEndTag, 1)

      'Read in the content of the element from the file for the function to return
      GetString = Trim(Mid(strHTML, intStart, (intEnd - intStart)))

    Else
      'There is no content for the element.
      GetString = ""
    End If
  End Function
%>
```

The function has three arguments, strStartTag, strEndTag, and strHTML. The strStartTag and strEndTag arguments will contain our <!—StartDate—> and <!—EndDate—> comments. The strHTML argument will contain the text of our HTML document that we're going to read with the ReadAll method.

Now all we have to do is loop through the folder, and search each of our HTML files.

```
<%
  Dim objFSO, objFolderFSO, myFolder
  Set objFSO = Server.CreateObject("Scripting.FileSystemObject")

  myFolder = Server.MapPath(".")

  'If directory does not exist, return an error.
  If NOT objFSO.FolderExists(MyFolder) Then
    Response.Write "Invalid folder: " & MyFolder
    Response.End
  End If

  Set objFolderFSO = objFSO.GetFolder(MyFolder)

  'Use a For Each ... Next loop to display the files
  Dim File, objFileFSO, objTextStream, myText
  For Each File in objFolderFSO.Files
    set objFileFSO = objFSO.GetFile(File.Path)
    set objTextStream = objFileFSO.OpenAsTextStream(1)
    myText = objTextStream.ReadAll
    Response.Write("<a href=""" & File.name & """>" &_
      GetString("<title>","</title>", myText) & "</a>, " &_
      GetString("<!—StartDate—>","<!—EndDate—>",myText) & "<br />")
  Next
%>
```

The finished page looks like this in the browser:

> You could add some file
> extension checks

Hopefully the gears are turning in your head now. This is a simplistic example, and will pick up the default.asp file as well. If you're familiar with Dreamweaver Templates you might remember that Dreamweaver uses comments for its template syntax. This means that you could search a folder of template files for a specific editable area and output that information, making it possible to build a site map for a folder or an entire site by looping through all of the files. You could also add some file extension checks to make sure you only list .html files or just .asp files.

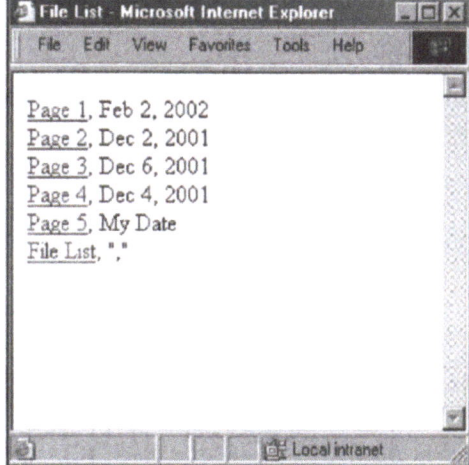

The results of our looping, file reading, and text manipulations

8

File Handling

Writing a Text File

Going back to our gallery example, what if we wanted to allow the client to change the description through a web page? We can do this using a few more methods ofz the `TextStream` objects. What we're going to do now is build an administrative page that will show the client what's currently in the `description.txt` file and allow them to add to the end of the file or overwrite the contents of the file.

First thing we need to do is build a page to display the text files available to edit and a form to make changes. We're going to start in the samw way we did on our gallery. We need a place to show links to the galleries, and a place to put our form. Here's the skeleton we're going to use; as you can see it's based on the `default.asp` file we created earlier. The only thing I changed is the link from `default.asp` to `manager.asp` in the subfolder loop:

```asp
<%@LANGUAGE="VBSCRIPT" CODEPAGE="1252"%>
<% Option Explicit %>
<?xml version="1.0" encoding="iso-8859-1"?>
<!DOCTYPE html PUBLIC "-//W3C//DTD XHTML 1.0 Transitional//EN"
"http://www.w3.org/TR/xhtml1/DTD/xhtml1-transitional.dtd">
<html xmlns="http://www.w3.org/1999/xhtml">
<head>
<title>Gallery Manager</title>
<meta http-equiv="Content-Type" content="text/html; charset=iso-8859-1">
<style type="text/css">
<!—CSS same as default.asp —>
</style>
</head>
<body>
<div id="GalleryNav"><%
'=======
'Variable Declaration
'=======

' Same as in default.asp

'=======
'Loop through subfolders
'=======
'Loop through all of the subfolders in our parent folder and output their names
'with a link to display the particular gallery.
For Each SubFolder In objFolder.SubFolders
   theName = SubFolder.Name 'Get the folder's name
   Response.Write("<a href=""manager.asp?gal=" & theName & """>" &_
    Replace(theName,"-"," ") & "</a>")
   'Is this the folder we're currently looking at, if so, add an indicator
   If galPath = theName Then Response.Write(" &laquo;")
   Response.Write("<br />")
Next
Set objFolder = Nothing
%></div>
<div id="GalleryPhotos">
    <% If Request.QueryString("gal") <> "" Then %>
Form goes here
<% Else %>
Choose a gallery.
<% End If %>
```

```
</div>
<div id="GalleryHeader"><h1>Gallery Manager</h1></div>
</body>
</html>
```

So now we need to build our form area. We're just going to have a form field that contains the current
`description.txt` content so it can either be replaced or appended to. This is what our form is going
to look like in Dreamweaver:

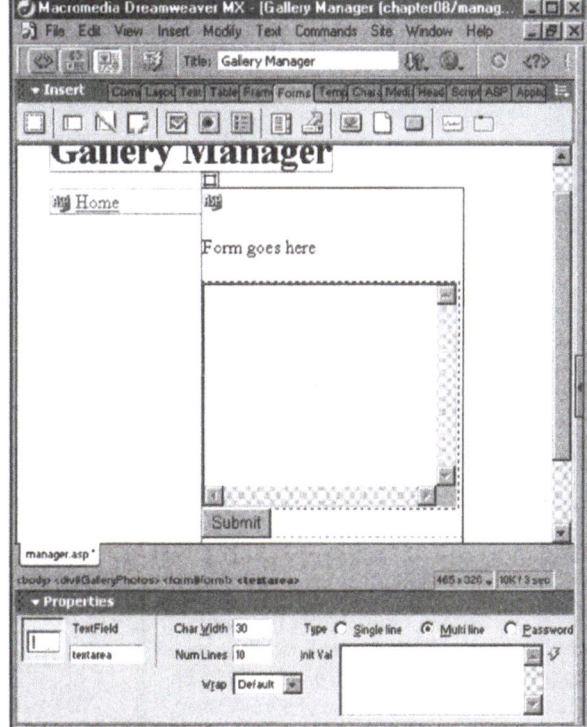

Our form, with submit button

Now that we have our form on the page
we need to pull in some more dynamic
variables. First, we need to set the
action of the form based on the
Querystring of the page, and second,
we need to pull in the contents of the
`description.txt` file if there is one.
First, the form tag; we need to make
sure that we submit it back to the page
with the same Querystring so we stay on
the same gallery's `description.txt`:

```
<% If Request.QueryString("gal") <> "" Then %>
  <p>Form goes here</p>
  <form action="manager.asp?<%= Request.QueryString %>" method="post" name="form1"
    id="form1">
    <textarea name="Description" cols="30" rows="10" id="Description"></textarea>
    <br />
    <input type="submit" name="Submit" value="Submit">
  </form>
<% Else %>
```

We can use `Request.QueryString` (without specifying an exact variable) to get the entire
Querystring. Next we need to pay attention to the `textarea`. We're going to reuse some code from
`default2.asp` to check for the existence of `description.txt`, and if it exists, fill our `textarea` with
the contents:

```
<%
Dim forReading : forReading = 1
Dim forWriting : forWriting = 2
Dim objFile, objTextStream
Dim textPath : textPath = Server.MapPath(galPathFull & "/description.txt")
%>
   <form action="manager.asp?<%= Request.QueryString %>" method="post" name="form1"
       id="form1">
     <textarea name="Description" cols="30" rows="10" id="Description"><%
     'Display our gallery description.
     If objFSO.FileExists(textPath) Then
       Set objFile = objFSO.GetFile(textPath)
       Set objTextStream = objFile.OpenAsTextStream(forReading)
       Response.Write(objTextStream.ReadAll)
       Set objFile = Nothing
       Set objTextStream = Nothing
     End If
   Set objFSO = Nothing
%></textarea>
     <br />
     <input type="submit" name="Submit" value="Submit" />
   </form>
```

I've created a `textPath` variable to hold the absolute path to `description.txt` since we're going to be using that path repeatedly

I've declared the variables before the text area and added two new variables. The `forReading` and `forWriting` just hold the numbers 1 and 2 so that we can easily see what we're doing with a text file when we use the `OpenAsTextStream` method. I've also created a `textPath` variable to hold the absolute path to `description.txt` since we're going to be using that path repeatedly. So now if we open our page in the browser and choose *Clogs*, we should see something like this:

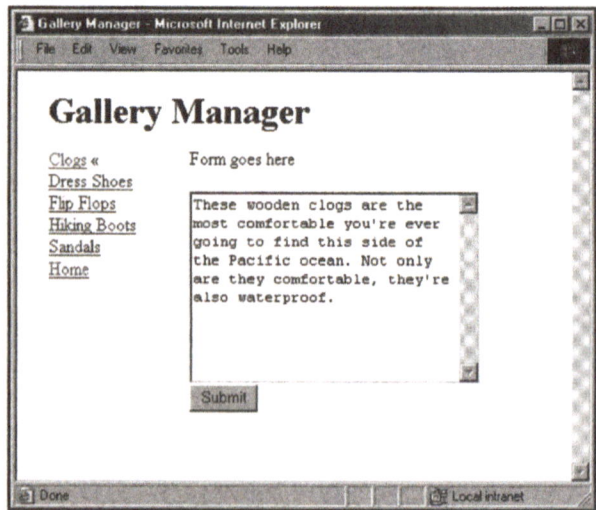

We already have a description for the Clogs gallery

Now we need to write our code for when the form is submitted. We have to do two things. First, we have to check and make sure that a `description.txt` file exists. If it does we just write in the new contents. If one doesn't exist, we need to create a new text file and then write in the new contents. So let's check to see that there's a valid text file; we can reuse some of the code from our `textarea`:

```
<%
Dim forReading : forReading = 1
Dim forWriting : forWriting = 2
Dim objFile, objTextStream
Dim textPath : textPath = Server.MapPath(galPathFull & "/description.txt")

If Request.Form("submit") <> "" Then 'check for form submission
  'Check for description.txt
  If NOT objFSO.FileExists(textPath) Then
    Set objFile = objFSO.CreateTextFile(textPath)
  End if
End If%>

  <form action="manager.asp?<%= Request.QueryString %>" method="post"
name="form1" id="form1">
```

If you get a *Permission Denied* error on the `Set objFile` line, make sure that the IUSR account has **Full Control** permissions on the directory you're trying to add the text file to. By default, most web hosts set the permissions to read-only, which means you won't be able to modify files or create new ones. If you're working locally, right-click your parent folder, `Shoes` for instance, and choose *Properties*, then *Security*. Make sure that the IUSR account has Full Control:

Once you get the new file creation working, if you submit the form you'll probably end up getting an *Input past end of file* error in your text area. This is because you're trying to read the contents of an empty text file. To prevent the error we're going to add `On Error Resume Next` directly before the text read, and to stop it from happening to future text files we're going to immediately add new content to our text file after creating it. So our final form looks like this:

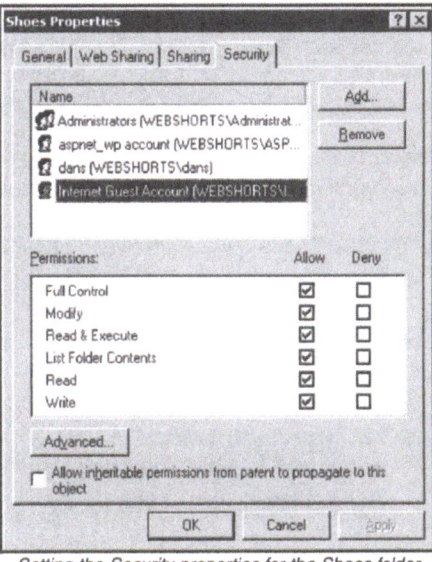

Setting the Security properties for the Shoes folder

```
<%
Dim forReading : forReading = 1
Dim forWriting : forWriting = 2
Dim objFile, objTextStream
Dim textPath : textPath = Server.MapPath(galPathFull & "/description.txt")

If Request.Form("submit") <> "" Then 'check for form submission
  'Check for description.txt
  If NOT objFSO.FileExists(textPath) Then
    Set objFile = objFSO.CreateTextFile(textPath)
  End if
```

```
   Set objFile = objFSO.OpenTextFile(textPath,forWriting)
   objFile.Write(Request.Form("Description"))
End If
%>
<form action="manager.asp?<%= Request.QueryString %>" method="post" name="form1"
    id="form1">
   <textarea name="Description" cols="30" rows="10" id="Description"><%
      'Display our gallery description.
      If objFSO.FileExists(textPath) Then
         Set objFile = objFSO.GetFile(textPath)
         Set objTextStream = objFile.OpenAsTextStream(forReading)
      On Error Resume Next
         Response.Write(objTextStream.ReadAll)
         Set objFile = Nothing
         Set objTextStream = Nothing
      End If
      Set objFSO = Nothing
%></textarea>
   <br />
   <input type="submit" name="Submit" value="Submit" />
</form>
```

And that's it. The `OpenTextFile` method takes two arguments. The name of the text file you want to open and what to open it for, in our case `forWriting`. We immediately use the `Write` method and write the contents of the `Description` form field to the text file.

We've covered quite a few of the properties and methods of the FSO object but there are a lot more. You can find them all at the MSDN Library along with examples and explanations:

http://msdn.microsoft.com/library/library/en-us/script56/html/fsooriScriptingRun-TimeReference.asp

Uploading Files

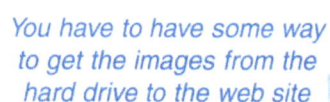
You have to have some way to get the images from the hard drive to the web site

Now that you have this wonderful gallery up and running, how are you going to manage it? If you're doing it yourself you certainly know how to use FTP to upload and manage files. But if you're turning the gallery over to a client who's not computer-literate you'll need to either teach them how to use FTP (at great expense and pain) or give them a way to do it all through a web form on their site. You have to have some way to get the images from your client's hard drive to the web site. This is a bit harder than it sounds due to the binary nature of files. By default, an ASP server doesn't have any mechanism for handling binary files and knowing how to piece them back together after they're sent from the client's web browser. The server has to know what to do with the binary file and where to put it.

That's where file upload scripts come into play. I'd like to say that the rest of this chapter would teach you how to build your own, but we don't have enough space, and there are so many good products already out there that it seems counterproductive to write our own. I'll give you links to a few server components (one of which is free), a few free pure ASP solutions, and finally a look at a commercial pure ASP upload extension for Dreamweaver.

The only preparation work you need to do to ensure you can upload files to your server is make sure that the file you're going to upload to has the proper permissions assigned. Most hosts allow the IUSR account (the user account that Internet users use) only read permission on a directory. In order to upload files to a directory the IUSR has to have at least write permission. In order to overwrite a file, they need at least modify permission. If the IUSR account doesn't have appropriate permissions the user will get a *Permission denied* error message.

You'll need to set the permissions to allow whatever operations you'd like the user to be able to perform. If you're testing locally, you can change your permissions by right-clicking the directory you want to upload to and choosing *Properties*. Click the *Security* tab and check the permission settings, as seen below:

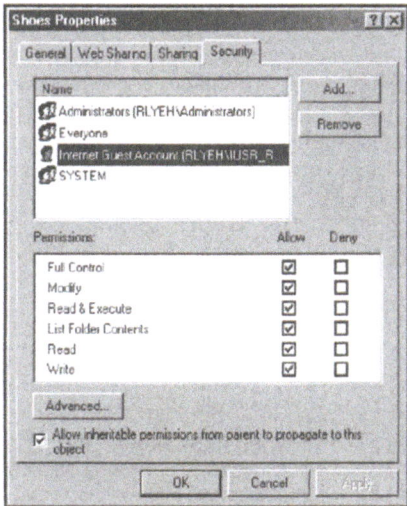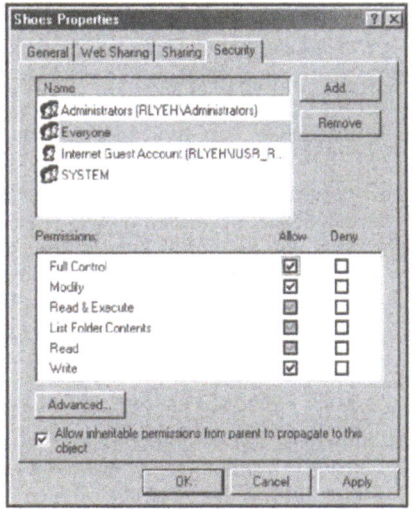

If you already have the *Everyone* group with *Full Control* or the *IUSR* group with *Full Control* you'll be able to upload files.

If you've removed the *Everyone* group or don't have the *IUSR* group, you'll need to add it. Click *Add* to find and add the `IUSR_machinename` account and give them the appropriate permissions.

Encoding

Another thing to watch out for is to make sure that you use the correct encoding when submitting a form for uploading a file. By default a web browser sends all of its information in plain text, since that's what is usually passed between client and server. In order to send files to the server the browser and server both need to know what to expect.

To set the proper encoding type, choose *multipart/form-data* from the *Enctype* drop-down in the form *Property Inspector*.

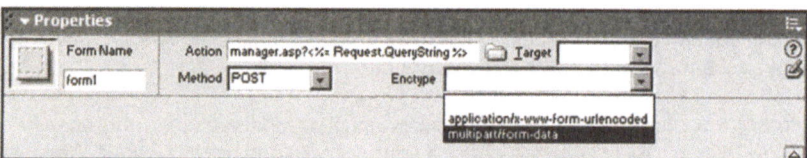

Upload Components

The best way to upload a file to a server is by using a professional third-party component to do the work for you. Windows 2000 and ASP don't have anything built in to handle this functionality. It can be done with pure ASP (I'll show you a free script and commercial Dreamweaver extension in a bit) but the preferred method is to use something server-side to handle the work for you. Here are a few components I've used in the past. I won't cover their syntax since every component works a little bit differently and the component sites have lots of in-depth coverage already.

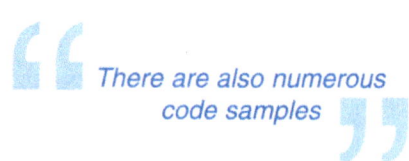

There are also numerous code samples

To find out which file upload components may be installed on your web server, you can use the component checker from PensaWorks (*http://www.pensaworks.com/prg_com.asp*). The checker checks for more than 300 different components so you may find at least one upload component your host may have installed.

aspSmartUpload

aspSmartUpload from *aspSmart.com* is free, and has been around for several years. If you're running your own server (or testing locally) you can download and install it for free from *http://www.aspsmart.com/aspSmartUpload/*. There are also numerous code samples for uploading (and downloading) multiple files.

ASPUpload

ASPUpload from *http://www.aspupload.com* is another long -established upload component. You can find a 30-day evaluation download at *http://www.aspupload.com/download.html*. The cost per server is $149.00. You can find instructions at *http://www.aspupload.com/manual.html*. The UltraSuite for Dreamweaver MX at *http://www.ultrasuite.com/products/us_aspvbs_dmx/* includes several extensions for working with ASPUpload.

SA-FileUp

SoftArtisan's FileUp (*http://www.softartisans.com/softartisans/saf.html*) is another robust component that includes support for checking unique filenames, uploading entire directories, and uploads to memory. You can download an evaluation version at *http://support.softartisans.com/eval.aspx*. SA-FileUp is $299.00 per server. The UltraSuite for Dreamweaver MX at *http://www.ultrasuite.com/products/us_aspvbs_dmx/* includes several extensions for working with SA-FileUp.

Pure ASP Solutions

There aren't a whole lot of pure ASP upload scripts. The only three that I've used consistently are Pure ASP File Upload from ASP 101 at *http://www.asp101.com/articles/jacob/scriptupload.asp*, a file upload class written by the guys at 4guysfromrolla at *http://www.4guysfromrolla.com/webtech/012401-1.shtml* and Pure ASP Upload for Dreamweaver at *http://dmxzone.com/index.asp?TypeId=3&CatId=69*. The links provided also supply instructions on how to use the upload code.

By far my favorite is Pure ASP Upload from DMXZone. It is a commercial extension but saves me so much time that I'd rather use it than the free alternatives. It also doesn't require any additional software on the server.

Summary

In this chapter we've introduced you to working with files and folders on your web server. The `FileSystemObject` gives you an entire new world to explore.

We first covered all of the objects and collections included in FSO and explained what each of them contains. After that we covered the `Server.MapPath` method, which isn't actually part of FSO but is used extensively for finding physical paths on the server.

Next we learned how to build a dynamic image gallery that introduced you to a large number of properties and methods for working with FSO. After that we covered both reading and writing text files, and built a small text file manager for our gallery.

Finally we looked at uploading files to the web server. We discussed a free server component and two commercial ones, and finally a few pure ASP solutions.

8

File Handling

9

- An introduction to XML

- Working with XML vocabularies in Dreamweaver MX

- Using XML with Dreamweaver templates

- Transforming XML with Extensible Stylesheet Language Transformations (XSLT) via ASP

Author: Dan Short

Using XML with ASP

It seems that every day a new product comes out with X in the name – Windows XP, Mac OS X (yes, I know it means 10 here, but it's still an X) and Dreamweaver MX. **XML** (or **Extensible Markup Language**) will certainly be new to some, but it has been around for a while now.

XML isn't a new programming language, and it's not (strictly speaking) a database (although there are XML-native databases): it's a simple way of storing information in a plain-text file using self-describing tags. XML is a markup language that can contain as many custom elements as you feel necessary to describe your data. That means that if we have an address in our XML file, we can stick it in an `<address>` element so we know instantly that it's an address.

" XML is a markup language that can contain as many custom elementss as you feel necessary to describe your data "

Because XML is a plain-text file, it's also completely platform-independent. This means that XML data is completely portable between UNIX, Windows, or Linux servers. This comes in handy if you need to share information between different sites on different servers.

In this chapter we're going to do the following:

- Explain what XML is, and how to define your XML files and work with them in Dreamweaver
- Look at how to work with XML and Dreamweaver templates
- Transform our XML into pretty HTML pages
- Go over how to display someone else's XML on your own site

" Because XML is a plain-text file, it's also completely platform-independent "

<defined>XML</defined>

XML stands for Extensible Markup Language, meaning that you can change the element set to meet your needs, adding new elements and attributes as necessary. Unlike HTML, you're not limited by a predefined set of elements, and your elements can actually describe the data that they contain.

In fact, the only thing an XML page has to contain is the **XML declaration** (`<?xml ... ?>`), and even this can be left off in some instances. The XML declaration firstly states that this is an XML document we are dealing with, and tells an XML Parser (such as IE6's built-in MSXML parser, or the MSXML server-side components, which we'll cover later) which version of XML the page is using. At the time of writing, you will probably only have to deal with `<?xml version="1.0"?>` – XML 1.0 is the current working standard, with XML 1.1 on the way (see *http://www.w3.org/XML/Core/* for more details).

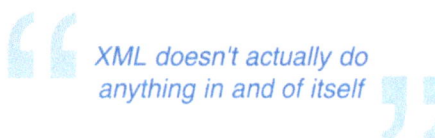
XML doesn't actually do anything in and of itself

By now you're probably still wondering what XML does. Well, XML doesn't actually do anything in and of itself. XML is a data storage medium that just happens to be in plain text. XML is more like a mini database than an HTML page, as its sole purpose is to store and describe data.

Because they are used for data storage and retrieval, your XML files must be *well formed* to ensure that they're easily portable from application to application. In fact, XML parsers are required to reject poorly formed XML documents in order to maintain the integrity of the language. We don't want the same thing that happened to HTML to happen to XML, where different browser manufacturers decided to do things in different ways. To be wellformed, your XML must follow the following rules:

- All elements must be closed – for example, `<br>` tags would need to be changed to `<br />`, and you couldn't get away with just having a `<p>` tag at the start of a paragraph (you would need a `</p>` tag at the end of the paragraph as well).

- XML element and attribute names are case-sensitive. In XML, `<mytag>` is a different element to `<myTag>`. Remember to watch your element and attribute name case as you build your XML. The case doesn't matter, since you're defining your own elements and attributes, but you should have a consistent naming convention throughout your document to make it easier to manage.

- XML elements must be properly nested. So `<strong><em>My tags</strong></em>` would cause an error – all elements must completely enclose all of their child elements. We'd need to change our example to `<strong><em>My tags</em></strong>`.

- Each XML document must have a root (or document) element. Just like your HTML pages have an <html> element containing all the other HTML content, all XML documents must have one and only one root element, which must contain all other child elements.

- Attribute values must always be quoted. In HTML you can get away with `<mytag value=1>`, but XML will throw a fit. All attribute values must be properly quoted, so instead we'd use `<mytag value="1">`.

- Attribute minimization isn't allowed. For example, in HTML you can define an attribute value to be equal to the attribute name, like this: `<input type="checkbox" checked>`. XML (and by inheritance, XHTML) doesn't allow this. You must explicitly declare both the attribute and its value, like this: `<input type="checkbox" checked="checked" />`.

Let's look at a simple example to demonstrate XML in action:

```xml
<?xml version="1.0" encoding="UTF-8"?>
<customer id="1">
  <name>Daniel Short</name>
  <address>
    <street>123 Oak Street</street>
    <city>Portland</city>
    <state>Oregon</state>
    <zip>97280</zip>
  </address>
</customer>
```

Notice that the elements describe exactly what they contain. The `<customer>` element contains the customer's customer ID and the `<address>` element contains child elements that contain all parts of their address: street, city, state, and zip. We can expand on this further by adding additional elements and attributes (attributes are extensible as well). Let's change our example so that the customer's first and last names are represented by attributes of the `<name>` element, rather than a separate element:

```xml
<?xml version="1.0" encoding="UTF-8"?>
<customer id="1">
  <name first="Daniel" last="Short" />
  <address>
    <street>123 Oak Street</street>
    <city>Portland</city>
    <state>Oregon</state>
    <zip>97280</zip>
  </address>
</customer>
```

We could also represent the first and last name as completely separate elements:

```xml
<firstname>Daniel</firstname>
<lastname>Short</lastname>
```

or as separate elements under a parent `<name>` element:

```xml
<name>
  <first>Daniel</first>
  <last>Short</last>
</name>
```

So as you can see, the XML language is infinitely mallable, allowing you to change it to suit your needs. We could continue to expand this XML pattern for as many customers as we want – we just have to add a single top-level element to contain all of our child elements. Let's add a `<customers>` element to contain all of our `<customer>` elements (see `address.xml` in the code download for this chapter):

```xml
<?xml version="1.0" encoding="UTF-8"?>
<customers>
  <customer id="1">
```

Using XML with ASP

```
<name>
      <first>Daniel</first>
      <last>Short</last>
   </name>
   <address>
      <street>123 Oak Street</street>
      <city>Portland</city>
      <state>Oregon</state>
      <zip>97280</zip>
   </address>
</customer>
<customer id="2">
   <name>
      <first>Omar</first>
      <last>Elbaga</last>
   </name>
   <address>
      <street>456 Pine Street</street>
      <city>Portland</city>
      <state>Oregon</state>
      <zip>97201</zip>
   </address>
</customer>
<customer id="2">
   <name>
      <first>Rob</first>
      <last>Turnbull</last>
   </name>
   <address>
      <street>789 Elm Street</street>
      <city>Portland</city>
      <state>Oregon</state>
      <zip>97219</zip>
   </address>
</customer>
</customers>
```

Working with XML Files

Working with XML files in Dreamweaver is like working with HTML files without Design View. Since you're just entering data (remember, XML doesn't do anything on its own), you only get Code View. You can, however, use all of Dreamweaver's code hinting technology to make it easier to work with your XML files.

Now you're probably thinking to yourself "but XML doesn't have any defined elements, how can I use Code Hints?" The answer is "no problem" – Dreamweaver's extensibility makes building your own custom tag libraries a cinch.

Let's return to our address example. We'll be working with the following custom elements:

- `<customers>`
- `<customer>`

- `<address>`
- `<name>`
- `<first>`
- `<last>`
- `<street>`
- `<city>`
- `<state>`
- `<zip>`

We might also need a few attributes, such as a `type` attribute for the address element to determine if it's a business or home address. Right now typing these elements into a new XML document doesn't do anything fancy, but with Dreamweaver's Tag Library we can add all of our custom elements and attributes and create our own code hints.

Building a Tag Library

The first thing we need to do is open the **Tag Library Editor**. You'll find it at *Edit > Tag Libraries...* When the *Tag Library Editor* first opens you'll see the HTML tag set expanded in the *Tags* window.

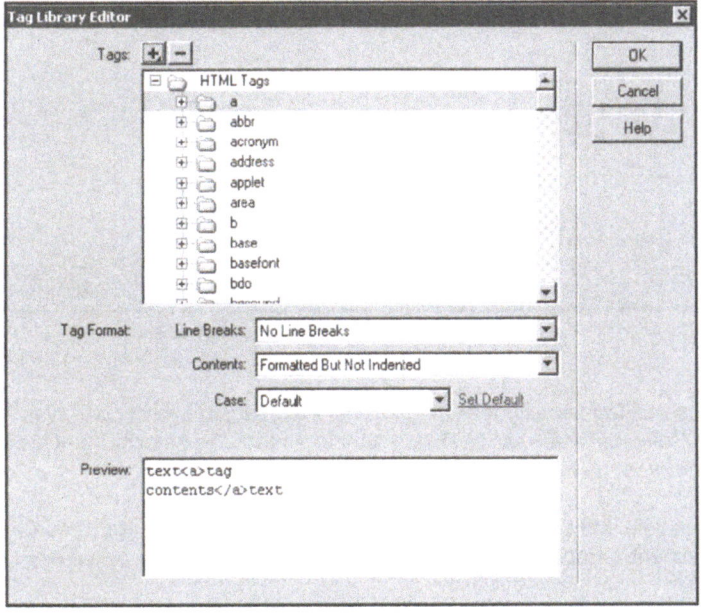

The Dreamweaver MX Tag Library Editor.

If you expand the first folder, you will see all of the attributes for the `<a>` element. Moving down the list you'll see every HTML element and every attribute that shows up in the *Code Hints* in *Code View*. Hopefully the gears are turning now and you can see how we can add our own custom elements for working with our XML files. To get started we need to add a brand-new library to the list. Click the *+* Icon and choose *New Tag Library*.

In the *New Tag Library* dialog, enter a name for the new Tag Library. This should just be a plain English description of the library so you know what kind of elements it will contain – we chose *Customer Information*.

After you click *OK* you'll see a new folder in the *Tags* window with your new name. If you look in the *Used In* window you should notice that *HTML* is checked by default. Uncheck *HTML* and scroll down to the bottom of the list and check the *XML* box. Your dialog should now look like this:

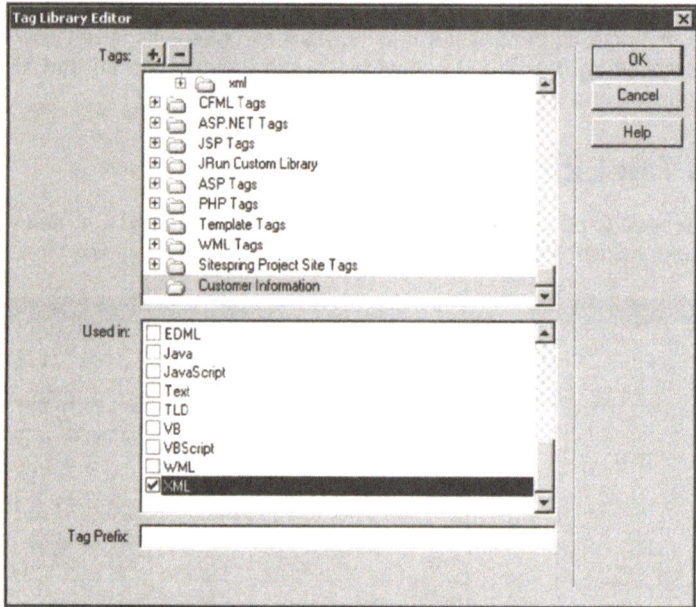

Adding our new Tag Library to the Tag Library Editor.

Now that we have our Tag Library defined, click the *+* icon again and choose *New Tags*. In the *New Tags* dialog the *Customer Information* library should already be selected. If it's not, just choose it from the *Tag Library* list menu.

In the *Tag Names* field you can enter a comma -separated list – here we need to enter the names of our XML elements, separated by commas, like so: `customers,customer,address,name, first,last,street,city,state,zip`

Also, it's a good idea to make sure that the *Have Matching End Tags* box is checked. If this box is checked, when you hit *Enter* after typing a tag it will add the appropriate closing tag. If you don't check this box, Dreamweaver won't take care of the close tags for you. The *New Tags* dialog box should now look like this:

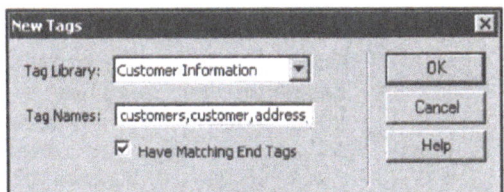

The New Tags dialog box.

After clicking *OK* you'll see all of the new elements listed under the *Customer Tags* library. You can click on each element and change the formatting attributes, an element at a time.

Now we need to add the `type` attribute for the `<address>` element and the `id` attribute for the `<customer>` element. First, click *address* in the *Tags* window, and click the + icon and choose *New Attributes*. To add our attribute, enter `type` in the *Attribute Names* field and click *OK*. Repeat the same action to add the `id` attribute to the `<customer>` element.

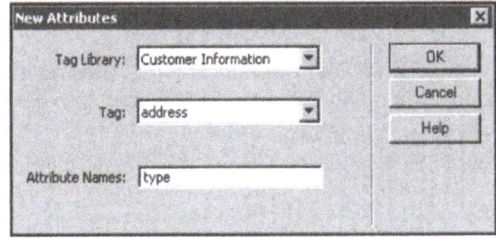

Adding a new attribute to our custom <address> element.

After you've added all the attributes, expand the `<address>` element entry in the *Tags* window and click the `type` attribute. We are now going to add a list of valid values for the `type` attribute. In the *Attribute Type* list menu, choose *Enumerated*. This causes the *Values* field to appear, so we can enter all of the address types we'd like to be available. This also takes a comma-separated list – enter `business,home,shipping` and click *OK* to exit the *Tag Library Editor*.

Now we can start entering new elements into our XML file. In Dreamweaver, open up `address.xml`, and add a new `<customer>` tag and a new `<address>` tag underneath it. After you type "`<address `" (notice the space) you should get a drop-down menu with the `type` attribute. Press *Enter* and you should see the list of available types in the *Code Hint* menu.

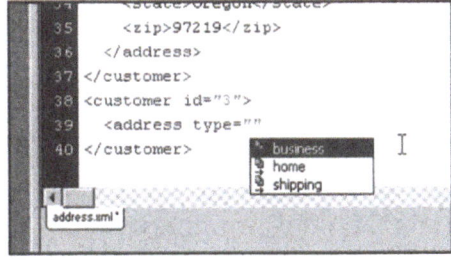

*The result of our hard work – Dreamweaver now helps us
with adding our elements to our XML pages.*

DTDs and Schemas

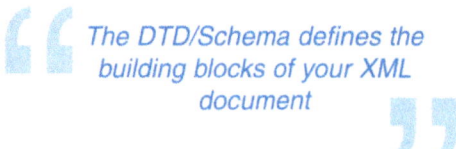

The DTD/Schema defines the building blocks of your XML document

For more information on writing and using XML Schemas, check out the W3C XML Schema primer, at http://www.w3.org/TR/xmlschema-0/, or check out a book such as Professional XML Schemas (Wrox Press, Jon Duckett et al, ISBN: 1861005474).

The purpose of DTDs and XML Schemas for XML is essentially the same as for an HTML DTD. The DTD/Schema defines the building blocks of your XML document. A DTD is a document type definition, meaning that it defines all of the allowable elements and attributes in your XML document and what type of data they can contain.

An XML Schema is simply an XML-based version of a DTD (being XML documents itself). The XML Schema is an alternative to DTDs and is also an official W3C Recommendation, which can be found at *http://www.w3.org/XML/Schema#dev*. We won't be covering how to write an XML Schema in this chapter because it's a long and complex subject. We will, however, show you how to use one to speed up building your tag libraries.

If you have an XML Schema or DTD for your XML documents, you can import it directly into the Tag Library. Dreamweaver's Schema importing facilities aren't perfect though. It will not import attributes, but at least you can get everything else imported in one go. Here's an example XML Schema built from our XML document (see `addressschema.xsd` in the code download, generated by XML Spy):

```xml
<?xml version="1.0" encoding="UTF-8"?>
<xs:schemaxmlns:xs="http://www.w3.org/2001/XMLSchema" elementFormDefault="qualified">
  <xs:element name="address">
    <xs:complexType>
      <xs:sequence>
        <xs:element ref="street"/>
        <xs:element ref="city"/>
        <xs:element ref="state"/>
        <xs:element ref="zip"/>
      </xs:sequence>
    </xs:complexType>
  </xs:element>
  <xs:element name="city" type="xs:string"/>
  <xs:element name="customer">
    <xs:complexType>
      <xs:sequence>
        <xs:element ref="name"/>
        <xs:element ref="address"/>
      </xs:sequence>
      <xs:attribute name="id" use="required" />
    </xs:complexType>
  </xs:element>
  <xs:element name="customers">
    <xs:complexType>
      <xs:sequence>
        <xs:element ref="customer" maxOccurs="unbounded"/>
      </xs:sequence>
    </xs:complexType>
  </xs:element>
```

```
  <xs:element name="first" type="xs:string"/>
  <xs:element name="last" type="xs:string"/>
  <xs:element name="name">
    <xs:complexType>
      <xs:sequence>
        <xs:element ref="first"/>
        <xs:element ref="last"/>
      </xs:sequence>
    </xs:complexType>
  </xs:element>
  <xs:element name="state" type="xs:string"/>
  <xs:element name="street" type="xs:string"/>
  <xs:element name="zip" type="xs:string"/>
</xs:schema>
```

Once you have your schema file, you can go back to the *Tag Library Editor* and import the file. Click the + icon and choose *DTDSchema* and *Import XML DTD or Schema*; now browse to your Schema file and click *OK*. Now all of your XML elements will be available inside a tag library with the same name as the Schema file.

XML and Templates

By far the most tedious part of XML is entering the data. If you're not pulling the information from a database or other source, then you have to enter it all manually. If you're building your own XML files, you also have to come up with all of the syntax on your own. If you're turning this task over to a less experienced developer (or simply hate writing tag after tag like me) then using Dreamweaver templates for this task might be a better alternative.

You can output XML data directly from Dreamweaver templates using the built-in template syntax. You can also use XML to move data into Dreamweaver templates, allowing you to generate XML data from some other data source (perhaps a database) and then have it imported into your templates to display on a static site.

The first thing we need is a template to work with. We're going to use the following template-based page (found as `template.htm` in the code download), which has an editable region for each of our XML elements:

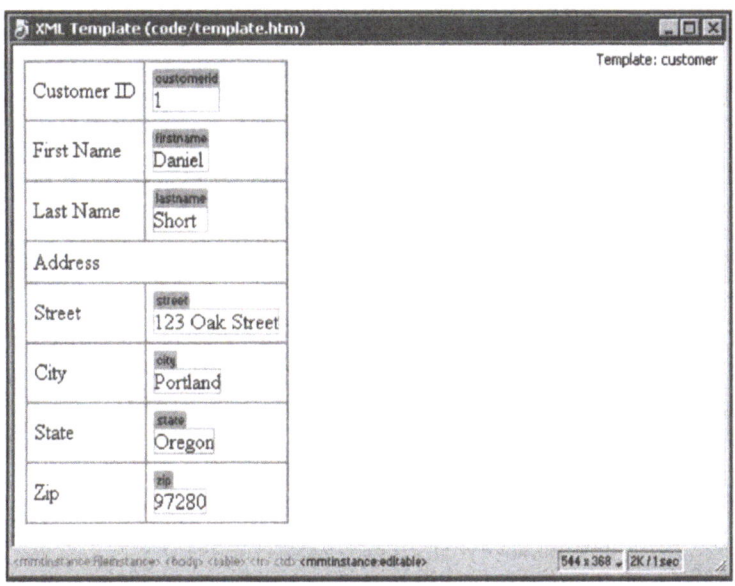

Our XML template-based page

Notice that we've named the template *customer* to match our `<customer>` element, and we have each editable area named to match an XML element we're going to use. When you export XML data from a template you have the option to use the editable regions as XML element names. It won't do nested elements, like we saw in our last XML example, but it will at least get you close.

In order to export the data, just choose *File > Export > Template Data as XML...* In the *Export Template Data as XML* dialog box you have two choices for your XML notation format, *Use Standard Dreamweaver XML Tags* and *Use Editable Region Names as XML Tags*:

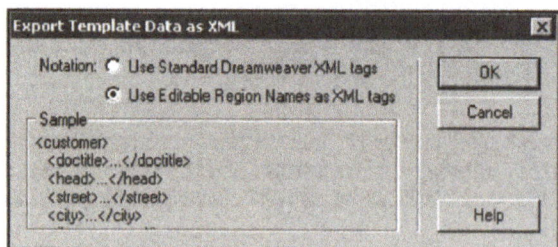

Export Template Data as XML

The first *Notation* option sets every editable region as a name of an `<item>` element, so an XML file using this first method would look something like this:

```
<?xml version="1.0"?>
<templateItems template="/Templates/customer.dwt" codeOutsideHTMLIsLocked="false">
    <item name="firstname"><![CDATA[Daniel]]></item>
    <item name="zip"><![CDATA[97280]]></item>
    <item name="head"></item>
    <item name="lastname"><![CDATA[Short]]></item>
    <item name="doctitle"><![CDATA[
<title>XML Template</title>
]]></item>
    <item name="street"><![CDATA[123 Oak Street]]></item>
    <item name="city"><![CDATA[Portland]]></item>
    <item name="state"><![CDATA[Oregon]]></item>
    <item name="customerid"><![CDATA[1]]></item>
</templateItems>
```

The `<templateItems>` element contains the name of the template we've applied to the page and whether code outside the `<html>` element is locked. Following that we have each editable region identified as a separate `<item>` element with the content set as CDATA.

CDATA *(character data) is a method of inserting data into an XML document that you don't want to be parsed along with the rest of the XML. This can include comments, or content like we have in this example. Everything inserted between the `<![CDATA[` and `]]>` containers will be ignored by an XML parser.*

Because content from an editable region of a template could conceivably contain elements that aren't terminated correctly (such as `<br>` instead of `<br />`), the CDATA makes sure we don't get any XML errors. You should also note that we have both the page `<title>`, and other data that was contained in the `<head>` of the document, including any `<meta>` elements.

The second *Notation* option (using the editable areas as names) is my preferred method, because the XML is more meaningful. In the first method, elements are just referred to as items, which is not very meaningful. However, with the second option you'll end up with an XML file like this:

```
<?xml version="1.0"?>
<customer template="/Templates/customer.dwt" codeOutsideHTMLIsLocked="false">
    <firstname><![CDATA[Daniel]]></firstname>
    <zip><![CDATA[97280]]></zip>
    <head></head>
    <lastname><![CDATA[Short]]></lastname>
    <doctitle><![CDATA[
<title>XML Template</title>
]]></doctitle>
    <street><![CDATA[123 Oak Street]]></street>
    <city><![CDATA[Portland]]></city>
    <state><![CDATA[Oregon]]></state>
    <customerid><![CDATA[1]]></customerid>
</customer>
```

In my opinion this XML is much easier to read. Our root element is `<customer>` since that's the name of our template file. Each editable region is then set as its own separate XML element. Click *OK*, and save your XML file with a sensible name.

So, now that we know how to export XML data we can go the opposite direction and import the same XML data. This means that we could generate a group of XML files from a database and import them directly into a template in Dreamweaver.

> We could generate a group of XML files from a database and import them directly into a template in Dreamweaver

When you have set up an appropriate template to import the data into (see the code download for a suitable `customer.dwt`), choose *File > Import > XML Into Template*. Browse to the XML file and click *OK*. Dreamweaver checks for the template attribute of the root element and imports all of your data into a new page based on that template. This means you could potentially pull data from a dynamic data source and import it directly into your static Dreamweaver templates, perhaps for use in Search Engine submissions.

9

Using XML with ASP

XSLT

Well, now that we're building these wonderful XML files, how do we get them into some type of presentable format? If you bring up an XML file directly in Internet Explorer you end up with something like the screenshot to the right::

Internet Explorer has a useful built-in stylesheet that allows you to view your XML in a useful expanding/collapsing markup tree, but not much else. Other browsers offer even less native XML support. So how do we present our XML in a more useful way?

That's where **Extensible Stylesheet Language Transformations** (**XSLT**) come in.

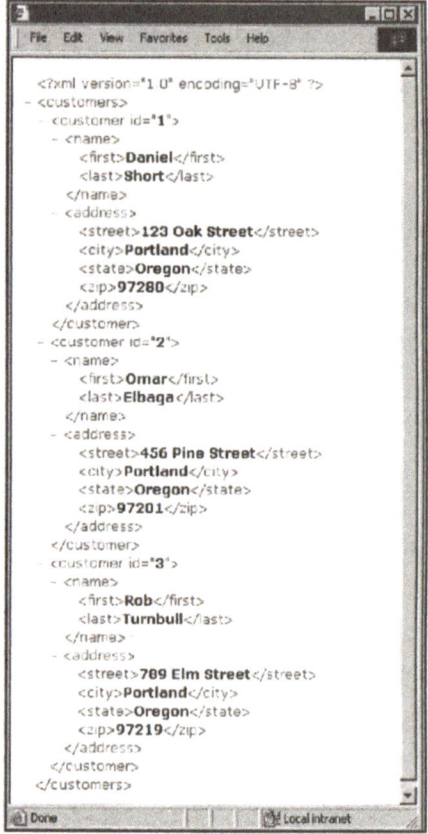

Our XML file, as displayed in Internet Explorer.

> *Using XSLT, you can not only style XML for display as HTML – you can also perform operations on your XML, changing the nature of the data to suit your needs*

XSLT can perform a similar function to cascading style sheets – like CSS, XSLT files can be applied to XML, and style the XML as you want before spitting the results out to the browser (as HTML). However, XSLT also offers a host of much more powerful functions. Using XSLT, you can not only style XML for display as HTML (or other markup languages, such as WML or cHTML for mobile devices). You can also perform operations on your XML, changing the nature of the data to suit your needs, and outputting the results as another XML file.

Along with XSLT comes its companion, **XPath** – XPath is a language designed to address specific parts of an XML document. XPath is used to traverse through the XML tree and pull out the data you want, based on the criteria specified. We'll be throwing a bit of that in here as well

In fact, it is common practice in the XML world to use XSLT and CSS in tandem, transforming your XML data using XSLT, then styling the result with CSS for display in a browser. This is useful for many reasons – it allows even better separation of content and presentation, and you could do your transformations on the server (say, using ASP), therefore saving client processing demands and bypassing the problem of browser support for XSLT (which is getting better these days); then you could do your styling on the client to save on some server load.

While I'm not going to write in-depth on XSLT and XPath, I'll show you enough to be dangerous and get you started. XSLT and XPath deserve an entire book of their own – these topics, check out a good XML book, such as *Practical XML for the Web* (*glasshaus, Alex Shiell et al, ISBN: 1904151086*).

Here's a sample XSLT file to transform our list of customers into a table (`address.xsl`):

```
<?xml version="1.0" encoding="UTF-8"?>
<xsl:stylesheet version="1.0" xmlns:xsl="http://www.w3.org/1999/XSL/Transform">
  <xsl:output method="html" />
  <xsl:template match="customers">
  <table>
    <xsl:attribute name="border">1</xsl:attribute>
    <xsl:attribute name="cellpadding">3</xsl:attribute>
    <tr>
      <th>Name</th>
      <th>Street</th>
      <th>City, State, Zip</th>
    </tr>
    <xsl:for-each select="customer">
      <tr>
        <td>
          <a>
            <xsl:attribute name="href">
              link.asp?id=<xsl:value-of select="@id" />
            </xsl:attribute>
            <xsl:value-of select="name/first" />
            <xsl:text> </xsl:text>
            <xsl:value-of select="name/last" />
          </a>
          <xsl:text> (</xsl:text>
          <xsl:value-of select="@id" />
          <xsl:text>)</xsl:text>
        </td>
        <td>
          <xsl:value-of select="address/street" />
        </td>
        <td>
          <xsl:value-of select="address/city" />
          <xsl:text> </xsl:text>
          <xsl:value-of select="address/state" />
          <xsl:text>, </xsl:text>
          <xsl:value-of select="address/zip" />
        </td>
      </tr>
    </xsl:for-each>
    </table>
  </xsl:template>
</xsl:stylesheet>
```

Because the XML language is self-describing, the XSLT elements are generally easy to understand just by looking at their names. However, to further aid understanding I'll give you a brief explanation of what each of the XSLT elements we've used actually does:

9

Using XML with ASP

```
<?xml version="1.0" encoding="UTF-8"?>
<xsl:stylesheet version="1.0" xmlns:xsl="http://www.w3.org/1999/XSL/Transform">
```

<xsl:stylesheet>: The <xsl:stylesheet> element tells whatever XML parser you're using that this document is indeed a stylesheet. It also determines what version of XSLT you're using and which namespace to use for the stylesheet.

```
<xsl:output method="html" />
```

<xsl:output>: The <xsl:output> element tells the parser what type of content to output. If you want XHTML output you should use method="xml". The <xsl:output> element can also determine indenting, whether to include the XML declaration in the output, and several other attributes.

<xsl:template>: The <xsl:template> element uses the match attribute to determine which XML records you are going to work with. Since we want to loop through all of the customers, we use match="customers" to get all of the data within the <customers> element. Now that we've determined which XML records to use we have access to all of the customers while using the <xsl:template> elements.

<xsl:attribute>: You'll need to use the <xsl:attribute> element to add attributes to HTML tags, especially if those attributes are going to be driven by your XML. Notice that inside the <table> element in our XSLT file we've added an attribute for the border and one for the cell spacing. Using the <xsl:attribute> element also allows you to enter complex attributes that might not be legal inside another XML element. You'd do the same if you wanted to add an id to a dynamic link as we are doing for our customer names.

<xsl:for-each>: You can treat the <xsl:for-each> element just like a For ... Each loop in VBScript. All this does is loop through each of the elements specified in the select statement. So <xsl:for-each select="customer"> means "loop through all of the customer elements". You just place all of the actions you want to perform on those records inside the <xsl:for-each> elements. Any selections or commands run inside the loop will be in the context of the current node in the loop.

<xsl:value-of>: Think of <xsl:value-of> as XSLT's equivalent of Response.Write. It means "grab this item and output it". The select attribute of <xsl:value-of> determines what will be output. Here are some examples explained:

- <xsl:value-of select="@id" />: Output the id of the current parent element, in our case <customer>

- <xsl:value-of select="name/first" />: Output the content of the <first> element inside the <name> element

- <xsl:value-of select="address/city" />: Output the content of the <city> element inside the <address> element

<xsl:text>: The <xsl:text> element just tells the parser to output the plain text inside the elements. This ensures that the text you output will look exactly as you want it, without stripping any whitespace, often something like this:

```
<xsl:value-of select="name/first" />
<xsl:text> </xsl:text>
<xsl:value-of select="name/last" />
```

will be output like this:

```
Daniel Short
```

Adding `<xsl:text> </xsl:text>` between the two `xsl:value-of` statements puts a nice display-friendly space between the first and last name:

Some things to look out for when working with XSLT files include making sure that all of your elements are closed correctly, and that you've used the correct encoding on the page. Improper encoding could prevent the parser from reading the file at all and you might just end up with a blank page in your browser. You can check to make sure XSLT syntax and document encoding are correct by loading up the XSLT file in an XML-compliant browser such as IE6. If it comes up as an XML tree (as we saw earlier), there should be no errors. Otherwise, the browser will note the errors that exist.

Now let's look at the fun part where we apply the XSLT to the XML to transform it.

Transforming XML

Transforming an XML file means simply applying the XSLT file to the XML file and outputting the results. There are quite a few ways to transform an XML file, including client-side JavaScript in modern XML-compliant browsers, a stylesheet `<link ... >` in the XML file, and ActiveX objects in Internet Explorer, but these are either non-dynamic, limiting their use, or require a specific browser or component on the client's machine, which can never truly be guaranteed. That's why I prefer to do my XML transformations on the server-side before sending them to the client, just like processing regular ASP.

Transforming an XML file means simply applying the XSLT file to the XML file and outputting the results

9

The first thing you need to do to start transforming XML is to make sure that you have the latest Microsoft XML components installed on the server. You can find out by running the Component Test from PensaWorks at *http://www.pensaworks.com/prg_com.asp?v=3*. Items 11-13 on the PensaWorks list are all Microsoft XML components. If you don't have the components installed you can download the latest versions from Microsoft, at the following URL:

http://msdn.microsoft.com/downloads/default.asp?url=/downloads/sample.asp?url=/msdn-files/027/001/766/msdncompositedoc.xml

Transforming Local Files

Once you're certain you have the XML components installed and ready to go, you'll need to make sure you have three things; a blank ASP file to do the transformation, an XML file to transform, and an XSL file to do the transforming. We've provided three sample pages in the code download for this chapter – `address.asp`, `address.xml`, and `address.xsl`.

The ASP code we're going to use is deceptively simple:

```
<body>
  <%
    'Declare our objects
    Dim xmlDocument, xslDocument
    'Set our objects to an XML Dom Object
    set xmlDocument = Server.CreateObject("MSXML2.DOMDocument.4.0")
    set xslDocument = Server.CreateObject("MSXML2.DOMDocument.4.0")

    'Set the XML document to asynchronous and load the XML file
    xmlDocument.async = false
    xmlDocument.load(Server.MapPath("address.xml"))

    'Set the XSL document to asynchronous and load the XSL file
    xslDocument.async = false
    xslDocument.load(Server.MapPath("address.xsl"))

    'Transform the document
    Response.Write(xmlDocument.transformNode(xslDocument.documentElement))
    'Destroy our objects
    set xmlDocument = Nothing
    set xslDocument = Nothing
  %>
</body>
```

Let's look at what we are doing here, step-by-step:

- First, we need to declare our variables and create two new objects. The first object, xmlDocument, will hold the content of our XML file. The second, xslDocument, will hold the contents of our XSL file. These are both MSXML objects.

- Next, we need to actually load the XML and XSLT documents. We set both of the documents to asynchronous mode by using the async property of the object. Setting async to False means that control won't be sent back to the page until the full document has been loaded into the object.

- After each object is set to asynchronous mode, we use the load method of the object to load the file. You'll need to provide the full path to the file, whether it's a location on the server's hard drive or the web address for a partner site's XML file (which we'll get to shortly). In this example we're using the Server.MapPath method to get the full drive location of the file (see *Chapter 8* for more on Server.MapPath).

- Finally, after we have both of our objects ready to go, we use the transformNode method of the xmlDocument object to transform the XML file using the XSLT in xslDocument. The documentElement property contains the root node of the XSLT file and all its children, meaning that it contains the entire XSLT document. In our example we're just writing it out with Response.Write. We could have just as easily stuffed the transformation into a variable and performed more operations against it, such as replacing characters or other string manipulation.

If we view `address.asp` in our browser we end up with this:

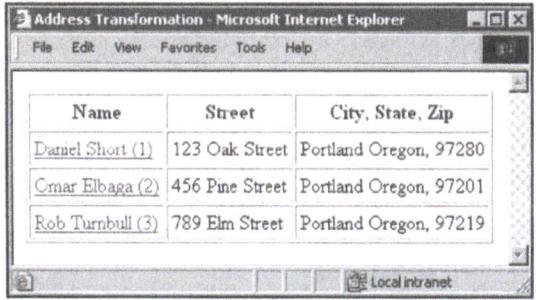

The result of our XML Transformation.

This screenshot shows the dynamic links pointing to a detail page for each customer. XSLT provides a completely portable solution for transforming your XML data, and is easy to use and maintain when it's exploited correctly.

XML for Data Portability

If you're used to working with databases, you know that there are issues with porting one database to another server and back. Your SQL Server database won't work with MySQL without a lot of manual labor, and that UNIX server you're working on might not have the correct drivers for working with Microsoft Access.

Another wonderful thing about XML is that it's completely platform-independent

This is another area where XML (and XSLT) can help: another wonderful thing about XML is that it's completely platform-independent. An XML file on a UNIX server is exactly the same as an XML file on a Windows server – end of story.

So how do you move an XML file between servers, and why would you want to? The main reason for sharing XML files between servers is syndication. Let's assume that your site provides late breaking news on the latest widgets in your industry. It could be possible to allow other widget-related sites to display your news headlines and link them back to your site, increasing your traffic and hopefully your profits. Using XML could be a cheap alternative to providing customized content for each widget-related site. Provide one XML file and leave it up to your syndication sites to convert the XML into a format fitting their site.

Transforming Remote Files

Transforming files on your own server is fine, but what about syndicating content as talked about above? We've probably all seen wonderful content on other sites that we'd like duplicated on our own, and provided that the other site can (and will) provide you with an XML feed, it's just as easy as transforming your local files.

Using XML with ASP

For an example, let's take a look at Macromedia's Designer and Developer Center at *http://www.macromedia.com/desdev*. Macromedia provides an XML feed for the DesDev Center that contains many of the top headlines along with links to the full articles. This is a great way to beef up content on a community site and also provides Macromedia with additional traffic.

So how do we make use of this? The first thing we need to do is take a look at the XML they're using, which is at *http://www.macromedia.com/desdev/resources/macromedia_resources.xml*. Here's a small snippet to give you an idea of what the XML file looks like:

```xml
<?xml version="1.0" ?>
<macromedia_resources>
  <resource type="Article">
    <title>The X(HTML) Files</title>
    <author>Daniel Short</author>
    <url>http://www.macromedia.com/desdev/mx/.../.../code_standards.html </url>
    <product name="Dreamweaver" />
  </resource>
  <resource type="Column">
    <title>Logged In: The End of Hassles</title>
    <author>Erik Larson</author>
    <url>http://www.macromedia.com/desdev/logged_in/elarson_contribute.html</url>
    <product name="Contribute" />
  </resource>
  <resource type="TechNote">
    <title>Using Section Anchors in Contribute</title>
    <author>Donald S. Booth</author>
    <url>http://www.macromedia.com/support/contribute/ts/.../anchors.htm</url>
    <product name="Contribute" />
  </resource>

  ...

</macromedia_resources>
```

As you've probably noticed, this isn't a whole lot different from the first XML file we built. We have a list of `<resource>` elements, each one identified as an individual resource of a specific type – a `Column`, a `TechNote`, or an `Article`. We also get the author, the title of the article, the full URL, and which product it's connected with. Here's a simple XSLT file to convert the feed to HTML (`desdev.xsl`):

```xml
<?xml version="1.0" encoding="UTF-8"?>
<xsl:stylesheet version="1.0" xmlns:xsl="http://www.w3.org/1999/XSL/Transform">
  <xsl:output method="html"/>
  <xsl:template match="macromedia_resources">
    <xsl:for-each select="resource">
      <xsl:sort select="@type" order="ascending"/>
      <xsl:if test="@type=not(@type=preceding-sibling::resource/@type)">
        <!-- The current type is different than the last type -->
        <xsl:choose>
          <xsl:when test="position()=1">
            <!-- This is the first record, add a title for the feed -->
            <h1>My XML Feed</h1>
          </xsl:when>
          <xsl:otherwise>
```

```
            <hr />
          </xsl:otherwise>
        </xsl:choose>
        <h2><xsl:value-of select="translate(@type, '_', ' ')"/>s</h2>
      </xsl:if>
      <a>
        <xsl:attribute name="href"><xsl:value-of select="url"/></xsl:attribute>
        <xsl:attribute name="target">_blank</xsl:attribute>
        <xsl:attribute name="title">
          Written by <xsl:value-of select="author"/>
        </xsl:attribute>
        <xsl:value-of select="title"/>
      </a>
      <br />
    </xsl:for-each>
  </xsl:template>
</xsl:stylesheet>
```

You may be scratching your head at this point. We've thrown in a few more XSLT elements in here, as well as a whole slew of XPath expressions. The first part should look familiar. We use an `<xsl:template>` to `match` the root element, `<macromedia_resources>`, and then use `<xsl:for-each>` to loop through each resource. After that we get to the new interesting part. Let's look at the new elements and expressions we've introduced here:

`<xsl:sort>`: The `<xsl:sort>` element sorts the XML records based on the criteria in the select attribute. In our case we're sorting by the `type` attribute of the `<resource>` element. This gets all of our articles, columns, and techNotes in groups for display purposes. The `order` attribute takes `ascending` or `descending` as valid values. You can add additional `<xsl:sort>` elements to sort by multiple XML elements.

`<xsl:if>`: An `xsl:if` statement is exactly like using an `If ... End If` statement in VBScript. You have an opening `<xsl:if>` tag with a `test` attribute. If the test proves true then the content between the `<xsl:if>` tags is processed. There is no `else` option with the `<xsl:if>` element – you'll see its equivalent shortly.

`preceding-sibling`: The `preceding-sibling` function is part of the XPath language. In this instance we've used it as a test to see if the current `type` attribute of the `<resource>` element matches the preceding `type` attribute. If it's not the same, then we know we either have the very first XML record, or we've switched from one type to another and need to output a new header for our category.

`<xsl:choose>`: The `<xsl:choose>` element, when combined with `<xsl:when>` and `<xsl:otherwise>` replicates the `If ... Else ... End If` structure of VBScript. `<xsl:choose>` will only contain the `<when>` and `<otherwise>` elements, and won't actually contain any content of its own.

`<xsl:when>`: The `<xsl:when>` element can only be used inside the `<xsl:choose>` block, and actually performs the desired test. In our case we're testing to see if the `position()` (a part of the XPath language) is equal to 1, that is, the first XML record. If the test proves true, then the content within the `<xsl:when>` tags is processed. If it's false, the `<xsl:otherwise>` block is processed, if there is one. If there is no `<xsl:otherwise>` then processing continues after the closing `</xsl:choose>` tag.

`<xsl:otherwise>`: This is the `else` part of the `<xsl:when>` test. This block is optional, and if present, will be processed when the test contained in `<xsl:when>` proves false.

`translate`: The `translate` function is an XPath function similar to the `Replace` function in VBScript. It takes three arguments:

- The first is the string you want to replace characters in – in our example it's the `type` attribute.

- The second argument is the string to search for

- The last argument is what to replace it with

Occasionally Macromedia has resource types with underscores in the name – our `translate` statement replaces the underscores with spaces for presentational purposes.

Now that we have our XML and XSLT sorted out, we just need an ASP file to do the processing for us. We only need to change three things from our previous example:

- We need to set a new property to tell the XML parser that we're grabbing a URL

- We need to give it the desired URL

- We need to change the location of our XSL file

Here's what our new ASP file looks like (`desdev.asp` in the code download):

```
<body>
<%
  Dim xmlDocument, xslDocument
  set xmlDocument = Server.CreateObject("MSXML2.DOMDocument.4.0")
  set xslDocument = Server.CreateObject("MSXML2.DOMDocument.4.0")

  xmlDocument.async = false
  xmlDocument.setProperty "ServerHTTPRequest", true
  Dim xmlURL
  xmlURL = "http://www.macromedia.com/desdev/resources/macromedia_resources.xml"
  xmlDocument.load(xmlURL)

  xslDocument.async = false
  xslDocument.load(Server.MapPath("desdev.xsl"))

  Response.Write xmlDocument.transformNode(xslDocument.documentElement)
  set xmlDocument = Nothing
  set xslDocument = Nothing
%>
</body>
```

The only new line on this page is the `setProperty` statement, which tells the XML parser that this is an HTTP request. That means that when the load method is called it will look for a URL, rather than a physical location on the drive. We've added the URL to a variable (for formatting the output page) and put that into our `xmlDocument.load` method. We've also pointed the `xslDocument` object at our new XSL file. If we browse to the `desdev.asp` page we should end up with a full listing of the resources, broken down by category.

If you happen to be unlucky enough to end up with a blank page, we can output some error-checking information to try and find out what might be wrong. Add the following code block after each of the `load` statements in `desdev.asp` (be sure to change `xmlDocument` to `xslDocument` after the second load statement):

```
If xmlDocument.parseError.errorCode <> 0 Then
  Response.Write("<br />Error Code: ")
  Response.Write(xmlDocument.parseError.errorCode)
  Response.Write("<br />Error Reason: ")
  Response.Write(xmlDocument.parseError.reason)
  Response.Write("<br />Error Line: ")
  Response.Write(xmlDocument.parseError.line)
End If
```

The full code for the new `desdev.asp` file can be found in the code download as `desdev_errorcheck.asp`. You'll now be able to check out any errors you get, to see exactly what the trouble is, and fix them more easily.

If you're error-free you should see something like this:

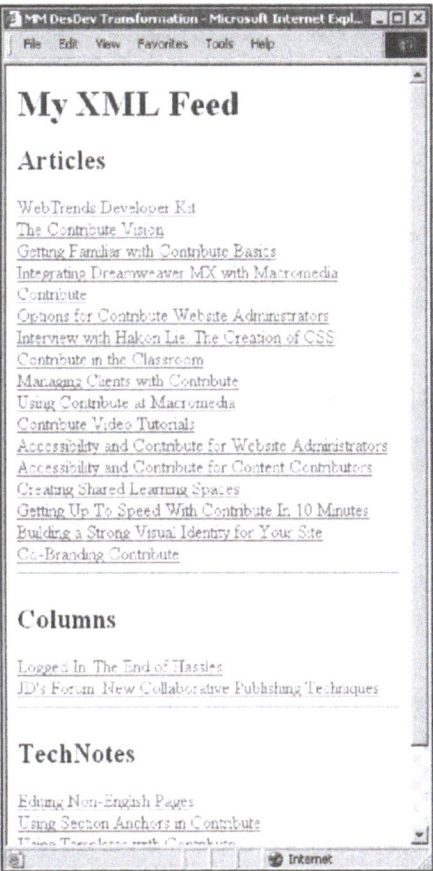

Our transformation of the Macromedia XML Newsfeed.

Things to Watch Out For

Probably the most annoying thing about working with XSL and XML is the lack of feedback from the XML parser. If all of your syntax is correct but you're referencing a element that doesn't exist, the XML parser will happily chug along and spit out a blank page. Dreamweaver also doesn't support color-coding or code hints in XSLT files, so it's often a good idea to use a separate dedicated editor to work with them. You'll also need to watch the case of your attribute and element name, as XML is case-sensitive.

As far as dedicated editors go, **XMLSpy** (see *http://www.xmlspy.com*) is probably the best around, but it is pricey ($399 as of the publishing of this book, home edition is $99 but more limited in functionality). A couple of good alternatives are:

- **XML CookTop** at *http://xmlcooktop.com*, which is completely free
- **XSelerator** from *http://www.topxml.com/xselerator/*, which retails at $125

The advantage to programs such as CookTop and XMLSpy is that you can check your work as you go, and they can help out with complex XPath functions and statements. Dreamweaver as an XML/XSL editor is low on the totem pole at the moment. This is the first edition to natively support XML files and they still have a little way to go till perfection. With continued feedback from us and other Dreamweaver users, the XML/XSL support should improve greatly in future versions.

More and more sites are now working with XHTML instead of good old HTML. You may have noticed that all of our examples use `<xsl:output method="html" />` to determine the output method. This means that the parser will change any XHTML elements into standard HTML.

For example, in our `desdev.xsl` example I'm using `<hr />` and `<br />` elements, but if you view the source of the page, you'll see `<hr>` and `<br>` instead, since the parser has converted all elements to old-style HTML. To get around this we need to make an adjustment to our `<xsl:output>` element:

```
<xsl:output method="xml" omit-xml-declaration="yes" />
```

Now when the parser runs through the XSL file it will generate valid XML, which also means we'll get valid XHTML. The `omit-xml-declaration` statement tells the parser not to output an additional `<?xml ... ?>` processing instruction, which is the default behavior for XML output. If you place regular XML elements inside a CDATA region the elements won't be converted to XML.

Summary

In this chapter we have looked at what XML is and how it can be used inside the Dreamweaver editing environment.

We've seen how to format XML documents and what makes a document well-formed. We also covered some common coding mistakes for XML documents, such as unbalanced elements and case-sensitivity. We looked at how to build your own custom tag library for working with XML files and how to import an XML Schema to speed up the tag library building process, as well as how to generate XML files from Dreamweaver templates.

Finally, we learned how to transform XML files using XPath and XSLT. We learned how to transform both local and remote XML files through the use of the server-side MSXML components to limit browser incompatibilities in our transformations.

9

Using XML with ASP

10

- The Session object, Application variables, and Session variables
- Session variable Server Behaviors
- Cookies, and cookie Server Behaviors

Author: Rob Turnbull

Sessions and Cookies

Many people argue that the use of Session variables and cookies in web applications is unnecessary. Any functionality provided by these items can just as easily be provided by database interactions or by utilizing Querystrings. This is true for the most part, but there are circumstances where using a Session variable or a cookie makes perfect sense, or indeed, is the only real option.

Take the example of a login page, for instance. Ideally, we would like to avoid forcing users to enter their login details at every visit, particularly for regularly visited pages. By using a cookie or two, we can eliminate the need to do this. We could provide a checkbox that allows the user to decide whether they want to be remembered or not; if it is selected, we simply store their personal login details in a couple of cookies. Next time they come to the page, they will be automatically logged in without having to entering any data.

This chapter will start by giving a bit of background on the `Session` object, and the collections, methods, events, and properties it makes available to us. Then we'll move on to the creation, modification, and deletion of Session variables, and we'll end the section by building some Server Behaviors that will help us out in situations such as our example above.

We'll then give the same treatment to cookies, showing how to create, modify, and delete them, along with the uses they have in areas such as improving login functionality these areas. We'll finish this section by building a Server Behavior that can be used in conjunction with a login form so it will remember us the next time we go to login. Then we will take a look at Application variables and how we can create and use them in the context of an *active users* counter that we can display on our web pages.

To round off the chapter, we'll take a quick look at a very useful Server Behavior that will be helpful to anyone who uses Session and Application variables in Dreamweaver MX.

Objects

ASP has several built-in objects that we can make use of in our web applications, as we saw in *Chapter 4*. You'll probably be familiar with some of them, but even then, you might not be aware of all their functionality. If you're not sure what an **object** is, refer back to *Chapter 4* for a quick refresher.

We'll cover the `Session` object in the following section of this chapter, since we've already seen the `Application`, `Request`, and `Response` objects in *Chapter 4*.

The Session Object

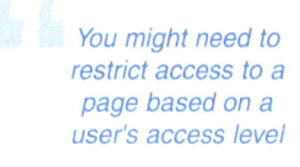

You might need to restrict access to a page based on a user's access level

By its very nature, the Internet is stateless. We might want to carry user information from one page to another as users browse through our site but, because of the statelessness of the medium, we cannot guarantee that this will always happen. If for example the user browses from page one to page two by clicking a link that you have coded to pass certain information along, that information will be available on page two. If, however, the user simply enters the URL of page two into their browser address bar, no information will be passed along and state is lost.

The `Session` object helps us to maintain state in situations such as these. We can store information about the user that each page might need and it won't matter if they type the URL in or click the link, the information will still be available. For example, you might need to restrict access to a page based on a user's access level. This is an ideal situation for Session usage as the user's level can be stored in a Session variable and then utilized to check if user should be allowed to access the page.

The `Session` object is automatically created for us by the server when a user browses to our web site. Each basic `Session` object requires approximately 10kb of memory on the server, and initially contains four items. They are:

- `CodePage`: This holds the number of the code page that your system is using for symbol mapping. Unless you're using non-Roman characters, such as Japanese, you'll not need to worry about setting this property.

- `LCID`: This is the locale identifier and is used to format dates correctly for the part of the world your server is in, among other things such as money and special characters. As with CodePage, you'll likely not need to worry about setting this variable on your server. To see a complete list of locale ID's, visit the following Microsoft web page:

  http://msdn.microsoft.com/library/en-us/script56/html/vsmscLCID.asp

- `SessionID`: This is a unique, read-only value, generated and used by the server to identify the user's current session. Each user who connects to the server will have their own SessionID assigned to them, and we can use this to follow them through the site, making it easier to personalize their browsing experience.

- `Timeout`: This is a value that you can set to determine the length of time in minutes that should pass before session information will expire. The default value is 20, but if you need to reduce it you can set it in the `global.asa` file, which we discuss briefly in the *Application Variables* section.

  There are advantages and disadvantages to shortening the Session timeout. For example, you might want a short timeout limit on a banking web site for security purposes. On a site that requires you to fill out forms, however, you wouldn't want to use a very short timeout because people might not have enough time to fill out the form.

Once you start adding your own variables into this object, the size will grow and the performance of the server will take a hit. On small-scale web sites, you probably won't notice this, but take the size up several notches to a site that receives hundreds of page requests per second and your server's performance will drop severely because of the amount of session data it needs to maintain.

As a quick and easy example to show the four initial session objects, create a web page with only the following code and then preview it.

```
<%@LANGUAGE="VBSCRIPT" CODEPAGE="1252"%>
<html>
  <head>
  <title>Initial Session Object</title>
  <meta http-equiv="Content-Type" content="text/html; charset=iso-8859-1">
</head>
  <body>
    <p>CodePage = <%=(Session.CodePage)%></p>
    <p>LCID = <%=(Session.LCID)%></p>
    <p>SessionID = <%=(Session.SessionID)%></p>
    <p>Timeout = <%=(Session.Timeout)%></p>
  </body>
</html>
```

Application Variables

This will show you the four session objects and their values for your particular location as shown in the following screenshot.

We will cover the creation, manipulation, and uses of these (and our own) Session variables in the *Session Variables* section.

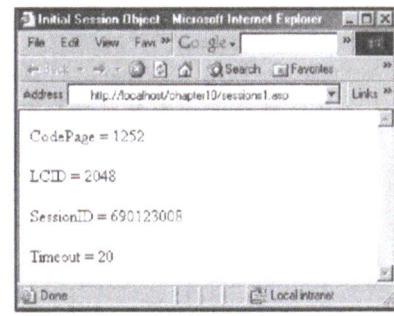

The server that processed this page was in England

Application variables are different from Session variables in that Session variables are maintained on a user-by-user basis and each user can only access their own Session variables, whereas Application variables are available to all users of the application.

The `global.asa` file gives us an opportunity to create application-level variables that individual users can access and update, and that are the same for every user of the site. You can create multiple `global.asa` files but you can only have one in any single location. You could create a file in each section of your site, for example, if you wanted to use different application-level variables in different sections.

A prime example of this type of activity is an active users counter. Using the `Application` object we can create and update an Application variable that will display the current number of visitors our site is experiencing. Let's take a look at how we would do this.

Active Users

To create the active users counter we need to create a `global.asa` file with the following code. This `global.asa` file should be stored in the site root. We don't use ASP delimiters (`<% %>`) in the `global.asa` file because all the content of this file is housed within a `<script>` element:

```
<script language="VBScript" runat="Server">
Sub Application_OnStart
  Session.Timeout = 20
  Application.Lock
  Application("Active") = 0
  Application.UnLock
End Sub
Sub Session_OnStart
  Application.Lock
  Application("Active") = Application("Active") + 1
  Application.UnLock
End Sub
Sub Session_OnEnd
  Application.Lock
  Application("Active") = Application("Active") - 1
  Application.UnLock
End Sub
</script>
```

Short and sweet!

What we have here is three events that will manage our active users counter. The `Application_OnStart` event is only ever fired when the application is started up for the first time. If that event occurs, we define an application-level variable, called `Active`, and assign it a value of `0` (zero).

The `Session_OnStart` event is fired every time a new user hits our web site. The server creates a new `Session` object for every user and, when that happens, we want our active users counter to be incremented by 1.

The `Session_OnEnd` event is fired whenever a session is terminated or times out. For example, when the user hits a page that abandons the session (termination), or the user simply closes their browser (timeout will occur after the defined timeout limit is reached). When either of these events occurs, we want our active users counter to be decremented by 1.

Each time the Application variable is updated, it is first locked, then the update takes place, and then it is unlocked again.

To display the active users counter on your web page, you would use the following code:

```
<%= Application("Active") %>
```

It really is as simple as that.

One thing to bear in mind is that this method is not a suitable solution for adding a constant hit counter to your site (one that counts all the hits over the course of time) because if the server were restarted, your counter would be too!

Another point to consider is the accuracy of this implementation. Because the `Session.Timeout` value is set to 20 minutes, your counter is unlikely to be exact all of the time since people can visit your site, get themselves added to the current users counter, and then leave a couple of minutes later, but they are still going to be counted as an active user for another 20 minutes. At least you get a rough estimate though.

Session Variables

Some swear by them, others swear at them! Session variables certainly have their uses, but are often overused by inexperienced web designers. For example, I have seen occasions where a form is used to collect users contact information and is then stuffed into a whole heap of Session variables to be carried over to the next page. This is just bad practice as this information could be gathered from the `Request` collection (`Request.Form`) or better yet, inserted into a database and retrieved on the next and subsequent pages that require any part of that information.

A better use of Session variables would be for storing information that needs to be carried with a user throughout their browsing experience on your site. For example, if they log in to your site, you would hold their username and perhaps an access level in Session variables for use on subsequent pages.

> *Another site cannot access your Session variables*

Session variables are only available to the application that created them. For instance, if a user browses to your web site and creates Session variables by logging in, then without logging out they browse to another site. That other site cannot access your Session variables (otherwise, what a security nightmare we would have!).

In this section we will look at creating, removing, and killing our own Session variables and then we will move on to creating Server Behaviors to speed that process up.

Creating Session Variables

Creating Session variables is very straightforward. You simply declare the variable name and assign it a value.

```
<% Session("svCustomerID") = "1" %>
```

That Session variable would be useless to everyone except the user with `CustomerID` number 1! To assign dynamic values, you would reference a Recordset:

```
<% Session("svCustomerID") = rsCustomers.Fields.Item("CustomerID").Value %>
```

The use of the lowercase `sv` prefix on the Session variable names is something that many developers use to identify that this is a Session variable and also to avoid naming conflicts that can otherwise occur.

You can overwrite the value contained in a Session variable by simply assigning a new value to it.

Sessions and Cookies

```
<% Session("svCustomerName") = "Rob" %>
<% Session("svCustomerName") = "Mike" %>
```

The Login User code creates two Session variables for us when we use this Server Behavior. They can prove to be very useful when you need to filter data on a page specific to a particular user, or perhaps restrict access to a page. These two variables are as follows:

```
Session("MM_Username")
```

```
Session("MM_UserAuthorization")
```

If you use the built-in Server Behaviors to create login pages and restrict access, then these Session variables are your friends. Make full use of them because they exist in your applications and are taking up server resources, so they ought to pay their way!

To write the values contained in Session variables out to the screen, use the `Response.Write` method:

```
<% Response.Write(Session("svCustomerName")) %>
```

or its shorthand equivalent:

```
<%= Session("svCustomerName") %>
```

Removing Session Variables

Removing Session variables has become easier since the advent of IIS5 (Internet Information Services), which brought with it ASP 3.0. With previous versions of IIS there was no way to actually remove a Session variable from the `Session` object. The only option available to you was to set its value to nothing (it still exists in the collection, taking up a small amount of valuable server resources):

```
<% Session("svVariableName") = "" %>
```

In IIS versions 5 and above, we have the `Contents` collection, which allows us to remove individual sessions from the collection, so we only need to maintain those that we really need, freeing up resources on the server. We do this using the following code:

```
<% Session.Contents.Remove("svVariableName") %>
```

We will cover the `RemoveAll` option in the next section.

Killing the Session

To remove all the Session variables in the `Session` object, you can use the `RemoveAll` method.

```
<% Session.Contents.RemoveAll() %>
```

RemoveAll is not available to users running anything less than IIS5.

This method removes all the Session variables from the `Session` object but does not destroy the actual object itself. You might need this functionality where your application uses the `SessionID` created by the `Session` object when it was first created.

If that is not the case, and you simply want to kill the entire object and start again, you would use:

```
<% Session.Abandon %>
```

Invoking the `Abandon` method does not immediately remove the `Session` object. It waits until the page that calls it has finished processing, so you could call the `Abandon` method at the start of a page and still reference your Session variables throughout the rest of that page without a problem. Once you move off that page, however, your `Session` object will be destroyed and a new one will be created in its place.

Session Variable Server Behaviors

For a quick lesson on using the Server Behavior Builder (SBB) to create Server Behaviors, check out *Chapter 6*, which covers this topic. From here on, it will be assumed that you are familiar with using the SBB in Dreamweaver MX.

We will show the code snippets and describe the steps you need to perform in order to create the following simple Server Behaviors:

- Create Session Variable
- Remove Session Variable
- Abandon the Session

Create Session Variable

This Server Behavior will enable us to create a Session variable with a name we specify and a value that is supplied from database content.

We only need to use a single line of code in the SBB for this Server Behavior (SB), which is as follows:

```
<% Session("SessionName") = recordset.Fields.Item("column").Value %>
```

Launch the SBB to create a new Server Behavior. Generate it in *ASP VBScript* and call it *Create Session Variable*.

Add a code block and enter the required code.

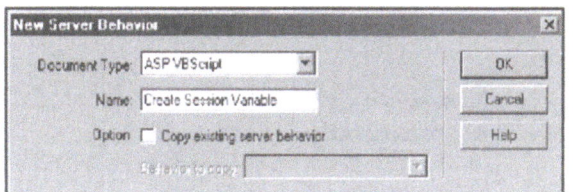

The first step in creating this simple Server Behavior

Replace `SessionName` in the code with a parameter called `Session name`. Replace `recordset` with a parameter called `Recordset` and `column` with a parameter called `Column`.

Set *Insert Code* to *Above the <html> Tag* and set *Relative Position* to *Just After the Recordsets*.

Tick the *Identifier* checkbox under the *Advanced* section and make sure this code block is selected in the *Code Block to Select* list:

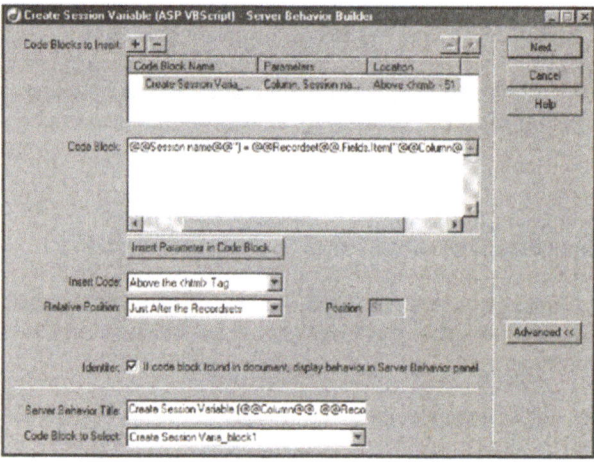

We're almost done telling Dreamweaver MX what we want to happen

Click *Next* to set the form element types. Set `Session name` to use *Text Field*, `Recordset` to use *Recordset Menu* and `column` to use *Recordset Field Menu*. They should be set in this order too, as it makes a sensibly structured form:

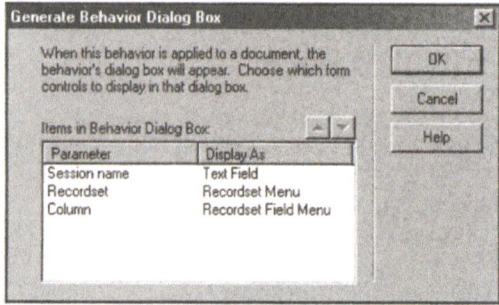

A sensible order for the parameters to be set in

Click *OK* to create the Server Behavior. When we use this Server Behavior, we'll be presented with the following dialog with which to specify our Session name, pick a Recordset, and select the column from which to draw the information:

If there isn't a Recordset on the page we want to use this Server Behavior on, Dreamweaver MX will warn us to create one before it lets us proceed.

If there isn't a Recordset, Dreamweaver MX will warn us

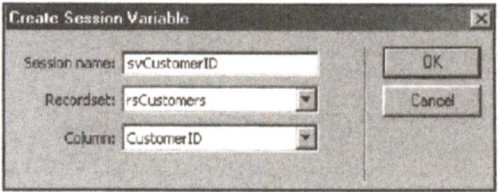

A likely selection of values for our parameters

Remove Session Variable

This Server Behavior will enable us to remove a specific Session variable. It will only work on IIS5 and above, as the method it employs does not exist on earlier versions of IIS. We only require a single line of code again, which is as follows:

```
<% Session.Contents.Remove("SessionName") %>
```

Launch the SBB to create a new Server Behavior. Generate it in ASP/VBScript and call it *Remove Session Variable*. Add a code block and enter the required code.

Replace SessionName in the code with a parameter called Session name.

Set *Insert Code* to *Above the <html> Tag* and set *Relative Position* to *The Beginning of the File*.

Tick the *Identifier* checkbox under the *Advanced* section and make sure this code block is selected in the *Code Block to Select* list, then click *Next* to set the form element types.

Set Session name to use the *Text Field* form element type and click *OK* to create the Server Behavior.

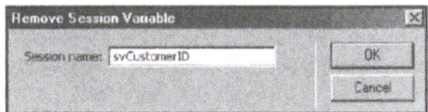

A simple form for a simple Server Behavior

Abandon the Session

This Server Behavior will abandon the entire session, thereby removing all Session variables at once. It only requires a single line of code again, which is as follows:

It only requires a single line of code

```
<% Session.Abandon() %>
```

Launch the SBB to create a new SB. Generate it in ASP/VBScript and call it *Abandon Session*. Add a code block and enter the required code.

Set the *Insert Code* list to *Above the <html> tag* and the *Relative Position* list to *The Beginning of the File*.

Tick the *Identifier* checkbox under the *Advanced* section and make sure this code block is selected in the *Code Block to Select* list, then click *OK* to create the Server Behavior.

This Server Behavior doesn't have a user interface because there's nothing for us to specify; it simply inserts the code into the document.

Sessions and Cookies

Cookies

Cookies are small text files that the server can send to the user, to be stored on their computer, and are intended for holding simple information. When the user makes a request with their browser to the site that set a cookie, it will include the cookie in the request. These days, cookies tend to be looked at with suspicion by many people because their legitimate uses have been usurped by large advertising companies who use them to find out as much about your surfing habits as they possibly can. That said, they do still remain quite a useful item; it's just unfortunate that people feel obliged to switch them off in their web browsers due to unscrupulous companies trying to be big brother.

> *We can only store the user's e-mail address if they give it to us in a form*

For many answers, tutorials, and scripts, visit *Cookie Central*, which has lots of great info. It also has a dedicated page for JavaScript cookies, which is certainly worth taking a look at. It can be found at the following address: *http://www.cookiecentral.com/content.phtml?area=2&id=7*.

Cookies are there to store information in order to help maintain a kind of 'state' in the stateless environment of HTTP. You can only store 4KB worth of information in a single cookie so you won't get masses of information in them. There is a couple of rules that have been laid down for cookies that Internet Explorer and Netscape Navigator both adhere to. They should only store up to 300 cookies (each) on your computer and no domain should be allowed to create more than 20 cookies on an individual user's computer. Despite the bad reputation that cookies have, they can't store any information that we don't have access to through our application – for example, we can only store the user's e-mail address if they give it to us in a form.

This section of the chapter will run through the creation of cookies and then move on to their removal. We'll wrap this section up by recreating my Login Cookies Server Behavior, which is useful for storing login information when a **remember me** feature is added to the form.

Creating Cookies

Just like creating Session variables, creating cookies is very straightforward. To create a cookie called `ckUsername` with a value of Rob, you would use this code:

```
<% Response.Cookies("ckUsername") = "Rob" %>
```

If we had a Recordset containing user names, we could dynamically create cookies for each user. The following line of code takes user names stored in a column called `Username` of a Recordset called `rsUser`:

```
<% Response.Cookies("ckUsername") = rsUser.Fields.Item("Username").Value %>
```

Iif you don't provide an expiry dates when you create cookies, they will expire when the current session ends. To provide an expiry date, you can use the following code:

```
<%
Response.Cookies("ckUsername") = rsUser.Fields.Item("Username").Value
Response.Cookies("ckUsername").Expires = Date() + 30
%>
```

This code sets the dynamic username value again, but this time specifies that it should expire 30 days from when it is set.

If you are trying to use cookies on a web site that uses multiple servers, you might find problems with the code displayed so far in this section because the cookies we have created are specific to the server that created them. To enable these cookies to be used on a site that spans multiple servers, you need to specify the `Domain` attribute, as shown next:

```
<%
Response.Cookies("ckUsername") = rsUser.Fields.Item("Username").Value
Response.Cookies("ckUsername").Domain = ".domain.com"
Response.Cookies("ckUsername").Expires = Date() + 30
%>
```

There are conditions that must be adhered to when using of the `Domain` attribute. You must use two periods in the name specified where it represents a top-level domain, and three dots for a second-level domain. The following illustrates this:

- Valid top-level domain references: `www.domain.com`, `.domain.com`

- Invalid top-level domain reference: `domain.com`

- Valid second-level domain references: `www.domain.co.uk`, `.domain.co.uk`

- Invalid second-level domain reference: `domain.co.uk`

If you need to create cookies that are only for a specific page or set of pages to use, you can use the `Path` attribute. The following example will set the `ckUsername` cookie to the value contained in a Recordset column, it will specify the domain and the path to the only pages in that domain that can use it. The path is stated relative to the root of the site.

```
<%
  Response.Cookies("ckUsername") = rsUser.Fields.Item("Username").Value
  Response.Cookies("ckUsername").Domain = www.domain.com
  Response.Cookies("ckUsername ").Path = "/path/to/the/pages/"
  Response.Cookies("ckUsername").Expires = Date() + 30
%>
```

The last attribute we can set in the cookie is `Secure`. This slightly misleading name does not mean that the cookie is going to be secure; what it means is that the cookie will only be set if the browser is viewing the page over a secure connection, such as *https://*.

Adding the Boolean value of `Secure` into the previous example would make our code look like this:

```
%
  Response.Cookies("ckUsername") = rsUser.Fields.Item("Username").Value
  Response.Cookies("ckUsername").Domain = www.domain.com
  Response.Cookies("ckUsername ").Path = "/path/to/the/pages/"
<  Response.Cookies("ckUsername ").Secure = True
  Response.Cookies("ckUsername").Expires = Date + 30
%>
```

Now that's quite a complex cookie!

Just to complicate matters further, cookies can also contain multiple values. These cookies are known as `Dictionary` cookies and are useful if you want to store data about one item that can have multiple values. As an example, let's take a user's first and last names. The `Dictionary` cookie would enable us to store both parts of the user's name in separate named values of the same cookie. The code to do this would look something like this:

> *Dictionary cookies can have multiple values*

```
<%
  Response.Cookies("ckUserDetails")("FirstName") = "Rob"
  Response.Cookies("ckUserDetails")("LastName") = "Turnbull"
%>
```

Much clearer!

Now we have covered the creation process, we need to know how to use the values that were written out to the cookie. To do this, we need to use both the `Response` object and the `Request` object, as follows:

```
<% Response.Write(Request.Cookies("ckUsername")) %>
```

Of course, we can also use the shorthand version:

```
<%= Request.Cookies("ckUsername") %>
```

To request the value from part of a `Dictionary` cookie, you would use the following code:

```
<%= Request.Cookies("ckUserDetails")("FirstName") %>
```

Removing Cookies

Once you've created some cookies on a user's computer, your site and only your site can use them for whatever purpose you had in mind. In the case of a login application, for example, you can create some cookies to store the user's login details so they don't have to type them in every time they visit.

On the login form, there will be a checkbox that the user can tick to be remembered in future. If they uncheck this checkbox at any time, they obviously no longer want to be remembered at your site and your code should know what to do about this.

You don't actually remove the cookie from the user's computer in code. What you do is remove the value that is stored in the cookie by setting its value to nothing: a zero-length string. For example, the following code will set the ckUsername value to a zero-length string:

```
<% Response.Cookies("ckUsername") = "" %>
```

Alternatively, you could force the cookie to expire by setting the `Expires` property to yesterday:

```
<% Response.Cookies("ckUsername").Expires = Date -1 %>
```

Cookie Server Behaviors

As we have previously discussed, we should write the final working code before starting the building process. The Server Behavior we are going to build is a replica of my Login Cookies Server Behavior.

It starts by checking that the login form has been submitted. If it hasn't nothing happens. Without this check in place, every time the page is visited, this code would run. If the form has been submitted, we then check to see if the user wants to be remembered (have they checked the *remember me* checkbox?). If they have, we can set about creating three cookies and setting their expiry dates to some point in the future; we'll decide how many days that should be when we apply the Server Behavior to the page.

> *We'll decide how many days that should be when we apply the Server Behavior to the page*

If the *remember me* checkbox is not checked, the code will expire the three cookies on the user's computer.

The working code for this Server Behavior is as follows:

```
<%
' *** Login Cookies Server Behavior by RobGT - http://robgt.com ***
IF Request("Form_Submit_Button") <> "" THEN
  IF Request.Form("Remember_Me_Checkbox") = "Checkbox_Value" THEN
    Response.Cookies("Username_Cookie_Name") = _
                    Request.Form("Username_Form_Element")
    Response.Cookies("Username_Cookie_Name ").Expires = Date + Cookie_Life
    Response.Cookies("Password_Cookie_Name ") = _
                    Request.Form("Password_Form_Element ")
    Response.Cookies("Password_Cookie_Name ").Expires = Date + Cookie_Life
    Response.Cookies("Remember_Me_Cookie_Name ") = _
                    Request.Form("Remember_Me_Checkbox ")
    Response.Cookies("Remember_Me_Cookie_Name ").Expires = Date + Cookie_Life
  ELSE
    Response.Cookies("Username_Cookie_Name ") = ""
    Response.Cookies("Username_Cookie_Name ").Expires = Date - 1
    Response.Cookies("Password_Cookie_Name ") = ""
    Response.Cookies("Password_Cookie_Name ").Expires = Date - 1
    Response.Cookies("Remember_Me_Cookie_Name ") = ""
    Response.Cookies("Remember_Me_Cookie_Name ").Expires = Date - 1
  END IF
END IF
%>
```

As you can see, the code is primed ready for the SBB. When we get it in there, all the parameters we'll need to replace will be easily found because of the naming we've used here. It also helps us to identify which elements' values need to be used in which area of the code.

Sessions and Cookies

Before we get to the building stage, we can make using the finished Server Behavior easier by including selection lists that contain the form elements on the web page that it is being applied to. If all we have to do is select the form element name from a list, there's less likelihood of us entering a form element name incorrectly and the Server Behavior not working.

Fortunately for us, one of the most prolific extension writers out there, Massimo Foti, has written some Server Behavior Builder extensions that, once installed, will give us the options of using form element select lists.

Download and install this extension from *http://www.massimocorner.com/*, click the *Ultradev* link and then click the *General* link. The extension you want is called *SBB Controls Form Menu 1.3*.

Let's build Login Cookies!

> *The Add Parameter button will offer to replace all instances of the same element*

Launch the SBB to create a new Server Behavior. Generate it in *ASP VBScript* and call it *Login Cookies*. Add a code block and enter the required code.

Make the following parameter replacements in the code. You will benefit from using the *Add Parameter* button when building this Server Behavior, because it will offer to replace all instances of the same element for you. And there are several instances of the same item to be replaced in this code.

Replace	With a parameter called
`Form_Submit_Button`	Submit button name
`Remember_Me_Checkbox`	Remember me checkbox name
`Checkbox_Value`	Remember me checkbox value
`Remember_Me_Cookie_Name`	Remember me cookie name
`Username_Form_Element`	Username form element name
`Username_Cookie_Name`	Username cookie name
`Password_Form_Element`	Password form element name
`Password_Cookie_Name`	Password cookie name
`Cookie_Life`	Cookie life in days

Set the *Insert Code* list to *Above the <html> Tag* and set the *Relative Position* list to *The Beginning of the File*.

Tick the *Identifier* checkbox under the *Advanced* section and make sure this code block is selected in the *Code Block to Select* list.

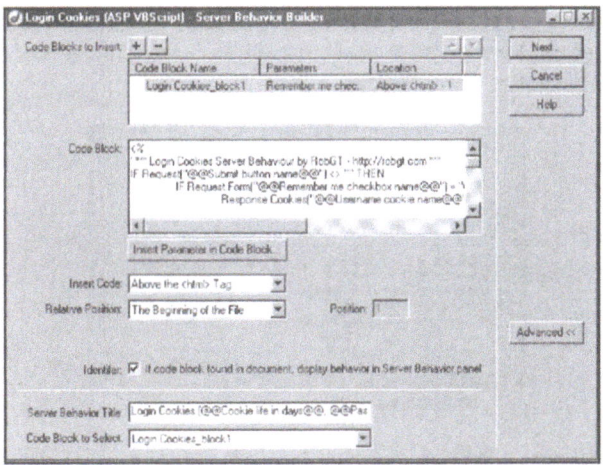
Lots of parameters to set in this code block

Click Next to set the form element types. The following table shows what form element should be selected for each parameter.

Parameter	Display As
Submit button name	Text Field
Remember me checkbox name	Form Fields Menu (tmt)
Remember me checkbox value	Text Field
Remember me cookie name	Text Field
Username form element name	Form Fields Menu (tmt)
Username cookie name	Text Field
Password form element name	Form Fields Menu (tmt)
Password cookie name	Text Field
Cookie life in days	Text Field

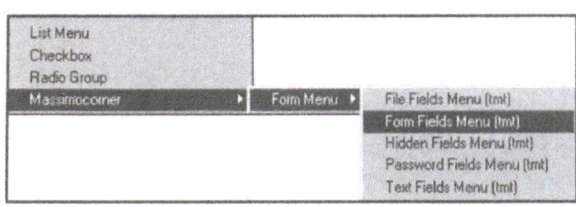
Accessing the Form Fields Menu

I think this order of the form elements is logical

10

Sessions and Cookies

Your form elements will be set in the order listed above (unless you order them differently of course.) I think this order of the form elements is logical but feel free to set them in your preferred order using the up and down arrow buttons in this dialog.

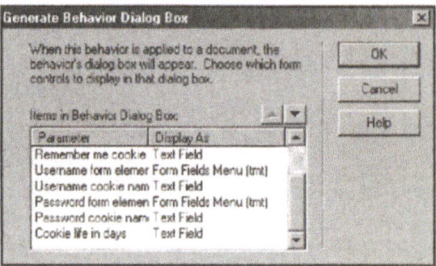

Ordering the parameters for the setup form

Once you are happy with the order, click *OK* to create the Server Behavior. When we run this Server Behavior, assuming we've got a form set up properly, we'll see the following dialog:

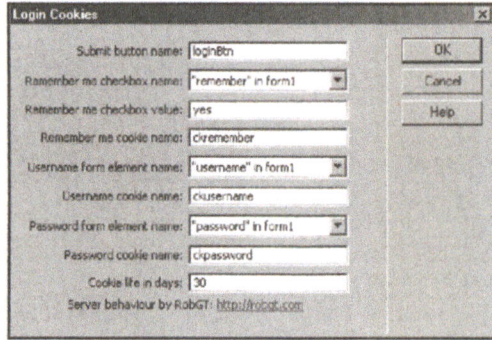

The Login Cookies Server Behavior needs a lot of information

Get All Data Sources Server Behavior

This Server Behavior by Tom Muck of The Dreamweaver Team (*http://www.dwteam.com*) will make a great addition to your extensions collection. One of the shortfalls of Dreamweaver MX is its lack of ability to share objects, such as Session variables between your web pages. It is freely available from either the *Macromedia special extensions* page located at:
http://www.macromedia.com/software/dreamweaver/special/extensions/, or on the Dreamweaver Team web site at *http://www.dwteam.com/Extensions/#DataSources*.

On one page you might have created some Session variables, on another page you might have created some Application variables. Unfortunately, Dreamweaver MX doesn't keep track of them in one place for you. This extension solves that problem. Once it is installed it offers two extra items in the *Bindings* list. They are:

- All Application Variables

- All Session Variables

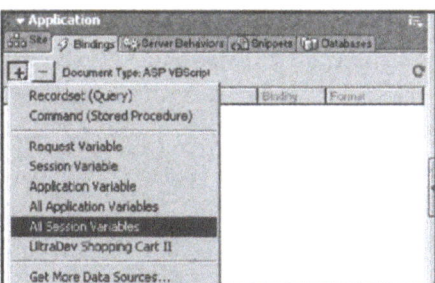

New items on the Bindings > + menu

When you select one of these bindings, a site-wide search is performed and all matches are pulled into the *Bindings* window. For example, selecting *All Session Variables* from this list will populate the *Bindings* panel with a *Session* object and list all the Session variables found in the site:

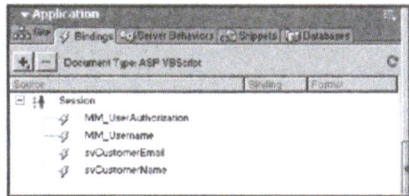

All Session Variables finds just that, all the Session variables on the site

Very useful!

Summary

We've taken a good look at the objects and their respective collections, methods, events, and properties that enable us to create, maintain, and remove Session and Application variables and cookies.

We've built a few simple but useful and timesaving Server Behaviors to help us in the creation and removal of Session Variables. We then built a Server Behavior for use with a login form that writes cookies to remember a user's login details, if they want them remembered.

We also built a simple **active users counter,** utilizing the `Application` object to create an application-level variable that we then used to display the number of people currently viewing our web site.

To round off the chapter we looked at a useful extension that gathers up all the Session and Application variables in our site and makes them available to us in the *Bindings* panel.

Hopefully, this chapter has given you an insight into the objects that you possibly use on a daily basis in your web applications, perhaps without having experienced some parts of them. This chapter intends to leave you thinking about how you might improve on your usage of Session variables and cookies in your web applications in order to streamline your server overheads and provide a better user experience.

11

- Introduction to Flash, and using Flash with ASP

- Creating a Flash MX/ASP Application via Dreamweaver MX

Author: Edward Apostol

Integrating Flash MX and ASP

Knowing how to use Macromedia Flash is becoming an integral skill amongst many web designers and developers.

In this chapter, you will find that Flash can be used to provide interactive interfaces for many applications, both web- and non-web based. From "splash pages", interactive banners, and even simple navigational buttons, to standalone lightweight games and presentations, Flash is involved in a wide range of activities.

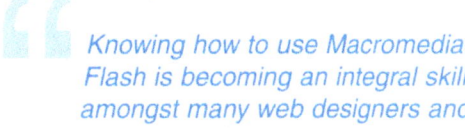

Knowing how to use Macromedia Flash is becoming an integral skill amongst many web designers and developers

This chapter explores how to make the most of the power of Flash with ASP, using Dreamweaver MX and the Flash MX development environment to deliver exciting applications. Specifically, we will cover:

- A brief history of Flash and its Traditional Uses
- "Flashes" of Flash already present in the Dreamweaver MX Environment
- Creating a Simple Application with Flash MX, Dreamweaver MX, and ASP

Note that exercises covered in this chapter have been built using Flash MX, although they will work equally well in Flash 5. Information on backward-compatibility between Flash 5 and Flash MX can be found at http://www.macromedia.com/support /flash/releasenotes/mx/rn_mx.html.

A Brief History of Flash

Initially conceived in 1996 (when it was referred to as FutureSplash), Flash was first utilized to create presentations that contained interesting animations, often including sounds and interactivity. Since then, Flash has grown to serve as a development platform for increasingly sophisticated application environments. Macromedia has employed the term "rich-media" to describe the level of interactivity that Flash can create between the user and the application.

Using Flash by Itself

Flash has been used by itself in the past to build self-contained interactive applications. This was probably satisfactory for applications such as small games, animation, or the construction of navigation bars where the data contained within the Flash Movie was updated infrequently, and only updated by the Flash developer.

However, businesses wanted to somehow combine Flash's dynamic content presentation with real-time data, perhaps obtained from a stock-ticker, a database, or through some other application. Communication with these applications often involved some form of middleware language, such as ASP. The diagram below shows the generic application architecture of a Flash-only application, compared to a Flash/ASP application:

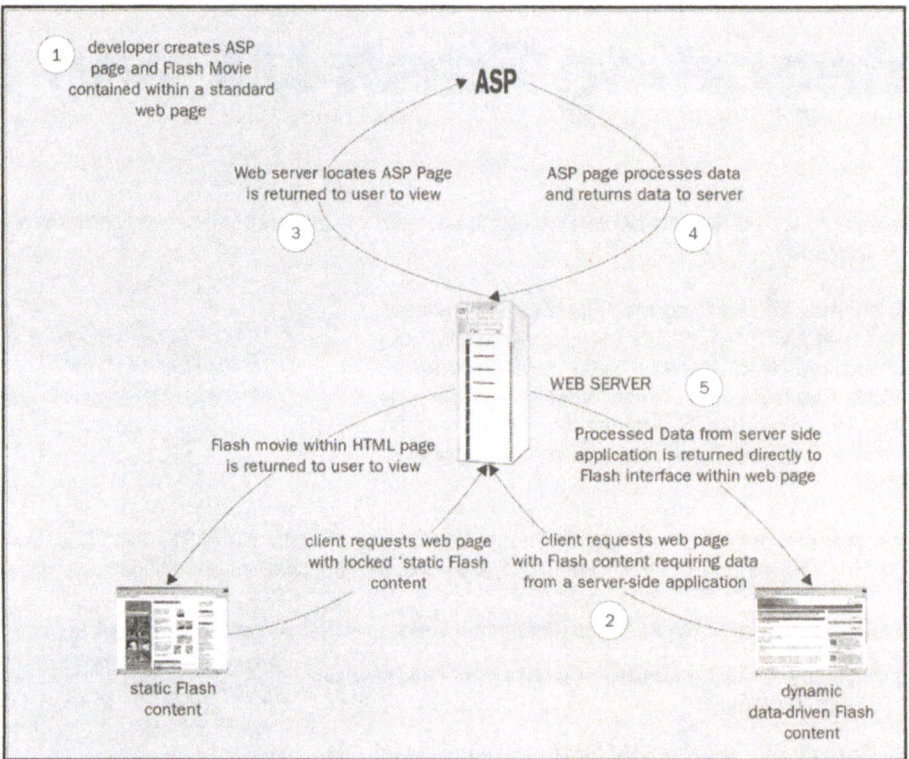

The static Flash page is pretty self-explanatory; however, let's look at the steps involved with the Flash/ASP web application:

- Step 1: The developer creates a web page with a user interface involving Flash content. This Flash content requires data processing (typically, user-input data, such as form data). The developer also creates an ASP page containing the necessary functionality to perform said data processing

- Step 2: The client requests the Flash-containing web page

- Step 3: When the data processing is required, the ASP is passed the data to process

- Step 4: The result is returned to the web server as an HTML stream

- Step 5: The web server then returns the data back to the Flash interface for display

The latest version of Flash, Flash MX, has shown significant advances in the way that it accesses server-side functionality. When coupled with a companion product called *Flash Communications Server* (see *http://www.macromedia.com/software/flashcom* for more details), Flash MX offers Flash-specific developers the necessary toolset to create dynamic applications (similar to those developed in traditional server-side languages) using only Flash.

However, this is a recent development, so it has yet to be seen where this path will lead. So for now, we will explore how Flash and ASP work together.

Using Flash with ASP

ASP provides a server-side solution that can act as a "middle-man" between a web page with a Flash-based interface and a data source (such as a database). ASP can also provide some sort of added dynamic interaction between the client browser and the application server.

> *ASP provides a server-side solution that can act as a "middle-man" between a web page with a Flash-based interface and a data source*

Flash's animation features provide the ability to help make easy and engaging interfaces with data sources and server-based applications, with distinct advantages over standard HTML. For example, in standard e-commerce-based web sites with HTML interfaces, a user usually has to go through several different pages in order to complete the shopping process, each page requiring load time. Flash, on the other hand, can preload all the data by invoking ActionScript commands that force the loading of data behind the scenes, and present the transaction within a single movie. When you launch a web page containing the Flash movie, the Flash movie itself does not need to reload in order to update its interface. Web pages on the other hand, usually need some sort of update or refresh action which may reload the entire page. Flash interfaces can receive and display updated data even as the interface changes, without reloading the Flash movie – this also reduces the risk of losing data between page loads.

When Flash and ASP are used together, there are generally two processes that take place – sending data from Flash to an ASP page so that data can be processed by ASP, and data being returned from an ASP-based application back to Flash.

Initiated by Flash

When Flash is used as a frontend, it can "initiate" the sending of data to a page containing ASP code. This process involves using Flash's internal language, ActionScript, to pass data to an ASP-coded page on the server. The ASP script could then return data using the `Response.Write` method to write out a string of data, which Flash MX can interpret. Let's take a look at some examples.

To begin with, let's look at a Flash movie that contains text fields and a *Submit* button. In a production scenario, this would be used as a front-end interface for a "search engine" type application.

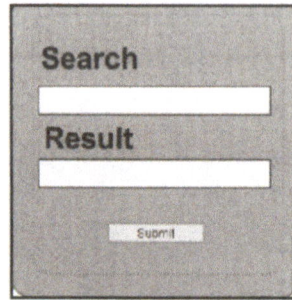

A simple Flash form.

In Flash MX, as in Dreamweaver MX, the *Properties* Panel reveals the properties of the various objects inserted onto the stage. In this example, there is an *Input Text* field called `strSearchText` (indicated within the *Var:* box) that will allow the user to enter data. There is also a *Result* field called `strResultsText`, which will return the results of the search. This field is called a *Dynamic Text Field* in Flash MX, and is not editable by the user.

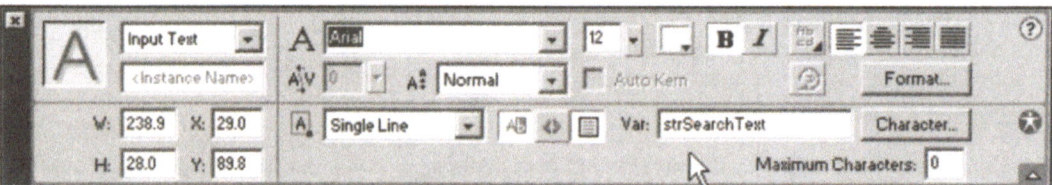

The Flash MX Properties Panel.

The ActionScript language is very similar to JavaScript. If you are already familiar with JavaScript, then learning ActionScript should not be too hard. Even if you are unfamiliar with it, you should be able to pick it up fairly quickly. For a good introduction to Flash, take a look at *Foundation Flash MX* (*Besley, Bhangal, and Farr, Friends of ED, ISBN 1-903450-10-1*), and for a more focused look at ActionScript (rather than the Flash interface), there's *Foundation ActionScript for Flash MX* (*Renow-Clark and Bhangal, Friends of ED, 1-903450-73-X*).

There is an ActionScript command called `loadVariablesNum`, used for information exchange between a Flash MX document and a server application, such as an ASP file. `loadVariablesNum` is often described as an *action* of a Flash movie that can be used to load data from an external URL. The syntax for the function is:

```
loadVariablesNum (url, level, [variables]);
```

- The *url* parameter is a string specifying the URL to load the variables from

- The *level* parameter specifies the level within the Flash MX movie that returned variables are loaded into. Think of a level as a plane within a Flash document that can hold variables, sounds, animations, and other data. Many levels of variables, sounds, and animations can exist within a single Flash document, and there are ways to reference data in a particular level if required. When you are looking at a Flash Movie, its background is often considered to be "level 0"

- The *variables* parameter is optional, but if it exists it specifies the method of string transmission or receiving as either sent via GET or POST methods. Basically, it determines the method by which variables within the Flash MX movie are sent to the specified URL

A usage example, placed within a Flash-based button (or *Flash pushbutton UI component*, as we will see later) is as follows:

```
on (release) {

  loadVariablesNum('results.ASP','_root','POST');
}
```

What we are saying is that when the user clicks and releases the mouse button, we load the variables from the script `results.asp` onto the principal level (actually, a *timeline*) of the Flash MX movie. We are also going to send the variables that exist in our Flash MX movie to the `results.asp` script using the `POST` method.

Similar to the `LoadVariablesNum` command is the `loadVariables` command, which can also retrieve data from an external file. It is different in that it can set the values for variables within a Flash movie, either in the Flash Player or in a target **Movie Clip**. Movie Clips are often described as instances of Flash Movies "in miniature". They have all the characteristics of a Flash Movie, but act as individual objects within the main Flash movie itself (rather like an instance of an ASP object, as opposed to the object itself). The syntax is quite similar:

```
on (release) {
  loadVariables('results.ASP',levelname -or- target Movie Clip,'POST');
}
```

A target Movie Clip (which the data is being sent to) would be referenced by a name assigned to it within the Flash program. The `LoadVariables` command can only specify target movie clip names when you are typing in Flash Programs in "Expert Mode" within the Flash ActionScript editor. Otherwise, `LoadVariablesNum` is used to specify levels in "Expert Mode".

When the data is actually sent to `results.asp`, the script will look something like this:

```
<%
  Dim whattolookfor, sendouttheresults
  whattolookfor=Request.Form ('strSearchText')
%>
```

All the script is doing is receiving the results of the `strSearchText` field via the `Request` object and passing them to a variable called `whattolookfor`. In ASP, a Flash-based form is treated like a standard HTML form, and thus we can use `Request.Form` to retrieve the information from the appropriate field.

Initiated by ASP (Back to Flash…the Return Trip)

Let's suppose that after some further processing within the same ASP page, you want to send the results of your search in the form of a text message (using the POST method) back to the Flash front end. After all, you have to tell the user whether a search result was found or not.

The ASP (continued from the previous code snippet above) that could be used to respond to the Flash interface's request for processing the information in the text fields might look something like this:

```
<%
' eja: create variable used to store the results of data processed by ASP
' eja: strResultsText is sent back to the Flash object via another variable in ASP
' eja: called sendouttheresults. We utilize the Write Method of the Response object
' eja: to achieve this task.

Dim strResultsText,sendouttheresults

' eja: some data processing here
' eja: for the sake of this example, theresults variable resolves to
' eja: the title of the book
theresults="ASP:Dynamic Dreamweaver MX"

' eja: sendouttheresults shows the preparation of sending the data in theresults
' eja: variable
' eja: and combines it with the expected variable to be used by Flash, strResultsText
sendouttheresults="strResultsText=" & theresults

' eja: The Response object is used to send the data in the sendouttheresults variable
' eja: When sending out the results using Response.Write
' eja: the MIME type by default is set to text/html
Response.Write sendouttheresults
%>
```

Remember that we set the variable name of the input box to strSearchText, and this value has been posted through to the script using the POST method. The results are returned from the ASP via a name/value pair strResultsText, which happens to be the name of the corresponding field in the Flash interface.

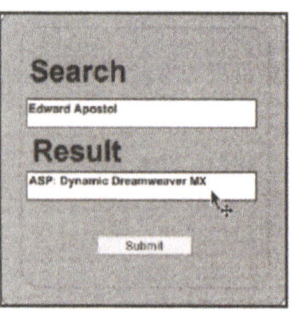

Our simple Flash form, with some result data passed to it from ASP.

The result from the script should immediately appear in the *Result* text box. The ASP code within the page sets the variable strResultsText, which is the variable name that we have assigned to the *Result* text box. The update occurs immediately.

Think of the possibilities: using this kind of methodology you could develop login functionality, or an e-commerce application with Flash-based animations.

In general, an ASP application can process data received from Flash and send the processed data back to Flash. All you need to know is how the data is going to be sent via ActionScript (loadVariablesNum) and how to send the data back (Response.Write). The obvious advantage of this approach is that this allows you to send data from Flash to an ASP application that can perform tasks that Flash normally cannot. In addition, the Flash interface can be designed to represent the data returned from an ASP application in an interesting and interactive manner.

Furthermore, data can be received by Flash MX as name/value pairs as discussed above, or even as tag-delimited XML data. Receiving the results of an application process written in ASP directly as XML data could potentially remove a translation step within Flash MX, as Flash MX is able to process XML data directly. Later on in this chapter you will see how Flash MX receives XML data initially generated from ASP code and use it to display information.

Flash MX in the Dreamweaver MX Environment

In this section we will take a brief look at how easy it is to use Flash content in web pages via Dreamweaver MX. The Dreamweaver MX environment already has aspects of Flash MX integrated within it, making interaction between the two even easier.

Inserting Flash

This is done via the obvious *Flash* options found under the *Media* tab of the *Insert* toolbar (or using the *Flash* icon under the *Common* tab of the *Insert* panel.)

To demonstrate inserting a Flash MX movie, simply use the Flash MX button on the *Insert* toolbar to insert a sample movie (dwmx.swf, found in the download) onto a blank HTML page. The *Properties* panel configures itself appropriately to show the characteristics of the newly inserted Flash MX movie.

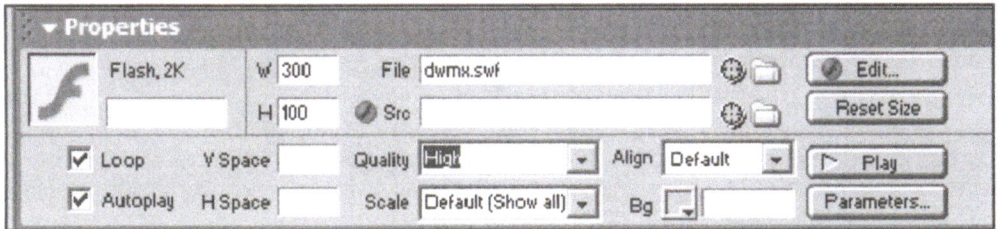

You should be able to see your Flash movie, shown as a grayed rectangle within the *Document* panel. If you press the *Play* button, the Flash Movie itself can be seen within the *Document* panel.

11

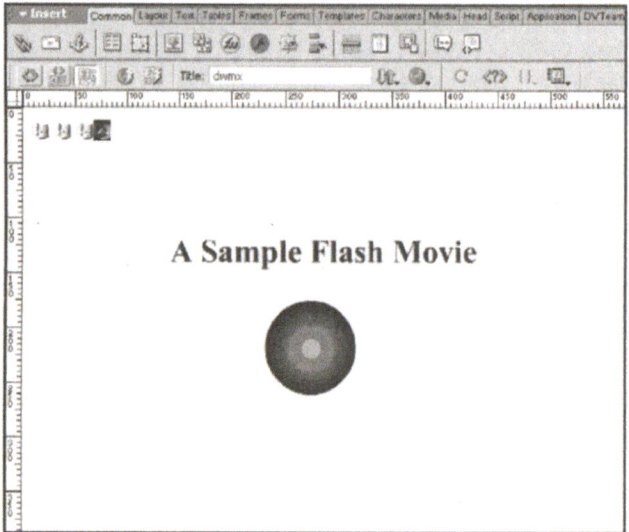

Embedding a Flash File into an HTML document using Dreamweaver MX.

When you insert the Flash MX movie, Dreamweaver MX automatically creates the code required to insert the Flash MX movie within the confines of the HTML-based web page:

```
<object classid="clsid:D27CDB6E-AE6D-11cf-96B8-444553540000" codebase=
"http://download.macromedia.com/pub/shockwave/cabs/flash/swflash.cab#version=6,0,29,0
" width="300" height="100">
  <param name="movie" value="sample.swf">
  <param name="quality" value="high">
  <embed src="dwmx.swf" quality="high"
pluginspace="http://www.macromedia.com/go/getflashplayer" type="application/x-
shockwave-flash" width="300" height="100"></embed>
</object>
```

The `<object>` element and its contents specify a multimedia object that is to be placed within the web page. In particular, these elements define several aspects of the Flash MX movie. The `classid` attribute simply refers to a unique identifier for the program (often referred to as an Active X Control) used to display this object, the Flash MX Player in this case. The `codebase` attribute contains a URL value that points to the location of the current Flash MX Player, if they do not have it already (this is only supported in the Internet Explorer browser – other browsers find the player via the `<embed>` element instead). Finally, the `height` and `width` attributes within the `<object>` tag set the height and width of the Flash MX movie.

The `<param>` elements are also only supported by the Internet Explorer browser, and fill in some further details about the nature of the object being embedded, such as the location of the object, and the quality to load it at.

Inserting Flash MX Buttons and Animated Flash MX Text

You can insert Flash buttons and text into your HTML pages via Dreamweaver MX without needing to launch Flash MX itself.

To insert a Flash MX button, choose *Insert > Interactive Images > Flash Button*, or use the *Flash Button* icon under the *Media* tab of the *Insert* panel. A dialog box will pop up, allowing you to alter the characteristics of the Flash MX button to be inserted, such as the button style, the button text, the button text font, the link, and the text color. After the appropriate options have been selected, your newly created Flash MX button will be placed into the document, to the left of the current location of the cursor.

Similarly, to insert Flash MX text choose *Insert > Interactive Images > Flash Text*, or use the *Flash Text* icon under the *Media* tab of the *Insert* panel. This allows us to insert Flash text links into your web pages. The text can be made to change color on an `onMouseover` event.

Now we have seen a bit about Flash, and how it interacts with Dreamweaver MX, let's get onto some real-world stuff – in the following example, we will walk through the Dreamweaver MX-aided development of a simple web-based application where Flash MX acts as a frontend to an ASP-based back end.

Creating a Simple Application with Flash MX and ASP via Dreamweaver MX

This section shows you how to build a CD/DVD catalog system with a Flash Front End, an ASP page that processes the data, and an XML file that acts as a data store.

A Brief Note About XML versus Databases

Why use XML in this exercise as opposed to a database? This exercise could easily be rewritten so that the ASP processing page commits the data to a database instead of an XML file. Well, we have chosen to use XML files, because they are easier to read, both by a human eye, and Flash itself – no data conversion is required.

Creating a User Interface Prototype in XHTML

Perhaps the best way to describe the Flash front end to our CD/DVD catalog system is to first conceptualize an interface in standard HTML. Below is a typical XHTML interface that would be suitable for the CD/DVD catalog (see `EnterData.html` in the code download):

```
<?xml version="1.0" encoding="iso-8859-1"?>
<!DOCTYPE html PUBLIC "-//W3C//DTD XHTML 1.0 Transitional//EN"
          "http://www.w3.org/TR/xhtml1/DTD/xhtml1-transitional.dtd">
<html xmlns="http://www.w3.org/1999/xhtml">
<head>
  <title>Enter CD/DVD Info</title>
```

```html
    <meta http-equiv="Content-Type" content="text/html; charset=iso-8859-1">
</head>

<body>
  <form action="process_entry.asp" method="post">
    <h3>Enter the CD/DVD Data here:</h3>
    <table width="500" border="0" cellspacing="0" cellpadding="0">
      <tr>
        <td><p>Format:<br />
          (enter CD or DVD) </p>
        </td>
        <td align="left" valign="top">
          <select name="strdisctype" id="strdisctype">

            <option value="DVD">DVD</option>

              <option value="CD">CD</option>
            </select>
        </td>
      </tr>
      <tr>
        <td>Disc Title :<br />
        </td>
        <td align="left" valign="top">
          <input name="strdisctitle" type="text" id="disctitle3" size="50" />
        </td>
      </tr>
      <tr>
        <td>Artist(s)/Cast:<br />
          (for more than 1 name, separate names by commas)
        </td>
        <td align="left" valign="top">
          <input name="strartistcast" type="text" id="address12" size="50" />
        </td>
      </tr>
      <tr>
        <td>Genre:</td>
        <td align="left" valign="top">
          <input name="strgenre" type="text" id="address22" size="50" />
        </td>
      </tr>
      <tr>
        <td>Catalog Number:</td>
        <td align="left" valign="top">
          <input name="strcatalognum" type="text" id="genre" size="50" />

        </td>

      </tr>
      <tr>
        <td>Date Acquired: (MM/DD/YY)</td>
        <td align="left" valign="top">
          <input name="strmonth" type="text" id="strmonth" size="3" />
          /
          <input name="strday" type="text" id="strday" size="3" />
          /
          <input name="stryear" type="text" id="stryear" size="3" /></td>
```

```
</tr>
    <tr>
      <td>Comments</td>
      <td align="left" valign="top">
        <textarea name="strcomments" id="strcomments"></textarea>
      </td>
    </tr>
  </table>

  <br />
  <br />
  <input type="submit" id="btnSub" name="btnSub" value="Submit" />
  <input type="reset" id="btnReset" name="btnReset" value="Reset" />
  <br />
</form>

</body>
</html>
```

Here is the page as it appears within the Dreamweaver MX interface:

Our HTML form prototype, as seen in Dreamweaver MX.

The HTML page can then serve as a "model" or "template" for your development. In fact, you could also use it as an alternative interface, for those people who wish to use a non-Flash interface.

Note that the `<form>` tag has an `action` attribute that passes the contents of the form to an ASP file called `process_entry.asp`. This will be the same page that the Flash interface will use.

Recreating the Form in Flash MX

Now onto the Flash interface itself – let's create the final Flash version of the form prototyped above. We'll call it `EnterData.fla`.

First, let's resize the stage and change its color to make it appear more vibrant. Select *Modify > Document* – the *Document Properties* dialog box will appear:

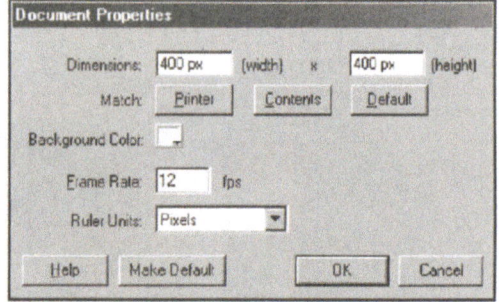

Change the *width* and *height* dimensions to 400 pixels by 400 pixels. We also changed the background color to the light yellow #FFFFCC.

The Flash MX DocumentProperties dialog.

Next, the *Timeline* is used to control content found within the stage, organized horizontally in *layers*. Choose *Insert > Layer* to insert a layer. Repeat the process three more times so there are four layers present in the timeline. From top to bottom, rename the layers *actions*, *text labels*, *form fields*, and *buttons*, as shown opposite:

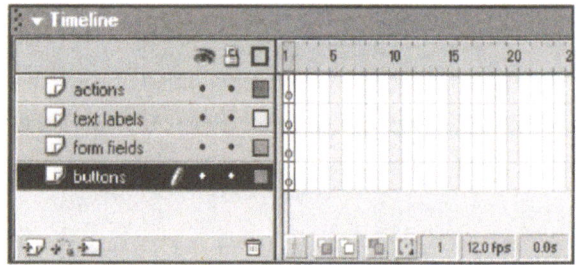

The Flash MX Timeline Panel.

Adding Text Labels

Select the *text labels* layer. Now select the text tool from the *Tools* panel. If you don't see the *Tools* panel in the environment, simply choose *Window > Tools*. Insert a static text label onto the stage by clicking your cursor at the appropriate location, and enter the text Enter *CD/DVD Data Here*, as shown here:

Use the *Properties* panel at the bottom to change the style of the text, and select *static text* from the *text type* pull-down menu:

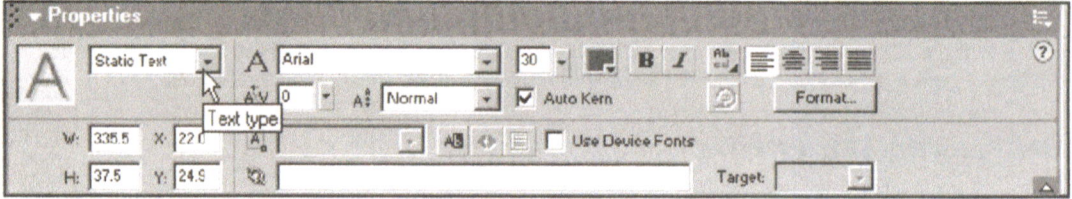

Keep adding more text labels; repeat the process above for each one, until the stage appears as shown below.

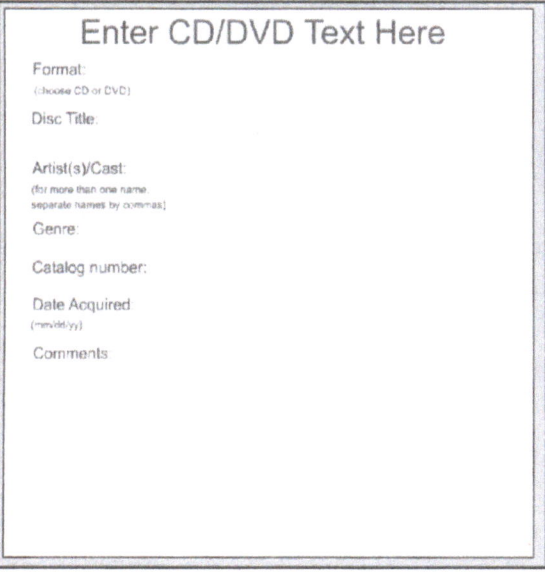

Our stage, with only the text labels added.

Setting up the Form Fields

With the form fields layer selected, insert the form fields for each appropriate label. Select *Input Text* as the style from the *Properties* pane, and insert text fields alongside *Disc Title*, *Artist(s)/Cast*, *Genre*, *Catalog Number*, *Date Acquired* (insert three beside this label), and *Comments*. Inserting text fields is also done using the text tool.

Next, using the *Var* input field of the *Properties* panel, insert variable names for each text field, as follows:

- *Disc Title*: `disctitle`
- *Artist(s)/Cast*: `artistcast`
- *Genre*: `genre`
- *Catalog Number*: `catnum`
- *Date Acquired*: `month`, `day`, and `year` (one for each of the three text fields, respectively)
- *Comments*: `comments`

Also, ensure that each field has the *Show Border Around Text* option selected as shown in the following screenshot, so you can see them when it is published:

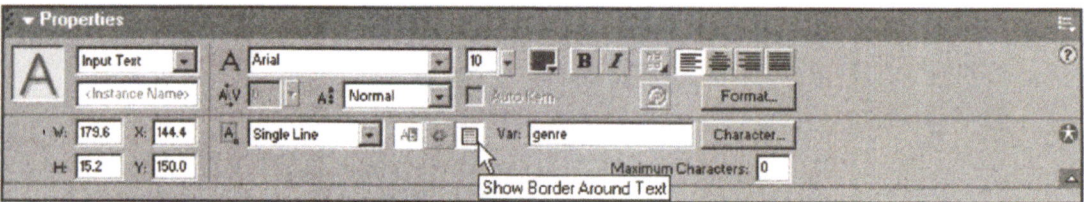

Our stage should now look something like this:

Enter CD/DVD Text Here

Format:
(choose CD or DVD)

Disc Title:

Artist(s)/Cast:
(for more than one name,
separate names by commas)

Genre:

Catalog number:

Date Acquired:
(mm/dd/yy)

Comments:

Our stage updated, with the text fields added too.

Adding UI Components

Flash MX comes with a new panel called the *UI Components* panel, which gives us access to predefined MovieClip objects that perform complex tasks. By default, the components included with Flash MX are MovieClips that act like elements of a standard HTML form. Drag the appropriate components required for this form and position them onto the stage, as shown opposite – the components you will be adding are the *ComboBox* for the *Format* field, and *Submit* and *Reset* buttons.

Enter CD/DVD Text Here

Format: _____ ▾
(choose CD or DVD)

Disc Title: [_____]

Artist(s)/Cast: [_____]
(for more than one name,
separate names by commas)

Genre:

Catalog number: [_____]

Date Acquired: [_] [_] [_]
(mm/dd/yy)

Comments:

Submit   Reset

Our stage further updated with UI Components.

However, we're not finished with our form yet – now we need to use the *Properties* panel to modify the properties of each component.

Select the *ComboBox* component on the stage, and in the *Properties* panel, click on the *Parameters* tab. For the instance name box, enter flistbox1. Note that this component is not called strdisctype (its HTML equivalent.) This is because in Flash, when we utilize a component, the component name identifies the component that will be used to send the selected item, not the variable. The variable used to store the selected item from flistbox1 will be added later in this exercise.

Next, click on the *Labels* and *Data* fields in the central area of the *Properties* panel, entering possible values of *CD* and *DVD* for each one, as shown below (the values themselves are entered in the *Values* dialog box that appears when you double-click the right-hand column containing the values, in the *Properties* panel):

▾ Properties			Properties	Parameters
Component	Editable	false		
strdisctype	Labels	[CD,DVD]		
	Data	[CD,DVD]		
W: 100.0 X: 145.3	Row Count	8		
H: 17.0 Y: 36.3	Change Handler			

Updating the properties of our ComboBox UI Component.

Now select the *Submit* button, and give it an instance name of *btnsubmit* and a label of *Submit*, as shown below:

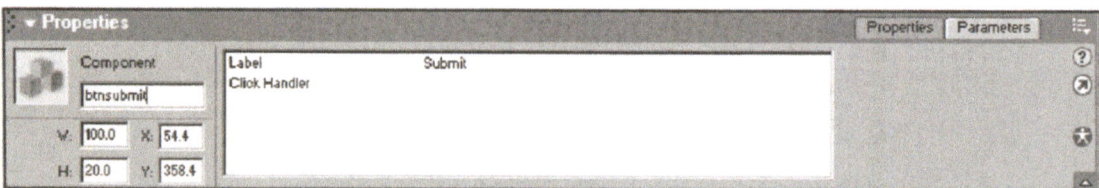

Updating the properties of our Submit button UI Component.

Note the *Click Handler* parameter in the *Properties* panel when the *Submit* button is selected – give it a value of *submitform*. By entering this value you are telling Flash MX to call a function called `submitform` within the ActionScript code. This function (which we'll see later) will be responsible for passing the contents of the Flash form to the ASP page for processing.

We need to do the same thing for the *Reset* button now – give the *Reset* button an instance name of *btnreset* and a label of *reset*, and give the *Click Handler* parameter for the *Reset* button a value of *clearfields*. This references an ActionScript function that is called when you click on the *Reset* button. The purpose of this function is to clear the fields of the Flash form. As with the `submitform` function, we'll be writing this ourselves, later on in the chapter.

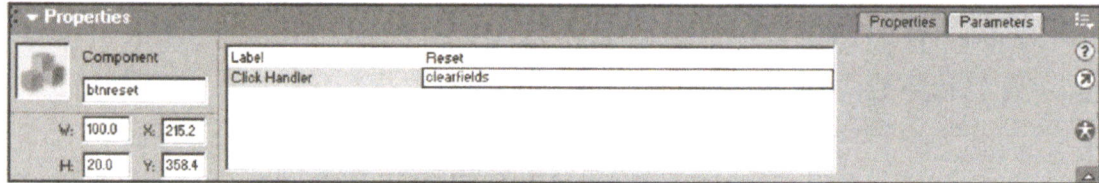

Updating the properties of our Reset button UI Component.

Adding Our ActionScript Functions

The last step in the creation of this form (for now) is to enter the ActionScript code to pass the contents of this form to the appropriate ASP page. The ASP page will then enter the data into an XML file.

Recall that the *Submit* button we created moments ago has a parameter in the *Properties* panel called *Click Handler* that describes a name of an ActionScript function to execute, which we called `submitform`. To create this function, select the actions layer.

Select *Frame 1* of the *Actions* layer. At the bottom of your Flash environment is the *Actions* panel, usually underneath the *Properties* panel – maximize the *Actions* panel by clicking on its arrow button on the upper-left corner of the panel. As you will be handcoding the ActionScript code, you need to make sure that the *Actions* panel is set to *Expert* mode. To go into *Expert* Mode, click the icon in the upper-right corner of the *Actions* panel to display the pop-up menu, and choose *Expert* Mode. At this time, you may also wish to choose *View Line Numbers*, which will help debug the code.

The *Actions* panel should now look like so:

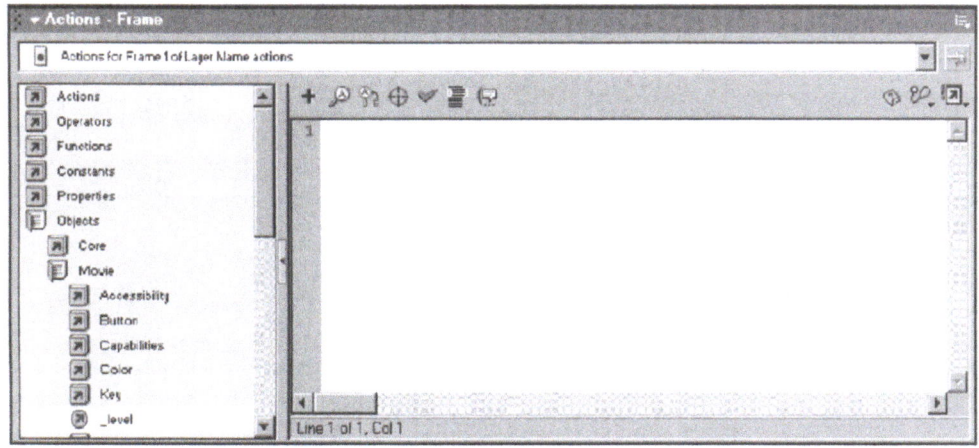

The Flash MX Actions Panel.

Add the following code to the *Script* area:

```
function submitform(){
// This function is triggered by clicking the submit button;
// Replace the URL with the URL to your web server.
loadVariablesNum("http://www.yourURL.com/aspflashdmx/process_entry.asp",0,"POST");
}


function clearfields(){
// this function resets the form and is triggered by the reset button;
flistbox1.setSelectedIndex(0);  // resets the list box back to CD
  disctitle=""; // resets the disc title var and clears the text field;
  artistcast=""; // resets the artist-cast field
  genre=""; // resets genre field
  catnum=""; // resets catalog number
  month="";
  day="";
  year=""; // resets the respective vars and fields
  comments=""; // resets the comments field
  results=""; // clears the results field
}


function getdiscformat(){
// This function is triggered when the user changes the list box.
// It will retrive the selected value and send it
// along with other variables to process_entry.asp
strdisctype=flistbox1.getSelectedItem().data
}

stop();
```

Note that you should replace *http://your.URL.com/aspflashdmx/* with the domain name of the web server that will host your files for this exercise, for example *http://localhost/chapter11/.* You could also relatively reference the link – this would have the advantage of allowing your web site to move from one server to another without necessarily breaking the links of your pages.

Let's take a look at the code in detail. Functions are created in ActionScript using the `function()` keyword. The curly braces contain the statements to be executed when this function is called. Our `submitform` function above is called when the *Submit* button is clicked (entered via the *ClickHandler* parameter in the *Properties* panel). Note that commands usually end with a semicolon in ActionScript – this is generally good practice.

The main statement to be executed in the first function (`submitform`) is the `loadVariablesNum` command. When you created the form fields in Flash, you specified variable names that were assigned to these form fields (within the *Properties* panel again) – each form field has a variable name. These variables in turn are located within a "level" of a Flash Movie; in this case it is the "main" level, level 0. Within the parentheses of the `loadVariablesNum` command you have the following arguments:

- The URL of the ASP page where you wish to send the variable information to

- The level in which the variables to be sent are located

- The method with which you choose to send this information, in this case, POST

In HTML, you would have assigned name variables to the `<input>` *form tags, set an action URL in the* `action` *attribute of the* `<form>` *element, and assigned a value of post to the* `method` *attribute to achieve the same effect.*

We could have just as easily used the GET method to send the data. If GET was chosen, the data would be passed as name/value pairs in the Querystring, and would need to be processed using ASP's `Request.QueryString` method. However, the GET method may not be appropriate if you do not wish to expose your data as it is being sent. In addition, it has a limit on the number of characters that can be sent. So in this case, the POST method is used.

The second function (`clearfields`) handles tasks to perform when the *Reset* button is clicked. In this case, all the variables (hence, all the text fields) are cleared or reset.

The third function, `getdiscformat`, is responsible for getting the selected item from the list box (`flistbox1`) and storing the value in a variable to be sent to ASP, called `strdisctype`.

Finally, the `stop();` line in ActionScript prevents the Flash document from proceeding to the next frame in the timeline. Recall that Flash was originally designed for animations and simple activity; as such, the *Timeline* panel is analogous to a movie with frames. We want Flash to stay within the frame that contains the form, much as we would like to have an HTML form stay within the web browser itself! If the `stop` command were not included, the Flash movie would proceed to the next frame, and since there is nothing there, the form would disappear from the stage!

When you publish a Flash movie, the file gets converted into a format that is playable by your browser's Flash Player, with a `.swf` extension. To preview your newly created form, choose *File > Publish Preview > Default (HTML)* from the Flash MX Menu. The form should look similar to the following:

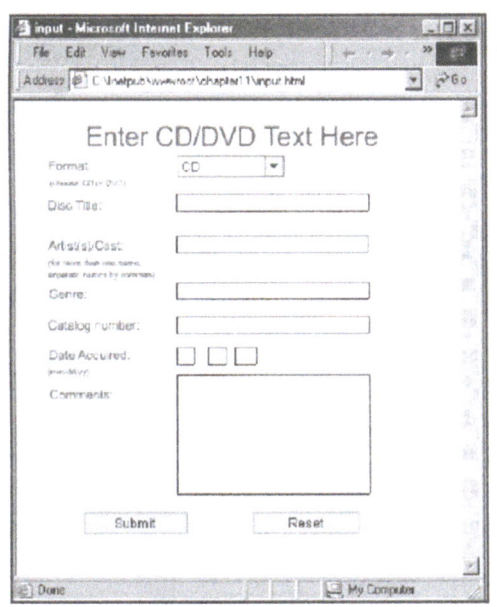

Now it's time to create our ASP file that will process the data from the form, `process_entry.asp`.

Our finished Flash form.

Creating the ASP to Handle the Form Data

In this exercise, our ASP development environment consisted of the following:

- Windows 2000 Professional, with a web directory to serve our application from – `C:\inetpub\wwwroot\chapter11`

- IIS 5.0 – Since this is a development PC, we set up the directory `chapter11` to have write permissions for the *INETPub* user (the user that accesses your web pages through your web server)

- The current version of the Microsoft XML Parser (Windows only), Microsoft XML Core Services 4.0 (MSXML 4.0), downloadable at *http://msdn.microsoft.com/downloads/ sample.asp?url=/msdn-files/027/001/766/msdncompositedoc.xml*

In Dreamweaver MX, create a new ASP VBScript page.

Remember that upon submission of our Flash form, the form contents are to be sent to our ASP page, and this page is to write the information into a data store. We could write the information to a database, but to make the data more universally accessible to other applications in the future, we are going to write the form contents to an XML file. Enter the code shown below in the Code View panel. Note that the code is heavily commented and fairly self-explanatory, but to aid understanding further, we've highlighted the actual code lines so they stand out from the comments.

```
<%
' **********************************************************************
' Script     : process_entry.asp
' Developed by : Edward Apostol
' Developed for: Dreamweaver MX Advanced ASP: Chapter 11 - Flash and ASP in DMX
```

```
' Version      : 1.0
' Modified     : November, 2002
' comments     :The "FlashFormtoXML" Function accepts two parameters.

'strXMLFilePath - The physical path where the XML file will be saved.
'strFileName - The name of the XML file that will be saved.

' ******************************************************************

Function FlashFormtoXML(strXMLFilePath, strFileName)

' Create variables

' Create a variable that stores the XML object
Dim objXMLDom

' Variable that will store the root tag
Dim objRoot

' Variable that will store the form field from Flash
Dim objField

' Variable that will store the current form field value
Dim objFieldValue

' Variable used to create Name attributes for the disc tag
Dim objattName

' Variable used to create an ID attribute that
' will be used to organize the CD/DVD entries
Dim objcatID

' Variable used to store the XML root tag
Dim objProcInstDim

' A counter variable used to assist in iterating
' through the form elements
Dim counter

' A variable used to store a message that is sent
' back to the Flash movie, indicating whether
' or not the writing was successful.
Dim statMsg

' A variable storing the message itself
Dim Msg

' Create an instance of the XML object.
Set objXMLDom = server.CreateObject("Microsoft.XMLDOM")
objXMLDom.preserveWhiteSpace = True

'Create your root element and append it to the XML document.
Set objRoot = objXMLDom.createElement("catalog")
objXMLDom.appendChild objRoot
```

```
'Iterate through the Form Collection of the Request Object.
For counter = 1 To Request.Form.Count
'Check to see if "btn" is in the name of the form element.
'  -or- if the element being passed is not a form element
'  (a Flash Function is actually a variable too in Flash)
'  Also, the Flash UI components have a var called 'fade'
'  that we do not want either
'If it is, then it is a button and we do not want to
'  add it to the XML document.

If (instr(1,Request.Form.Key(counter),"btn") = 0) Then
    If (Request.Form(counter)<>"[type Function]") Then
    If (instr(1,Request.Form.Key(counter),"Fade") = 0)
    Then

    'Create an element, "disc".

    Set objField = objXMLDom.createElement("disc")


    'Create an attribute, "name".

    Set objattName = objXMLDom.createAttribute("name")

    ' Set the value of the name attribute equal to the name of
    ' the current form field.

    objattName.Text = Request.Form.Key(counter)

    ' The setAttributeNode method will append and commit the
    ' id attribute to the disc element.

    objField.setAttributeNode objattName

    'Create another attribute, "catID". This just orders the elements.

    Set objcatID = objXMLDom.createAttribute("catID")

    'Set the value of the catID attribute.

    objcatID.Text = counter

    'Append the catID attribute to the disc element.

    objField.setAttributeNode objcatID

    ' Create a new element, "value", which will store the
    ' value of the current form field element being
    ' evaluated within this loop.

    Set objFieldValue = objXMLDom.createElement("value")

    ' Set the value of the "value" element equal to
    ' the value of the current field in the Form Collection.

    objFieldValue.Text = Request.Form(counter)

    ' Append the disc element as a child of the root element.

    objRoot.appendChild objField
```

```
        'Append the value element as a child of the field element.
          objField.appendChild objFieldValue

        End If
        End if

        ' the Next loop will cause this program to reiterate through
        ' the remaining form field elements.

        Next

        'Create the XML processing instruction.
        Set objProcInst = objXMLDom.createProcessingInstruction("xml", "version='1.0'")

        'Append the processing instruction to the XML document.
        objXMLDom.insertBefore objProcInst,objXMLDom.childNodes(0)

        'Save the XML document.
        objXMLDom.save strXMLFilePath & "\" & strFileName

        'Release all of your object references.
        Set objXMLDom = Nothing
        Set objRoot = Nothing
        Set objField = Nothing
        Set objFieldValue = Nothing
        Set objattName = Nothing
        Set objcatID = Nothing
        Set objProcInst = Nothing
        End Function


        'Do not break on an error.
        On Error Resume Next

        ' Call the FlashFormtoXML function, passing in the physical path to
        ' save the file to and the name that you wish to use for the file.
        ' In the first item, specify the drive and directory which you want to
        ' save the file to.
        ' In the second item, specify the filename of the XML file you wish
        ' to use to store your CD/DVD content.
        ' NOTE!!! In a live production server, you should NEVER have
        ' write privileges given to the same directory that hosts
        ' your web site itself! Your ISP or your Network Administrator
        ' may arrange a directory for you, similar to a directory
        ' where databases are stored.

        FlashFormtoXML "c:\inetpub\wwwroot\chapter11","cdDVDcatalog.XML"

        ' Test to see if an error occurred; if so, let the user know
        ' by sending a message back to the Flash Interface.
        ' Otherwise, tell the user that the operation was successful.

        If err.Number <> 0 then
        msg="Errors occurred while saving your form submission."
        msg = msg & " error - " & err.Description
        msg = msg & "; error number is " & err.Number

        Else
          msg="Your form submission has been saved."
        End If
```

```
    statMsg="results=" & msg

    response.Write statMsg

%>
```

Save the file as `process_entry.asp` in the `chapter11` directory.

So far, you have created a Flash-based form that allows the user to enter data related to CDs and DVDs. When the user hits the *Submit* button in the form, the form contents are sent to the page `process_entry.asp`.

The code within `process_entry.asp` creates an XML object and adds the necessary elements and fields to this object. Based on the data processed within the ASP page, a message is prepared at the end of the script, and the message is sent back to Flash.

Return to Flash

Our last steps consist of returning to the Flash environment and creating the necessary interface to receive the message that will let the user know whether the information was successfully written. In addition, we will physically check the directory `chapter11` to confirm that the XML file was successfully created.

In Flash MX, open the Flash document you were editing previously, `EnterData.fla`. In the timeline, add a new layer called *Results*:

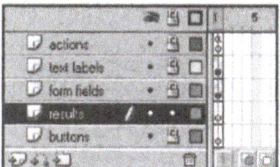

The Timeline Panel with the new Results layer.

With this layer selected, use the *Tools* panel to insert a new text field onto the stage, just below the *Submit* and *Reset* buttons, and centrally aligned. This new text field will serve to receive the verification message. Using the *Properties* panel, make sure the text field is a *Dynamic Text* field, and add the variable name *results* to the *Var* box. Use the width and height boxes to size the width of the field appropriately so that it can contain any messages sent from the ASP page. Our stage and *Properties* panel should now look something like this:

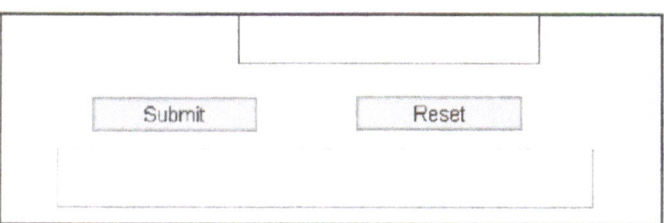

Save our updated `EnterData.fla` file, this time in the `chapter11` directory we created earlier. Now go to *File > Publish* to create our `.swf` file.

Saving the .fla file in the web directory prior to testing ensures that the Flash Movie will be placed in the correct directory upon publishing.

You should now be able to test the flash movie directly within the Flash environment. Press `ctrl-enter`, and the Flash environment changes to Preview Mode, where you can preview the Flash Movie as if it were running live. Try filling in some sample information within the text fields, and hit the *Submit* button. You can also test the *Reset* button at this time to see that the form fields are indeed cleared. The following screenshot shows sample information being input, and the results after clicking the *Submit* button.

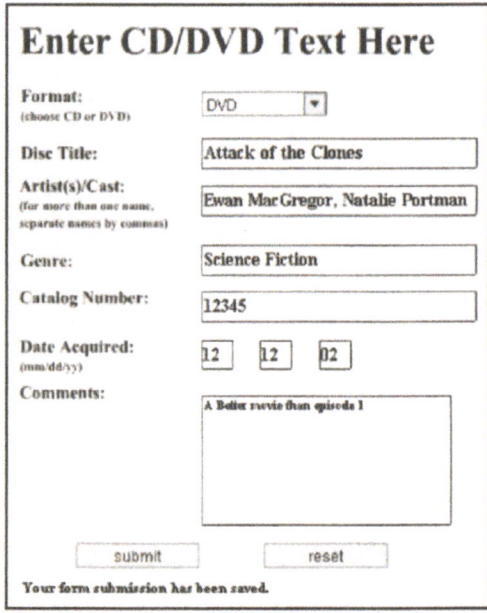

Our Flash form, with a successful submission message passed back from ASP

If you get the message at the bottom saying *Your form submission has been saved*, you are about 90% done! Not only does this indicate that your form data has been saved, but the message shows that your data was successfully received by the ASP page, and processed correctly. However, if you get an error message such as the following:

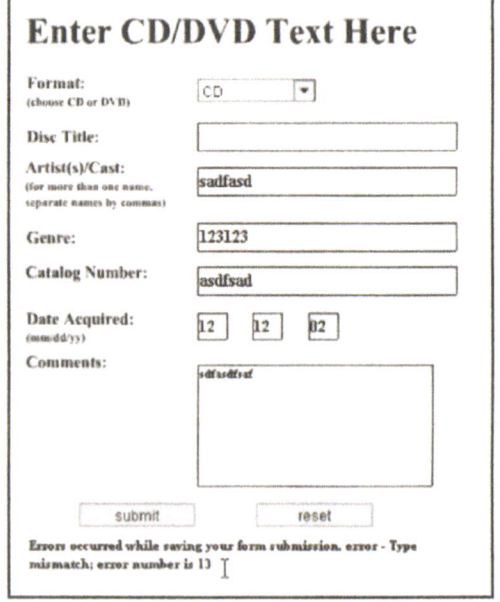

Our Flash form, showing that an error has occurred in data submission.

you should realize that an error occurring at this point will have been sent from the ASP page, `process_entry.asp`, therefore you need to open up that file again and troubleshoot it. In the above case, a type mismatch error is often a syntax error, perhaps from a misspelled command or the presence of a character, such as a quote, in a place where it shouldn't be.

The last check to perform is to locate and open the XML file itself for review. Go to the `chapter11` directory and find `cdDVDcatalog.xml`. If you can't find it, then you need to look at the ASP file again – the `save` method of the XML object may not be spelled correctly or it may reference the wrong directory.

Once you successfully locate the XML document, open up the document in a text editor – the code should look similar to the following screenshot:

A sample XML document created by our Flash/ASP application

We have now successfully performed our goals of passing information from Flash to an ASP page, processing that information and writing it to an XML file, and sending a message from the ASP back to the Flash interface to indicate a successful result (or not).

Adding More Functionality

Now that you know that you can create pages in Dreamweaver MX that create an XML file, how about creating a page that allows you to modify entries in the XML file? Remove entries from the XML file? Search through the contents of the XML file? And how about performing these tasks all within an animated Flash interface? These enhancements are all possible.

Located in the download for this chapter is a complete application for you to explore, contained within `cddvdcatalog.zip`. Unzip the contents of the file to your web server's root directory. The following files are contained within the `.zip` archive:

- `cddvdcatalog.fla` – The Flash development file for the CD/DVD catalog application

- `cddvdcatalog.swf` – The finalized version of the CD/DVD catalog application ready for the web

- `cddvdcatalog.html` – The HTML page that will contain the Flash interface

- `cdDVDcatalog.xml` – The sample catalog

- `search.asp` – An ASP page with code to search through the XML file and send the results back to the Flash interface

- `process_entry2.asp` – A modified version of the exercise file `process_entry.asp`, which contains the code required to add new entries to the XML catalog

- `modify_read.asp` – An ASP page with code to read the XML file and send to Flash

- `modify_write2.asp` – An ASP page with code to retrieve the modified data from the Flash interface via the modify entry option and write the data back to the XML file

- `delete_entry.asp` – An ASP page responsible for deleting an entry selected via the Flash Interface

- `readme.txt` – guide on how to explore the Flash files using Flash MX and the ASP files using Dreamweaver MX

Several other files have also been added, in the form of external ActionScript files (with the extension `.as`). To make life easier for Dreamweaver MX users who apply Flash, Dreamweaver MX supports the creation and editing of ActionScript files that are referenced by a Flash Movie. Our files are as follows:

- `enterdata.as` – modified code previously in the `enterdata` frame of the Flash Movie, now externalized

- `loadxmldata.as` – used to retrieve XML data sent from an ASP page

- `mod_process_xml.as` – used to process received XML data from an ASP Page to the Flash movie

- `mod_search_xml.as` – scripts used during the search process within the Flash movie

- `mod_delete_xml.as` – scripts used during the delete entry process within the Flash movie

Opening up the Flash movie will reveal interfaces over several different frames within the timeline, in addition to a slightly modified version of the *Add New Entry* interface created in this chapter. Each frame that contained a form interface now contains ActionScript code included via the `#include` pragma directive. This allows us to reference an external ActionScript text file.

Dreamweaver MX will save you a significant amount of time when typing in Flash ActionScript code because its coding environment supports code hinting and auto-insert for many of Flash MX's ActionScript commands

Creating external ActionScript files in Dreamweaver MX is a straightforward process – simply go to *File > New* in the Dreamweaver MX menu. In the *New Document* dialog box, select *Other*, and in the *Other* column you will see *ActionScript* listed:

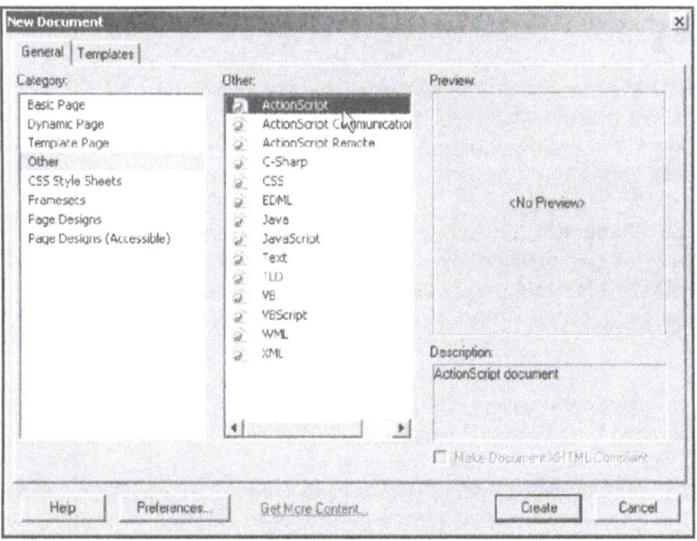

Creating an ActionScript document in Dreamweaver MX

Clicking on the *Create* button will then create your new ActionScript document. Dreamweaver MX will save you a significant amount of time when typing in Flash ActionScript code because its coding environment supports code hinting and auto-insert for many of Flash MX's ActionScript commands, as seen below:

Working with ActionScript in Dreamweaver MX.

You should therefore be able to explore many of the Flash application's functions within Dreamweaver MX itself.

The core ASP pages included in the application will modify, add, search for, or delete data from the XML file. When exploring the code, you will find that most of it is heavily commented, plus there is a `readme.txt` file included, to provide you with more help.

Summary

In this chapter we have dealt with various ways that we can integrate ASP and Flash MX using Dreamweaver MX. We began with a brief history of Flash, including the traditional methods used to pass data between a Flash Document and an ASP page. We then explored Dreamweaver MX's integrated Flash MX support.

Next, we moved on to complete a simple exercise demonstrating the development of an application that takes data from a Flash-based form and passes the information to an ASP page, constructed in Dreamweaver MX. The ASP page then creates an XML document containing the information, and sends a message back to the Flash frontend, and informs the user whether the writing was successful or not.

As a conclusion to the chapter we presented an expanded form of the CD/DVD catalog application to explore, summarizing these general concepts:

This completed application (*cddvdcatalog*) allows us to enter new CDs/DVDs into a catalog, view the catalog, search the catalog and present the search results, modify an existing entry, and remove entries from the catalog. Further exploration of these files will help you to better understand the relationship Dreamweaver and Flash have in terms of developing great looking, functionally sound, interactive applications.

Integrating Flash and ASP MX

Case Study 1

- Building a simple weblog, including:

  - A SQL Server database to store our blog information

  - Admin pages to enter the information we want to display

  - Display pages to display our information

Author: Rob Turnbull

A Simple Blogging System

WebLogs are everywhere these days, or so it seems. Everyone has got something to say and, thanks to the Internet, an easy way to say it.

A WebLog, or Blog as they are more commonly known, is basically a kind of online diary. You can post your thoughts, feelings, and suggestions about anything and everything and make it viewable by the world. You might want to think about what you're going to say before you say it, of course. You can also view a blog as a simple content management system.

The idea of this case study is to build a simple blogging system that enables us to add and edit items and to display those items in such a way as to make it easy for the user to navigate.

There are a few things we need in order to get a simple blog up and running.

- A database in which to store our blog data, although we could just as easily use a flat file instead.
- The pages to display our blog data to the viewers. The pages that make up this system will need to look attractive so we'll need to create a CSS file to style them.

We only need three pages to achieve this goal:

- A homepage, which can display the latest blog entries.
- A page to display all the entries for a selected month.
- A page to display an individual day's content.

Each of these pages needs to contain a calendar that derives its links from the database and forms the basic navigation for the blog system. The only link that you don't need to include in the calendar is a link back to your homepage. In our simple blog system there is a file called `calendar.asp` that includes all the necessary code to generate our database-driven calendar. We simply include it on the pages that need it (the display pages).

The final item we need is a secure online administration system to get our blog data into the database.

This should include:

- A login page to keep the admin system secure
- An admin homepage that lists the current entries
- Pages for adding new entries
- Pages for editing existing entries

Note that all the files you need for this case study are available to download from http://www.glasshaus.com/.

The homepage listing should be a list of links that enable editing the selected item.

The Database

For a very basic blog system, such as ours, we only need two tables: one to store our blog entries, and one for our login information. This system will utilize a SQL Server database.

The table we store the blog entries in will have the following columns and data types:

Column name	Data Type	Length	Allow Nulls
BlogID	int	4	No
BlogHeadline	varchar	255	No
BlogHTML	text	16	No
BlogDate	datetime	8	No
BlogIncluded	bit	1	No

We don't want to allow Null values to be entered into the database so we set all the columns to not accept them. The BlogID column should be set as the **Primary Key** column and should be an Identity column to ensure that this column is always unique.

We won't be entering anything in the BlogDate column; we want it to self-populate with the current date and time when a new record is entered. We'll use the getdate() function in the default value column to achieve this.

BlogIncluded is a bit data type column and will decide whether or not a blog entry can be displayed on the web page. We want to display all our entries as they're added so the default value for the column should be 1. Save this table as tblBlog and make sure you assign SELECT, INSERT, UPDATE, and DELETE permissions to the *IUSR* account so that the web site can access and modify the data.

The login table needs to store our username and password so we can secure the admin pages with a login system. This table should have the following columns and data types:

Column name	Data Type	Length	Allow Nulls
ID	int	4	No
Username	varchar	50	No
Password	varchar	50	No

The ID column should be set as the **Primary Key** column and should be an Identity column.

Save this table as tblAccess. You only need to assign SELECT permissions to the *IUSR* account so that the web site can access the data. We won't be adding, editing, or deleting any data in this table from the web site.

Once you have saved this table, open it up, add your username and password to the table, and then close it again. We will now be able to use this information in our application.

A Basic Site Map

The purpose of this basic site map is to illustrate the simplicity of the entire site structure and to give you an extra point of reference to see where individual files are supposed to be stored as they are created and added to the site.

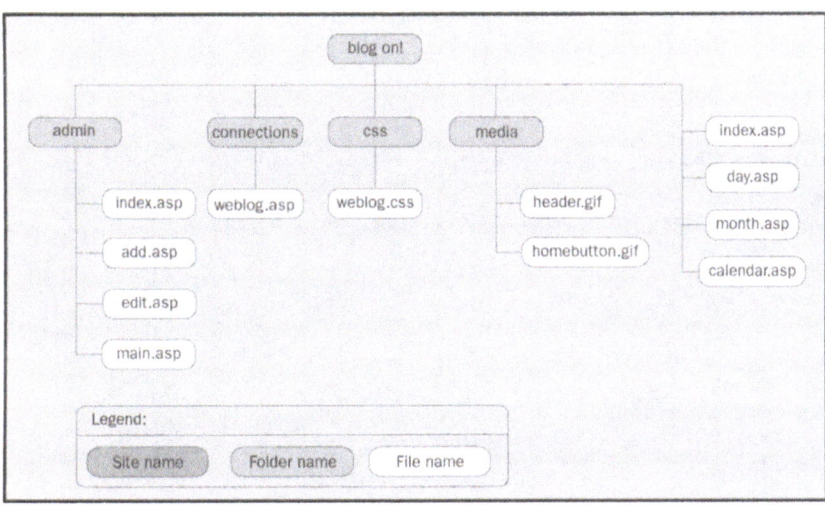

C1

The Cascading Stylesheet

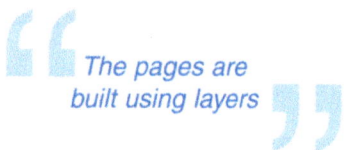

*The pages are
built using layers*

We will create several styles for use in the blog pages to give us the flexibility we want in making the content look good to the end users. The pages are built using layers, and we are going to cater for having different link styles in the page by setting up contextual styles.

The stylesheet code is as follows, broken into sections for the different `<div>` areas we'll be using:

```css
BODY {
    font-family: Verdana, Arial, Helvetica, sans-serif;
}
H1 {
    font-family: Verdana, Arial, Helvetica, sans-serif;
    font-size: 14px;
    font-weight: bold;
    margin: 3px 0px 3px 5px;
    color : #336666;
}

.underlined{
    border-bottom : 1px solid #CCCCCC;
}

.date{
    font-family: Verdana, Arial, Helvetica, sans-serif;
    font-size: 12px;
    color: #333333;
}

img {
    border : 0px;
    display : block;
}
```

For the `mainLayer` area:

```css
#mainLayer {
    font-family: "Trebuchet MS", Arial, Helvetica, sans-serif;
    font-size : 14px;
    padding-left : 10px;
    padding-right : 20px
}

#mainLayer p {
    line-height : 150%;
    margin : 6px 0px 10px 0px;
    font-size: 12px;
    color: #333333;
}

#mainLayer H1 {
    font-size: 12px;
    margin: 0px 0px 5px 0px;
    color : #666666;
}
```

For links:

```css
a:link {
  font-size: 12px;
  font-weight: bold;   color: #3300CC;

  text-decoration: none
}

a:visited {
  font-weight: bold;
  color: #3300CC;
  text-decoration: none
}

a:hover {
  font-weight: bold;
  color: #330066;
  text-decoration: underline;
}

a:active {
  font-weight: bold;
  color: #3300CC;
  text-decoration: none
}
```

For the `dateLayer` **area:**

```css
#dateLayer{
  font-family: Verdana, Arial, Helvetica, sans-serif;
  font-size: 12px;
  border: 1px solid #CCCCCC;
}

#dateLayer H1 {
  font-family: Verdana, Arial, Helvetica, sans-serif;
  font-size: 12px;
  margin: 0px 0px 0px 0px;
  color : #000000;
}

#dateLayer a:link {
  font-size: 12px;
  font-weight : bold;
  color: #000000;
  text-decoration: none;
  display : block;
  width: 100%;
}

#dateLayer a:visited {
  font-size: 12px;
  font-weight : bold;
  color: #000000;
```

```
#dateLayer a:hover {
  font-size: 12px;
  font-weight : bold;
  color: #FFFFFF;
  text-decoration: none;
  display : block;
  width: 100%;
  background : #330066;
}

#dateLayer a:active {
  font-size: 12px;
  font-weight : bold;
  color: #000000;
  text-decoration: none;
}
  text-decoration: none;
  display : block;
  width: 100%;
}
```

This is entirely dependent upon the reader using a modern browser that uses the stylesheet, of course. For users of browsers that don't support stylesheets, the site should degrade gracefully.

As shown in the code above, we have declared styles that will be specific to `dateLayer` and to `mainLayer`. We also style the `<body>`, `<h1>`, and `<img>` to ensure that our document is presented to the user in the way we intend.

Having built your stylesheet, you need to save it. As seen on the site map we are going to call it `weblog.css`. The file should be saved into the *CSS* folder within your site files.

The Admin Pages

Before we can display our blog content to the world, we need to put the content into the database. To do that, we will use a simple admin system consisting of four pages. This section assumes that you have already created the `admin` folder within your Dreamweaver MX site. All the web pages created for the administration of the site will be saved in the `admin` folder.

For all of the pages in this site to function correctly, they need to be able to talk to the database. In Dreamweaver MX, the quickest way to enable that is to open the *Databases* panel, click + and create the required connection there. Upon completion, your connection will be saved in the `Connections` folder of your site. Our connection is called `weblog`, surprisingly enough!

The Admin Login Page

Create a new page and save it as `index.asp`, in the `admin` folder. Draw a layer on the screen and enter these settings in the property inspector for it:

LayerID	headerLayer
Left	0px
Top	0px
Width	213px
Height	38px
Z-Index	1
Visibility	Default
Tag	DIV

This layer is for the header image, which we should insert now. Place your cursor into the layer and insert an image by selecting *Insert > Image*, pressing *ctrl+alt+I*, or clicking the *Image* icon on the *Insert* bar. Select header.gif from the media folder and click *OK*:

Draw a second layer on the screen and enter these settings in the property inspector for it.

LayerID	homeLayer
Left	10 px
Top	85px
Height	20px
Z-Index	2
Visibility	Default
Tag	DIV

This layer is for the home icon, which will link to the homepage of the display pages. Put your cursor into the layer and insert an image by selecting *Insert > Image*, pressing *ctrl+alt+I* or clicking the *Image* icon on the *Insert* bar. Select homebutton.gif from the media folder and click *OK*.

In the property inspector, type ../index.asp as the link (we could browse for the file but it doesn't exist yet), type *Home* as the alt text and remove the border attribute (Dreamweaver MX adds a zero border value but we don't want it – our CSS takes care of this for us):

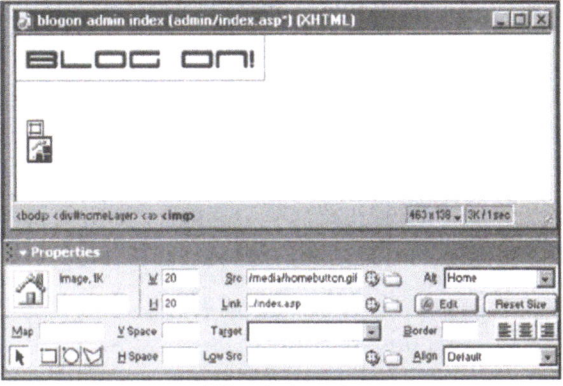

Adding the home icon

Draw a third layer on the screen and enter these settings in the property inspector for it.

LayerID	mainHeaderLayer
Left	40px
Top	85px
Width	20px
Z-Index	3
Visibility	Default
Tag	DIV

Now would be a good time to attach the stylesheet

This layer is just going to let us know where we are in the site. As this is the login page, type *Login* into the layer. In the *Properties* inspector for the text, select the Heading 1 format. Now would be a good time to attach the stylesheet to the page to bring that heading into line.

Bring the *CSS Styles* panel to the front by pressing *Shift+F11*, or clicking the *CSS Styles* tab. Click the *Attach Style Sheet* icon at the bottom of the *CSS Styles* panel and select `weblog.css` from the `css` folder in the site. Leave *Add As Link* selected and click *OK*.

Once your stylesheet has been added to the page, your heading (*Login*) should appear smaller in size and have acquired a green color, just as the CSS tells the browser to display it:

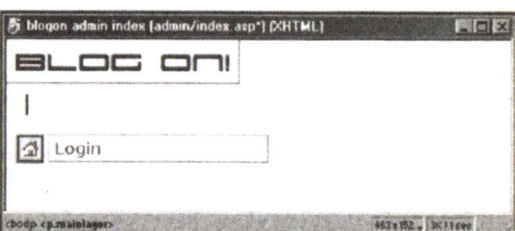

The new styled heading

Now we need to add the actual login form to the page. Draw a fourth layer on the screen and enter these settings in the property inspector for it.

Note the capital L in the middle of `mainLayer`*. This is important because in our stylesheet we defined an ID style that will apply itself automatically to the layers in these pages called* `mainLayer` *and* `dateLayer`*.*

LayerID	mainLayer
Left	30px
Top	130px
Width	370px
Z-Index	4
Visibility	Default
Tag	DIV

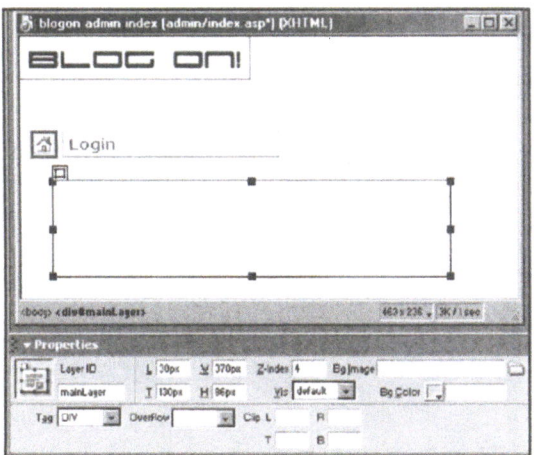

The fourth layer for our form

Click to put the cursor inside the layer and add a `<form>` element by clicking *Insert > Form*, or use the icon on the *Forms* tab of the *Insert* bar. Leave the form properties at their defaults. Click inside the form on the page and insert a table with the following properties.

Rows	5
Cell padding	0
Columns	2
Cell spacing	0
Width	350px
Border	0

- Merge the top row, enter *Login failed* as the cell content and set the format to Heading 1.

- In the second row, enter *Username* in the first column and add a textbox form element into the second column. Call the textbox `username`, and give it a value of `<%= Request.Cookies("ckusername") %>`.

- In the third row, enter *Password* in the first column and add a textbox form element into the second column. Call the textbox, `password`, and give it a value of `<%= Request.Cookies("ckpassword") %>`.

- n the fourth row, enter *Remember* in the first column and add a checkbox form element into the second column. Call the checkbox, remember, and give it a value of yes. We'll get to the cookies for those form elements in a moment.

- In the bottom row of the table, second column, insert a submit button. Call it `loginBtn` and set the label to *Login*.

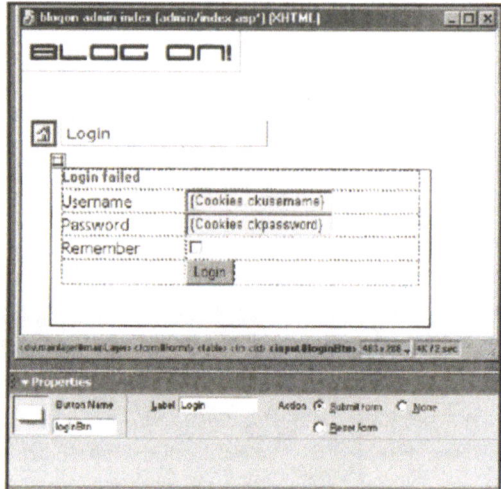

The basics of the form

Select the middle three rows containing `username`, `password`, and `remember` (words and form elements), and apply the *Paragraph* format. Now apply the *Log In User* Server Behavior by clicking *Server Behaviors > + > User Authentication > Log In User* and complete the dialog as follows:

Get Input From Form	form1
Username Field	username
Password Field	password
Validate Using Connection	weblog
Table	dbo.tblAccess
Username Column	Username
Password Column	Password
If Login Succeeds, Go To	main.asp
If Login Fails, Go To	index.asp?lf=true

Click *OK* to apply the Server Behavior to the page.

Note where we're telling the code to go if the login fails: back to the same page with a querystring. We'll check for this in our code once we've dealt with the cookies we'll be using. If you haven't already downloaded your free copy of Login Cookies, go and do so now from *http://robgt.com/products/*. It makes adding "remember me" functionality to your login pages very easy. Alternatively, if you'd prefer to build your own copy, *Chapter 10* runs through the complete process of building this Server Behavior.

If you download and install the *Login Cookies* Server Behavior, apply it by clicking *Server Behaviors > + > RobGT > Login Cookies* and completing the dialog as follows:

Submit button name	loginBtn
Remember me checkbox name	remember
Remember me checkbox value	yes
Remember me cookie name	ckremember
Username form element name	username
Username cookie name	ckusername
Password form element name	password
Password cookie name	ckpassword
Cookie life in days	30

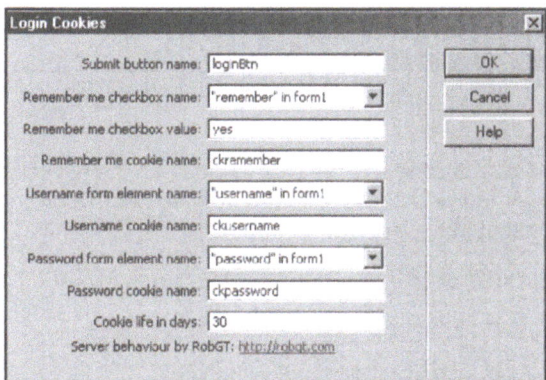

The Login Cookies setup dialog

Click *OK* to apply the *Login Cookies* Server Behavior to the page.

The final thing we need to add to this page is the code to hide the *login failed* message unless the login has actually failed. Select the entire first row and wrap it with the following code in Code View, so your finished code for that row looks like this:

```
<% IF Request("lf") = "true" THEN %>
        <tr>
          <td colspan="2"><h1>Login failed!</h1></td>
        </tr>
<% END IF %>
```

In the *Log In User* Server Behavior, we specified that we would return to this page in case of login failure, including the query string `"lf=true"`. If we access the page without this parameter, we don't see the *login failed* message. That's it; we've built our login page. Now save it and close it.

The Admin Main Page

To save us time in the page creation process, we can simply copy and modify the login page. One way to do this is to open the index.asp page and click in the Design View to give the page focus. Now right-click on the *Name* tab at the bottom left of the page, select *Save As…* and in the dialog that pops up, save the page as main.asp. Now we're automatically editing main.asp.

The first thing we need to do is strip the page of everything we don't need. Basically we only need the layers, everything else can go. Click the *Server Behaviors* tab to focus that panel. Click the *Log In User* Server Behavior in the list and remove it by clicking the minus button. Do the same for the *Login Cookies* Server Behavior to remove that:

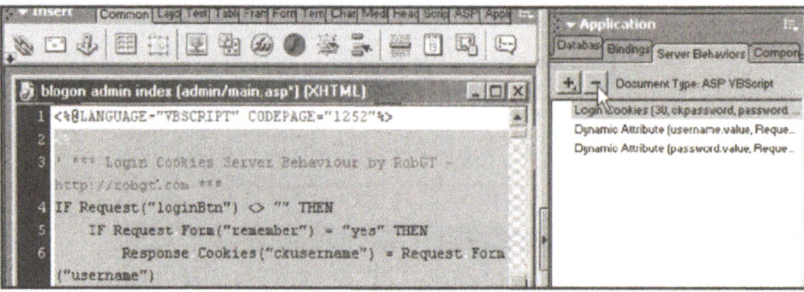

Look at the code you're about to delete

Next, click inside the form on the page and the click `<table>` on the tag selector. Then hit the *delete* key. Right-click the `<form>` tag and select *Remove Tag*. Go into Code View and check that the following code has been removed:

```
<% IF Request("lf") = "true" THEN %>
<% END IF %>
```

It should have been but, if not, remove it now.

Now we have our bare bones page on which we will build the main admin page. Type *Admin home* in the place of *Login*, in the mainHeaderLayer:

The start of a new page

Click inside the `mainLayer` and type the word *Add*. In the property inspector, type `add.asp` in the link box to make this a link. Return the cursor to the `mainLayer` and press *Enter* to go to the next paragraph in the layer.

Now we need to create the Recordset that this page needs in order to show us our current entries. Click *Bindings > + > Recordset (Query)*. The settings we need are as follows:

Name	rsB
Connection	weblog

Create the SQL statement that will grab all the records from the blog table (`tblBlog`) in your database and order them in reverse date order, so that the latest entry will be at the top of the pile.

```
SELECT *
FROM dbo.tblBlog
ORDER BY BlogDate DESC
```

Now bind `BlogHeadline` to the page below the *Add* link, press *shift+enter* to add a `<br />` to the page, then bind `BlogDate` to the page:

Select the `BlogHeadline` binding on the page and click the folder icon in the property inspector next to the link box. We are going to link this to the edit page, which doesn't yet exist.

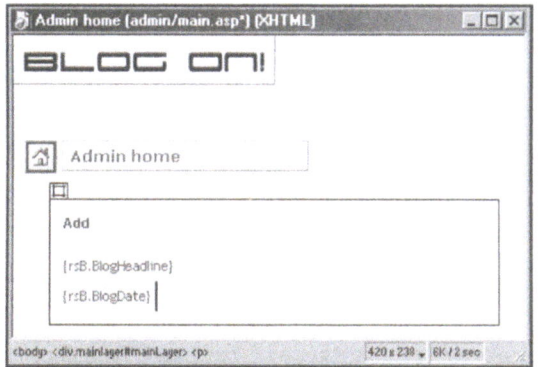

We'll be displaying data from the database here

In the filename area, type `edit.asp`, then click the *Parameters* button. Click + and click in the *Name* column of the row that has just been added to the dialog. Type `bid` as the name of the parameter. Click in the *Value* column, click the lightning bolt icon and select *BlogID* from the dialog, click *OK*, *OK* again, and *OK* a third time to close the link dialog completely.

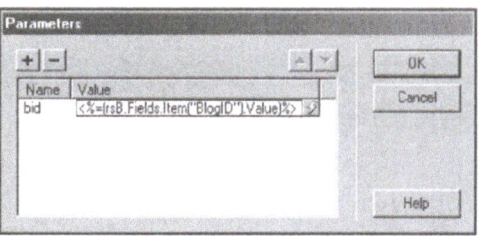

Adding parameters

Your complete link should look like this:

```
edit.asp?bid=<%=(rsB.Fields.Item("BlogID").Value)%>
```

Now select the date and the headline bindings on the page by dragging the cursor over them, then click the `<p>` tag on the right side of the *Tag Selector* bar to select the entire paragraph that contains these two elements. Now apply the *Repeat Region* Server Behavior to the selection choosing to *Show All Records*.

A Simple Blogging System

C1

p

303

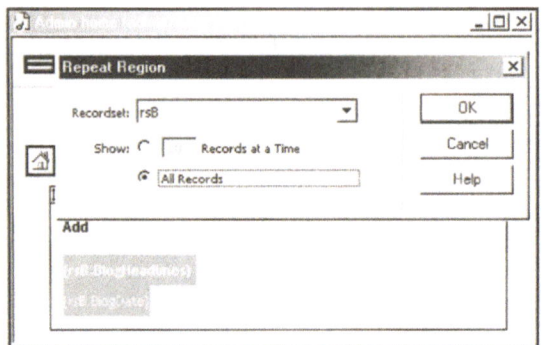

Dreamweaver will add code here to make the highlighted text repeat for all the records in the Recordset

If someone tries to access these pages directly, we need to stop them

The last thing we need to add to this page is the *Restrict Access* Server Behavior. We are already using the *Log In User* Server Behavior to ensure only the administrator can access the pages, but if someone tries to access these pages directly, we need to stop them and redirect them to the login page.

Click *Server Behaviors > + > User Authentication > Restrict Access To Page*. In the *If Access Denied, Go To:* textbox, select the admin index page or type `index.asp`, and leave *Restrict Access Based On Username And Password* selected.

That's all we need to do for this page. Save it and we're done.

The Admin Add Content Page

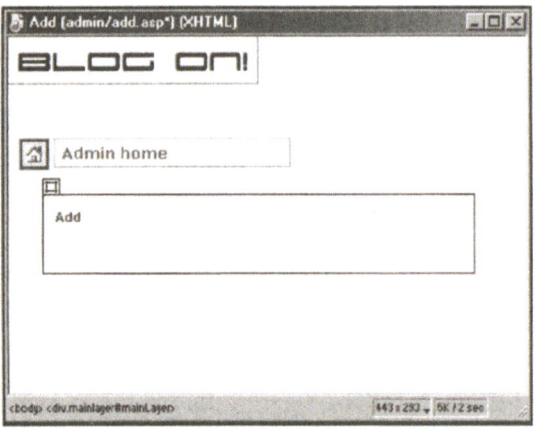

Another page almost ready to start

To save page creation time again, make a copy of `main.asp` and save it as `add.asp`.

Now remove the code that we don't want on this new page. Starting with the repeat region, click it in the list of Server Behaviors applied to the page in the *Server Behavior* panel and remove it by clicking the − button. Next, remove the Recordset from the page; we don't need it when we're adding records. Finally, remove the data bindings from the page (`BlogHeadline` and `BlogDate`).

```
<p><a href="edit.asp?bid="></a><br>
</p>
```

Now go into the code and remove the last bit that has been left behind that we don't want. It will look like this:

> One less step needed this time around

We can leave the *Restrict Access To Page* Server Behavior applied to the page because we'll need it here too. One less step needed this time around. You should basically be left with all of your layers, the heading, and the *Add item* link. Great, now we can get on with building our new page.

- The *Add* page will be easier for us to use if it's a little wider so it can accommodate the form elements at a reasonable size. Click the border of the `mainLayer` to bring up the properties of the layer and change the width to 530px.

- Change the heading for the page from *Admin home* to *Add new*.

- Change the *Add item* link to read: *Complete the form or click* back and make the word *back* a link back to the previous page by adding `javascript:history.go(-1);` into the link box.

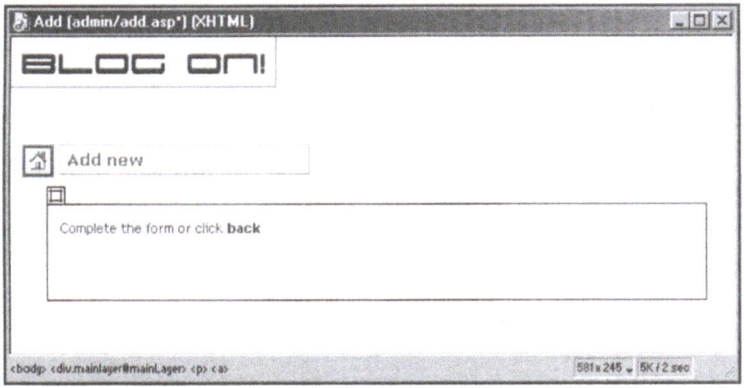

That's the easiest bit done

On the next line below the *back* link, add a form element to the page and then add a table inside that with the following properties:

Rows	7
Columns	2
Width	500px
Cell padding	0
Cell spacing	0
Border	0

- In the first row, column 1, type Headline.

- Merge the second row and add a textbox form element called `headline`.

- In the third row, column 1, type *Body text*.

- Merge the fourth row and add a multi-line textbox form element called `bodytext`. To give us plenty of room for adding text, make this text area 65 characters wide and 12 lines deep.

- Leave row 5 blank.

- In the sixth row, column 1, type *Included*. In column 2 add a checkbox form element called `included` with a value of 1. Set its Initial State to *Checked*. This will save us a step every time we add an item because the form will set each new item to be included on the web site.

- In the seventh row, column 1, add a submit button called `submit` with a label of *Submit*.

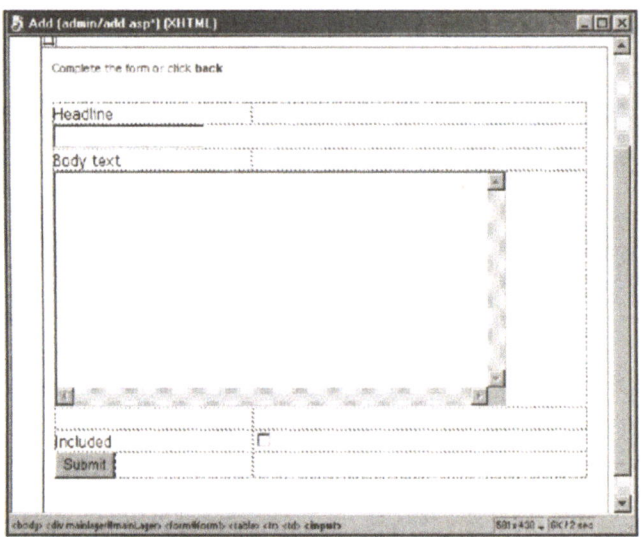

That's the appearance of the form dealt with

Connection	weblog
Insert Into Table	dbo.tblBlog
After Inserting, Go To	main.asp
Get Values From	form1
Form Elements	headline inserts into column "BlogHeadline" (Text)
	bodytext inserts into column "BlogHTML" (Text)
	included inserts into column "BlogIncluded" (Checkbox 1,0)

With the form in place, all we need to do is add the *Insert Record* Server Behavior to the page. To do this, click *Server Behaviors > + > Insert Record* and complete the dialog as follows:

Click *OK* to apply the Server Behavior to the page. That's it, this page is complete. Save your work.

The Admin Edit Content Page

The edit page is almost identical to the add page so this won't take long at all. Make a copy of `add.asp` and save it as `edit.asp`. Remove the *Insert Record* Server Behavior and we're ready to build the edit page!

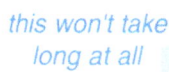

this won't take long at all

Change the heading from *Add new* to *Edit existing*. We need to create a Recordset to enable us to use the *Update Record* Server Behavior. Click *Bindings > + > Recordset (Query)* and build a Recordset called `rsEB` using the `weblog` connection with the following SQL code:

```
SELECT *
FROM dbo.tblBlog
WHERE BlogID = varBID
```

The variable setup is as follows:

The variable called `varBID` will be replaced at runtime by the value we request from the querystring element called `bid`. If no `bid` value is passed in the querystring, the default value of 0 is used and the Recordset will be empty because no records in the database will have a `BlogID` of 0.

Name	varBID
Default Value	0
Run-time Value	Request("bid")

Now we need to bind the database columns to the form elements. Click the `BlogHeadline` data binding and drag it onto the *headline* form element, then drag the `BlogHTML` binding onto the *bodytext* form element.

Select the *included* checkbox and click the *Dynamic* button in the property inspector. In the resulting dialog, click the lightning bolt icon next to the *Check If* textbox and select the `BlogIncluded` column of the Recordset, then click *OK*. In the *Equal To* textbox, type *True* and click *OK*.

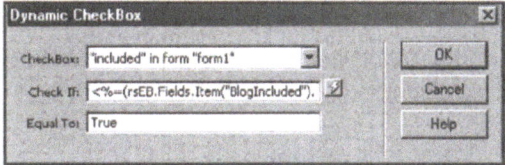

Now we need to apply the *Update Record* Server Behavior. Click *Server Behaviors > + > Update Record* and complete the dialog as follows:

Connection	weblog
Table To Update	dbo.tblBlog
Select Record From	rsEB
Unique Key Column	BlogID
After Inserting, Go To	main.asp
Get Values From	form1
Form Elements	headline updates column "BlogHeadline" (Text)
	bodytext updates column "BlogHTML" (Text)
	included updates column "BlogIncluded" (Checkbox 1,0)

Click *OK* to apply the Server Behavior to the page and that's it completed. Save the page.

Summing Up the Admin Pages

You can easily create paragraphs of text and then select words to create any links that you might need. Just remember to copy the content and the opening and closing paragraph tags otherwise your code will have problems on the display pages from improperly marked up HTML.

With these pages in place, we can start adding content to the database.

It should be noted here that if you want to have anything more than simply plain text in your blog display pages (for example if you want to include hyperlinks, images, and bold or italic text), you will need to create that content with the proper HTML markup. You can write this out by hand if you want to, or you could open a new blank page in Dreamweaver MX, write your blog content on that page, and then copy the code from the Code View of this page and paste it into the admin system. The display pages will display it all beautifully thanks to the CSS.

The Display Pages

Once we have added some content into our database through the admin pages, we are going to need to display it. There are only three pages required to do this, which will give our users some nice and simple functionality.

Each of these three pages requires the inclusion of a calendar, which provides all of the site navigation except for the link to the homepage. `calendar.asp` is the file that contains all the code required to build our calendar and dynamically add the links where relevant data exists in the database. For example, if data exists for November 20th 2002 in the database, then the calendar will display a link for that date.

One important point to note about the calendar code is the setup of the variable called `varBlogStartDate`, which is used to determine which month links to show on the calendar.

The Homepage

To quickly remove all the code we don't want on this page, click Server Behaviors to focus that panel and simply drag the cursor over all the entries in the list, then delete them all by clicking the minus button.

As shown on the site map, this page sits directly under the root of the site, as it will be the first page the users see when they access this site online.

To speed up the creation process, and save us repeating the same work over again, open up `main.asp` from the admin folder and save it as `index.asp` in the site root. Be careful and make sure you're saving this file in the site root and not in the admin folder or you will overwrite your login page! We'll want to get rid of all the Server Behaviors we used on `main.asp`.

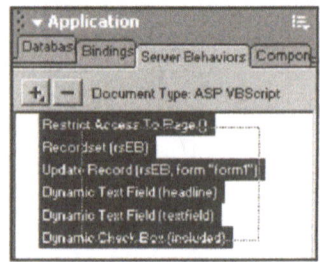

Dragging the cursor over the entries is easier than selecting them individually

Having deleted all that code, go into Code View and remove the remaining link that is no longer needed. It looks like this:

```
<p><a href="edit.asp?bid="></a><br>
</p>
```

Remove the *Add* link and text, then change the heading text from *Admin home* to *The last five entries*. We should be left with an almost blank page with our homepage heading and all but one of the layers in place.

To include the calendar code on the page, go into Code View and scroll to the top of the document. You should see the language declaration code on the first line. Add a blank link beneath that in the code and then click *Insert > Script Objects > Server-Side Include.* In the following dialog, choose `calendar.asp` located in the site root, leave *Relative To Document* selected, then click *OK.* You can find a copy of `calendar.asp` in the code download for this chapter. The original version was written by John Pramik and is available from *http://www.aspfree.net/authors/johnp/cal_small.asp,* although I've made some modifications to enable database-driven content.

> *You can find a copy of calendar.asp in the code download for this chapter; I've made some modifications to enable database-driven content*

The following code should be added to your page:

```
<!--#include file="calendar.asp" -->
```

This will add a new Recordset into your *Bindings* panel. The reason for this is that the code in the `calendar.asp` page contains a Recordset and Dreamweaver MX has parsed the content of that included file. You don't need to worry about that Recordset (`rsDates`).

Now we need to add the final extra layer to accommodate our calendar. Draw a layer on the screen and enter these settings in the property inspector for it:

LayerID	dateLayer
Left	450px
Top	130px
Width	200px
Z-Index	5
Visibility	Default
Tag	DIV

This calendar will look nice because of the stylesheet we created earlier. We defined an ID style called `dateLayer`, which will be automatically applied to this layer because it uses this ID. Displaying the calendar on the page requires a minimal amount of code at this point. Go into Code View and locate the `dateLayer`, then enter the following code inside the layer.

```
<TABLE WIDTH="200px">
<%=cal%>
</TABLE>
```

Your entire `dateLayer` code should look like this:

```
<div id="dateLayer"
    style="position:absolute; left:450px; top:130px; width:200px; z-index:5">
<TABLE WIDTH="200px">
<%=cal%>
</TABLE></div>
```

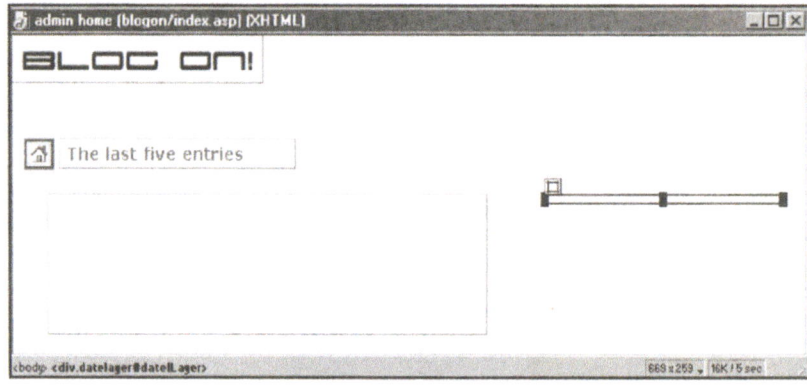

Just got to add the blog entries, and change the page title

Now we can add the content from the database into the main layer.

Click *Bindings > + > Recordset (Query)* and create a Recordset in the *Advanced Recordset builder* called `rsContent` using the `weblog` connection with the following SQL:

```
SELECT TOP 5 *
FROM dbo.tblBlog
WHERE BlogIncluded = 1
ORDER BY BlogDate DESC
```

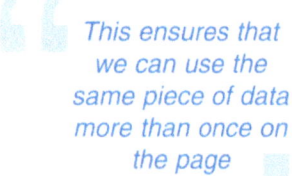

This ensures that we can use the same piece of data more than once on the page

Click OK to create the Recordset, then go immediately to the *Properties* inspector and change the Recordset *Cursor Type* to *Static*. This ensures that we can use the same piece of data more than once on the page, and we need to do this for the date and time displays for each record.

We retrieve the top five records in this case for a slight speed benefit. We could bring back all the records in the database and use a repeat region on the page to display the top five, but if there are a lot of records, this could take a long time and would be a waste of resources.

Click inside the `mainLayer`, highlight `BlogDate` from the `rsContent` Recordset, and click *Insert* (circled in the following screenshot). At the end of the highlighted `BlogDate` line in the *Bindings* pane, click the drop-down to format the data bound on the page. Select *Date/Time > Monday, January 17, 2000*.

Now click in the `mainLayer` after that `BlogDate` data binding and add a space, then a hyphen, and then another space. We're going to add the time at the end of that line, so click `BlogDate` in the *Bindings* panel again and click *Insert*. This time, when selecting the data format, select *Date/Time > 14:35*. This will give us a final date and time that looks like this:

Sunday, October 20, 2002 - 14:17

Return to the mainLayer and press *Enter* to add a new paragraph after the date and time, then click the cursor somewhere inside the date and time paragraph, and apply the underlined CSS style to it. Click in the empty paragraph underneath the date and time (which should now be underlined thanks to the CSS style) and bind the BlogHeadline to the page. Apply the Heading 1 format to it.

Now we need to apply a repeat region to the page to display all five of the records that this Recordset can contain. Drag the cursor over the BlogHeadline and the date and time bindings on the page to select it all and then click *Server Behaviors > + > Repeat Region*. Make sure you choose rsContent as the Recordset to use, then click *Show: All Records* and click *OK* to apply the Server Behavior to the page.

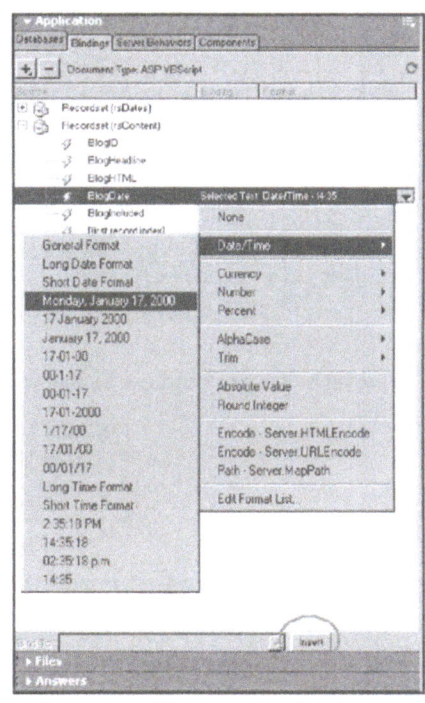

Dreamweaver MX gives us lots of choice in our data formatting

The final layout of this page in the Design View of Dreamweaver MX should look like this:

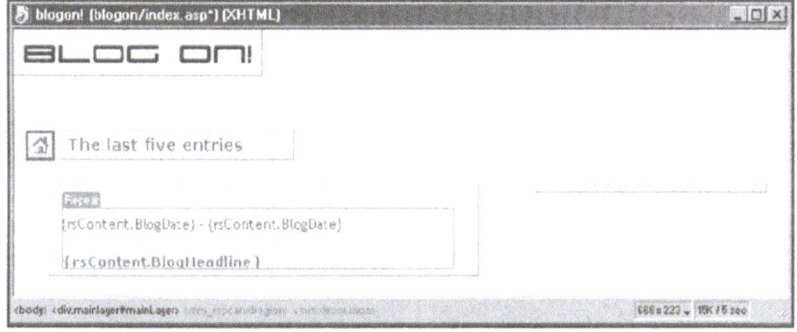

The finished homepage design

That's the homepage completed, save it and we're ready to move on to the page for displaying a month.

The Month Page

The month page is almost exactly the same as the homepage; just the content Recordset is tweaked to give us the right month's content to display on the page and a little code is added to the heading.

Open `index.asp` display page and save it as `month.asp`.

The first and most important thing to do is to make the necessary changes to the Recordset, which as before will require the *Advanced* interface. The SQL code for the `rsContent` Recordset should now look like this:

```
SELECT *
FROM dbo.tblBlog
WHERE DatePart(mm, BlogDate) = 'vDisplayMonth'
      AND DatePart(yyyy, BlogDate) = 'vDisplayYear'
      AND BlogIncluded = 1
ORDER BY BlogDate DESC
```

The variables you need are as follows:

Name	Default Value	Run-time Value
vDisplayMonth	00	DisplayMonth
vDisplayYear	0000	DisplayYear

Click OK to apply these changes to the Recordset.

Delete the heading The *last five entries...* and replace it with *All entries for* . Note the extra space at the end of the heading; we're going to add the month name to the end by using the following code:

```
<%=MonthName(Month(DisplayDate))%>
```

Next, add a new line after the `BlogHeadline` data binding in the main layer and bind `BlogHTML` to the page. For ease of reading multiple entries on this page I would suggest adding an extra blank paragraph after the `BlogHTML` binding just to space out the entries.

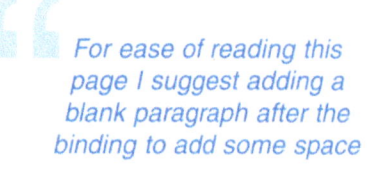

For ease of reading this page I suggest adding a blank paragraph after the binding to add some space

To briefly explain what's going on in this Recordset, we require only those records from the database that match the selected month in the selected year. To do this we use the DatePart function of SQL and compare the values held in the variables DisplayMonth and DisplayYear to the relevant part of BlogDate from the records in the database.

The final layout of this page in the Design View of Dreamweaver MX should look like this:

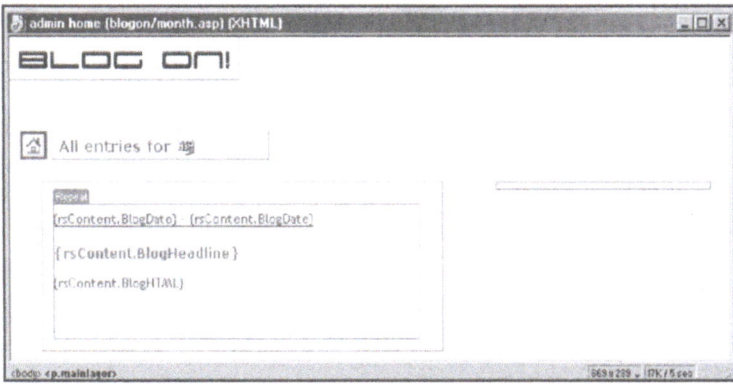

That's the month page completed, save it and we'll go to the final page to show a day of blog entries.

The Day Page

Not surprisingly, the day page is not a million miles away from the month page!

Open the `month.asp` page and save it as `day.asp`.

There's only a small change to make to the `rsContent` Recordset and we make this change to ensure that we only retrieve content from the database that is relevant to the selected day.

The `rsContent` SQL should be changed to the following:

```
SELECT *
FROM dbo.tblBlog
WHERE DatePart(dd, BlogDate) = 'vDay'
      AND DatePart(mm, BlogDate) = 'vDisplayMonth'
      AND DatePart(yyyy, BlogDate) = 'vDisplayYear'
      AND BlogIncluded = 1
ORDER BY BlogDate DESC
```

The variables you need are as follows:

Name	Default Value	Run-time Value
vDisplayMonth	00	DisplayMonth
vDisplayYear	0000	DisplayYear
vDay	00	varDay

Click *OK* to apply these changes to the Recordset.

Now delete the heading *All entries for*, including the ASP code we used on the month page. We are going to bind the current date to the page in place of the heading, as all the content on this page will be relevant only to this specific date. Make sure your cursor is inside the heading layer, then select *Bindings > rsContent > BlogDate* and click *Bind* to add the date to the page. Format the date by clicking the gray arrow icon in the *Bindings* panel in the *Format* column and selecting *Date/Time > Monday, January 17, 2000.*

Now we can remove the date from the main layer, as we don't need it twice; we can just leave the time on display. Highlight the date data binding and the hyphen in the main layer and delete them. The final layout of this page in the Design View of Dreamweaver MX should look like this:

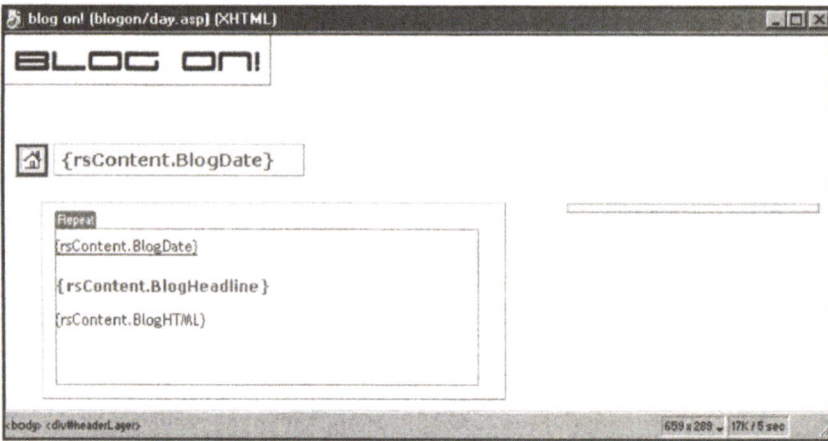

The finished design of the day page

That's the day page completed, and the site as well. Save the page, and we're done building.

Summing Up the Display Pages

...each individual day's entries are accessed by clicking the individual date links

Your users can now view all of your blog content by day, by month, or by looking at the last five entries that you made.

The navigation of all of these pages is taken care of by the calendar code, whereby each month is accessible by clicking the month name in the calendar and then each individual day's entries are accessed by clicking the individual date links.

The display pages are really very simple but achieve the objectives of the initial task at the same time.

The Next Level

As was stated at the beginning of this case study, this is a simple blogging system. There are several areas that can be easily identified as candidates for improvement and then there are the extra items that can be added to enhance the user experience.

Room for Improvement

One of the first things that could be improved upon is the month's display page. Currently it just displays all of the blog entries for the selected month in one long page. What might be a better choice would be to display a defined number of blog entries on the page and introduce Recordset paging to reduce the length of the page.

Another advancement on the month page might be to add a link next to each blog entry that could take you to the day page to display that selected blog entry. You would need to ensure that the variable it passed in the querystring to the day page was correctly formatted in order to filter the database correctly.

Study the calendar code to see how those links are assembled.

Additional Functionality

After your blog has been running for a while, if you've been busy blogging you might build up a very large number of entries.

You could consider adding more elements to your blog system to make it easier for your users to find the data they are looking for, and interact with your posts. These are just a few simple suggestions:

- A search mechanism to search the headlines and the HTML data for the users' search criteria.

- A search by date range to return entries between two user-specified dates.

- A commenting system that allows your users to comment on your blog posts. This would require a third database table to store comments related to blog entries.

It doesn't take much to see opportunities for improving an application such as this so feel free to experiment.

Summary

In this chapter we've walked through creating a basic blogging system using Dreamweaver MX.

We built a secure online admin system that populates the blog and then we built the actual blog pages that display the information. We also produced a stylesheet to make sure the pages will be displayed in an appealing yet simple visual style.

There are many areas in which this simple system can be upgraded – we even listed a few ideas that could be fairly easily integrated into this system – but as a simple solution, I hope you find that it works very well.

Happy blogging!

Case Study 2

- Building an online message forum, including:

  - An Access database backend

  - Pages for registering, and logging in and out

  - Pages for posting messages and replies, editing posts, and deleting posts

Author: Omar Elbaga

Message Forum

Introduction

In this case study you will learn how to build an online forum from the ground up, starting with the database and moving on to the web pages. We will not discuss too much theory in this chapter but rather a practical application of the ASP principles we've learned from the previous chapters. In this case study you will:

- Build an Access database back end for an online forum

- Create front-end pages of a complete dynamic forum using – of course – Dreamweaver MX

- Learn how to tweak the application to enhance your forum

Any discussion forum revolves around a few general principles that are quite easy to implement (we'll discuss these in a moment). Beyond these principles, web developers add personal tweaks here and there to make the forum more accessible, user-friendly, and scalable. As a web developer you will find ways to change the flow of your forums according to your own style. For example, you might like to give your users the option to receive an e-mail notification for any replies posted in topics they've created, or topics they've replied to, or even subscribed to. These additional features are not very hard to implement and each web developer decides what they want to add to their forum to make it friendlier.

How the Forum Will Work

When building any database-based application we need to think of what we want from it. What do we want to happen with this forum?

> *As a web developer you will find ways to change the flow of your forums according to your own style.*

Specific Forums: Subject Matter

First, we want a group of forums that revolve around a specific subject matter. Normally, the Webmaster creates the categories they want the forum to revolve around. These have no real bearing on the flow of the pages or creation of the database unless the subject matter is extremely complicated. You may want your forums to be about Health, Cars, Politics, Computers, Web Programming, or any number of possible topics. As you know, you may not even have the option of creating the subject matter as you might be building it for a client who wants a specific topic. Hence we need to create a simple table that stores these forums, which we'll call `forums`.

Forums Need Topics

Now that we have a table that stores the forum subjects, we want users to be able to create topics within them. Hence we need another table that stores this information. What data do we want to collect regarding the topic? We need a title, body of text, username of the submitter for identification, date/time of submission, and the forum that the topic is related to. We'll call this table `forum_topics`.

Topics Need Replies

The last of the information we need to collect are the replies to the topics. We need to collect details about the replies very similar to those we have collected for the topics: Title, body of text, date/time of submission, username of the submitter for identification, and the topic that the reply is related to. We'll call this table `forum_replies`.

Don't Forget About the Users

Finally, a forum needs users to post; our database needs a table to store users. I'm sure you are familiar with this kind of table already. We'll use it to collect the username, password, first name, last name, a group level for each user, date/time of registration, and e-mail. We'll call this table `users`.

How Does the Forum Flow?

The forum in general revolves around a few simple database inserts and queries. There is not much beyond that. It isn't much different from a guest book except that the surfers who post need to register a username. Users who think they are "posting" a topic or even "replying" to one are merely inserting a comment into a database field that we then display on a separate page. If you know the concept of inserting text into a database and displaying text from a database, you have all the principles needed to build a discussion forum.

> *If you know the concept of inserting text into a database and displaying text from a database, you have all the principles needed to build a discussion forum.*

The forum we will create consists firstly of a database, but before we discuss the database let's just briefly go over the flow of the pages. The forum will consist of eight essential pages. I will divide them up into three main database-related categories:

- Displaying text
- Inserting text
- Editing text

Displaying Text from a Database

The three pages we'll be using to display the text from the database are as follows:

- `forums.asp` – The page that lists the forums.
- `topics.asp` – The page that lists the topics related to a specific forum.
- `replies.asp` – The page that lists the replies related to a specific topic.

Inserting Text into a Database

The two pages we'll be using to insert text into the database are as follows:

- `post_topic.asp` – The page that allows the user to insert a topic related to a specific forum.
- `post_reply.asp` – The page that allows the user to insert a reply related to a specific topic.

Editing Text in Database

The three pages we'll be using to edit text in the database are as follows:

- `edit_topic.asp` – The page that allows the user to delete his or her topic related to a specific forum.
- `edit_reply.asp` –The page that allows the user to delete his or her reply related to a specific topic.
- `delete_posts.asp` – The page that allows the user to delete his or her topic related to a specific forum. Depending on the referential integrity you enforce in the database, this can also automatically delete all replies related to a deleted topic.

Relating Posts to Users

We also need to create three additional pages, no directly related to the forum, which are the registration, login, and logout pages. Surfers have to register a username saved in the database so that all their posts are identified. This is really the only reason why you would have surfers register usernames to post in the forum. Otherwise, posts would be arbitrary and we would have no way of relating topics to users. It also stops users pretending to be other people and would be required if we were to extend the site to send out e-mails. Hence, we will create three more pages:

C2

- `register.asp` - The page that allows a surfer to register for a username in order to begin posting.

- `login.asp` - The page that allows a surfer to login with a username in order to relate posts to him or her.

- `logout.asp` - The page that allows a logged-in user to log out.

The **registration**, **login**, and **logout** pages are also important when it comes to testing the application because in order to post you should be logged in as a user. When testing you should also create at least two usernames so you can test posting and replying between two different users. This will require you to log in, post, log out, log back in as a different user, post a reply, and log back out, and then log back in as the first user and repeat. You will have to do this several times to make sure everything is working properly. We will get into this later, but now let's discuss how we want the forum to work.

The Foundation, the Database

We will be using Microsoft Access to build the database. Open Access at this stage, create a new database and name it `dynamicforums_data.mdb`.

The forums Table

Create a new table, called `forums`, as follows:

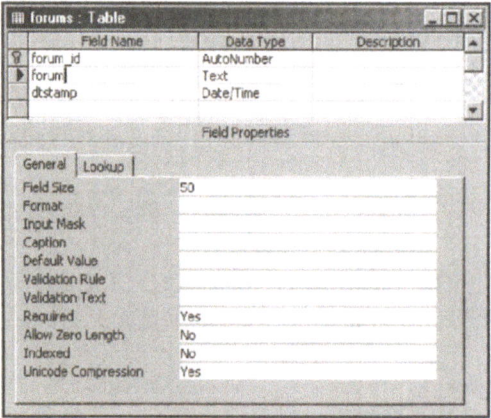

The forums table.

Make the `forum_id` column the primary key. Make the `forum` column *Required* (set this option to *Yes* in the Field Properties) and not *Allow Zero Length* (set this option to *No*). We'll give the `dtstamp` column a *Default Value* of `Now()`.

This will automatically generate the current date and time for each new record inserted into the table without us having to insert it manually from the form on the web page. Save this table as `forums` and close it.

The forum_topics Table

Create a new table in Design View and save it as `forum_topics`. Create the table as follows:

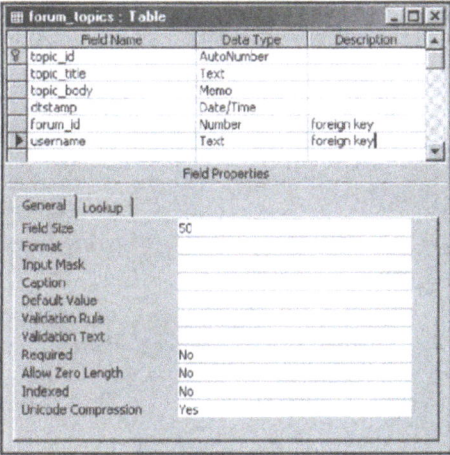

The forum_topics table.

Make the `topic_id` column the primary key. Make the `topic_title` column *Required*, and not *Allow Zero Length*. Again, we'll make the `dtstamp` column have a *Default Value* of `Now()`. Save the table and close it.

The forum_replies Table

Create a new table, save it as `forum_replies`. Create the table as follows:

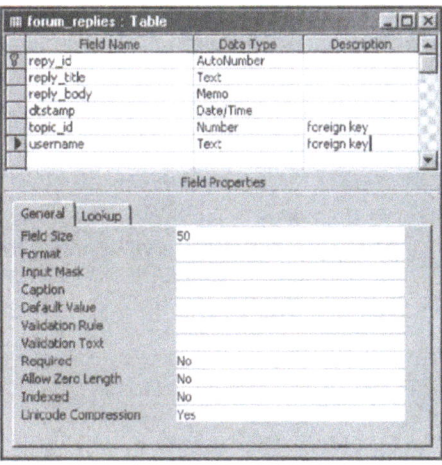

The forum_replies table.

Make the `reply_id` column the primary key. Make the `reply_title` column *Required*, and not *Allow Zero Length*. Again, we'll give the `dtstamp` column a *Default Value* of `Now()`. Save the table and close it.

The users Table

Create a new table in Design View and save it as `users`. Create the table as follows:

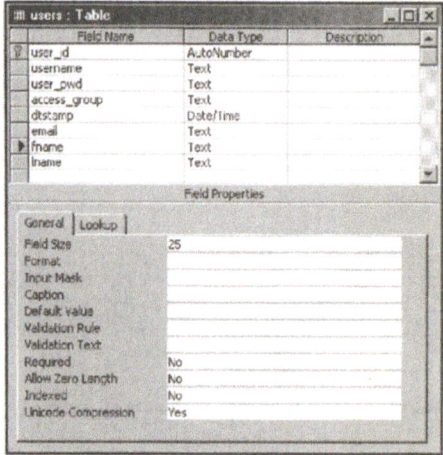

The users table.

Make the `user_id` column the **Primary Key**. Make the `username` column *Required*, and set *Allow Zero Length* to *No*. Do the same for the `user_pwd` field. Again, we'll give the `dtstamp` column a *Default Value* of `Now()`. Set the *Default Value* of the `access_group` field to `"member"`.

Every user who registers will automatically be considered a "member". Later we can change this from within the database to "admin" for a specific user who will serve as an administrator. This is so we can perform certain actions in our web application according to the access level a user has. For example, only an administrator might have access to a particular page; we can then query the database to see the value stored in this column to find out if the user is an administrator or simply a member and redirect accordingly.

You may wish to limit the number of characters in the `email`, `fname`, and `lname` columns. You can do so by inputting a number from 1-255 in the *Field Size* option of *Field Properties*. Save the table and close it. You may also decide whether or not the first name and last name are required. This is your choice, based on the data that is important for you as the web developer or for the clients you are building the forum for.

Database Table Relationships

Now that we have created our tables, we need to understand a couple of relationships between the tables. Notice that both the `forum_topics` and `forum_replies` include foreign keys. The foreign key stores the autonumber of the previous table. The foreign key called `forum_id` in the `forum_topics` table will store the `forum_id` number that resides in the `forums` table.

Likewise, the foreign key called `topic_id` in the `forum_replies` table will store the `topic_id` number that resides in the `forum_topics` table.

These numbers will be inserted from the form on the actual web page. These keys are very important because they literally connect topics to forums and replies to topics. Without them, we could not relate any post to another.

Another relationship exists, this time based on the `username` column that resides in both the `forum_topics` and `forum_replies` tables. This column in both tables serves as a foreign key to the `username` stored in the `users` table. This key is also important because it attaches every post to a particular user. This will also be inserted from a form on the web page without the user necessarily knowing it. We will get into this when we begin building the actual pages.

Select the relationships icon in Access and show all tables.

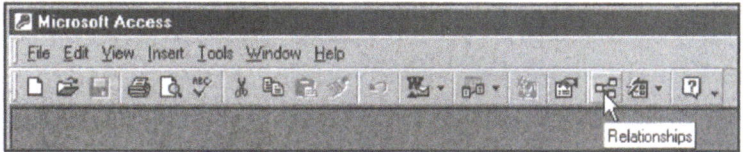

Create the relationships between the columns that we have just created; you can drag the column from one table onto its corresponding key, and Access will present you with a dialog in which you can specify the relationship. Here is a look at the relationships in Access:

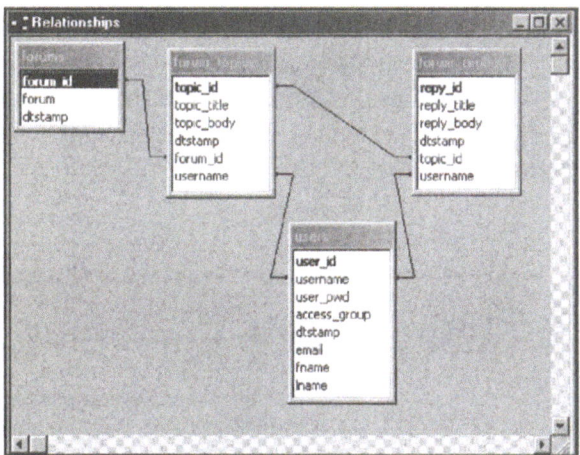

The relationships between the tables.

If you want to make sure that all related replies are deleted when a particular topic is removed, then you can enforce referential integrity here. You can right-click the line that connects the `topic_id` column in the `forum_topics` table to the `topic_id` column in the `forum_replies` tables and select *Edit Relationship*. When the dialog box opens, you should check off the two options: *Enforce Referential Integrity* and *Cascade Delete Related Records*.

If you select Cascade Delete Related Records, Access will delete related records in related tables.

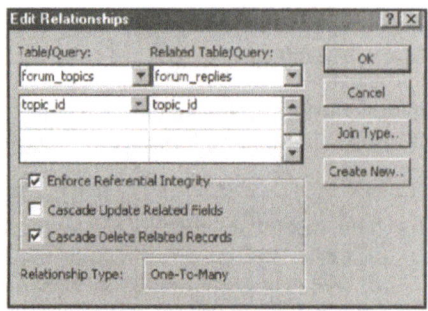

In this case study I have chosen not to do so because I normally like replies to remain even if a user deletes his or her topics. Many forums delete the whole topic.

Populating the Database

We have now completed all the necessary tables needed to run our forum. Before we move on to building the actual web pages, we need to populate our database with some basic information. At the very least, we need to populate the `forums` tables with some forum subjects and the `users` table with a couple of users. The subject matter you choose to populate the `forums` table with is entirely up to you; it will not affect the creation of our web pages. I will populate my forum with health-related topics. I populated the `forums` table with the following forums: Diet, Exercise, Grooming, Women's Issues, Recipes, Open Talk Zone, Pregnancy, and Weight Loss.

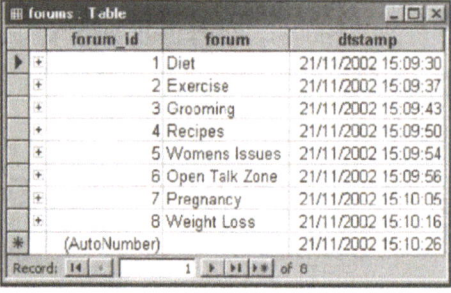

> At the very least, we need to populate the forums tables with some forum subjects and the users table with a couple of users.

We also need to populate the `users` table with a couple of users. Remember that we used the text "`member`" as the default value of the `access_group` column so the users added will automatically be given "member" status.

Make sure to add yourself first and use the text "`admin`" for your access group; do this manually. We use this to distinguish between someone who has administrative rights and other "regular" users. From this point on, we are done with the database and can move on to Dreamweaver MX to build our pages.

The Connection

We have to do a few more things before we begin working on the forum pages. Before moving on, create a directory on your computer where you will store the forum pages and then create a virtual directory that maps to that directory in IIS (do this by right-clicking on the folder and going to *Properties > Web Sharing*). I named the physical directory `dmxasp_forum` and the virtual directory `dmxaspforum`.

Within the directory that you will keep your forum pages in, create a folder called *db* and place the `dynamicforums_data.mdb` database in this directory.

As you may already know, now we need to create a connection to the database from within Dreamweaver. After creating a local site in Dreamweaver that maps to the physical directory you've created for the forum pages, from the *Application* panel select *Custom Connection String* from the plus sign on the *Databases* tab. Enter `conn_dmxaspforum_oledb` for the *Connection Name* and the following string for the *Connection String*:

When you decide to deploy this forum online, be sure never to put the actual database within a virtual directory, otherwise a user may find and download the database. Always place the database in a physical directory, usually directly above the root of your virtual site.

```
Provider=Microsoft.Jet.OLEDB.4.0;Data Source=C:\Path To
Database\dynamicforums_data.mdb;
```

Notice, in the above code, the part of the string that maps to the database:

```
C:\Path To Database\dynamicforums_data.mdb;
```

Make sure this reflects the path to the physical directory on your own computer.

Tell Dreamweaver to connect *Using Driver On This Machine*. Test the connection to make sure the connection is successful and then hit *OK*. If the connection is unsuccessful double-check that the path to the database is correct. Also make sure that your local host is running. Once successfully connected, we can move on to creating the forum pages.

The Pages

Feel free to design your pages as you like. Keep in mind that we won't be getting into design issues, but sticking more with the scripting.

empty.asp

Before we begin creating any of the main pages you should create this page and save it in the same directory as the other pages; we will be redirecting new browser windows to this page often. For example, we will load pages that post new topics and replies in new windows. When the user submits the form, we want to close the new window and refresh the main window so that the new post appears automatically. This page will have the JavaScript that does just that. Create a new ASP VBScript document and save it as `empty.asp`. Add the following JavaScript to the `<body>` tag:

```
<body onLoad="window.opener.location.reload();window.close();">
```

You can close this page and basically forget it, but make sure it remains in the directory with all the other forum pages we will be creating.

login.asp

Create a new ASP VBScript web page and save it as `login.asp`. In the main body of your page, create a login form with two text fields and one submit button. The first text field will be where the user enters the username and the second text field will be where the user enters the password. Name the first text field `txtusername` and the second text field `txtpassword`. Label the submit button as `Login`.

Now from the *Application* panel select *Server Behaviors > + > User Authentication > Log In User*. When the dialog box opens, fill in the fields according to the picture below. Make sure that the `username` field reflects the `username` field in the form, `txtusername`, and the `password` field reflects the `password` in the form, `txtpassword`. Also be sure that once you've selected the connection (`conn_dmxaspforum_oledb`) and table (`users`), the `Username` column reflects the `username` column of the database, `username`, and the `password` column reflects the `password` column of the database, `user_pwd`. If a login succeeds send the user to `forums.asp` and if it fails send the user back to `login.asp`. Restrict access based on `username`, `password`, and `access level` (*Get Level From* should be `access_group`):

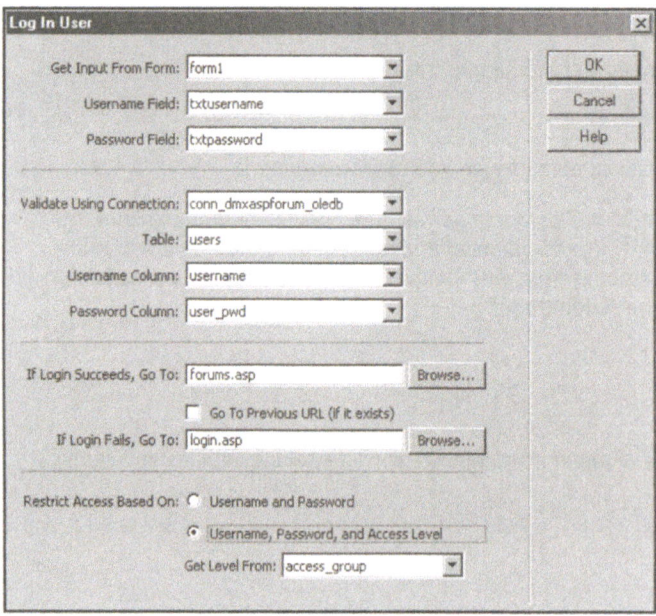

Let's add some more code. Switch to Code View and you should notice at the top the big block of login code Dreamweaver has created. You should also see the connection include. Directly above the connection but below the page directive add the following code:

```
<%@LANGUAGE="VBSCRIPT" CODEPAGE="1252"%>

<%
If Session("MM_Username") <> "" Then
  Response.Redirect "forums.asp"
End If
%>
<!--#include file="Connections/conn_dmxaspforum_oledb.asp" -->
```

The `login.asp` page is only for users who need to log in; users who are already logged in don't need to come here again until they log out. To avoid users attempting to access the login page while already logged-in (or even running into it by accident and thinking they weren't logged-in already) the code above redirects a logged-in user to the `forums.asp` page. You could redirect to a page of your choice, although sending them back to `forums.asp` seems to make sense.

The Dreamweaver login code creates a Session variable named `MM_Username` that stores the logged-in user's username as its value to identify a successful user. Refer to *Chapter 10* to learn more about Session variables. If this variable exists it means the user must have passed the login code successfully otherwise it would not have been created.

One more thing we want to do is create a few cookies to remember some data about a user so we don't have to keep querying the database to retrieve throughout the other web pages. Let's store the user's first name, e-mail, and access group in three different cookies. We can do this only if the user has successfully passed the Dreamweaver login so we need to find the spot in the login code block where the user has passed. You should notice at around line 29 the following code:

```
If Not MM_rsUser.EOF Or Not MM_rsUser.BOF Then
    ' username and password match - this is a valid user
    Session("MM_Username") = MM_valUsername
```

After the first line, the user has entered a successful username / password pair and Dreamweaver creates the Session variable for the username. From here we can create our own variables. First we'll need to grab the information from the database, so find the line:

```
MM_rsUser.Source = "SELECT username, user_pwd"
```

and replace it with:

```
MM_rsUser.Source = "SELECT username, user_pwd, fname, email, access_group"
```

Let's create the three cookies we mentioned above now. Add the following code directly below the last line:

```
If Not MM_rsUser.EOF Or Not MM_rsUser.BOF Then
    ' username and password match - this is a valid user
    Session("MM_Username") = MM_valUsername
Response.Cookies("ckfname") = Trim(CStr(MM_rsUser.Fields.Item("fname").Value))
Response.Cookies("ckemail") = Trim(CStr(MM_rsUser.Fields.Item("email").Value))
Response.Cookies("ckaccessgroup") = _
                Trim(CStr(MM_rsUser.Fields.Item("access_group").Value))
    If (MM_fldUserAuthorization <> "") Then
```

We now have created three cookies: `ckfname`, `ckemail`, and `ckaccessgroup`. Note that the user must have cookies enabled in the browser for these to be set properly. Save the login page: we're not going to add any more functionality. Here is a look at my login page:

Now that you've altered the code by hand, be careful about altering the page by clicking on Server Behaviors. This will cause Dreamweaver to "Correct" the code, leading to problems later on.

The welcome page in a browser.

logout.asp

Since we've built a login page, we'd better build the `logout.asp` page, as we will also need this when testing the pages. Create a new ASP VBScript web page and save it as `logout.asp`. Select *Server Behaviors > + > User Authentication > Log Out User*. When the dialog box opens, select the second option to log out when the page is loaded and redirect to the `login.asp` page (we will replace this below) and hit *OK*.

Switch to Code View and change the Dreamweaver code to the following:

```
<%
' *** Logout the current user.
MM_logoutRedirectPage = Request.ServerVariables("HTTP_REFERER")
Session.Contents.Remove("MM_Username")
Session.Contents.Remove("MM_UserAuthorization")
Response.Cookies("ckaccessgroup") = ""
Response.Cookies("ckemail") = ""
Response.Cookies("ckfname") = ""
If (MM_logoutRedirectPage <> "") Then Response.Redirect(MM_logoutRedirectPage)
%>
```

We've replaced the redirect page from a static one (`login.asp`) to the referrer URL (`HTTP_REFERER`), which would be the page the user came from. This is so the user who logs out while viewing a post can be redirected back to the post they were viewing after logging out. We then add our own Logout variables to destroy the cookies we created. Save and close this page and let's move on.

register.asp

The `register.asp` page allows our users to register to post. Create a new ASP VBScript page and save it as `register.asp`.

Insert a form and within this create a table with seven rows and two columns. In the top first column of the top row put the text "*Become a member*". In the first column of the next row put the label text *Username* and in the second column put a text field called `username`. In the next row put a label text *Password* and a password text field called `user_pwd`. In the next row add a label of *First Name* and a text field called `fname`. The following row is a label of *Last Name* and a text field called `lname`. The row after that contains a label of *Email* and a text field called `email`. In the last row of the table put a submit button. This form will hold the information our new user wishes to use.

Go to the *Design* panel and select *Behaviors > + > Validate Form*. Make all the fields required, and the `email` field to be a valid e-mail address.

Now we want the form to insert a user record into our database. Highlight the form and go to *Server Behaviors > Insert Record*. Select the `conn_dmxaspforum` connection and choose the `users` table. Set *After Insert Goto* to `forums.asp`. The form elements should automatically be set to the relevant fields of the database. Hit *OK* to complete this addition.

Before we can use this page however we want to make sure that no usernames are duplicated. To do this we add another server behavior from *Server Behaviors > + > User Authentication > Check New Username*. Set the *User Name* field to `username` and the *If Already Exists Goto* to `register.asp`. Use the browse button to add a parameter called `exists` with a value of `"that username already exists"`. Next, go to Code View and add the following to the second column of the first row:

```
<%=request.querystring("exists")%>
```

Now, if the user tries to use an existing username he is redirected to the registration page and given a warning. We also want a user to be redirected to the forum if they try to register and are already logged in. To do this add the following code directly after the ASP directive:

```
<%
If Session("MM_Username") <> "" Then
   Response.Redirect "forums.asp"
End If
%>
```

The final page should look something like this:

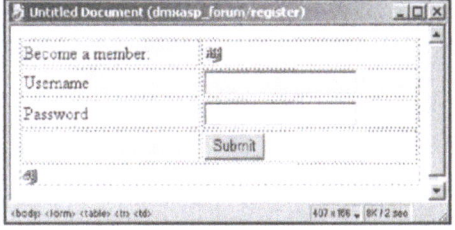

The registration page in a browser.

forums.asp

The `forums.asp` page serves as the main page of the entire forum; it displays the forum subjects from the database. Create a new ASP VBScript web page and save it as `forums.asp`.

Before we begin this document in Dreamweaver let's add some generic links that should go on all pages. This will be a personal welcoming message, login, and logout link. We want to show the welcoming message and logout to users who are logged in and the login link to users who are not. Put these links somewhere at the top of your page design. Here is the code to use:

```
<% If Session("MM_Username") = "" Then %>
<a href="login.asp">login</a> | <a href="register.asp">register</a>
<% End If %>
<% If Session("MM_Username") <> "" Then %>
Welcome <%=Request.Cookies("ckfname") %>!
<a href="logout.asp">logout</a>
<% End If %>
```

Now select *Server Behaviors > Recordset*. Name the Recordset `rsgetforums` and select the `conn_dmxaspforum_oledb` connection. Insert the following SQL in the SQL text field using the *Advanced* option:

```
SELECT forum_id, forum, dtstamp
FROM forums
ORDER BY forum_id ASC
```

In the main body of your page, insert a table with one row and two columns. Place your cursor in the left column and from the *Bindings* window drag the `forum` column from the `rsgetforums` Recordset into the column. Highlight the dynamic text and from the *Properties* panel, choose browse, type in `topics.asp`, then use the parameters button to add the `forum_id` parameter that should receive its value from the `forum_id` field of the `rsgetforums` Recordset. The URL should look like this:

```
topics.asp?forum_id=<%=(rsgetforums.Fields.Item("forum_id").Value)%>
```

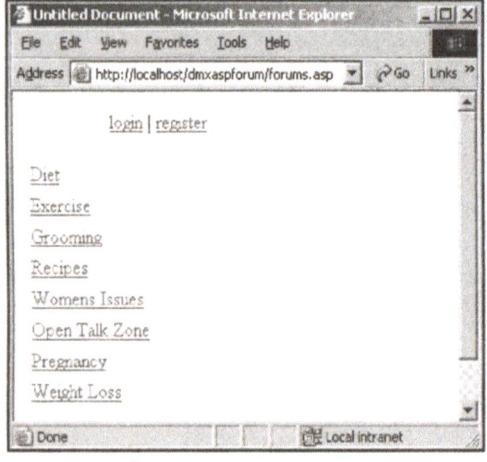

The forums page in a browser.

This goes to the `topics.asp`, passing the `forum_id` to the next page in the querystring. The next page will display the topics according to the forum selected from this page. Now highlight the table row and select *Server Behaviors > Repeat Region*. Select the `rsgetforums` recordset from the drop-down menu and choose the option to display all records. Test the page in your browser to see the display of the forums; it'll look something like this:

Leave the second column empty as we will use it later in the chapter, and we're done for the moment; save and close the file.

topics.asp

The `topics.asp` will display topics related to the forum selected from the previous page. Create a new ASP VBScript web page and save it as `topics.asp`.

In the main body of your page insert a table with five rows and one column. Split the third and fourth rows into four columns. Label the columns of the third row with the following labels: `Topics`, `User`, `Date`, `Replies`. Type the following text in the last row (fifth): `No topics have been posted for this chapter`.

![The topics page layout showing Untitled Document (dmxaspforum/topics.asp*) (XHTML) with Topics, User, Date, Replies columns and text "No topics have been posted for this chapter"]

The topics page layout.

Place your cursor in the top row and type the text: *New Topic*. Highlight this text and then link the text with the following URL:

```
javascript:void(0)
```

With this text still highlighted and from the *Design* panel select *Behaviors > + > Open Browser Window*. When the dialog box opens select the `post_topic.asp` page and be sure to also add a parameter to the URL named `forum_id` with the following value:

```
<%=(Request.QueryString("forum_id"))%>
```

Name the window: `winnewtopic`. Give the window the width and height of your choice and check your preferred attributes. Click *OK*, set the behavior to trigger `onClick`, and the final code should look something like the following:

```
<a href="javascript:void(0)"
onClick="MM_openBrWindow('post_topic.asp?forum_id=<%=(Request.QueryString("forum_id")
)%>','winnewtopic','status=yes,scrollbars=yes,resizable=yes,width=650,height=410')"><
b>New Topic</b></a>
```

This will open the `post_topic.asp` page (which we will create next) passing the `forum_id` in the querystring.

Now let's create the Recordset to retrieve the topics for the forum that was selected from the previous page. Notice that we have the `forum_id` passed in the querystring of this page. So now we want to query the `forum_topics` table and retrieve the topics related to the `forum_id` passed in the querystring. We will also join the two tables so that we can maintain the forum name in the Recordset along with the forum ID.

Message Forum

C2

Select *Bindings > + > Recordset*. Name the Recordset `rsgettopics` and select the `conn_dmxaspforum_oledb` connection. Put the following SQL in the SQL text field:

```
SELECT forum_topics.topic_id, forum_topics.topic_title, forum_topics.dtstamp,
       forum_topics.username, forums.forum, forums.forum_id
FROM forum_topics, forums
WHERE forum_topics.forum_id = MMColParam AND forum_topics.forum_id = forums.forum_id
```

Add a variable called `MMColParam` with a *Default Value* of `0` and a *Run-time value* of `Request.QueryString("forum_id")` and hit *OK*. This definition gives a value to the `MMColParam` variable that appears in the recordset. We filter the forum topics by the `MMColParam` variable that holds the `forum_id` passed in the querystring as its value:

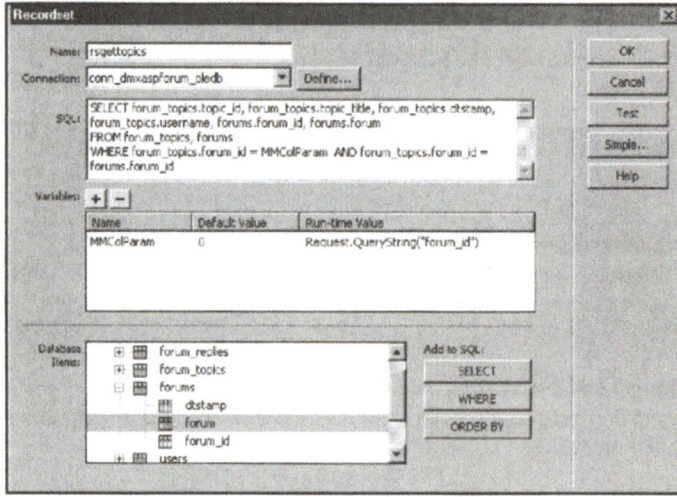

The Recordset dialog.

Let's populate the table with the dynamic text now. From the *Bindings* window drag the `forum` column to the right of the `New Topic` text in the first row of the table. Next, drag the other columns into their appropriate columns of the fourth row, except the replies, as we haven't created the Recordset for this yet.

Highlight the `topic_title` dynamic text in the first column of the fourth row and from *Properties* link it to the `replies.asp` page. Click the parameters button to add two parameters. The first one should be `topic_id` whose value should come from the `topic_id` column of the `rsgettopics` Recordset and the second should be named `forum_id` whose value should come from the `forum_id` column of the `rsgettopics` Recordset. Click *OK* to close the two dialog boxes. The final URL code should look like this:

```
<a
href="replies.asp?topic_id=<%=(rsgettopics.Fields.Item("topic_id").Value)%>&forum_id=
<%=(rsgettopics.Fields.Item("forum_id").Value)%>">
<%=(rsgettopics.Fields.Item("topic_title").Value)%>
</a>
```

This allows the user to click the topic title, which will take them to the `replies.asp` page (which we haven't created yet) that will display the replies associated with the topic selected from this page. Notice that the link passes `topic_id` and `forum_id` in the querystring for retrieval on the next page.

You will also need to drag the `username` and `dtstamp` from the `rsgettopics` in the *Bindings* panel into the correct cells of the table.

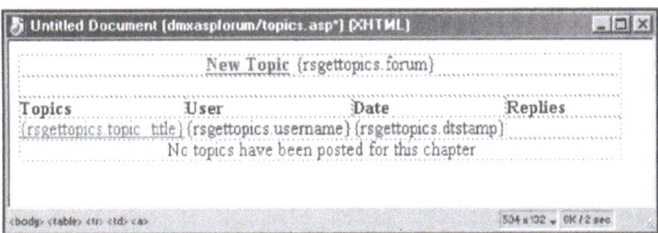

The topics page in Dreamweaver.

Lastly we need to show the topics only if any exist for the forum selected. Highlight the forum dynamic text in the first row beside the New Topic text and select *Server Behaviors > + > Show Region > Show Region If Recordset Is Not Empty* and select the `rsgettopics` Recordset and hit *OK*. This will mean we don't show the forum name if there are no topics, only the link to create a new topic.

Now highlight the fourth row and follow the same exact step as above by using the *Show If Recordset Is Not Empty* Behavior. The data will now only show if topics exist. Finally, highlight the fifth row and select *Server Behaviors > + > Show Region > Show If Recordset Is Empty* and select the `rsgettopics` Recordset and hit *OK*. Here is a look at the form in my document:

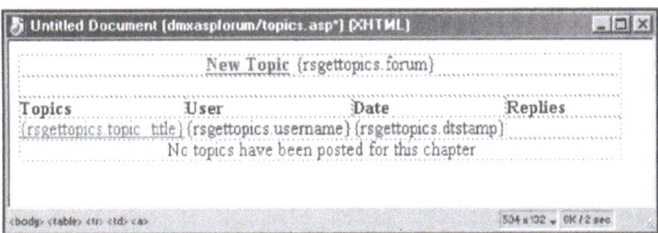

The topics page in Dreamweaver.

Now switch to Code View and find the following code that should be the last few lines of code in your page:

```
<%
rsgettopics.Close()
Set rsgettopics = Nothing
%>
```

This is the code that closes the Recordset. In the form above, we've surrounded the dynamic text that attempts to display data from this Recordset with a conditional region to not display if the Recordset comes up empty. Similarly we need to make sure this code that attempts to close the Recordset does not display if the Recordset comes up empty. Surround the code with the following `If` statement:

```
<% If Not rsgettopics.EOF Or Not rsgettopics.BOF Then %>
<%
rsgettopics.Close()
Set rsgettopics = Nothing
%>
<% End If %>
```

We will come back to this page later to create the code for showing the number of replies.

post_topic.asp

Users now need the ability to actually create their own topics. We created a link to this page on the `topics.asp` page that passes the `forum_id` in the querystring. This identifies the forum the user desired to insert a topic into.

Create a new ASP VBScript web page and save it as `post_topic.asp`. In the main body of your page insert a form and then place a table with three rows and two columns inside this form. Place the following text to appear above the form: *Post New Topic (Note: Please no HTML tags. Thank you.).*

In the first column of the first row place the text: `Title`. In the second column of the first row, insert a text field and name it `topic_title`. In the first column of the second row place the text: `Body`. In the second column of the second row, insert a text area field and name it `topic_body`.

In the second column of the third row insert a submit button and a regular button. Label the submit button with the text: *Post New Topic*. Label the second button with the text: *Cancel*. Select the cancel button and from the *Design* panel select *Behaviors > + > Go To URL*.

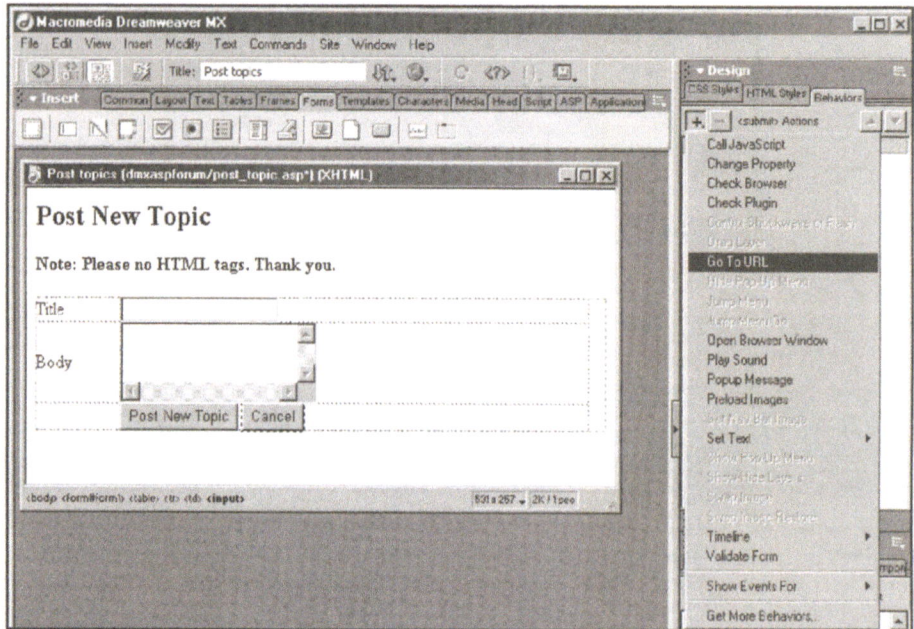

post_topics.asp in Dreamweaver, showing the Behaviors menu.

When the dialog box opens select `main window` for the *Open In* option and send to the `empty.asp` page that we created earlier; remember this will close the pop-up and refresh the main window.

Since this is a page for posting a new topic, we'll need to insert the values from the form into the `forum_topics` database table. If you recall, this table also needs to collect the `username` and `forum_id`. These values are available to us to add to the form. The username is in a Session variable named `MM_Username` which was created upon logging in and the `forum_id` is in the querystring of the URL. Make sure you place your cursor inside the form and insert two hidden fields. Label the first one `username` and give it the following value:

```
<%=Session("MM_Username")%>
```

Label the second field `forum_id`, and give it the following value:

```
<%=Request.QueryString("forum_id")%>
```

Our form is now complete, apart from submitting to the database.

We need to insert the values of this form into the `forum_topics` database table. Select *Server Behaviors > + > Insert Record*. When the dialog box opens select the `conn_dmxaspforum_oledb` connection. Insert into the `forum_topics` table. After inserting, send to `empty.asp`.

The form elements should automatically appear to insert into the appropriate database columns because we named the elements the same as the columns. Hit *OK* to close the dialog box.

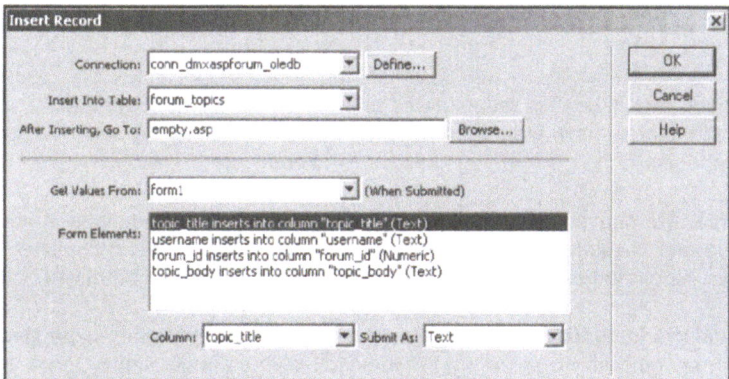

The Insert Record dialog.

Now we'll add Dreamweaver's *Validate Form* behavior to this form to ensure users enter values for the title and body. Highlight the form and from the *Design* panel select *Behaviors > + > Validate Form*. Make both the `topic_title` and `topic_body` fields required and hit *OK*.

Message Forum

C2

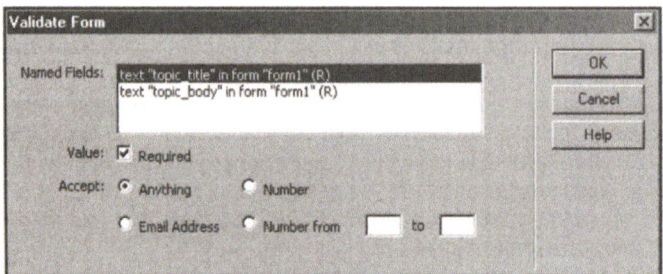

The Validate Form dialog.

Finally let's make sure that only a logged-in user can access this page. Add the following code to the top of your document in Code View. It should be placed directly below the ASP page directive:

```
<%
If Session("MM_Username") = "" Then
Response.Write "You must be logged in to use this page"
Response.End
End If
%>
```

This code prints to the screen the text: *You must be logged in to use this page* and ends the ASP page immediately if no Session variable exists for the user who has attempted to access the page.

Pause: Test the Application

So far we have created the `login.asp`, `forums.asp`, `topics.asp`, and `post_topic.asp` pages. From this point you should be able to log in and post topics in desired forums at the very least. This is what we need to test out now. Test each page one by one; assume the role of a surfer and log in to begin posting topics.

Most often, errors are caused by a faulty Recordset or misnaming variables. If you encounter a problem go back and check that the Recordset code matches the code in this book. Also be sure that the dynamic text on the page matches the database columns being retrieved in the Recordset.

I recommend that you frequently back up your documents, especially when debugging, because as you debug you may perform an action that is irreversible or you may simply forget how to reverse steps you've taken while debugging. Before you begin manipulating any code, back up your documents.

Before you begin manipulating any code, back up your documents.

Also attempt to access the `post_topic.asp` page while being logged out to be sure that the page is unavailable to logged-out users. Log in and create a few topics in various forums. When you are satisfied with the testing move on to build the next set of pages. We still have to create the `replies.asp`, `post_reply.asp`, `edit_topic.asp`, `edit_reply.asp`, and `delete_topic.asp` pages.

replies.asp

If you recall from the `topics.asp` page we linked the topic title to this page passing the `topic_id` in the querystring. On this page we will retrieve the `topic_id` from the querystring and filter the replies that relate to the selected topic. We also want to display the topic selected on this page and then display the replies underneath the topic. Let's begin creating the document. We will first create the design part and then go in to add the Recordset's and dynamic text.

Static Layout

Create a new ASP VBScript web page and save it as `replies.asp`. In the main body of your page insert four tables stacked over each other vertically. The second table should be split into two rows and the fourth table should be split into three rows. The first and third could remain as one row each.

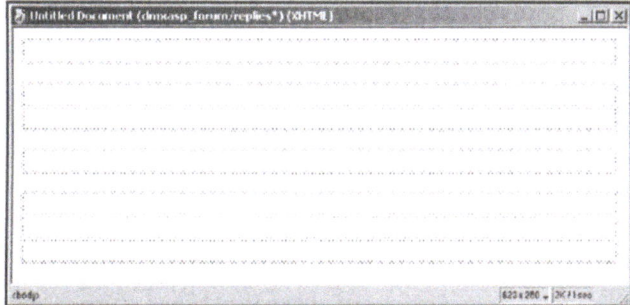

The replies.asp page in Dreamweaver.

Place your cursor in the first table and add the following text:

    Back To Topic | Reply

Place your cursor in the first row of the second table and add the text:

    Original Post by dt_username edit | delete
    posted on dt_date   dt_date2

Place your cursor in the second row of the second table and add the text:

    dt_topic_title
    dt_topic_body

Place your cursor in the third table and add the text:

    No Replies have been submitted yet. Return

Place your cursor in the first row of the fourth table and add the text:

    Reply Message by dt_username edit | delete
    posted on dt_date   dt_date2

> *Don't be confused by the text items beginning dt_; it serves as a temporary placeholder that will be replaced by dynamic text.*

Message Forum

Place your cursor in the second row of the fourth table and add the text:

dt_reply_title

Finally, place your cursor in the third row of the fourth table and add the text:

dt_reply_body

The page should look like this:

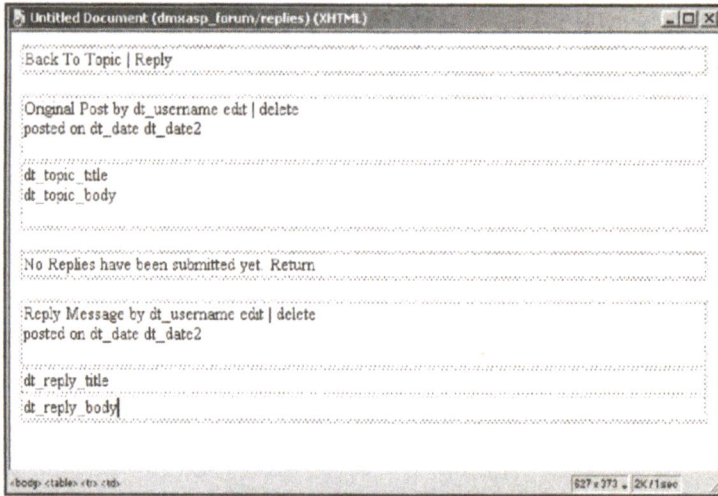

replies.asp in Dreamweaver.

Dynamic Functionality

Now let's add the dynamic functionality. Highlight the text *Back To Topic* in the first table and from the *Properties* panel choose *browse*, type in `topics.asp`, then use the parameters button to add the `forum_id` parameter which should have the following value:
```
<%=Request.QueryString("forum_id")%>
```

The final URL should look like this:

```
topics.asp?forum_id=<%=Request.QueryString("forum_id")%>
```

Also link the text `Return` in the third table with the same link. This retrieves the `forum_id` in the current URL's querystring and passes it back to the `topics.asp` page with the `forum_id` attached. If you simply link back to the `topics.asp` without passing the `forum_id`, the topics will display according to the default value of 0. Because there isn't a `forum_id` of 0 in the database, we'd see a blank topic page.

Let's retrieve the topic selected first. From the *Application* Panel select *Server Behaviors > + > Recordset*. When the dialog box opens, name the Recordset `rsgettopic` and select the `conn_dmxaspforum_oledb` connection. Insert the following SQL in the SQL text field:

```
SELECT topic_id, topic_title, topic_body, username, dtstamp
FROM forum_topics
WHERE topic_id = MMColParam
```

Add the following variable called MMColParam, with a *Default Value* of 0 and a *Run-time Value* of Request.QueryString("topic_id") and hit *OK*. This tells the query to only get the information for the topic specified.

In the second HTML table, replace the text dt_username with the username column from the *Bindings* window. Replace both texts dt_date and dt_date2 with the dtstamp column. Format the first date to display the date and format the second date to display the time. This can be done by highlighting the dynamic text in the document and selecting the arrow pointing downward to the right of the database column in the *Bindings* window:

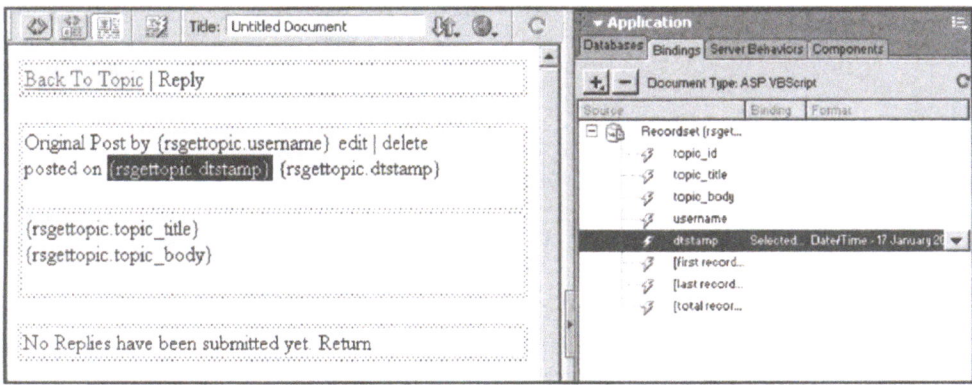

replies.asp in Dreamweaver showing the Bindings window.

In the second row of the second table replace the dt_topic_title with the topic_title database column and the dt_topic_body with the topic_body database column. You can test that the topic displays by going back to the forums page, and then selecting a topic. The topic should appear at the top of the replies.asp page. The replies will not appear below because we haven't created the code yet, neither have we created the post_reply.asp page to allow replies. Here's one we prepared earlier:

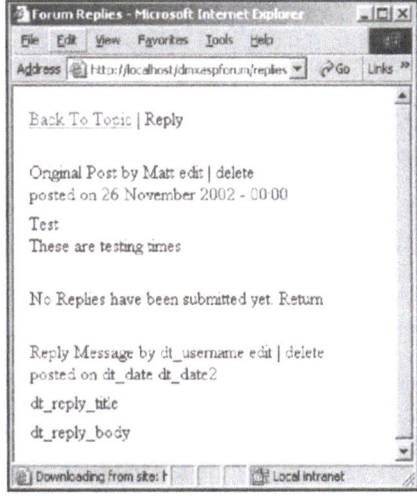

replies.asp in a web browser.

Let's retrieve the replies now. From the *Application* panel select *Server Behaviors > + > Recordset*. When the dialog box opens, name the Recordset `rsgetreplies` and select the `conn_dmxaspforum_oledb` connection. Insert the following SQL in the SQL text field:

```
SELECT reply_id, reply_title, reply_body, dtstamp, topic_id, username
FROM forum_replies
WHERE topic_id = MMColParam1
```

Add a variable called `MMColParam1` with a value of `Request.QueryString("topic_id")` and default of 0, and hit *OK*:

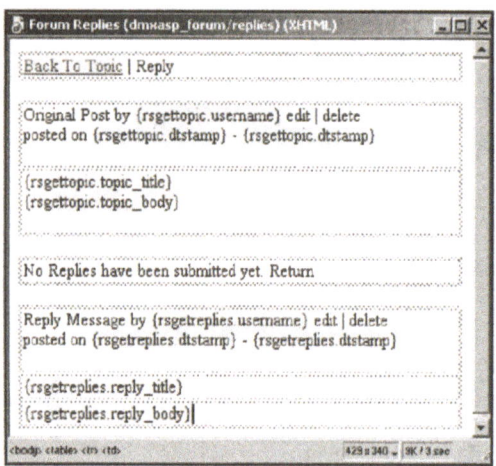

replies.asp in Dreamweaver.

In the first row of the fourth table, replace the text `dt_username` with the `username` of the `rsgetreplies` Recordset – **not** the `rsgettopic` Recordset. Next replace both `dt_date` and `dt_date2` with the `dtstamp` column from the `rsgetreplies` Recordset. Format them the way you formatted the dates of the `rsgettopic` Recordset.

In the second row of this table replace the text `dt_reply_title` with the `reply_title` column and in the third row replace the `dt_reply_body` with the `reply_body` column.

Go back to the text *Reply* in the first table. Link it with the following URL:

```
javascript:void(0)
```

Let's have this link open in a new window. Highlight this text and from the *Design* panel select *Behaviors > + > Open Browser Window*. Fill out the values according to your liking but make sure to link the URL in the dialog box with the following:

```
post_reply.asp?topic_id=<%=(rsgettopic.Fields.Item("topic_id").Value)%>&replyto=<%=(rsgettopic.Fields.Item("topic_title").Value)%>
```

This passes the `topic_id` and `topic_title` to the `post_reply.asp` page. You'll want to change the default event of `onmouseover` to `onClick`.

Now let's show regions depending on what the Recordset returns. Since the URL for the `Reply` link is built on values from the `rsgettopic` Recordset, we should hide this if the `rsgettopic` Recordset turns out empty. As a note, it should not really turn out empty because it was selected from the previous page and we are merely displaying it again on this page, but let's say someone comes to this page directly without going through the `topics.asp` page, an error will be thrown on the page. As the web programmer we need to think of all possible outcomes and code to make the application more user-friendly.

Highlight the *Reply* text and select *Server Behaviors > + > Show Region > Show Region If Recordset Is Not Empty*. Select the `rsgettopic` Recordset from the menu and hit *OK*.

Next, highlight the entire second table and give it the same functionality; select *Server Behaviors > + > Show Region > Show Region If Recordset Is Not Empty*. Select the `rsgettopic` Recordset from the menu and hit *OK*.

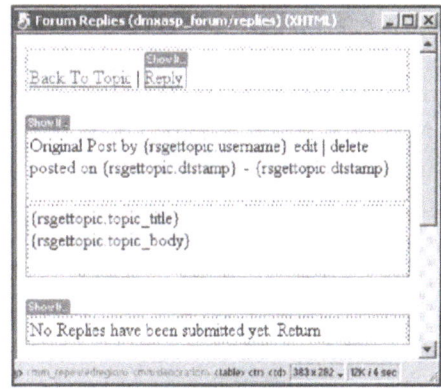

Third, highlight the entire third table and select *Server Behaviors > + > Show Region > Show Region If Recordset Is Empty*. Select the `rsgetreplies` recordset from the menu and hit *OK*. This text should appear if there are no replies to display. Again, this makes the page more user-friendly if it is reached accidentally.

.replies.asp in Dreamweaver with the Show If regions added.

Before we add show region functionality to the fourth table we need it to repeat in the case of multiple replies. Highlight the entire fourth table and select *Server Behaviors > + > Repeat Region*. When the dialog box pops up select the `rsgetreplies` Recordset from the menu and choose the option to display all records. Now highlight the entire table **including** the repeat region and select *Server Behaviors > + > Show Region > Show Region If Recordset Is Not Empty*. Select the `rsgetreplies` Recordset from the menu and hit *OK*.

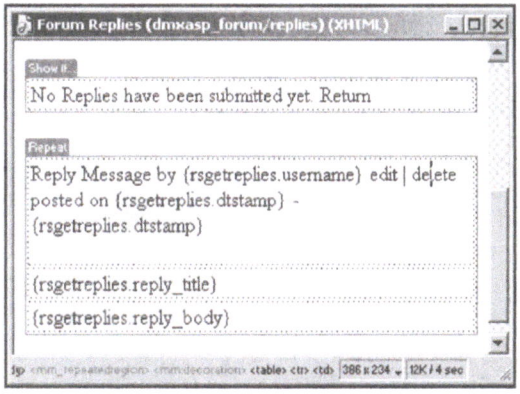

replies.asp in Dreamweaver showing the repeat region.

We are done with this page; we will leave the edit and delete links empty for now, until we create the linking pages. Let's move on to allow users to post replies.

post_reply.asp

Users now need the ability to actually reply to topics. We created a link to this page on the `replies.asp` page that passes the `topic_id` in the querystring. This identifies the topic the user desires to insert a reply into.

Create a new ASP VBScript web page and save it as `post_reply.asp`. In the main body of your page insert a form and then place a table with three rows and two columns inside this form. Switch to Code View and place the following text to appear above the form:

```
Posting Reply to "<%=Trim(Request.QueryString("replyto"))%>"<br />
(Note: Please no HTML tags. Thank you.)
```

In the first column of the first row place the text: `Title`. In the second column of the first row, insert a text field and name it `reply_title`. In the first column of the second row place the text: `Body`. In the second column of the second row, insert a text area field and name it `reply_body`. In the second column of the second row insert a submit button and a regular button. Label the submit button with the text: *Post Reply*. Label the second button with the text: *Cancel*. Select this button and from the *Design* panel select *Behaviors > + > Go To URL*. When the dialog box opens select `main window` for the *Open In* option and send to `empty.asp` as we've done before.

We need to insert these values into the `forum_replies` database table. If you recall, this table needs to collect the `username` and `topic_id`. These values are available to us to add to the form. The username is in a Session variable named `MM_Username`, which was created upon logging in, and the `topic_id` is in the querystring of the URL. Make sure you place your cursor inside the form and insert two hidden variables. Label the first one `username` and give it the following value:

```
<%=Session("MM_Username")%>
```

Name the second one `topic_id` and give it the following value:

```
<%=Request.QueryString("topic_id")%>
```

Our form is now complete.

post_reply.asp in Dreamweaver.

We need to have the values of this form insert into the `forum_replies` database table. Select *Server Behaviors > + > Insert Record*. When the dialog box opens select the `conn_dmxaspforum_oledb` connection. Insert into the `forum_replies` table. *After Inserting, Go To* `empty.asp`. The form elements should automatically appear to insert into the appropriate database columns because we named the elements the same as the columns, but check that the dialog appears as in the following screenshot. Hit *OK* to close the dialog box:

The Insert Record dialog box.

Let's add Dreamweaver's *Validate Form* behavior to this form to ensure users enter values for the title and body. Highlight the form and from the *Design* panel select *Behaviors > + > Validate Form*. Make both the title and body fields required and hit *OK*.

Finally let's make sure that only a logged-in user can access this page as we did with the `post_topic.asp` page. Add the following code to the top of your document in Code View. It should be placed directly below the ASP page directive:

```
<%
If Session("MM_Username") = "" Then
Response.Write "You must be logged in to use this page"
Response.End
End If
%>
```

This code prints to the screen the text: *You must be logged in to use this page* and ends the ASP page immediately if the Session variable does not exist for the user who has attempted to access the page.

Preparing for edit_topic.asp

You may recall that the edit link is on the `replies.asp` page. We need to create this link so load that page in Dreamweaver before creating the `edit_topic.asp` page. Find the `edit` text in the second table that displays the topic. Link it with the following code:

```
javascript:void(0);
```

We need it to open a new window. From the *Design* panel select *Behaviors > + > Open Browser Window*. For the URL to display, browse for the `edit_topic.asp` page and be sure to use the parameter button to pass a parameter named `topic_id` whose value should come from the `topic_id` column of the `rsgettopic` recordset. You can select it by hitting the lightning bolt icon. Hit *OK*. The URL should look like this:

```
edit_topic.asp?topic_id=<%=rsgettopic.Fields.Item("topic_id").Value%>
```

C2

Fill in the options as you desire and hit *OK*. In Code View change the event to `onClick`, and surround the entire `edit` link with the following code:

```
<% If Session("MM_Username") <> "" AND Session("MM_Username") =
trim(rsgettopic.Fields.Item("username").Value) Then %>
<a href="javascript:void(0);"
onclick="MM_openBrWindow('edit_topic.asp?topic_id=<%=rsgettopic.Fields.Item("topic_id
").Value%>','','scrollbars=yes,resizable=yes')">edit</a>
<% End If %>
```

This shows the link only if the `username` session exists and equals the `username` of the original poster of the topic. Otherwise, it does not appear.

As for the `delete` text highlight it and from *Properties* browse for the `delete_posts.asp` and then hit the *Parameters* button. Add two parameters. Name the first `topic_id` and select its value as the `topic_id` column from the `rsgettopic` Recordset. Name the second parameter `forum_id` and type the following code as its value: `<%=Request.QueryString("forum_id")%>`. The final URL should look like this:

```
delete_posts.asp?topic_id=<%=(rsgettopic.Fields.Item("topic_id").Value)%>&forum_id=<%
=Request.QueryString("forum_id")%>
```

Surround the entire `delete` link with the following code:

```
<% If Request.Cookies("ckaccessgroup") = "admin" AND Session("MM_Username") <> ""
Then %>
<ahref="delete_posts.asp?topic_id=<%=(rsgettopic.Fields.Item("topic_id").Value)%>&
forum_id=<%=Request.QueryString("forum_id")%>">delete</a>
<% End If %>
```

This displays the link only if the access group of the logged-in user equals admin. We will only allow administrators the option to delete posts. Some forums allow the person who created a post to delete it as well.

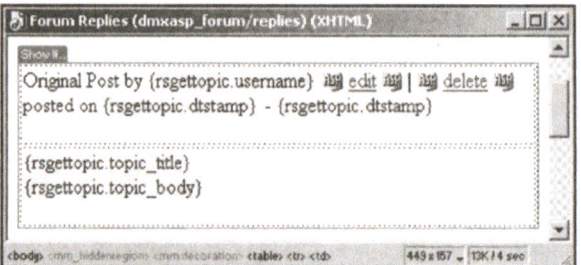

The top of replies.asp in Dreamweaver with the edit and delete code added.

Next, go to the set of `edit` and `delete` texts in the fourth table on the page that displays the reply data. Link the `edit` text with the following code:

```
javascript:void(0);
```

From the *Design* panel select *Behaviors > + > Open Browser Window*. Browse for the `edit_reply.asp` page for the URL to display, add one parameter named `reply_id`, and select its value from the `reply_id` column of the `rsgetreplies` recordset. The final URL to display should look like this:

```
edit_reply.asp?reply_id=<%=(rsgetreplies.Fields.Item("reply_id").Value)%>
```

Hit *OK* to close the dialog box. In Code View surround the entire `edit` link with the following code:

```
<% If Session("MM_Username") <> "" AND Session("MM_Username") =
trim(rsgetreplies.Fields.Item("username").Value) Then %>
<a href="javascript:void(0);"
onclick="MM_openBrWindow('edit_reply.asp?reply_id=<%=(rsgetreplies.Fields.Item("reply
_id").Value)%>','','scrollbars=yes,resizable=yes')">edit</a>
<% End If %>
```

As for the `delete` text, highlight it and from the *Properties* panel, browse for the file `delete_posts.asp`. Also add 2 parameters to the URL. Name the first parameter `reply_id` and select its value as the `reply_id` column from the `rsgetreplies` Recordset. Name the second `forum_id` and type the following as its value: `<%=Request.QueryString("forum_id")%>`. The final URL should look like this:

```
delete_posts.asp?reply_id=<%=(rsgetreplies.Fields.Item("reply_id").Value)%>&forum_id=
<%=Request.QueryString("forum_id")%>
```

Surround the entire `delete` link with the following code:

```
<% If Request.Cookies("ckaccessgroup") = "admin" AND Session("MM_Username") <> ""
Then %>
<                                                                                    a
href="delete_posts.asp?reply_id=<%=(rsgetreplies.Fields.Item("reply_id").Value)%>&for
um_id=<%=Request.QueryString("forum_id")%>">delete</a>
<% End If %>
```

the bottom of replies.asp in Dreamweaver with the edit and delete code added.

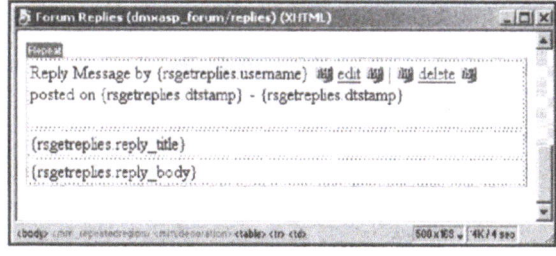

edit_topic.asp

Now create a new ASP VBScript web page and save it as `edit_topic.asp`. In the main body of your document insert a form, and with that a table with four rows and two columns. In the first column of the first row add the text: *Edit Topic Title*. In the second column of the first row insert a text field named `topic_title`.

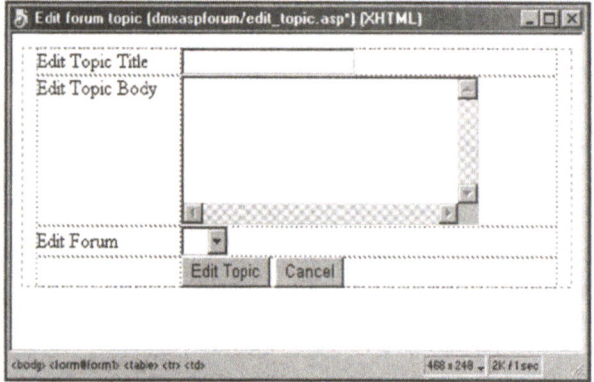

edit_topic.asp in Dreamweaver.

In the first column of the second row add the text: *Edit Topic Body*. In the second column of the second row insert a text area named `topic_body`. In the first column of the third row add the text: `Edit Forum`. In the second column of the third row insert a List/Menu named `forum_id`. In the second column of the fourth row insert a submit button. Label it *Edit Topic*. Add another button, label it *Cancel*, and add the Dreamweaver behavior to it called *Go To URL*. When the dialog box opens, have it open in the main window and use the `empty.asp` page for the URL.

Now let's create the Recordset to retrieve the topic. Select *Server Behaviors > + > Recordset*. When the dialog box opens, name the Recordset `rsgettopic` and select the `conn_dmxaspforum_oledb` connection. Insert the following SQL in the SQL text field:

```
SELECT topic_title, topic_body, forum_id, topic_id, username
FROM forum_topics
WHERE username = 'MMColParam' AND topic_id = MMColParam1
```

Don't quote `MMColParam1` *because this is a numeric value. If you quote it, the database will think it's a string and won't be able to match it to the numeric data type for the* `topic_id` *column.*

Add two new variables: `MMColParam` with a *Default Value* of `x` and a *Run-time Value* of `Session("MM_Username")`; and `MMColParam1`, with a *Default Value* of `0` and a *Run-time Value* of `Request.QueryString("topic_id")`.

This SQL retrieves the topic passed in the querystring and only the topic whose creator's `username` matches the `username` stored in the Session variable of the logged-in user, because users can only edit their own topics. Filtering the topics by username is also very important, otherwise a user can simply load this page and manually manipulate the querystring value to retrieve a topic and edit it.

From *Bindings* drag the `topic_title` column onto the `topic_title` text field and the `topic_body` column onto the `topic_body` text area.

edit_topic.asp in Dreamweaver with the dynamic text added.

We also want the user to be able to place the topic in a different forum in case he or she placed it in the wrong forum by accident. Let's retrieve the forums and populate the List/Menu with them. We need to create a Recordset to retrieve the forums first. Select *Server Behaviors > + > Recordset*. When the dialog box opens, name the Recordset `rsgetforums` and select the `conn_dmxaspforum_oledb` connection. Insert the following SQL in the SQL text field:

```
SELECT forum_id, forum
FROM forums
ORDER BY forum_id ASC
```

Highlight the list/menu in the form and from the *Properties* panel hit the button labeled *Dynamic*.
Select the `rsgetforums` Recordset for the options. Use the `forum_id` column as the values and the
`forum` column as the labels. Set the *Select Value Equal To* text field to have the following code:

```
<%= rsgettopic.Fields.Item("forum_id").Value %>
```

What this last option does is make sure that the topic is already loaded by default

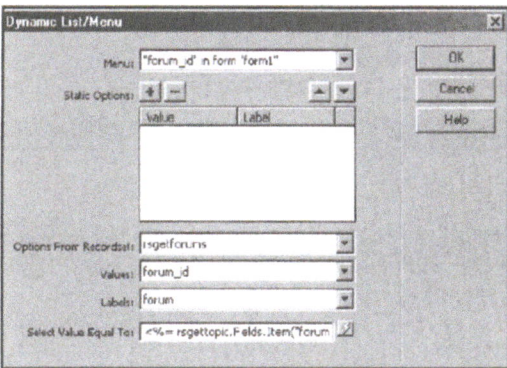

The Dynamic List/Menu dialog.

Finally we need to create the code to update the topic. Thankfully Dreamweaver can generate this
for us. Highlight the form and select *Server Behaviors > + > Update Record*. When the dialog box
opens, select the `conn_dmxaspforum_oledb` connection. Update the `forum_topics` table. Set *Select
Record From* to the `rsgettopic` Recordset. Use the `topic_id` as the *Unique Key Column*. After
updating, send to `empty.asp`. Make sure the form elements go into the appropriate columns in the
dialog box. Hit *OK*.

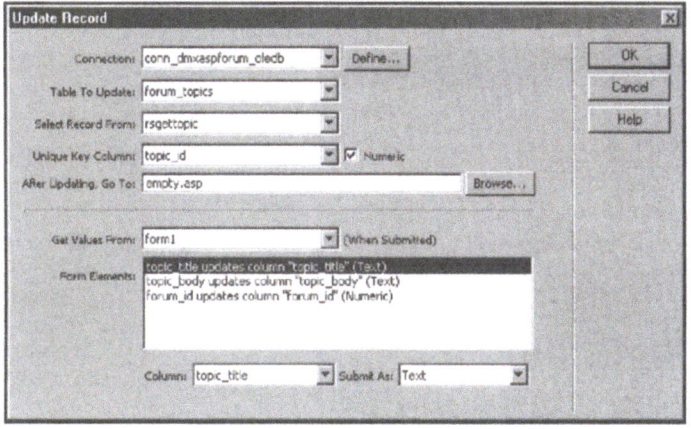

The Update Record dialog.

C2

Our `edit_topic.asp` page is now complete, and looks something like this:

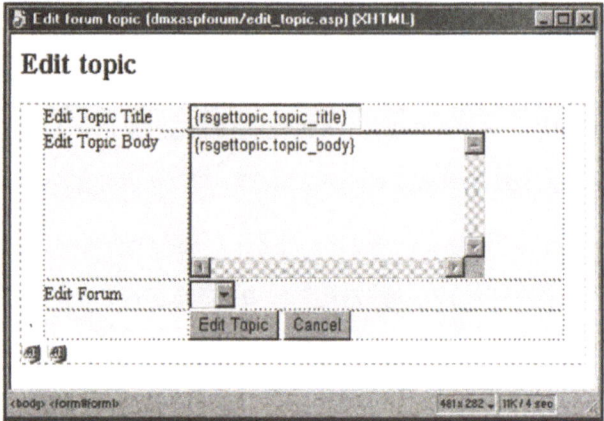

edit_topic.asp in Dreamweaver.

Users can now select the edit link from the `replies.asp` page to edit topics they have created. Test this page out now by logging in and attempting to edit a topic you've created from the `replies.asp` page. Let's allow users to edit replies now.

edit_reply.asp

This page will follow instructions very similar to the `edit_topic.asp` page except that it won't include the option of moving the post into another forum (replies are associated with topics) and it will retrieve data from the `forum_replies` table instead of the `forum_topics` table.

Create a new ASP VBScript web page and save it as `edit_reply.asp`. In the main body of your document insert a form, into which add a table with three rows and two columns for each row. In the first column of the first row add the text: *Edit Reply Title*. In the second column of the first row insert a text field named `reply_title`. In the first column of the second row add the text: *Edit Reply Body*. In the second column of the second row insert a text area named `reply_body`.

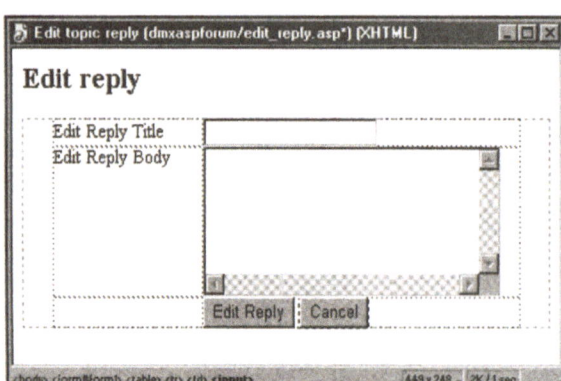

edit_reply.asp in Dreamweaver.

In the second column of the third row insert a submit button and a regular button. Label the submit button *Edit Reply*. Select the regular button, label it *Cancel* and add the Design behavior *Go To URL*. When the dialog box opens, have the URL open in the main window and use the `empty.asp` page for the URL.

Now let's create the Recordset to retrieve the topic. *Select Server Behaviors > + > Recordset.* When the dialog box opens, name the Recordset `rsgetreply` and select the `conn_dmxaspforum_oledb` connection. Insert the following SQL in the SQL text field:

```
SELECT reply_id, reply_title, reply_body
FROM forum_replies
WHERE username = 'MMColParam' AND reply_id = MMColParam1
```

Add the following variables: `MMColParam` with a *Default Value* of `x` and a *Run-time Value* of `Session("MM_Username")`; and `MMColParam1` with a *Default Value* of `o` and a *Run-time Value* of `Request.QueryString("reply_id")`.

From *Bindings* drag the `reply_title` column onto the `reply_title` text field and the `reply_body` column onto the `reply_body` text area.

Highlight the form and select *Server Behaviors > + > Update Record.* When the dialog box opens, select the `conn_dmxaspforum_oledb` connection. Update the `forum_replies` table. Select the record from the `rsgetreply` Recordset. Use the `reply_id` as the *Unique Key Column.* After updating, send to `empty.asp`. Make sure the form elements go into the appropriate columns in the dialog box. Hit *OK.*

Our `edit_reply.asp` page is now complete.

edit_reply..asp in Dreamweaver.

Users can now select the *edit* link from the `replies.asp` page to edit replies along with topics they may have created. Test this page out now by logging in, replying to some topics, and attempting to edit replies you've created from the `replies.asp` page.

delete_posts.asp

We will add two commands to this page. The first command will be to delete a selected topic and the second will be able to delete a selected reply. Again all selections are coming from the `replies.asp` page through querystrings attached to the URL for retrieval on this page. This page will have no design functionality but only ASP code. The page uses the following code:

```asp
<%
If Session("MM_Username") = "" OR Request.Cookies("ckaccessgroup") <> "admin" Then
Response.Write "You are not authorized to access this page"
Response.End
End If
%>


<!--#include file="Connections/conn_dmxaspforum_oledb.asp" -->
<%
'code to delete a topic
if(Request.QueryString("topic_id") <> "") then
cmd_delete_topic__MMColParam = Request.QueryString("topic_id")
set cmd_delete_topic = Server.CreateObject("ADODB.Command")
cmd_delete_topic.ActiveConnection = MM_conn_dmxaspforum_oledb_STRING
cmd_delete_topic.CommandText = "DELETE FROM forum_topics  WHERE topic_id = " +
Replace(cmd_delete_topic__MMColParam, "'", "''") + ""
cmd_delete_topic.CommandType = 1
cmd_delete_topic.CommandTimeout = 0
cmd_delete_topic.Prepared = true
cmd_delete_topic.Execute()
Response.Redirect Request.ServerVariables("HTTP_REFERER")
end if

'code to delete a reply

if(Request.QueryString("reply_id") <> "") then
cmd_delete_reply__MMColParam1 = Request.QueryString("reply_id")
set cmd_delete_reply = Server.CreateObject("ADODB.Command")
cmd_delete_reply.ActiveConnection = MM_conn_dmxaspforum_oledb_STRING
cmd_delete_reply.CommandText = "DELETE FROM forum_replies  WHERE reply_id =
MMColParam1 "
cmd_delete_reply.CommandType = 1
cmd_delete_reply.CommandTimeout = 0
cmd_delete_reply.Prepared = true
cmd_delete_reply.Execute()
Response.Redirect Request.ServerVariables("HTTP_REFERER")
end if
%>
```

Firstly the code checks to see if the user is a valid admin. If it is then it checks to see if a particular variable is passed in the querystring and then executes the correct SQL to delete the requisite record.

We are now done with the forum page and our forum is complete. You can test out the forum by logging in and out, and posting topics and replies. Try to test two users who have a discussion about something, to make sure the permissions for editing work correctly.

Showing the Number of Posts

Now we will add an extra feature to our forum to make it more user-friendly. Specifically, we'll be adding the following extra feature to show the number of posts.

Let's display the number of topics in each forum and the number of replies in each topic. The number of topics will appear on the `forums.asp` page and the number of replies will appear on the `topics.asp` page. Load the `forums.asp` page in Dreamweaver MX. In this page you should have created a table with one row and two columns. We left the right column empty; we will use it here to display the number of topics in each forum.

We need to create the Recordset that counts the number of topics in each topic. *Select Server Behaviors > + > Recordset*. When the dialog box opens, name the Recordset `rsgettopicstotal`, select the `conn_dmxaspforum_oledb` connection, and insert the following SQL in the SQL field:

```
SELECT Count(forum_topics.forum_id) AS CountOfTopics
FROM forum_topics
WHERE forum_topics.forum_id = MMColParam
```

Add a variable called `MMColParam` with a *Default Value* of `1` and a *Run-time Value* of `rsgetforums("forum_id")`.

This SQL filters the `forum_topics` table with the `forum_id` being retrieved from the other Recordset on the page called `rsgetforums`. From the *Bindings* window drag the `CountOfTopics` column in to the second column of the HTML table in your document. Surround the `CountOfTopics` dynamic text with brackets.

Dreamweaver should have added two ASP code blocks to the top of your page. The first one declares and initializes the `MMColParam` variable for use in the `rsgettopicstotal` Recordset, and does so as follows:

```
<%
Dim rsgettopicstotal__MMColParam
rsgettopicstotal__MMColParam = "1"
If (rsgetforums("forum_id") <> "") Then
  rsgettopicstotal__MMColParam = rsgetforums("forum_id")
End If
%>
```

The second declares and fills the recordset `rsgettopicstotal`, as follows:

```
<%
Dim rsgettopicstotal
Dim rsgettopicstotal_numRows

Set rsgettopicstotal = Server.CreateObject("ADODB.Recordset")
rsgettopicstotal.ActiveConnection = MM_conn_dmxaspforum_oledb_STRING
rsgettopicstotal.Source = "SELECT Count(forum_topics.forum_id) AS CountOfTopics
FROM forum_topics  WHERE forum_topics.forum_id = " +
Replace(rsgettopicstotal__MMColParam, "'", "''") + ""
rsgettopicstotal.CursorType = 0
rsgettopicstotal.CursorLocation = 2
rsgettopicstotal.LockType = 1
rsgettopicstotal.Open()

rsgettopicstotal_numRows = 0
%>
```

In Code View drag and drop these two blocks to appear right before the dynamic text **within** the repeat region of the table row. This ASP code needs to repeat along with the repeat of the forums in order to display a count for each forum, which is why we're moving it. The page should now look something like the following:

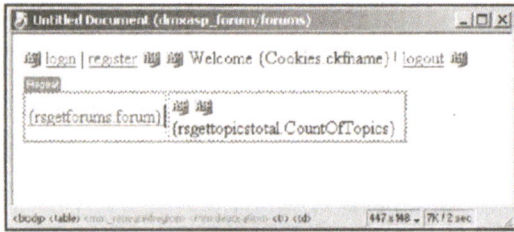

forums.asp in Dreamweaver with the topic count added.

When we browse to the page on the site, we can see it has worked:

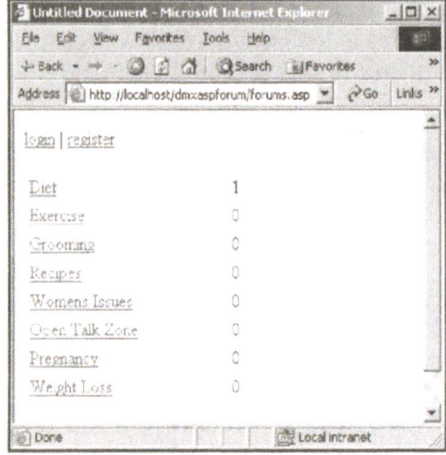

forums.asp in a browser.

Now let's display the number of replies for each topic on the `topics.asp`. We will use SQL similar to what we used for the above page. Load the `topics.asp` in Dreamweaver MX.

Select *Server Behaviors > + > Recordset*. When the dialog box opens, name the Recordset `rsgetrepliestotal`, select the `conn_dmxaspforum_oledb` connection, and insert the following SQL in the SQL field:

```
SELECT Count(forum_replies.topic_id) AS CountOfReplies
FROM forum_replies
WHERE forum_replies.topic_id = MMColParam
```

Add a variable called `MMColParam` with a *Default Value* of `1` and a *Run-time Value* of `rsgettopics("topic_id")`.

You should have a table with four columns. The second row of the fourth column was left empty for this section. From the *Bindings* window drag the `CountOfReplies` column into the fourth column. Again, Dreamweaver will have generated two code blocks at the top of the document. The first one declares and initializes the `MMColParam` for use in the `rsgetrepliestotal` Recordset, as follows:

```
<%
Dim rsgetrepliestotal__MMColParam
rsgetrepliestotal__MMColParam = "1"
If (rsgettopics("topic_id") <> "") Then
  rsgetrepliestotal__MMColParam = rsgettopics("topic_id")
End If
%>
```

The second block declares and initializes the `rsgetrepliestotal` Recordset, and begins as follows (remember to get the whole block):

```
<%
Dim rsgetrepliestotal
Dim rsgetrepliestotal_numRows

Set rsgetrepliestotal = Server.CreateObject("ADODB.Recordset")
```

Drag these blocks to reside right before this dynamic text **within** the *Show If* region, for the same reason as we did on `forums.asp`, so that the Recordset will be executed for each topic:

topics.asp in Dreamweaver with the replies count added.

Switch to Code View and scroll to the bottom of your page to the code that destroys the Recordsets. You should see the original `rsgettopics` Recordset along with the `If` statement we added earlier while building the `topics.asp` page so that it doesn't attempt to destroy a Recordset that doesn't exist. Since we created a new Recordset on this page called `rsgettotalreplies` you will see code that destroys that Recordset also:

```
<% If Not rsgettopics.EOF Or Not rsgettopics.BOF Then %>
<%
rsgettopics.Close()
Set rsgettopics = Nothing
%>
<% End If %>
<%
rsgettotalreplies.Close()
Set rsgettotalreplies = Nothing
%>
```

Make sure to drag and drop the code that destroys the `rsgettotalreplies` Recordset into the `If` statement as well:

```
<% If Not rsgettopics.EOF Or Not rsgettopics.BOF Then %>
<%
rsgettopics.Close()
Set rsgettopics = Nothing
%>
<%
rsgettotalreplies.Close()
Set rsgettotalreplies = Nothing
%>
<% End If %>
```

The resulting page should look something like this when viewed:

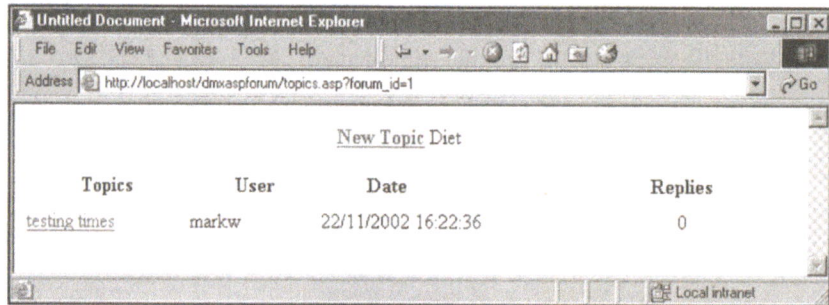

topics.asp in a web browser.

Summary

In this case study we have built an entire forum from scratch. We have taken a look at the fundamentals behind many forums including a detailed look at the database foundation. We saw the database tables required for most forums and the relationships needed between the tables.

From here we have also added features to our forum to show the number of topics in forums and the number of replies in topics. We have built a complete database for our forum, and all the pages required to run it.

Now that you have the basic structure for the forum, expanding it is a relatively easy task. Using similar functionality to that given above you can add all sorts of information to the forum, such as configuring the forum to report on the date of the last reply.

Index

A Guide to the Index

The index is arranged in word-by-word order (so that New York would appear before Newark). Unmodified headings indicate the main treatments of topics and acronyms have been preferred to their expansions as main entries on the grounds that they are easier to recall or to work out. Dreamweaver MX has occasionally been abbreviated to DMX to save space. Comments specifically about the index should be sent to *billj@glasshaus.com*

B

E

G

H

V

W

X

Notes

Notes

Also from glasshaus:

glasshaus
web professional to web professional

Dynamic Dreamweaver MX

Rob Turnbull, Bob Regan, Omar Elbaga,
Paul Boon, Rachel Andrew

1-904151-10-8

US: $29.99
C : $46.99
UK: £21.99

July 2002

This book gets you up to speed on using Macromedia Dreamweaver MX, the new version of Macromedia's premier visual web site design tool, to produce dynamic, creative, visually stunning sites that comply with web standards and accessibility guidelines. It gets straight to the heart of the matter so you spend less time reading, and more time building your site.

- **Rachel Andrew** is a member of the Web Standards Project's Dreamweaver Task Force, responsible for improving Dreamweaver's standards compliance and accessibility

- **Omar Elbaga** started out as a fine artist and moved to computer graphic arts. He is also a member of Team Macromedia

- **Alan Foley** is an Assistant Professor of Instructional Technology who teaches and consults on web accessibility and usability issues

- **Bob Regan** is the Senior Product Manager for Accessibility at Macromedia

- **Rob Turnbull** is also a member of Team Macromedia

Also from glasshaus:

glasshaus

web professional to web professional

Dreamweaver MX:
PHP Web Development

Bruno Mairlot, Gareth Downes-Powell
Tim Green

1-904151-11-6

US: $39.99
C : $61.99
UK: £28.99

July 2002

Web Professionals have been calling for years for Dreamweaver/ UltraDev to support PHP, as it's the premier free open-source server-side scripting language. With Macromedia's landmark new release of Dreamweaver, PHP is fully supported in the familiar Dreamweaver visual environment.

It's a no-fluff 400 pages, so you can learn enough PHP to make real dynamic web pages, spending less time reading and more time on the job. It uses an example project, a hotel reservation system, that is built up through the chapters to demonstrate the concepts explained

Aimed at web professionals who want to use Dreamweaver MX to produce PHP web sites, it doesn't assume any knowledge of PHP, and it doesn't hold your hand when talking about Dreamweaver, so experience of Dreamweaver would be useful. It assumes knowledge of HTML and Web design.

"the VERY best book I have ever seen dealing with databases and web programming."

- Matt Brown, Dreamweaver and Contribute Community Manager, Macromedia

Also from glasshaus:

labor-saving devices for web professionals

1-904151-18-3
Practical Web Traffic Analysis

1-904151-15-9
Web Graphics for Non-Designers

1-904151-08-6
Practical XML for the Web

1-904151-20-5
Practical Web Database Design

1-904151-02-7
Usable Web Menus

1-904151-09-4
Usable Forms for the Web

1-904151-14-0
Usable Shopping Carts

1-904151-03-5
Usability: The Site Speaks for Itself

1-904151-04-3
Cascading Style Sheets

1-904151-05-1
Practical JavaScript for the Usable Web

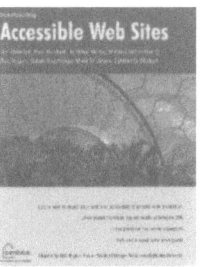

1-904151-00-0
Accessible Web Sites

1-904151-17-5
Fundamental Web Design and Development Skills

glasshaus books: labor-saving devices for web professionals